THE NEW DEMOCRACY
Challenging the Social Order in Industrial Ontario, 1914–1925

The period during and after the First World War was marked by tremendous labour unrest in Canada, not only in Winnipeg where the General Strike of 1919 was a watershed, but across the country. James Naylor focuses on southern Ontario, in the industrial heartland of Canada, as key to understanding the character of this phase of labour history.

In the 1919 provincial election, the Independent Labor Party of Ontario swept most of the province's industrial constituencies outside Toronto and formed a coalition government with the organized farmers. Strike activity soared to unprecedented levels. The Toronto Trades Council organized a general strike, and new forms of industrial unionism began to emerge. If these events lacked some of the drama of those in the West, they did reflect both an increasingly articulate working-class view of democracy and labour's determination not to be overlooked in post-war reconstruction.

Naylor examines a number of issues: the nature of working-class views of democracy and the state; conflicts between existing and emerging forms of working-class organization; the role of women in these movements; the logic of participation in the electoral process; and the dynamic between 'industrial' and 'political' activity in the context of a liberal-democratic system. He also considers the response of employers and government with a view to understanding the 'negotiated' character of post-war reconstruction in the conflict between social classes.

JAMES NAYLOR is a member of the Department of History, University of Winnipeg.

James Naylor

THE NEW DEMOCRACY
Challenging the Social Order in Industrial Ontario, 1914–1925

UNIVERSITY OF TORONTO PRESS
Toronto Buffalo London

© University of Toronto Press 1991
Toronto Buffalo London
Printed in Canada

ISBN 0-8020-5953-8 (cloth)
ISBN 0-8020-6886-3 (paper)

Printed on acid-free paper

Canadian Cataloguing in Publication Data

Naylor, James, 1954-
    The new democracy: challenging the social order in
    industrial Ontario, 1914-1925

    Includes index.
    ISBN 0-8020-5953-8 (bound) ISBN 0-8020-6886-3 (pbk.)

    1. Working class – Ontario – History.   I. Title.

    HD8109.052N3 1991   305.5'62'09713   C91-094581-0

This book has been published with the help of a grant
from the Social Science Federation of Canada, using
funds provided by the Social Sciences and Humanities
Research Council of Canada.

For Wendy

Contents

Acknowledgments

However long one sits alone in an archive or at a computer, historical writing is a collective project, and it gives me pleasure to be able to thank those who have facilitated my research and prodded my thinking. I am indebted to the archivists and librarians at the National Archives of Canada, the National Library of Canada, the Labour Canada Library, the Archives of Ontario, the Regional Collection at the University of Western Ontario, Queen's University Archives, the Thomas Fisher Rare Book Room at the University of Toronto, the Provincial Archives of Manitoba, and Special Collections at the University of British Columbia Library, as well as to the staffs of several local libraries who provided generous assistance. Funding for research came from the Social Sciences and Humanities Research Council, Labour Canada, and the Canadian Association of University Teachers.

My interest in pursuing such a study took root at the universities of Manitoba and Winnipeg, and I owe an intellectual debt to Peter Bailey, Gerald Friesen, Ross McCormack, Ed Rea, Doug Sprague, Lionel Steiman, and Tom Vadney. In particular, the infectious passion that Mark Gabbert and Henry Heller have for understanding the past, and the present, helped spark my own efforts. At York University, I would like to thank Irving Abella, Christopher Armstrong, Ramsay Cook, Paul Craven, Susan Houston, David Shugarman, and Reg Whitaker. Greg Kealey provided thoughtful and useful comments on producing a book manuscript from my dissertation, while Geoffrey Ewen, Mary Nolan, and Allen Seager have had occasion to comment on aspects of my research.

The Toronto Labour Studies Research Group played an important role in providing an exciting intellectual environment. Ruth Frager, Franca Iacovetta, Lynne Marks, Ian Radforth, Mark Rosenfeld, and Bob Storey, along with the other members, provided a forum that was, at the same time, challenging and supportive. Finally, I would like to thank three people in particular. Tom Traves served as a model dissertation supervisor, helping me confront problems both large and small. To Craig Heron I owe a special thanks for generously sharing both his insights and his enthusiasm. Finally, I thank Wendy Boyd for her sustained patience, support, and interest in this work. This book is dedicated to her.

THE NEW DEMOCRACY

Introduction

Nineteen nineteen was a pivotal year in working-class history. In Canada, it was the year of the Winnipeg General Strike and the birth of the One Big Union. Everywhere, it seemed, the labour movement was undergoing an astounding transformation. In North America and Europe, general strikes, insurrections, soviets, workers' councils, industrial unions, and a myriad of socialist parties were emerging out of the ashes of the First World War, often taking inspiration from the Bolsheviks in Russia. Although the extent of this radicalization varied greatly, few would have accused Lloyd George of alarmism in his assessment that the 'whole existing order in its political, social and economic aspects is questioned by the masses of the population from one end of Europe to the other.'[1] On both sides of the Atlantic, this historic moment quickly passed. Historians have been left to attempt to understand the emergence and demise of this wave of working-class activity. What spurred these workers into action and what did they hope to achieve? What kind of class consciousness was reflected in these struggles, and why were they, in most cases, so unsuccessful?

An examination of the industrial cities of southern Ontario provides a useful window into this world. Contrary to the impression created by a generation of Canadian labour historians, the great class battles of 1919 were not fought solely on the western front.[2] Certainly it was in the mining towns of British Columbia that socialist consciousness was most pervasive, and no conflict in the country matched the determination and drama of the Winnipeg General Strike. Regional and industrial distinctions were many and ought not to be overlooked. Yet the social crisis of 1919, the result of years of war and decades of class conflict, was national and international in its scope. To understand its outcome, historians must explore its breadth and diversity.

Historians who view class conflict as exceptional and seek an explanation for it in extraordinary conditions on a frontier fringe find it comforting to exaggerate the regional contrast, but to do so is to fail to account for the deep social divisions and class conflicts in southern Ontario. Most notably, David Bercuson has clung tenaciously to the view that western radicalism was unique; that it had no parallel in central and eastern Canada.[3] Such a claim, however, is based on a misreading of historians such as Gregory Kealey who, in response to the 'western exceptionalists,' has demonstrated that a wave of militancy broke over the entire country at the end of the First World War, boosting the stock of radicals within the labour movement.[4] Kealey implies no uniformity to this movement, nor does he make any claims for the existence of any ideological consistency among Canadian workers. If this is what he meant by a national 'labour revolt' (as Bercuson seems to suggest), then such an argument would, indeed, be absurd.

Rather, as Kealey and others[5] have recognized, Canadian workers were in revolt against a social order associated with greed, profiteering, inflation, the assault on workers' skills and autonomy, and incipient 'kaiserism' in Ottawa. Indeed, large numbers of Canadian workers came to consider the meaningless tragedy of world war as the inevitable manifestation of capitalism. Such views fuelled the wave of post-war strikes, industrial unions, mass protests, and labour parties. Everywhere, and not least in the West, the ideological configurations that emerged were complex. Revolutionary, reformist, and labourist ideologies vied for attention across the country.

As this study is intended to demonstrate, Ontario fit this pattern. The number of strikers enumerated in a study of strike activity in ten major Ontario cities between 1901 and 1914 was surpassed in just three years from 1918 to 1920.[6] But outside western Canada, the local and regional peculiarities that shaped these struggles have scarcely been elucidated.[7] Events in Ontario, for instance, cannot be understood without an examination of electoral activity that was not only successful at the polls, but also instrumental in challenging the local basis of working-class activity and in forging a provincial labour movement. The trajectory and defeat of the 'Canadian labour revolt' requires a careful examination of the workers' movement in southern Ontario. If it was far from quiescent, as we argue, why was it unable to maintain its gains and lend support to workers across the country? What happened in Ontario?

Southern Ontario workers were no less angry than westerners about the profiteering and corruption they saw around them. They were no less concerned about the future of their jobs and their crafts as production methods were altered and new, less skilled, immigrant and women workers entered their shops; no less sickened and frustrated by the carnage in Europe that grew to unimagined proportions, and no less wary of wartime powers claimed by a federal state whose presence in society had traditionally been minor. Moreover, the region of Canada that this study examines – urban southern Ontario from Windsor to Peterborough – was in the heartland of industrial Canada. Here, in a score of smaller centres, as well as the major industrial centres of Toronto and Hamilton, manufacturing throve in the latter half of the nineteenth century. By 1914, the rapid industrial development of the previous two decades had increasingly concentrated within this region; centres throughout southern Ontario were recognized as the Canadian home of 'Modern Industry.'[8] If capitalism had created, as the socialists argued, an agency of social change in the industrial working class, the likely focus of decisive class battles would be the industrial cities of southern Ontario.

Wartime conflicts forged a regional working class capable of acting collectively on a number of fronts. Union membership soared, new organizational forms were proposed and debated, and independent working-class political action was undertaken on a much larger and more successful scale than ever before. The conflict, however, had its specific character. Southern Ontario workers had a long tradition of craft unionism, and the nature of industrial cities and working-class communities was quite different from that in the West (although hardly homogeneous in either case). In this region, existing and emerging forms of labour organization confronted each other from the outset of this new wave of militancy. Moreover, events in the region elicited a different response from employers. In short, workers and bosses in southern Ontario fought in a different arena and under different circumstances than elsewhere. Building on their own experiences at work and in the war, workers developed their own vision of post-war 'reconstruction.' Indeed Ontario, like so many other settings in this exciting time, provides an example of the creative potential of a workers' movement freed from the constraints of 'normalcy,' and free to dream of a new, more equitable, social order. Central to this notion of 'reconstruction' was a conception – captured in the title of one of the region's lively and articulate labour papers, *The New Democracy* – that the international struggle for democracy must be brought home; kaiserism must not flourish in Canada as it had in Germany. The definition of the new democracy was itself an object of struggle.

As in the West, Ontario workers entered the conflict as a class. Collective action was, after all, the only effective means of overcoming the political powerlessness that for decades had plagued workers' hopes of benefiting from the fruits of the Industrial Revolution. A sense of betrayal at the hands of the 'old parties' encouraged such a move; workers' own sense of common purpose determined the form it would take. But collective action itself shaped the view of both the democracy that ought to emerge from the tragedy in Europe and the perceived growth of autocracy at home. Conflicts between social classes became articulated in a dialogue over democracy. Through strikes and elections workers formulated a view of a new democracy at odds with their employers' version, and capital responded with a defence of 'British democracy' and the status quo.

The very scale of the conflict, which saw the direct representatives of workers and farmers displace the Tories in the provincial legislature and mass strikes for unprecedented goals in the cities, reveals much about the nature of class relations in the region and the way in which workers developed and articulated their aspirations. More than this, the future of social relations and political culture in the province would be shaped by such conflict. While the dominant ideology of the labour movement did not foresee a revolution in the social order, the extent of social mobilization unleashed a force stronger than anyone imagined. Employers responded rapidly.

The social explosion that this study examines was, by its nature, complex. The tumultuous events of the era opened new avenues of thought and action to thousands of workers whose lives had been confined to a much narrower stage. Historical processes are never tidy; moments of crisis are even less so. This complexity is augmented by the appearance, in the course of the war, of two seemingly autonomous working-class movements. Most immediately apparent was the emergence of the 'industrial' movement, as militant trade unionists increasingly came to champion the establishment of large industrial unions and began to countenance the use of the general strike as a weapon against intransigent employers. At the same time, a 'political' movement sought working-class emancipation on the electoral terrain. Through the instrument of the Independent Labor Party, this 'labourist'[9] current hoped to free the parliamentary system from the grip of profiteers and the machinations of the political parties. Thus liberated, elected legislatures would heed the needs and wishes of the working masses as they had manifestly failed to do in the past, particularly during the war.

As we shall demonstrate, these two movements operated in quite distinct realms; the factory and the legislature were autonomous terrains in the eyes of Ontario workers. Unlike workers in the West, where the harsh deployment of military and judicial powers made the state a more open player in industrial strife, Ontario workers were more likely to view the state as a neutral and potentially friendly force.[10] The transformation of the state through the ballot box, rather than its overthrow, appealed to large and growing numbers of Ontario workers. Although, as we shall argue, the industrial and electoral movements stood or fell together, they operated separately and under quite different rules. This is all the more notable given that each movement represented the same constituency, shared the same leadership, and voiced similar aspirations.

That the 'political' and the 'economic' realms should be considered distinct had important implications and requires some explanation. The democracy familiar to Ontario workers was liberal democracy as it functioned in a capitalist social order. It was this democracy, with its promise of universal suffrage and entrenched civil liberties, that was apparently threatened by the increased powers of the federal state under the War Measures Act. And it was this democracy that the labour movement undertook to rescue from the 'propertied interests' while, at the same time, appending to it labour's own notions of direct working-class representation. Liberal democracy, however, cannot be separated from the social order within which it emerged. It directly reflects, in fact, a distinction between 'economic' and 'political' spheres under capitalism that was faithfully reflected in labourist ideology.

What distinguishes capitalism from other forms of class society is the means by which surplus labour is appropriated by capital. In pre-capitalist class societies rulers perform this task in an 'extra-economic' fashion, through direct coercion, traditional duties and tithes, and so on. However, unlike pre-capitalist or petty-commodity producers, workers under capitalism have no access to the means of production other than by selling their labour-power – their ability to labour – to capitalists who can supply them with the raw materials and instruments with which to labour. In this context, surplus value is created in the process of production and becomes the property of the capitalist. Since an exchange has taken place in the labour contract between legally free agents, such a relationship can be viewed as 'economic' rather than as a 'political' appropriation of the workers' product. Consequently, workplace struggles are viewed as economic, not political, contests. Moreover, the necessary connections between economic and political power are obscured. The wage form, commented Marx, appears as the real value of labour and thereby 'extinguishes any trace of the division of the working-day into necessary labour and surplus-labour, into paid and unpaid labour.'[11] Thus, it is not immediately apparent that the labour process (as opposed to control of the political apparatus of the state) is the source of power in capitalist society. Since the social surplus must be both produced in the workplace and realized in the market, the source of profit and of the social domination of capital over labour is further obscured.

The primary social decisions within a capitalist society, particularly in relation to the allocation of resources and labour and the distribution of wealth, are rooted in private 'economic' mechanisms. This leaves a relatively constrained 'political' sphere, which is considered to be autonomous from the production process. An illustration should suffice. A liberal democracy such as Canada is considered democratic because of the existence of a set of institutions and procedures – primarily universal suffrage and sovereign legislatures. That such institutions do not directly govern the economic sphere does not disqualify Canada as a member of the 'democratic' world. But who would argue that such democratic procedures extend to the workplace? Rather, 'freedom' in the economic realm means something quite different. It refers to the ability of economic forces to govern relatively unfettered.

This separation of social power between economic and political spheres creates a strategic dilemma for working-class movements. How can workers transform their collective economic power to challenge political power? Ellen Meiksins Wood has gone so far as to argue that this ' "structural" separation may, indeed, be the most effective defence mechanism available to capital.'[12] Recognizing this, socialists have long argued that economic and political power go hand-in-hand in capitalist society and have attempted to develop strategies that reflect this recognition. Labourism, however, was not socialism. For the majority of politically active workers in southern Ontario, liberation was sought through electoral means, which they considered the key to social power. By contrast, workplace 'economic' relations were to be ameliorated through industrial action by the appropriate means: trade-union activity. The persistence of this ideological distinction and the concomitant commitment to the rules of liberal democracy were central features of the regional labour movement in this period. This is not to argue that Ontario itself was 'exceptional,' any more than that there was a 'uniform' revolt across Canada.[13] The working-class currents we examine were present across the country, although in unique combination. Nowhere else was the relative strength of labourism greater, and nowhere else were the hopes of workers pinned so greatly upon their elected representatives. In the end, we shall argue that so stark a distinction between economic and political action was untenable for a labour movement in an advanced capitalist society, and labourism passed into oblivion.

Not only did this conceptual distinction have important consequences for the labour movement; it necessarily affects the structure of this volume. The industrial and electoral labour movements will, for the sake of clarity, be examined somewhat separately. This study opens with an examination of the 'economic front' and of the determinants of trade-union activity during the war, arguing that workers' response to the war and to the new powers claimed by the federal government established the framework of union activity during and after the war. Chapter two focuses on the culmination of this development: the movement for greater and more effective labour unity through industrial unionism, most dramatically during the Toronto General Strike. Chapters three and four trace the development of working-class political action through the nascent Independent Labor Party leading to its apogee, the election of the farmer-labour government of Ontario in October 1919. Chapter five examines the participation of working-class women in the struggle for the 'new democracy.' Such an investigation is important since the object of working-class political action was not confined to the workplace, but aimed at the improvement of working-class family and community life. Moreover, the achievement of women's suffrage had a resonance in a labour movement clamouring for democracy. The experiences of working-class women who gained access to the 'political' sphere is illustrative both of the broadening definition of democracy and, as we shall see, of the unwillingness of the labour movement to expand the conceptual limits of democracy beyond the realm of what they considered political to include the household.

Chapter six looks at employer and government responses to growing labour militancy and politicization, and particularly at their interest in corporate welfarism and 'industrial democracy.' It argues that the scale of the challenge was great enough to prompt employers to undertake new strategies and, most interestingly, to appropriate the rhetoric of democracy in their confrontation with labour on the economic front. As it became apparent that workers were confronting capital as a class, employers themselves drew together. Chapter seven, then, is a study of collective employer response. It raises the question of whether a new social order based on a new industrial-relations regime, perhaps a form of 'tripartism' involving the state in a direct role, was in the offing. Such a prospect was welcomed by many trade unionists. Its establishment, however, was blocked by employers who foresaw that the labour movement would use such a regime to legitimate its class interests and secure the organizational gains it had made during and after the war. Chapter eight studies the experience of labourist participation in government in order to explain its failure as a political current. In the eyes of a constituency still dedicated to its own version of liberal democracy, workers achieved their greatest victory and suffered their most substantial defeat.

A series of important industrial defeats, the consequence of increased unemployment as well as the failure of labour's political and industrial strategies, sealed the fate of even such a truncated image of the 'new democracy.' In the conclusion, I examine the failure of labour's new democracy as a prelude to the exceptionally narrow political culture of the 1920s. This was the bedrock upon which 'Tory-blue Ontario' was reconstructed. Canadian historians have failed to recognize the options that presented themselves – and were defeated – in the short period from 1914 to the mid-1920s.[14]

The flowering of social history in the past two decades requires that historians be circumspect in claiming that they can explain working-class behaviour in a single study. While many aspects of social conflict in southern Ontario will be examined, the texture of a community study cannot be replicated here. The home, community, fraternal club, school, and street all contributed to the context within which the events discussed here developed, but for the most part remain outside the scope of this study. The role many immigrant workers played in these events awaits the work of historians with language skills and an insight into different communities. While the part played by immigrants is discussed here, the sources available – largely union and government documents – view these communities from the outside. There is much to be learned about such aspects of the growth and evolution of the working class in twentieth-century Canada. This is the study of a critical period in its development.

Part One

THE INDUSTRIAL FRONT

1 Workers, Unions, and War

'... the war was fought to make the world safe for hypocrisy.'
Electrical worker, St Catharines, Ontario, 1924[1]

'Mr. Workingman, war has hit men hard and made them think deeply.'[2]
The labour propagandist who wrote in these terms about the First
World War had observed workers' efforts to understand the sources
of the terrible conflict and grasp its consequences for their own lives,
for their families, workmates, community, and country. There was
much to find confusing. Sacrifice, hardship, and service in the name
of the high ideals of civilization and democracy for which the Empire
claimed to stand became commonplace. Trade unions in Toronto alone
saw 3,500 members facing an uncertain fate in the trenches of France
by the end of the first year of war.[3] Gradually, however, contrasting
images entered the picture. In Europe, the scale of sacrifice taxed the
imagination. On the home front, hardship often seemed to be caused
less by the demands of war than by the avarice of those seeking to take
advantage of it – the profiteer mocked the ideal of service. Worse yet,
democracy and civilization were themselves at risk. Ironically, the war
to defeat militarism and autocracy seemed to be breeding those very
evils in Canada.

For workers, particularly in the industrial heartland of southern Ontario, the pre-war struggle to retain shop-floor power and build effective unions was suddenly cast upon a new and unpromising terrain.
The pace of industrial development and of the concentration and con-
solidation of business enterprises forced workers to confront stronger,
more diversified firms with a wider range of resources with which to
resist their demands. Now the war economy provided a new impetus
to growth while at the same time undermining workers' ability to respond. The industrial demands of modern warfare presented employ-

ers with a duty to eliminate 'inefficiencies' and an opportunity to extend a policy of 'dilution of labour' or replacement of skilled craftworkers with semi-skilled and unskilled workers proficient in a more limited range of tasks. Craftworkers' skill, the currency in which they dealt with their bosses, was threatened with rapid debasement. Moreover, workers' complaints about such threats, or about increased living costs or housing shortages, were overshadowed by the national crusade to defeat 'the Hun.'

Workers faced many problems with few ready solutions. The lessons of pre-war working-class struggles, focused as they were on community and workplace, grew less and less applicable. The extent of the problems workers faced extended far beyond the confines of city or factory. A single strike could make this clear. No longer was the opponent simply 'the boss.' More and more workers confronted faceless boards of directors in Toronto – boards able to rally behind them the forces of a dominant ideology that devalued workers' concerns as trivial or selfish in a world devastated by war – and a state whose presence was felt as never before.[4] The world had changed, and workers found they had to accommodate themselves to a wider stage if they hoped to have an impact.

Slowly, and with difficulty, the labour movement in southern Ontario came to articulate a response to its altered circumstances. Workers' views of the war neither directly mirrored the dominant ideology nor were entirely independent of it. This phenomenon can best be understood as a process of negotiation whereby the dominant ideas of service and democracy were measured against workers' own collective experiences, as well as their objective position within a society divided by class. By the conclusion of the war, it was apparent that 'making the world safe for democracy' held different meanings for different social classes. For labour it implied an untrammelled right to self-organization and action, as well as an end to the social privileges enjoyed by a few. Of course, workers were hardly unanimous regarding the relative importance of these goals or the best means of obtaining them, but such aspirations were clearly visible in their response to the war and its aftermath. This chapter examines the evolution of the union movement in the course of the First World War.[5]

The Ambiguous Legacy of Craft Unionism

Organized Ontario workers confronted the war as heirs to a substantial tradition of working-class organization and struggle. Several older leaders still remembered the enthusiasm and egalitarianism of the Holy and Noble Order of the Knights of Labor that had swept the province three decades earlier.[6] The nobility of useful labour would persist in the rhetoric of labour journalists such as Joseph Marks, yet the nineteenth century seemed an archaic and foreign place to the organized workers of 1914. Stolid and businesslike craft unions, affiliated to the American Federation of Labor (AFL) and the Trades and Labor Congress of Canada (TLCC), had displaced the Knights. While ritual and fraternalism persisted in craft unions, and broad reform programs were debated, the unions' primary purpose was more prosaic. In the tradition of AFL president Samuel Gompers, craft unions tended to eschew broader social goals and united workers more narrowly by craft, excluding those without recognized skills. The movement culture identified by Gregory Kealey and Bryan Palmer in their study of the Knights in Ontario was only a pale reflection of itself after the 1880s.[7]

Nevertheless, craft unionism in Ontario cannot be dismissed as simple pragmatic 'bread-and-butter' unionism. Craft unions had been well rooted in particular industries before, and during, the hey-day of the Knights and exhibited many of the qualities of the latter.[8] And, as Robert Babcock has documented, craft unions could attract considerable enthusiasm. The industrial boom of the early twentieth century was focused in central Canada, and southern Ontario workers quickly took advantage of the delayed prosperity long promised by John A. Macdonald's National Policy to organize to defend themselves. From 1897 to 1902 the number of local unions in Ontario more than tripled to over six hundred. Almost three of every five AFL union locals in Canada were in southern Ontario.[9]

As Craig Heron and Bryan Palmer have demonstrated, these craftworkers struggled tenaciously to defend their skill and autonomy in the face of increased mechanization, concentration of capital, and new managerial strategies in Canadian industry. At issue were not narrowly defined economic issues, but the encroachment of new factory disciplines and organization that threatened to rob skilled workers of their prized currency: the monopoly of valuable skills. At issue were craftworkers' standard of living, autonomy, community, and 'manly' self-respect. Like the Knights, these workers were fighting to defend and further a way of life rooted in their workplaces and communities. In this battle, workers relied upon the strategies their unions had developed in the nineteenth century, and Ontario workers struck to defend the apprenticeship system, to maintain established workplace procedures against mechanization, and, of course, to repel assaults on their unions. And despite Gompers' own opposition to broader social activity and electoral politics, AFL unionists in Ontario regularly experimented in such fields. Hamilton labour had its own independent representative sitting in the Ontario Legislature from 1906. By the First World War, Ontario workers, then, had a rich and varied tradition of struggle and well-established notions of workplace justice and honour.[10]

Yet this was a tenuous possession in the economic maelstrom of the Laurier era. If the nineteenth century seemed remote to the workers in this study, that remoteness was largely due to the dramatic transformation of the regional economy, a process that outpaced workers' organizations. Although the notion that the Canadian economy suffered a 'great depression' from 1873 to 1896 has come under fire, historians and economists agree that the subsequent period did represent a unique period of expansion and transformation of industrial capitalism. W.A. Mackintosh estimated that the net value of production in manufacturing more than doubled from 1900 to 1910 and again by 1923. Urquhart and Buckley's estimates suggest a fivefold increase in the gross value of production in manufacturing in Canada from 1900 to 1917. R.C. Brown and Ramsay Cook captured the regional focus of the expansion of manufacturing 'from south-central Ontario through the peninsula' where 'hardly a week passed without the announcement of a new company being formed, a new factory being built, and hundreds of new men being hired to man the production lines.' Ian Drummond further notes that, within Ontario, this growth was 'remarkably wide ranging' in terms of the industries effected as well as being geographically dispersed through the region. Toronto and Hamilton attracted the most industries, but a number of smaller centres also emerged as significant industrial cities. Berlin, Brantford, Galt, Guelph, Oshawa, Peterborough, St Catharines, St Thomas, Sarnia, Stratford, Windsor, and Woodstock are enumerated by Drummond; all fall within the parameters of this study.[11] Smaller centres, especially those with local industries based on water power, were more vulnerable. Eastern Ontario declined in industrial significance.

Most importantly, these were not merely changes of scale. On the basis of innovative technologies and radically new products, whole new sectors of manufacturing arose. A 'second industrial revolution' was in the making. Just as iron and steam characterized earlier industrialization, a broader array of steel, electrical, rubber and chemical industries emerged as the dominant industries of the new century.[12] In 1900 the automobile industry was non-existent; a decade later it employed 2,400 workers. The electrical industry grew sixfold in the decade, while iron and steel quintupled production.[13] Such new industries drew upon few craft traditions and, at best, unions recruited only small numbers of the workers they employed, generally the most skilled. The vast numbers of unskilled and 'semi-skilled' workers in the chaotic labour market of the early twentieth century were beyond the grasp of AFL unions. Such workers had few identifiable skills to defend or to use as bargaining chips. Establishing secure unions in such industries seemed impossible. Few unions tried. Craig Heron's recent study of the Canadian steel industry demonstrates the difficulties. Steel companies recruited workers without traditions of craftsmanship or organization and tapped a labour market of workers without a long-term commitment to the local community or industry. On the shop floor, an often tyrannical foreman ruled his petty empire and workers had little autonomous power upon which to build a craft tradition. While semi-skilled workers soon acquired invaluable 'know-how,' they were less successful in gaining recognition of such knowledge as a craft.[14] The electrical industry was similar. The majority of workers in the new plants built by companies such as Canadian General Electric or Westinghouse were not 'electricians' as defined by the International Brotherhood of Electrical Workers. How could a craft union organize them, while still demanding recognition of the fully trained electrician?

As these examples demonstrate, technological innovation was not the only change unions had to face. New industries and old were dominated by huge corporations whose control rested far from the place of production. Local manufacturers ceded ground to the symbol of the new age of 'monopoly capitalism': the financier. In the United States, the Morgan and Rockefeller empires had already become the targets of populist outrage. In Canada, Max Aitken, the future Lord Beaverbrook, was perhaps the best known of this breed, and the names of mergers he constructed epitomized monopolist aspirations: the Steel Company of Canada, Canada Cement, and the Canadian Car and Foundry Company. Aitken was hardly alone. In 1913, the *Grain Growers' Guide* listed him as only one of the forty-two 'aristocrats' associated with the large banks and railways in Toronto and Montreal who, it charged, had come to own Canada. The *Guide* had cause for alarm. In the previous four years Canada had undergone its first full-scale merger movement. Between 1909 and 1913, 97 mergers involving 221 firms with combined assets of more than $200 million took place. The cumulative effect was unmistakable. In 1901, firms with more than $1 million in sales accounted for only 15 per cent of total manufactured output. In 1921, that proportion surpassed 50 per cent. In

southern Ontario, control was often even more remote, as the protective tariff finally bore fruit in attracting giant American corporations.
Firms such as International Harvester, United States Rubber, Swift,
Ford, and Goodyear emerged as major employers in the region. As
Palmer has concluded, the century that, which in Laurier's famous
declaration was to belong to Canada 'belonged, more correctly, to
monopoly capital.'[15] Faced with a rising tide of concentrated economic
power, craft unionism strove to tread water. In Hamilton, where so
many of such firms were located, the number of craft unions stagnated
in the decade before the war. Michael Piva has noted a similar situation
in Toronto.[16]

Nor were the workers who came to toil in these and older industries
necessarily familiar to craft unionists. Increasingly, they were workers
from southern or eastern Europe who came for a season, or a few
years, to earn enough money to establish themselves in their homelands
or in the Canadian West. These were men without the sort of long-
term commitment to a job or a trade that had motivated craft unionism.
Rather, they responded to the mercurial demands of the Canadian and
international economies. Moreover, as sojourners, theirs was a life apart.
Overwhelmingly male and single, they inhabited the 'foreign colonies'
that sprang up near large industrial plants. Near the Steel Company
in Hamilton, social investigators counted 232 men, 19 women, and 12
children living in seventeen houses. Included in the number were Italians, Bulgarians, Poles, Rumanians, and Macedonians.[17] Census figures
are notoriously inaccurate in this regard. Immigrant transiency, language difficulties on the part of census takers, as well as the changing
map of central Europe combine to make statistics unreliable. John
Zucci's count of Italians in Toronto demonstrates the degree to which
census figures were underestimates as well as the failure of the census
to distinguish between permanent residents and sojourners. The census
does make clear the differences within the region, however. Far more
immigrants came to centres with greater opportunities, such as Toronto or Hamilton, while cities like Peterborough or London largely
retained their Anglo-Celtic character. In different cities and industries,
unionists were challenged to organize a rapidly changing working class
that lacked common experiences.[18]

If unions had difficulty dealing with new problems, they were overwhelmed with an old one: unemployment. The particularly sharp economic depression of 1913–14 devastated labour's ranks and undermined
much of whatever control over the labour market it had been able to
attain. The wave of industrial unrest analysed by Heron and Palmer

appeared to be exhausted; estimated union membership in the province as a whole fell by more than 25 per cent. The problem was most serious in Toronto, where 1914 began with perhaps 15,000 unemployed. Rather than spurring economic growth, the war initially dislocated the revival then underway.[19] However strong its traditions in southern Ontario, organized labour was not in an advantageous position to press its claims in 1914.

Confronting Militarism

Ontario's workers naturally viewed the cataclysmic international events through the lens of their own history. Not only were workers incredulous of their employers' sudden professions of service and self-sacrifice, but they also grew to interpret the aims of the war in light of the ideals for which the labour movement had long fought. This was particularly the case as the two struggles shared a common language; each sought to redress injustices, restrain the abuse of power, and defend democracy. The failure of wartime appeals to patriotism to derail labour's struggles can best be explained by the fact that workers did not consider their own actions unpatriotic. One was the extension of the other. Fighting profiteers and would-be kaisers at home was consistent with opposing the enemy abroad. Democracy and freedom had a specific content for workers who faced powerful and (in the language of the day) autocratic employers. Workers' war aims could not be confined to the trenches of Europe. The language of war gave them ammunition for domestic battles.

The tendency of workers to respond to events according to their own class experiences was apparent before the war. Trade unionists' initial response to the gathering storm clouds was informed by the principles of working-class solidarity and internationalism. From 1911 the TLCC supported a plan of international general strikes in the event of war. Although rhetoric would outstrip action, such a policy was consistent with the AFL's participation in international pacifist bodies. Moreover, such sentiments persisted even as war broke out; on 4 August 1914, TLCC president J.C. Watters declared that the 'policy of the Labour party is to make war against war and we are proud of Keir Hardie's proposal that there should be a great international strike against war.' Although the TLCC executive never mounted any real opposition to the war and declared its support of Britain and France as bastions of democracy, it is noteworthy that it felt forced to defend its inactivity by claiming that 'the working class in one country alone cannot stop war.'[20] It also pledged its willingness to work towards an early peace.

While Thomas Socknat's study of Canadian pacifism has awakened us to a long history of anti-war sentiment, specifically working-class attitudes to war have received scant attention. Evidence that the TLCC's positions represented the real concerns of many trade unionists and not just its national leaders is to be found in the actions of local trades and labour councils. Prior to the war, those working-class concerns that were not limited to a particular craft tended to find their focus in city trades councils. In contrast to the TLCC, which met only once a year, trades councils more immediately reflected developing currents, since they usually met fortnightly and delegates were in regular communication with their locals. By 1914, concern about militarism was a regular theme in a number of cities. The London Trades and Labor Council (TLC), for instance, strongly opposed the teaching of military drill in schools as fostering a spirit of militarism. The Toronto District Labor Council (TDLC) expressed similar views in 1916, unanimously denouncing the Board of Education for spreading a 'monstrous doctrine' by encouraging such exercises, and was angered when the board refused to hear its delegation. The Brantford and Peterborough TLCs challenged jingoism and the establishment of home guards.[21]

The paradox of attempting to maintain an anti-militarist stance during a war that was being fought, ostensibly, against militarism, soon fractured any prospect of labour unanimity. Moreover, the labour movement itself added little to clarify the concept. Harriet Dunlop Prenter, soon to be a central figure in the labour political movement, reflected one particularly idealist current of thought when she attacked church ministers for supporting military training in schools: 'After all, militarism is not a system: it is a spirit, and if we allow this thing now, we are denying the very principle for which our men are dying in Europe.'[22] At the same time, vague anti-militarism was flexible enough to allow for a range of attitudes towards the war. The London TLC, for instance, abandoned its past practice of refusing to allow bands in military uniform to participate in Labour Day parades and grimly declared: 'It is clearly recognized ... that when mobilization has actually taken place and a state of war exists the time to enter sensible and useful opposition to the war has passed. This has been the policy of the Socialists in Germany, France and other countries involved in the present conflict who have had to bow to the inevitable without endorsing the principle of war and armaments in themselves.'[23] This tone of critical support for the war soon gained dominance throughout

southern Ontario. The old tensions persisted, but military action was
the order of the day. At a recruiting meeting held in the Toronto
Labour Temple in 1916, for example, a Lieutenant-Colonel Wright
created a most favourable impression by declaring his opposition to
militarism of both the Prussian and British varieties. The situation, he
concluded, demanded that workers vanquish the former first, but the
latter too would be addressed in due course.[24]

This measured response to the war contrasts sharply with at least
one historian's assertion that 'Ontario's urban residents could hardly
contain their patriotic enthusiasm.'[25] The Toronto District Labor
Council, for instance, opposed the intimidation of single men by military recruiters, and 'hunger-scription' caused by continued unemployment. Most importantly, labour opposed the 'paper patriotism' of
the employers when it was the workers who were being called upon
to assume the risks and costs of the war. Particularly galling was the
example of employers notorious for paying low-wages who, while making a great show of their contributions to the Patriotic Fund, cut workers' wages. Equally disturbing was the practice of companies such as
the Grand Trunk Railway of collecting 'voluntary' contributions from
their employees, many of whom valued their jobs and 'doubtless think
it may not be healthy to keep their name off the list.'[26]

Such practices reinforced an attitude that helps explain working-class
actions during and after the conflict. When an employer in Owen
Sound cut wages and provoked an iron moulders' strike in October
1914, he was denounced as 'unpatriotic'[27] for placing profit and self-
interest not only above the war but also above the well-being of his
workers. Already, workers were defining for themselves the 'national
interest' and implicitly formulating their own set of war aims. The
refusal of workers to respond to patriotic appeals to accept lower wages,
longer hours, deskilling, and the limiting of union power can be explained in large part by a contrary notion of 'patriotism' that was shaped
by workers' own experience. Working-class support for the war was
contingent upon a belief that it was not simply a militarist adventure
pursued in the interests of capital, but a campaign for goals consistent
with their own interests. Events over four years, however, would fuel
workers' wariness. For most workers, convinced of the justice of the
Empire's cause though they may have been, the war would come to
have two fronts – national and class – both fought under the banner
of democracy.

None of this should imply unanimity among workers, although the
mass actions that the armistice would bring indicate that many currents

in the workers' movement shared a common trajectory. The localism that characterized the pre-war union movement can be seen reflected in the various city trades councils. The Hamilton TLC represents one end of this spectrum; it was unanimous and enthusiastic in its support of the local recruiting league.[28] The same issue, however, tore the Toronto District Labor Council apart. When TDLC secretary T.A. Stevenson made a recruitment proposal, a delegate was quickly on his feet suggesting that 'the capitalist class ought to be left alone to fight its own battles.' The next speaker pointed to the example of the British Labour Party in arguing that the recruiting drive should be supported. A third argued that labour should be represented on the recruiting league to prevent 'bogus patriots out after war profits' from misrepresenting the views of the workers. In the end, the TDLC voted eighteen to twelve to participate, but sent as one of its two representatives cigar maker Thomas Black, an outspoken opponent of militarism.[29]

This contrast between localities is best explained by the relative influence of socialists in each centre. In Toronto, the Social Democratic Party of Canada (SDP) had built an organization of about 1,000 members on the eve of the war and gained some influence on the TDLC. In the 1914 municipal election, it ran a slate of thirteen candidates and succeeded in electing James Simpson to the city's Board of Control with 20,695 votes, the highest ever recorded by any candidate to the post. Still, even in Toronto socialism was a minority current, although with significant political influence within the labour movement. In contrast to the vague anti-militarism that had wider currency among organized workers, socialism offered both an analysis and a strategy for action against the war. The SDP characterized the war as a fight for markets between capitalists and appealed to the workers of Canada 'to refrain from lending any assistance in the war.' SDP locals followed suit, declaring that the workers' war was against capital. Toronto socialists regularly spoke on topics such as 'The Truth about the War' or the 'Economic Causes of the War.'[30]

In London, as well, a Radical Club functioning with participation of local unionists sponsored a number of anti-war speakers and received fair publicity in the local press.[31] However, as the mobilization for the war progressed, this political space inexorably shrank. An important speech by Simpson in February 1915 must have reflected the sentiments of many. Although socialists were organized to remove the root causes of war, he argued, their strength had been greatly overestimated. Then, like socialist leaders in most other belligerent countries,

Simpson went a step further and rose to the defence of the war effort. This speech reflected strongly divided loyalties. On the one hand, the war was described as playing a positive role in the inevitable movement of capitalism towards socialism typical of the mechanistic thinking of the Second International. True, France, the United States, and Britain were capitalist, but unlike Russia, Germany, and Austria, they were not reactionary. Regimes of the latter category curtailed democratic rights that would hasten the free development of the working-class movement necessary for the attainment of socialism. One of the products of an allied victory, Simpson argued, would be the continued development of industrial capitalism in Russia; the progress of world history required support for the Empire's cause.

On the other hand, Simpson praised British socialists for their 'educational propaganda' against the war despite their lack of any organized opposition to their government's war policy. That Simpson could defend such an inherently contradictory position – supporting the war effort but favouring propaganda against it – reveals the confusion and political drift of many socialists. At the end of the speech, a member of the small, revolutionary Socialist Party of North America asked Simpson why he did not call for a general strike against the war. The answer demonstrated resignation more than principled support for the war. It would be folly, the speaker suggested, to call such a strike given the consciousness of the workers. For inspiration, Simpson could only point to German anti-war socialist Karl Liebknecht, who had stood by his working-class principles against both the state and his party.[32] As far as southern Ontario was concerned, coherent opposition to the war had dissolved.

Whatever its disposition towards the war, labour was seriously concerned with the more pressing issue of unemployment. Yet the ubiquitous presence of the war already overshadowed its unemployment relief efforts. In January 1915, fund-raising entertainment at Massey Hall organized by the TDLC on behalf of the unemployed reflected the inroads being made by the war upon popular culture, even among organized labour. Following renditions of 'The Death of Nelson' and 'We'll Never Let the Old Flag Fall,' the audience was treated to a recitation of 'The Empire Flag' by an entertainer enfolded in the Union Jack.[33] Ironically, even those whose message was that the problems of workers at home should not be forgotten in the enthusiasm of the war were learning to speak in a patriotic language that, for the moment, lacked a vocabulary to address their concerns.

Confronting the War Economy

In time military demands fuelled economic recovery as millions of dollars were poured into the economy for munitions and war-supply production. This was particularly the case in southern Ontario where most of the orders of the Shell Committee and its successor, the Imperial Munitions Board (IMB), were placed.[34] Although workers tended to join their employers in clamouring for such work, unions quickly ascertained that the maintenance of union wages and conditions was far from a guiding principle in the letting of contracts.[35] Run by capitalists, and under constant pressure to ensure the regular production of war materials, the Shell Committee, and later the IMB, proved unsympathetic to workers' complaints. By early 1915, clothing-workers' unions drew attention to the poor conditions under which uniforms were being made and a machinists' union delegation went to Ottawa in an attempt to ensure better wages for its members engaged in the production of shells. Trades councils throughout the region took up the fight in defence of local affiliates working on IMB contracts.[36]

Such action proved futile. In response to wage cuts by some local war contractors, delegates to the Toronto District Labor Council heaped abuse on the federal Department of Labour. The anger expressed reflected a feeling of betrayal, as the department had been viewed by many as labour's avenue into the inner workings of the government. Union leaders declared the department a 'joke' calling the minister of labour 'the one wallflower in the Cabinet who had really nothing to do.'[37] However, Labour minister Thomas W. Crothers' plea that the issues upon which unions were demanding action were beyond his jurisdiction was not entirely disingenuous. The creation of various boards and commissions by the government marked a devolution of authority away from Parliament and, in the eyes of labour, away from any real form of democratic control. It was a disturbing trend unionists were also confronting on a municipal level.[38] The creation of the IMB in late November 1915 placed a vast amount of power and money in the hands of a small group of businessmen, firmly led (as Michael Bliss has demonstrated) by Toronto millionaire meat-packer Joseph W. Flavelle. In this case, the problem was compounded by the fact that the IMB was an agent of the British Ministry of Munitions and not directly responsible to the Canadian government.[39] Small wonder that labour did not know where to turn to remonstrate against the abuses suffered at the hands of IMB contractors.

Organized labour's initial strategy to ensure the maintenance of wages and conditions was to demand 'fair-wage' clauses in war contracts. Such clauses would require employers to pay wages that were comparable to those of similar workers in the district. This policy had been familiar to workers ever since the federal government had declared itself in favour of a fair-wage system by a resolution of the House of Commons in 1900 and had implemented it on public-works projects. In order to determine local wage levels and prepare schedules of wages to be applied to particular jobs, the Department of Labour maintained a small force of fair-wage officers. This system had its shortcomings. Most obviously, the determination of local wage levels, or more particularly the specification of the analogous group of workers whose wages were to be considered the standard, was open to dispute. Generally, workers sought to have union wage levels recognized as 'fair wages,' a not unreasonable argument since it was usually unionists on public works who were in a position to make their demands heard, and they hoped not to be compared with unorganized workers. Although the system did not guarantee a favourable response to workers' demands, it did hold some advantages for labour. Most importantly, the system provided an arena within which workers could press their claims and receive a hearing. Moreover, it directly involved the government in the person of the fair-wage officer, rather than forcing workers simply to confront a contractor who could claim that his hands were tied by the terms agreed to with the government.

Trade unionists assumed that the Department of Labour would follow this long-established policy as the federal government undertook to supply military requirements. When it became clear that neither the Shell Committee nor the IMB intended to be guided by this precedent, the labour movement, and particularly the International Association of Machinists (IAM), undertook a concerted campaign in defence of the fair-wage system. A test case was made of the Canada Foundry Company in Toronto where machinists were working on shell contracts for ten to twelve hours a day for wages as low as sixteen to twenty-five cents an hour.[40] As an integral part of the Canadian General Electric and Allis-Chalmers merger of 1913, the target exemplified the growing oligopolies that labour confronted. Moreover, this combination of companies was controlled by a long-time *bête noire* of organized labour, Senator Frederic Nicholls. His vocal and unbending defence of the open shop appeared calculated to draw fire from organized labour.[41] Only the threat of a strike brought any response at all. The federal Department of Labour investigated and confirmed that conditions were as the unions had claimed, adding that Nicholls 'was firm in his statement that he would not alter the working conditions and that he was prepared to let the men strike and fight it out to a finish.'[42]

The Canada Foundry situation was not unique. The intervention of the Department of Labour headed off a strike at the John Inglis Company plant. Notably one of the major issues in dispute in this case was the classification and wage rate of unskilled 'operators or specialists' who threatened to replace skilled machinists. The IAM was persuaded to allow the management to determine the proficiency of specialists, but the IMB's interest in eliminating the control of skilled workers through 'scientific management' techniques of closely timing and supervising tasks threatened craft unionism at its core. The long run of standardized shrapnel shells produced in Ontario created a new potential for deskilling.[43] As disputes threatened to multiply, officers of the TLCC and the international unions took their case directly to the federal cabinet. In January 1916 they presented their demand that a Fair Wage Board be established to set and enforce schedules.

Their argument was stated in a defensive voice. 'We would be remiss in our duty,' they suggested, 'if we did not point out that the demands for patriotic service at this time makes it almost impossible for the workers to protest against unfair conditions without being charged with unpatriotic action. For that reason the government should recognize the seriousness of their obligations to prevent employers from taking advantage of the war conditions to increase the exploitation of their employes.'[44] In what was to appear as a direct snub to the leadership of the labour movement, the government ignored this advice and, to add injury to the insult, acted directly against the wishes of the unions by using its powers under the War Measures Act to extend the terms of the Industrial Disputes Investigation Act (IDIA) to cover munitions workers. The requirement, under the IDIA, that strikes or lockouts be delayed pending compulsory conciliation could only hamstring workers who, in a context of widespread labour scarcity, were finally gaining some leverage in the labour market. As IAM international vice-president J.A. McClelland pointed out, the Borden government was acting inconsistently in claiming that it had no jurisdiction over imperial authorities while taking the 'drastic action' of bringing munitions workers under the IDIA.[45]

The extension of the IDIA suddenly revealed a developing rift in the trade union movement between many of its leaders and the membership. It became apparent that the TLCC executive had been aware that such action was being considered but had failed to alert the membership, relying instead on its own efforts at lobbying the government.

The TDLC unanimously censured the TLCC executive, and the Hamilton TLC asked exactly how long it had been aware that the IDIA was to be extended to the munitions industries and why it had failed to notify the TLCC affiliates. Implicit in such actions was a criticism of the bureaucratic mode of functioning adopted by the TLCC leaders. Instead of relying on an informed and active membership to ensure that workers' demands would not be ignored, they had overestimated the strength of their own personal powers of persuasion within the corridors of Parliament. As lobbyists, they could be easily ignored. Interestingly, the idea of a Fair Wage Board, as opposed to the simple inclusion of fair-wage clauses in IMB contracts, had little support beyond the executive of the TLCC.[46] The establishment of a permanent board, which would include representatives of labour, once again reflected bureaucratic thinking.

By March 1916, matters were coming to a head. In Toronto the IAM had been particularly successful, having organized six hundred munitions workers in ten months and signed agreements giving workers a nine-hour day with more than fifty of the city's contract shops. Given the scarcity of skilled workers and the demands of munitions production, many Toronto employers acted in accord with the assessment of the vice-president of Steel and Radiation, Limited, that labour's demands were not 'altogether unreasonable' and that 'this was no time for manufacturers to "split hairs" with labour.' Employers were, however, far from unanimous on this score. When the IAM approached Canada Foundry demanding parity with other plants that had settled for the nine-hour day, the company responded by dismissing a number of its six hundred workers, claiming lack of work for them to do. Nicholls later admitted that this was not true and that work was being contracted out to other manufacturers. The reaction of the Toronto District Lodge of the IAM contrasted sharply with the TLCC's activities in Ottawa. It threatened to call a general strike of all Toronto machinists in support of the Canada Foundry workers.[47]

Hamilton munitions workers were less successful than their Toronto counterparts in gaining any concessions from the employers. Increased membership and the example of gains in many Toronto plants convinced the IAM that the moment for a successful assault on Hamilton employers had arrived.[48] Faced with the threat of city-wide munitions strikes in two of the main industrial centres in Canada, the Borden government was finally motivated to act. A royal commission chaired by Judge Colin Snyder, along with William Inglis of the John Inglis Company and McClelland of the IAM, was established to investigate the situation in both cities. In itself, this was a victory for labour. Although the government hoped to postpone any strikes, and perhaps defuse the entire situation, its action was not without risk. Thomas Findlay, president of the Massey-Harris Company, itself a major munitions producer, felt that 'such a Commission, at the present time, in Toronto, would be like carrying fire into a powder magazine' by bringing 'to a head differences that might otherwise be avoided.' By providing a platform for workers to air their grievances, the commission would enable workers' resentment to become focused. The vice-president of National Steel Car in Hamilton also felt that the entire process played into the hands of the unions.[49]

The report of the commission did indeed favour the workers. Although Inglis refused to go along with the recommendation for the nine-hour day, it was unanimously determined that workers' wage demands were justified.[50] Toronto employers were not averse to this decision, since many had already conceded these conditions. Hamilton manufacturers, however, dug in their heels. On 12 June, perhaps 2,000 munitions workers struck the city's major industrial employers.

The Hamilton munitions strike has been studied in detail by Myer Siemiatycki, so its details will not be reviewed here.[51] It is, however, worthwhile noting some features that were common in subsequent wartime conflicts. The first of these was the popularity of unionism. Although figures are unclear, at least four hundred unorganized workers participated in the strike from the outset, and perhaps many more.[52] Although we are often confined to discussing organized unionists' attitudes to the war and wartime class relations, there is abundant evidence that unorganized workers willingly followed the lead of the unions when the opportunity arose. The ideas expressed by labour papers and working-class orators proved to have a broad resonance among workers.

Secondly, the impetus for the strike came directly from rank-and-file unionists rather than the union leadership. Department of Labour fair-wage officer E.N. Compton wired Ottawa that the munitions workers were beyond the control of local union officers. He commented that he 'had never seen the men so determined and anxious to quit work, and I have heard [Richard] Riley [the Union Business Agent] and McClelland [the International Vice-President] abused in round terms. A number from the National Steel Car Company threatened to take a holiday but wiser counsel prevailed.'[53] Riley and McClelland were not considered to be conservative union leaders and were not opposed to the strike. On this occasion they were merely attempting to postpone the strike until negotiations were concluded. In September 1915 the *Industrial Banner* had commented that only the moderation of the workers had prevented a series of munitions strikes.[54] That situation no longer obtained.

Thirdly, confrontations tended quickly to overflow the bounds of an individual shop or employer. Machinists throughout Toronto had threatened to strike in sympathy with workers at Canada Foundry, while in Hamilton, the entire trade was drawn into battle. Initially, this was due to feelings of solidarity engendered in the rapidly expanding and relatively homogeneous munitions industry, but subsequent events reflected a growing tendency for workers to perceive their interests as a class, raising the possibilities that various disputes would erupt into confrontations involving large numbers of workers.

A fourth feature of this strike was the greater intervention on the part of the state. Besides the establishment of the royal commission, the federal Department of Labour sent Compton to Hamilton to mediate the dispute.[55] This reflected a growing tendency of the department to use its fair-wage officers as roving trouble-shooters. Compton found himself mediating countless potential eruptions throughout southern Ontario in the years that followed.[56] This widening role for the Department of Labour stemmed from the fact that a single dispute could spark a wider conflagration. However, intervention, it should be observed, was purely pragmatic; the failure to codify the role of individuals such as Compton within a new legal system of labour relations will be discussed later.

Fifthly, the strike revealed a greater degree of organization on the part of employers. As the strike was about to begin, an 'Employers' Association of Hamilton' was formed. Its declaration of principles included the following points:

> 1. To secure for employers and employes freedom of contract in the matter of employment, irrespective of membership in this or kindred associations ...
> 3. To oppose restriction of output, sympathetic strikes, and boycotts ...
> 5. To prevent interference with those seeking work ...

It was, in short, an open shop association formed to fight trade unionism. A similar organization was founded in Toronto in 1902,[57] but few existed elsewhere. By 1919, they were to act effectively in Hamilton, Toronto, and Kitchener. The question of capitalist class organization and strategy would emerge as a particularly hot issue during the first year following the armistice.

The sixth element worth noting was the censorship of news about working-class activity. It was soon apparent that the prime motive in censoring news of the strike was not strictly military but was mainly an effort to prevent the strike from spreading beyond Hamilton, particularly to Toronto. Chief press censor Col. E.J. Chambers admitted as much in private correspondence. The *Industrial Banner* concluded that the government was attempting to undermine working-class solidarity and isolate the Hamilton strikers by censoring news of the strike; at considerable risk it published full accounts of the conflict.[58]

Finally, the relative ineffectiveness of patriotic appeals aimed at persuading the workers to abandon their struggle was particularly noteworthy. The Employers' Association placed advertisements in Hamilton papers claiming that the strike 'has been wholly inspired, developed and encouraged by paid officials of alien labor interests, WHO HAVE ABSOLUTELY NO CONCERN IN THE CAUSE FOR WHICH BRITAIN IS FIGHTING.'[59] The *Industrial Banner's* response to this was blunt. Since it was the employers who rejected the report of the royal commission and provoked the strike, they 'should be the ones to demonstrate their patriotism.'[60] Workers appear not to have been swayed by these types of appeals, and few returned to work. The strike revealed a working-class immunity to jingoistic enthusiasms that has already been noted in the actions of local trades councils. Workers took the war emergency seriously, but they were not willing to allow manufacturers to take advantage of the war to profit at their expense. As a leader of the machinists' union declared, such strikes were in solidarity with their brothers-in-arms. It was organized labour's responsibility to preserve working conditions and wages at home for the day the soldiers returned.[61] Implicitly, they were fighting the obnoxious by-products of war, jingoism and profiteering. They were also defending their own class interests.

The Hamilton munitions workers lost their strike. As a consequence, events in Hamilton began to diverge in an even more marked way from Toronto, where unions, as yet, had suffered no major defeat. Hamilton munitions workers had taken the plunge by conducting a major strike in wartime, and were unsuccessful. A strike of such magnitude was not repeated for the duration of the war. But working-class scepticism about the goals of employers had deepened. With the fundamental grievances still to be resolved, rough times lay ahead.

Trade Union Leadership under Pressure

While employers had prevailed in the Hamilton strike, they looked to
the future with little confidence and turned to Ottawa for support.
The Canadian Manufacturers' Association (CMA) and its journal, *Industrial Canada*, campaigned for state intervention in order to relieve
growing labour-market pressures and undercut the leverage workers
had gained. Proposals included the suspension of the Lord's Day Act
to allow seven-day work weeks and the relaxation of immigration re-
strictions by suspending the Alien Labor Act. The Toronto branch of
the CMA demanded a national registration of labour as a means of
regulating the labour market, particularly for skilled workers. The
Financial Post urged similar action.[62] For its part, the Trades and Labor
Congress clung to the long-established mechanism of fair-wage clauses
as a means of defusing a tense industrial situation.

The employers' proposals, Labour minister Thomas Crothers recognized, were clearly provocative. For the moment, the option presented by labour held greater promise. At the end of 1916 the
Conservative government recognized the possibility of offering organized labour something, perhaps fair-wage clauses, as a *quid pro quo* for
its support for registration and perhaps even conscription. This course
was blocked by the IMB. Flavelle had argued, before the Hamilton
strike, that placing fair-wage provisions in new IMB contracts would
cause conflict in plants already working on contracts that did not have
such clauses.[63] His real objection, however, was that fair-wage clauses
would tend to make the IMB a direct player in labour disputes and
provide a focus for working-class action. As Flavelle wrote to his director of munitions labour, Mark H. Irish, 'We are in the country to
observe the conditions which are present in the country and not to
attempt to interpret for manufacturers what their duty is to organized
labour ... I do not want to create a situation where they [organized
workers] can come to us over the head of the contractors, or to say
that our Department of Labour made promises to them.'[64] Not only
was Flavelle hoping, as Bliss points out,[65] to prevent the IMB from
becoming any more of a lightning-rod for working-class frustrations
than it already was, but he was also seeking to maintain a degree of
working-class disorganization by ensuring that conflicts occurred, as
much as possible, at the level of individual firms. As we shall see, the
fear that the establishment of any new industrial relations system might
provide an occasion for workers to participate in a more unified manner

– beyond the level of an individual enterprise – became a preoccupation of capital after the war.

The Borden government, true to form, did not consult labour in its plans to institute National Service Registration in 1916. The TLCC was still very much on the outside looking in with respect to government policy. At the IMB, the situation was not much different; Flavelle instructed Irish not to see labour leader Tom Moore, 'because you will only have an irritating and stormy interview.'[66] Conscription, in the spring of 1917, laid bare the strategic prostration of the established trade union leadership.[67] Verbal radicalism combined with inaction demonstrated both a perceived threat to its authority in the labour movement and its unwillingness or inability to mobilize trade unionists against the government. The threat posed by conscription was twofold. Firstly, it threatened severely to constrain trade-union action. At an earlier meeting with the federal government, McClelland had voiced a widespread concern that the implicit corollary of military conscription was 'industrial conscription.' Certainly *Industrial Canada's* pleading for precisely such a policy provided a basis for such fears.[68] Even if workers were not strictly tied to their jobs by statute, their mobility would be effectively curtailed if they were liable for military service if they left their employment. Labour would no longer be able to benefit as it had from conditions of labour scarcity. Secondly, union leaders had an additional problem of their own; their credibility was at stake. Having failed to win any concessions from the government or the IMB, and having acquiesced in the war and, in December 1916, national registration, they had been forced to establish a fall-back position on the issue of conscription. TLCC president J.C. Watters, in an official statement, argued that registration did not contravene the congress's war policy. He added, however, that: 'Should the government undertake to adopt military or even industrial conscription a wholly different state of affairs would obtain. The action of the Vancouver convention, reaffirmed at Toronto, clearly sets forth the position of the congress in unqualified opposition to conscription.'[69] This left little room to manoeuvre. In 1916, the union leaders had accepted both the extension of the IDIA and registration. Now, a year later, the risks of inactivity had grown, for both the trade-union movement and their own positions.

Unfortunately, by the time the congress leaders got their long-awaited interview with Borden, conscription was practically an accomplished fact. They chose instead to focus on the IMB's labour policy.[70] If anything was to be gained, it was on that front. The TLCC executive called a conference of eighty international trade union officers, including the unaffiliated railway brotherhoods, to begin on 1 June. This response fulfilled several objectives. The TLCC executive could no longer be accused of not notifying affiliates, as had occurred the previous year, and also could deflect any blame if it was unsuccessful. Also, by placing the issue in the hands of affiliates, 'direct action could be taken.'[71] The TLCC itself was a 'purely legislative' body that could not call strikes. The leaders of the international unions jealously guarded this prerogative, claiming that a central body might use it irresponsibly. The mechanism of a conference allowed this restriction to be side-stepped without being removed. At the same time, the TLCC leadership was able to retain some control over the composition of the conference. The international unions, not union locals or trades councils, chose the representatives.

The statement drafted by the TLCC conference took direct aim at the Imperial Munitions Board. It cited examples of the 'hostile attitude' of the IMB to organized labour, pointing to long hours and low wages on IMB contracts as well as what it considered the 'unnecessary dilution of labor' by encouraging the hiring of unskilled, and particularly female, workers to replace skilled men at lower wages. Interestingly, it demanded that the IMB be reorganized with direct trade-union representation: a reflection of the thinking that had led the TLCC executive to demand fair-wage boards with union members. The conference also expressed itself as 'emphatically opposed to the proposed conscription measure and demanded action in reducing the high cost of living.'[72]

Still no action to press these demands was proposed and, not surprisingly, Flavelle was unmoved. He repeated to the prime minister that a fair-wage policy would be 'unwise,' arguing that manufacturers might ask to be released from munitions contracts if new labour conditions were forced on them.[73] Mark Irish, not sharing his superior's myopic aversion to unions, had a more sophisticated understanding of developments in the trade union movement. He recognized that union leaders were under great pressure from the rank and file of their organizations to produce some benefits and that they shared with the IMB an interest in preventing a rebellion from below and its resulting disruption of production. In an incisive assessment, he argued that

the leaders of organized Labour have always credited to themselves the ability of securing alleged concessions. True these concessions in reality are negligible in their benefits, but they form a peg upon which Labour Leaders are enabled to hang their claims to future consideration by the rank and file.

In this regard they have found themselves helpless with the Munitions Board and recognizing among the workpeople, engaged in the production of Munitions, a large body over which they have no control, and another large body over which their control is gradually weakening, these Labour Leaders have become alarmed lest their re-election to Office is in jeopardy.

Little would be lost by the IMB's granting of such clauses, Irish argued, because the union leadership 'knows just as well as you that the Clause is no good except at a Union Meeting.'[74]

Labour minister Thomas Crothers held similar, if less cynical, views. He felt that Flavelle had, with one unnamed exception, co-operated with the department to ensure 'fair conditions' and that there were few real grounds for complaint. But 'I have never been able, for the life of me,' he added, 'to see any reasonable objections to the fair wage clause being put in these contracts.' A report by Crothers' deputy minister, F.A. Acland, claimed that informal investigation of grievances, along with the machinery provided by the Industrial Disputes Investigation Act, was sufficient and would only be duplicated by fair-wage measures. Given Flavelle's obstinacy and Acland's assurances, the Government let the issue slide. Flavelle, as it turned out, was less sanguine. He undertook a survey of munitions contracts in order to determine what measures were being taken on a plant-by-plant basis to avoid conflict and urged some measure of 'co-operation' with workers. While responses were mixed, the comments of some of the larger employers portended conflict. The John Inglis Company claimed that it was '[a]lmost impossible to co-operate with present class of help as they appear to be getting too much money and don't want to work,' while the Midland Engine Works Company claimed that 'not 5% of men are moved by any sentiment of love of country and the dollar is the only thing that counts.' The Canada Forge Company also reported continued unrest.[75]

Confronting the State

The stalemate was prolonged by the 1917 federal election, after which the situation appeared, suddenly, to shift. Recognizing that conscription would intensify labour-market pressures, and concerned about mounting industrial unrest, the Borden government was under some pressure to re-evaluate its attitude towards labour. The author of the new policy, it appears, was the former leader of the Ontario Liberal Party, Newton Wesley Rowell. A prominent social reformer, Rowell was committed to conciliatory methods as a means of attaining industrial peace and was potentially open to recognizing key labour concerns. Consequently, the War Committee of Cabinet, in which Rowell played a prominent role, proposed that a major conference with labour take place in January 1918. The *Industrial Banner* proclaimed that the government finally had realized its mistake in ignoring the trade-union movement. The labour contingent, which eventually numbered about sixty, was chosen by the TLCC executive and comprised mainly officers and business agents of the international unions.[76] Following the conference, the TLCC executive expressed great satisfaction at its outcome and declared that the government's 'attitude is now one of co-operation with the organized Labour movement.'[77] What was gained? The Borden government, for its part, received at least tacit approval for registration and the Military Service Act. For the unions, the answer is not as clear. Statements issued afterwards made no mention of the IMB or, surprisingly, of the fair-wage issue. The labour representatives had been given the opportunity to present a range of demands and proposals, but the government refused to commit itself to specific actions.[78]

What labour did win was a promise that unions would be represented 'on all advisory committees and commissions which would have to do with the prosecution of the war, or the reconstruction period after the war, and in which Labour was affected.'[79] For the labour leaders present, this was an invitation to participate in the running of wartime Canada, since much of the task had been handed over by Parliament to such bodies. Despite the paucity of immediate gains, this was a historic compromise, albeit of a thoroughly bureaucratic nature. A handful of individuals from the labour movement, chosen unilaterally by the government rather than the trade unions, were promised a role within the state. If any benefits were to fall to the trade union ranks, it would depend upon the skill and persistence of these appointees and the good will of the government.

The labour participants in this conference had a high estimation of their ability to wrench real gains from the government without mobilizing the movement as a whole. Such a bureaucratic approach was reinforced by developments in the United States, where apparently successful tripartite bodies made up of labour, capital, and government had been established by the Wilson administration. There, labour was recognized as a central player in the war effort, and its demands, it seemed, were being heard. Even before the war, the U.S. Commission on Industrial Relations had allowed the AFL to expose 'industrial feudalism' and win a number of legislative changes that it had long demanded. This was followed by the participation of AFL president Samuel Gompers on the seven-member advisory Council of National Defence, and several administrative bodies were created with AFL participation, culminating in the establishment of the National War Labor Board in April 1918. Labour and capital agreed that the system resulted in material gains for American workers, and it was praised in the journals of the international unions for Canadian workers to read. On the negative side, at least for radicals in the movement, it also provided the opportunity for the repression of the enemies of both the AFL and the state, the Industrial Workers of the World.[80]

The AFL's support for Wilson and the Democratic Party, and its subsequent willingness to trade industrial peace – insofar as it could guarantee it – for participation in the state, provoked a certain amount of interest in a number of quarters in Canada. In January 1918, a committee of Canadian business figures, established by the government and chaired by Frank P. Jones of Canada Cement, examined the Wilson administration's industrial policies and reported sympathetically on the co-operation between the AFL and the government. The conference with union leaders represented at least a tentative step in that direction by the Borden government. This appeared to be confirmed when Gompers was honoured with an invitation to address the House of Commons. The AFL president told Parliament that the unions and the state had a common interest in the outcome of the international crisis and that since the declaration of war 'there has not been a difference of opinion between the policy of the Government of the United States and the organized bodies of working people.' The promise of active trade union support for the Union government's war policies was being offered. The Department of Labour signalled its interest by distributing Gompers' address to union locals throughout Canada.[81]

The success of this new relationship – and the credibility of those labour leaders who accepted it – depended upon the making of concrete concessions to the labour movement. Initial indications were not promising. As early as 31 January 1918 the TLCC complained of the weak trade-union representation on the government-appointed committee investigating the wartime labour policy of the United States government. By April, moreover, little action had been taken, and pressure from the ranks of the trade-union movement was being felt in a new and potentially serious wave of strikes. Prompted partly by the Borden government's refusal to raise letter carriers' wages in the face of increasing living costs, a TLCC delegation called upon the cabinet and complained that it was reneging on its promise to appoint trade unionists to various government bodies. Specifically, the TLCC demanded representation on the Food Control Board, the proposed Central Immigration Authority to be established in Britain, and the War Purchasing Board. All these, they argued, had a direct impact on Canadian workers. Within cabinet, Gideon Robertson, former trade-union leader and now a Conservative senator, argued strongly that such appointments be made, but the action taken fell short of the TLCC's expectations.[82]

In May, the Labour Sub-committee of the Reconstruction and Development Committee of the federal cabinet was broadened to function as a tripartite body chaired by Senator Robertson and including labour experts Herbert J. Daly of the Canadian Manufacturers' Association and TLCC president J.C. Watters. Its mandate was, however, essentially investigative. Rather than intervening directly in disputes, as the National War Labor Board did in the United States, this committee was instructed to report to the cabinet on means 'to promote co-operation and harmonious relations between employer and employee.'[83] As we shall see in part three, the Labour Sub-committee would play a slightly more innovative role in the post-war period. In the meantime, it was content to report that the main cause of working-class unrest was the decline in real wages caused by wartime inflation. This was a safe conclusion. Anonymous economic forces, rather than employers, were primarily to blame.[84]

As late as June 1918, as prominent a figure as Mark Irish was unable to determine whether the government intended to follow the American example and establish a body along the lines of the National War Labor Board. It is noteworthy that he tended to favour the idea. Irish was concerned that labour was, in fact, not simply interested in wage levels, but was beginning to challenge the prerogatives of employers to run their firms as they saw fit. Although 'wages are always injected,' he noted, 'the demands of Labour are rather along the lines of imposing upon the Employer intolerable conditions related to hours, pay days, and, worst of all, the right to select his own Employees and dilute his Factory with women.' In his view some sort of government response aimed at preventing work stoppages, even if it tended to 'boost wages inordinately' in the short term, was urgently required.[85]

By July, the time the Borden government had purchased by making hollow promises to labour had expired. Recognizing that 'industrial unrest during the past few months has become more general than formerly,' particularly in munitions work, and that the provisions of the Industrial Disputes Investigation Act covering these workers were being ignored with impunity, the government took a slightly different tack. By Order in Council, a new labour policy incorporating a statement of principles was announced. On the face of it, it addressed a wide range of grievances. It declared that all workers were entitled to ample wages, that rates should be at least as high as in other comparable firms in the district (i.e., fair wages), and that workers' health and safety should not be jeopardized by the demands of war production. And, it officially recognized, for the first time, the workers' right to organize themselves in a union without fear of reprisal or discharge.[86]

However, for a workers' movement that had experienced the betrayal of the promises inherent in the January accord, the government's action was transparent. The Order in Council's high-sounding principles, in fact, lacked any substance at all. There was no machinery for enforcing any of its terms, nor was any proposed. Employers continued to fire workers for union activity and seemed to do so with increasing regularity. E.N. Compton was at the time trying to settle a strike at the York Knitting Mills in Toronto that, he argued, had been provoked by the employer's firing of unionists in an attempt to smash the union. In Kitchener, an attempt to organize Canada's premier rubber company, Canadian Consolidated, had recently failed when organizers were fired; furthermore, an anti-union black list was maintained by the Kitchener Manufacturers' Association. Even the IMB ignored the Order in Council, firing a union steward of the carpenters' union from its Canadian Aeroplanes plant in Toronto. A meeting of the Canadian Manufacturers' Association executive in November expressed resentment at interference in the affairs of employers, and the federal labour minister was informed that the dismissal of employees for joining unions 'is a matter in which the Government should be absolutely impartial.'[87]

Not only was the Order in Council's ostensible recognition of unions immediately labelled a dead letter, it exacerbated resentment by reminding trade unionists of the protection that they did not, in fact, enjoy. Moreover, the government's real intentions were soon revealed in subsequent orders under the War Measures Act. It clamped down on violations of the IDIA and, in September, charged the Dominion Police with IDIA enforcement. Other Orders in Council required that all male Canadians be 'regularly engaged in some useful occupation,' forbade criticisms of the war effort, and outlawed speculation regarding the motives behind the war upon penalty of a $5,000 fine or five years' imprisonment. In September, Orders in Council banned a wide range of socialist organizations and their publications as well as non-religious meetings held in specified languages other than English or French. The sole measure that could be interpreted as consistent with the government's purported policy in support of trade-union recognition and the development of tripartism was the establishment in August 1918 of the Railway Board of Adjustment No. 1, which provided for regularized collective bargaining between the railway brotherhoods and the railways.[88] It took at least a vague threat of a national tie-up of the transportation system during wartime to provide the sort of pressure to which the government responded.

Finally, as the war was drawing to an end, the government, again by Order in Council, banned strikes in their entirety, establishing the Labour Board of Appeal as a final body before which to seek redress of grievances if the decision of a Board of Conciliation under the IDIA should prove insufficient.[89] The labour movement had received no significant response from the Borden government to its requests and demands in more than four years of war. A month before the armistice, the sole weapon that had proved of any real value – the strike – was outlawed. As an allied victory appeared on the horizon, workers were forced to wonder what this portended for peace-time Canada and their quest for 'democracy.' Even Parliament had been ignored as the country experienced 'government by Order in Council' under the sweeping powers of the War Measures Act.

Conclusion

On 11 November 1918 the armistice was signed. Civic celebrations and parades reflected the joy and relief that the terrible conflict had ended. But for workers, the future was uncertain. The problems of deskilling and, now, a potential return to the unemployment of 1914 remained to be addressed. Moreover, the struggle for democracy was unresolved. The federal government, using extraordinary powers, had directed its repression not against the profiteers but against workers and their organizations.

Finally, the trade-union leadership was itself under challenge from within the ranks of its own movement. As early as the Hamilton munitions strike, it was apparent that local conflicts threatened to bypass the control of established union leaders. The events of 1918 further challenged their credibility. As it became clear that the January rapprochement between the TLCC and the government brought few benefits to workers, it became easier to suggest that a 'job-hunting' leadership had been lured by the promise of personal prestige and security.[90] Most of the leadership of the international unions had chosen not to prepare a major co-ordinated industrial confrontation with the state and instead grabbed at the opportunity to exercise personal influence on government policy at the level of wartime boards and committees. By October 1918 it was obvious to all that the results of this strategy had proved negligible, and consequently the credibility of the labour leadership was severely damaged.

As the war ended, the consequences of these developments remained unclear. Throughout this period, the workers' movement had been subject to contradictory pressures. The events of the past four years had drawn workers together through common experiences, but the concentration of economic power and the threat of deskilling had, if anything, increased. Moreover, the war had skewed economic development, potentially dividing workers even further. Certain sectors, which have been the focus of examination to this point, became hypertrophied as a result of the material demands of the war. This was particularly true of the metal trades as the result of the demand for shells by the IMB. The manufacture of other war materials of course, such as aeroplane engines at the Russell Motor Car Company in Toronto, required similar skills. The IAM estimated that the number of machinists in Toronto, the most numerous craft in the industry, climbed from 2,500 to close to 4,000 in the course of the war.

There were similar developments in other trades. The men's garment industry, for instance, responded to an apparently endless demand for uniforms. The Amalgamated Clothing Workers in Toronto was able, before its counterparts in the major American centres, to win a forty-four hour week and an arbitration agreement with the Associated Clothing Manufacturers of Toronto; the union grew from 200 members to 1,300 in eighteen months. By 1919, it had more than 3,000 members in that city and 700 in Hamilton. Even work-forces less closely associated with the war benefited. The Toronto streetrailway workers union gained recognition and was able to win important job protection during the war. In this case, the IMB was particularly concerned, as trouble threatened in 1917, that a strike would hamper war production throughout the city. In London, the street-railway union, which had been smashed before the war, was reorganized and was moderately successful in gaining its demands.[91]

However, other sectors fared less well. The building trades, the strongest bastion of craft unionism, were particularly hard hit. The pre-war depression and then the war itself had a negative impact on the entire industry.[92] In other sectors, the war only accelerated long-term decline. The Cigar Makers International Union was forced into a series of protracted defensive strikes.

The war economy, then, had a widely uneven impact on different trades and localities. Nevertheless, the war also had a powerful unifying effect, propelling workers into conflict with their employers and the state on a number of fronts. This impulse was to be reflected in post-war movements towards industrial unionism and sympathetic strikes. Nevertheless, even though a deeper class-consciousness held the promise of a 'new democracy' in the era of reconstruction, the different traditions and experiences of workers would prove to be a difficult legacy from which to fashion an effective strategy.

2 Beyond Craft Unionism: The Post-war Industrial Challenge

'It is going to be Winnipeg all over again.'
Toronto Metal Trades Council president R.C. Brown, 1919[1]

In the spring and summer of 1919, southern Ontario's workers were finally free to vent their anger on a political and social system that had repeatedly failed to respond to their demands. It was soon apparent that the armistice had brought no solutions to the problems that, three years earlier, had provoked the uprising of Hamilton machinists. In part, it meant that Canada's rulers were no longer able to attempt to play the trump cards of sacrifice and patriotism to silence workers' demands for social justice and decent living conditions. Moreover, the period of reconstruction, which had come to occupy people's thoughts so much in the last months of the war, had suddenly arrived. Still, there were no immediate prospects of a solution to the housing crisis, nor of relief from the burden of high prices. And, after two or three years of plentiful employment and commensurate leverage in the labour market, there was fear of a relapse to the depressed conditions of 1913 to 1915.

The post-war industrial crisis, which assumed its most severe form in Toronto, was both generalized throughout the region and firmly built upon a string of disputes dating from the Hamilton strike in 1916. Labour's defeat, on that occasion, shaped the contours of future battles. Hamilton workers, in fact, would be particularly slow in recovering and would play a marginal role in post-war battles at the point of production (although holding centre stage in working-class independent electoral politics). The workers' movement was severely chastened, and confrontations of this scale were not a feature of class relations in southern Ontario for the balance of the war. Nevertheless, strike activity, which tended to level off in 1917, albeit at a rather high level, climbed to new heights as the war drew to an end. In the region as a whole, the number of worker-days lost in strikes climbed from 25,000 in 1915 to more than 120,000 in 1918 and to an astounding 850,000 in 1919. In the early years of the war, only slightly more than 1,000 workers a year went on strike. In 1918 more than 9,000 struck; in 1919, well over 35,000 walked off their jobs. Unprecedented working-class militancy greeted the end of the war.[2]

This militancy was successful and therefore contagious. This was particularly so among metal workers, who had emerged as the vanguard of the regional labour movement. Although stymied in Hamilton, the machinists secured the nine-hour day in Toronto and firmly established their union's presence in important locations such as London's contract shops and the Grand Trunk shops in Stratford. A new confidence manifested itself in December 1918 in a decision made by the machinists' Provincial Council to demand an eight-hour day and forty-four hour week, as well as a clear definition of the craft to protect themselves against deskilling.[3] Members of the International Moulders' Union (IMU) came to similar conclusions. Before the war, this 'craft-bound' union held out against the Toronto District Labor Council's (TDLC) endorsement of industrial unionism. Wartime confrontations, such as a month-long strike in Brantford against the huge farm machinery firms in 1917, tended to diminish craft exclusiveness. Following moulders' strikes throughout the region, the IMU emerged from the war rejuvenated and powerful to play a major part in the post-war metal trades federations.[4]

Skilled workers were not the only ones touched by these developments. The rapid organization and successful strike of 1,500 civic workers in Toronto in 1918 demonstrated that unskilled workers could form effective 'Federal Labor Unions' (the AFL's organizational solution for those lacking the skills to join existing craft unions).[5] The struggles of each of these groups of workers reinforced lessons of class solidarity and militancy, lessons that often conflicted with the exclusivist traditions of craft unionism. Moreover, sectors of the labour force that had no such traditions were organizing and striking. Both workers and bosses wondered where this tendency would lead. Would a militant and inclusive form of industrial unionism take hold among a significant sector of the region's workers? Perhaps even the western-based One Big Union would bring its brand of radical all-grades unionism to Ontario.[6] To many, this (or something similar) seemed a more effective weapon with which to confront the relatively centralized and powerful capitalism that had taken root in southern Ontario in the previous two decades. The answer came quickly in the Toronto General Strike of late spring 1919 and in the movement towards the amalgamation of craft unions that became an important feature of the southern Ontario labour movement in the tumultuous year that followed the armistice.

The Transformation of the Labour Movement: Toronto

In the final weeks of the war, the Borden government's Orders in Council banning strikes and severely limiting other forms of activity sparked an angry response from trade unionists. While labour organizations were divided and often disoriented in their response to the war, they shared a common determination that in the war's wake would come 'real democracy.'[7] Regardless of the degree of support given to the war effort, it was agreed that the sacrifices would mean little if 'kaiserism' were to take root in Canada. The suspension of democratic rights on the eve of victory spelt a warning. 'There is a danger that while the people of the countries in Europe that up to now have been under the iron heel of despotism are throwing off the yoke of their oppressors, the workers in Canada, unless they wake up, may find themselves still further enslaved.'[8] When Social Democratic Party leader Isaac Bainbridge was arrested for seditious libel for his publication of anti-war literature, the Brantford TLC and the TDLC came quickly, and in the latter case, unanimously, to his defence. The case was, in fact, handled in a particularly ham-handed manner by the courts. Originally arrested in April 1917, held without bail, and eventually found guilty, Bainbridge received a suspended sentence. As he had pointed out to the jury, the articles that led to his arrest had been published in other allied nations without having led to convictions. On 12 September, he was again arrested, convicted of seditious libel, and sentenced to the prison farm at Burwash.

On appeal, it was ruled that the indictment had been improperly attained, and the prisoner was released after having served three months. But Bainbridge was immediately ordered to appear once again before the judge who had originally granted him a suspended sentence, at which point he was again charged with the original crime, although now under the Criminal Code rather than the Order in Council. He was sentenced to a further three months' imprisonment. It was not difficult to draw the conclusion that, as Bainbridge's letter from prison to the *Industrial Banner* stated, 'this is not a prosecution, but a persecution.'[9] Moreover, this was not the end. Although freed by order of the minister of justice in June 1918, Bainbridge was among dozens of socialists arrested in raids by the Dominion police across the province on the night of 20 October 1918.[10] None of this augured well for the 'democracy' for which the war had been fought.

The prohibition of strikes was particularly offensive, undermining as it did labour's last line of defence against inflation and 'industrial autocracy.' As we have seen, the leadership of the Trades and Labor Congress and of the international unions had pursued a strategy of attempting to interest the federal government in a policy of consultation by appointing labour representatives to various committees and commissions. The Borden government's actions revealed how little this course had achieved. In fact, the federal agency created to settle disputes, the Labour Board of Appeal, proved particularly irksome to Toronto workers. In rapid succession, it rolled back awards made by boards of conciliation under the Industrial Disputes Investigation Act (IDIA) in the cases of Toronto blacksmiths, ship's carpenters, and pattern makers, and, in the case of Canadian Express Company employees, ruled against the eight-hour day. In April 1919, the TDLC unanimously condemned the body, calling for its abolition.[11]

The greatest opposition to the actions of the federal government developed in Toronto, deepening the factional disputes that Michael Piva has identified in the District Labor Council.[12] On 16 November 1918, a mass meeting called by the TDLC to protest the Orders in Council packed the Labour Temple. The officers of the TDLC were openly unenthusiastic about the protest and, citing the recent revocation of some of the more objectionable orders, attempted to cancel the meeting. The hall exploded in shouts of 'traitor' and 'fakir.' Herbert Lewis, a socialist leader of the machinists' union, moved: 'That this meeting register a vigorous protest against government by Order-in-Council, which prohibited free speech, the holding of public meetings, and the unfettered use of the press, that the Cabinet was simply a committee of Parliament, and that it had illegally usurped the representatives of the people.'[13] TDLC president A. Conn attempted to rule the motion out of order on the grounds that the meeting was called only to protest the no-strike Order in Council that had been rescinded. Finally, when Lewis suggested that the war had been ended by German workers rising in revolt, rather than by allied arms, Conn decided that enough was enough and adjourned the meeting. However, only when lights in the hall were turned out was the meeting stopped, and even then it continued informally on the street outside the Labour Temple for another two and a half hours.

The 'official' version of the event presents an interesting comment on the composition of the labour movement.

> [I]t was apparent that an organized effort was engineered to pack the labor headquarters and this was shown conclusively when even before 7.30 p.m. hundreds of people, largely of foreign origin, forced their way into the assembly hall and jammed it to the doors. When President Conn assumed the chair it was clearly apparent that many in the audience were not trades unionists, a large number of women were present who could not possibly have belonged to any trades union, and it was clearly to be seen that any business transacted would not be representative of the sentiments of the trades union movement of the city.

It was apparent not only that the left was becoming an organized force, but also that the relative sex and ethnic exclusivity of craft unionism was about to be challenged. However, as the battle immediately spilled over into the TDLC itself, it is also apparent that the sentiments expressed at the meeting were already reflected within Toronto's unions. The actions of the council's executive in stopping the meeting were, in fact, the subject of the TDLC's next three meetings. By the third meeting a dispute over delegates' credentials led to two hours of pandemonium, and the meeting degenerated into a war of song, with socialists cheering the Bolsheviks and singing 'The Red Flag' and conservatives cheering St Patrick, followed by a rendition of 'Auld Lang Syne'![14]

The semi-annual election of officers of the TDLC in January 1919 provided the first major test of strength in the battle over the political direction organized labour was to follow. The presence of an unprecedented 258 accredited delegates attests to the interest created by recent events and the effectiveness of the campaign for the two slates. With some hyperbole, a conservative leaflet described the election as 'a struggle ... as to whether the international trade union movement or the Socialist supporters of Trotsky and the Russian Bolsheviki shall control the District Labor Council.' On this occasion, the conservative forces led by Arthur O'Leary and W.J. Hevey won handily, but a number of developments soon undermined their dominance.[15]

The first of these was the widening scope of protests against continued arrests under the Orders in Council banning specified literature and left-wing organizations. These moves provoked two of the largest unions in the province into action: the machinists and the carpenters. The first case involved Arthur Skidmore, a railway machinist and executive member of the Stratford Trades Council. In late December 1918 Skidmore was sentenced to thirty days in jail plus a five hundred dollar fine (or a further six months) for possessing two copies of *Canadian Forward*, the paper of the SDP, published prior to the ban. In Stratford the response was immediate; the local trades council unanimously voted to call the city's workers out on a general strike to obtain Skidmore's release. In Toronto, Machinists Lodge 438, whose president was Herbert Lewis, voted to demand that the machinists' Toronto District Lodge call all its members out on strike. In turn that body, representing 4,000 Toronto machinists, voted to ask the TDLC to call a general strike. Before it could act, however, the federal government intervened and Skidmore was released from jail and his fine remitted. Ontario workers had tasted their own collective power.[16]

Similar cases followed. In Toronto, an ex-police officer and munitions worker, Charles Watson, was found with a variety of socialist literature and sentenced to three years and five hundred dollars. A week later, hundreds of members of the carpenters' union attended Police Court to see one of their members, Harry Cheesman, sentenced to six months: a lighter sentence, explained the magistrate, as Cheesman was only a 'tool' rather than 'an active agent.'[17] The consequence of these arrests was to mobilize a much broader layer of workers than had packed the Labour Temple two months earlier to protest the no-strike ban. Large protest meetings were held in rapid succession. On Sunday, 12 January, 1,200 attended a Workers' Political Defense League protest, and subsequent mass meetings were organized by the Building Trades League on Monday night, the Carpenters' District Council on Tuesday, and the machinists on Wednesday. Most interesting was the carpenters' meeting, which attracted 3,000 to Massey Hall. Tom Moore, president of the Trades and Labor Congress 'had the worst time of any of the speakers.' Despite his promise to work for the freeing of political prisoners, his avowed commitment to 'constitutional means' raised storms of opposition from several hundred in the audience.[18] Ten days later, before the carpenters could present their petition with more than 10,000 names, Watson and Cheesman had their sentences drastically reduced, to thirty and fifteen days, respectively. The lessons taught by the Skidmore case had been reinforced.

While the abrogation of civil rights was a major catalyst in radicalizing large numbers of Toronto workers,[19] the transformation of the organized labour movement was to have even greater consequences. A favourable labour market, along with a greater commitment to organizing previously unorganized sectors, combined to create organizational breakthroughs for the unions and political triumphs for the left. Once again, the machinists were the key to this process. During the war, the trade had experienced rapid expansion, and machinists' lodges grew rapidly, particularly Lodge 438 based in Allis-Chalmers and other large shops of the city's west end. Moreover, the International Association of Machinists (IAM) made an important turn to organizing less-skilled 'specialists' – including, for the first time, women – hired during the war to work on specified machines. The rapid growth of specialists' Lodge 1005 reflected a preliminary step towards challenging some of the assumptions of craft unionism.[20] The impetus to organize these workers was, however, an ambiguous one. Certainly, organizing the specialists was an effective means by which skilled craftsmen could defend themselves from 'diluted' labour. But the skilled machinists who took part in a major strike at the Willys-Overland airplane works in support of two fired women workers in June 1918 saw no contradiction in claiming that they 'gained nothing by striking' and only 'wished to help those who were lower down, the specialists and the women.' After the war, the machinists demanded that no further specialists be hired and that existing specialists receive the existing machinists' rate after four years' service.[21]

The machinists' success in broadening their organization and in winning the nine-hour day led them to conclude that the long-sought eight-hour day could be won through the unity of all metal-trades workers. Their numerical strength and strategic clarity led them to play a central role in the Metal Trades Council of twelve crafts established in January 1919. A similar body had existed before the war, but had collapsed in the aftermath of the machinists' defeat in 1907 and because of the pre-war depression. The post-war federation was seen to be substantially different. For the first time, the federation presented the employers with a common schedule based upon the machinists' demands for an eight-hour day, with a half holiday Saturdays, double time for overtime, shift differentials, and the closed shop. In the eyes of the *Globe* and of the Employers' Association, this was industrial unionism.[22]

The machinists also exemplified the process of radicalization that was occurring unevenly across the Toronto labour movement. As the war neared an end, debate raged at all levels of the union; noon-hour educational classes were even held at larger factories, and the tactic of a general strike was raised for discussion as early as July 1918. By January 1919, the machinists formed a solid left bloc on the Toronto District Labor Council and, as we have seen, were prepared to launch a general strike against 'government by order in council.'[23] Moreover, a major portion of the IAM was already prepared to call a general strike for the six-hour day.[24] Most revealing of the growing sentiment of Toronto machinists, though, was their response to the One Big Union. Local machinists on the Canadian Pacific Railway voted 162 to 11 in favour of the OBU, while other lodges invited OBU speakers to address them. Lodge 438 heard a full report on the Calgary conference from local machinist Thomas Mellilieu and voted unanimously to endorse the OBU. Toronto locals of the British-based Amalgamated Society of Engineers were openly enthusiastic, and each local instructed its executive to write to Vancouver for OBU literature and information on affiliation. The Toronto District Council of the United Brotherhood of Carpenters and Joiners ordered 15,000 OBU pamphlets in defiance of a threat by its international president to withdraw its charter.[25] By May, long-time socialist Fred Peel told the *Toronto World* of the 'fascination' that the OBU held for many workers: '[it] is my opinion that what opposition has been expressed to the One Big Union idea or to the principle of industrial trade unionism does not express the sentiment of the rank and file of the labor movement by any means, altho [*sic*] self-interest and fossilized ideas may obtain amongst a few men identified with the labor movement.'[26] If this was true for any section of Toronto workers, it was the machinists. Through its new organ, the *Ontario Labor News*, the Metal Trades Federation assailed the established 'per capita eating' leaders of the trade union movement for retarding the progress of labour. R.J. Johns, a leader of the OBU, felt that the city's machinists were ripe for the new organization.[27]

Following the lead of the metal trades, the prospect of craft-union federation leading to an industrial form of organization became a common theme for discussion throughout 1919 and into 1920. Toronto's shipyards reflected this tendency. Empowered by the emergence of new locals of painters and of steam-fitters, as well as a large contingent of machinists, an audacious Marine Trades Federation emerged and soon covered twenty shipbuilding yards from the lakehead to the Atlantic. In turn, the federation itself helped to organize new locals of its affiliated crafts in Collingwood, Midland, Bridgeburg, Niagara Falls, and of course, Toronto. In keeping with its intention of organizing all workers in the shipyards, the federation also proclaimed its intention of establishing a new union, the Federal Labor Union, for unskilled labourers. Significantly, the shipbuilders went beyond the Metal Trades Federation in demanding a common wage for all trades of eighty cents an hour, with lower rates for helpers and labourers. This egalitarianism did not entirely enhance the federation's position, however. The Boilermakers' and Iron Shipbuilders' Union Local 128 in Toronto, composed of highly skilled and relatively highly paid craft workers was to have nothing to do with the Marine Trades Federation nor with the general strike in May and June. In May 1919, major strikes at the British American Shipbuilding Company in Welland and the Polson and Allis-Chalmers shipyards in Toronto won shorter workdays and the recognition of the unions, although recognition of the federation was not achieved. In 1920, this huge industrial federation of workers throughout central and eastern Canada again demanded a single agreement containing an egalitarian wage structure.[28]

The building trades travelled even farther along a similar route. The industry recovered quickly from a long building slump during the war, and other conditions provided an impetus to rapid growth. In March 1919, the Toronto Carpenters' District Council moved to centralize union organization in the building trades and to shift decision-making power away from the international unions to the local Building Trades League. A large meeting of Toronto carpenters decided to initiate the creation of a $25,000 strike fund, raised by a local assessment on building-trades workers, that would be under the control of the league. As the *Industrial Banner* explained, 'the object of this move is to place the Building Trades League in a position to take immediate action in small labor disputes, where it might not be advisable to wait for international support or sanction of a strike.'[29] It is evident that there was a substantial feeling that it was going to be necessary to circumvent the control that international union officials had over access to strike funds: a prerequisite to sympathetic strike action. That such actions were seriously considered by building-trades workers was evident in the spring of 1919 as affiliated unions authorized the Building Trades League to call out all 7,400 workers in the industry in Toronto in support of the striking painters' union.[30] The building trades stood strongly behind the striking metal trades. The painters, for instance, had long enjoyed the eight-hour day, but were willing to strike in sympathy with those who did not. At a demonstration in support of the metal workers, their banner read: 'What we have we want for others.'[31]

The transformation of a number of existing unions into powerful and self-confident federations paralleled the emergence of a number of dynamic new unions. In most cases these were unskilled workers, such as the civic workers, or the teamsters employed by the railway forwarding companies who had engaged in strikes in the past, but always without the aid of a union. In 1919, they were able to form a union of 700 members and win recognition from their employers. Telephone operators, whose 1907 strike had failed in the face of inaction on the part of the International Brotherhood of Electrical Workers and intransigence by the employer, were successfully organized into a union of more than 700 members and obtained important improvements in conditions. A union of bank workers started with 300 members and claimed to have organized over 50 per cent of the city's bank clerks by the end of 1919. Unions of waitresses and of domestic servants attracted women workers previously viewed as unorganizable.[32]

The largest numbers of new unionists came from the mass production industries with large, heterogeneous, work-forces. For instance, probably more than a thousand rubber workers were organized in April and May 1919.[33] The most dramatic breakthrough occurred, however, in the city's meat-packing plants. Given a new lease on life by the achievement of the eight-hour day in Chicago, the Amalgamated Meat Cutters and Butcher Workmen of America had grown tenfold during the last two years of the war. In Toronto, the union was organized in May 1918 with twenty-two members and grew slowly. In a six-week period in the spring of 1919, however, membership exploded. When the union went on strike to force recognition by the 'big five' meat-packers, it was able to claim more than 3,000 members; 900 more joined in the course of the conflict. Overnight it became the largest local union in Toronto. Moreover, the butcher workers' union exemplified the changes taking place in the union movement. A large number of its members were women and immigrants; they had even performed the 'impossible' task of organizing Chinese immigrants. Under the leadership of socialist Louis Braithwaite, the butcher workers substantially augmented the radical forces in the Toronto labor movement. The arrival of thirty-five butcher workers' delegates in April 1919 was seen as an integral part of a left-wing 'coup' in the Toronto District Labor Council. A month later, they were eligible for seventy-nine delegates.[34]

The TDLC was integral to the rapid expansion of the city's unions and in April it responded to the challenge by increasing the size of its organization committee from five to twenty-one members – mostly radicals. Socialists also played major roles in the new unions. Isaac Bainbridge, for instance, was elected secretary of the new Federal Labor Union, which attracted more than a thousand unskilled workers to its organizing meeting in May. On May Day, Jimmie Simpson told the audience that between four and five thousand Toronto workers had joined unions in the past week. Herbert Lewis later claimed that ten thousand joined in the two months preceding the general strike call in late May.[35] While these figures contained, perhaps, an element of hyperbole (it is impossible to know), they represented a substantial shift in the relationship of forces in the local labour movement. Well before the end of the war, Herbert J. Daly, a leader of the Toronto branch of he Canadian Manufacturers' Association, commented: 'The older unions were will [sic] controlled; it is the newer organizations that are the disturbing element.'[36] Combined with the changes evident in some of the 'older unions,' employers had much to find disturbing.

The Toronto General Strike

Buoyed by all these developments and an overwhelming mandate from the unions involved, 4,000 metal-trades workers in 232 factories began their strike on May Day. Their goal was the eight-hour day and recognition of their federation. The events of the preceding months had encouraged optimism, but there was recognition that the road would be difficult. A month earlier, the unions had sent their demands to the firms involved; on 17 April, they received a single reply from James G. Merrick, secretary of the Employers' Association, refusing all their demands. There would be no breach in the employers' front as there had been in 1916. Responding to red-baiting, the metal-trades unions had strong grounds to claim that it was in fact they who were fighting the One Big Union – employers![37]

As Metal Trades Council president R.C. Brown told the TDLC, the Employers' Association was testing the city's labour movement; a united response was necessary.[38] Yet every step revealed the disunity of Toronto labour. On 13 May, the Metal Trades Council came to the TDLC with a motion calling for a city-wide general strike. Left-wing leader John MacDonald, underestimating the sentiment of the meeting, proposed limited mass strikes of perhaps one or two days' duration each week. Machinists', butcher workers', and carpenters' delegates demanded a full general strike. A Russian immigrant among the delegates appealed to the ethnocentrism of the audience: 'I'm asking you as a foreigner, aren't you going to be ashamed to work nine or ten hours a day when the foreigner which you don't like is only working eight hours?' The meeting, noted the *Toronto Daily Star*, 'shouted its laughing approbation.'[39]

Yet a number of delegates, led by the large Street Railway Employees' Union, strongly opposed 'precipitate action.' W.D. Robbins, the union's financial secretary and a Conservative member of Toronto's

Board of Control, led the opposition. Robbins was already unpopular among a growing segment of the city's labour movement. Active in the labour movement since the 1890s, and first elected as an alderman in 1912, he had opposed a post-war international labour conference if it meant sitting with 'Huns' and had welcomed the introduction of conscription in 1917 as a long overdue measure. More recently he had opposed lifting the banning order against the SDP and had berated police chief H.J. Grasset for refusing to close buildings permanently as a penalty for renting space to socialists. Not surprisingly, Toronto unionists active in establishing a local labour party repeatedly refused to endorse his candidacy for city council.[40] To the TDLC, he pointed to the consequences of striking without the sanction of the international unions, most notably the possibility of losing their union pensions. Carpenters' leader John Doggett 'replied that if pensions caused workers to starve it was time the international unions did away with the pensions.' While the left dismissed Robbins' comments as 'the usual 18th century drivel which one generally hears from what is termed by the press, "a sane labor man," '[41] his position reflected an outlook that, as events would reveal, retained credibility in sections of the labour movement. Agreement as to the next step was, however, reached; a convention of all unions in Toronto was called for 20 May to consider the question of a general strike. Around the city, hastily called meetings of local unions discussed the question and chose delegates to the convention. Newspapers published regular tallies of who supported the strike and who did not. Carpenters, rubber workers, painters, teamsters, butcher workers, cigar makers, and civic workers supported the general strike; plumbers, boilermakers, and boot-and-shoe workers opposed it.[42]

Meanwhile, it appeared that a general strike was developing of its own accord. On 4 May, more than 3,000 butcher workers had walked out demanding recognition from the big five packers. Three days later, the Toronto *Telegram* calculated that 8,525 workers, at 250 firms, were on strike in the city and that almost 8,000 others were in the process of negotiating. The *Star* put the latter figure at 14,000.[43] On 17 May, 5,000 workers rallied in the rain at Queen's Park in a show of force before the convention. While the demonstrators obeyed the new city by-law banning red flags and non-English signs, such conditions stood as reminders of the campaign against 'autocratic government' that had provoked the movement a few months earlier. A veterans' banner read: 'We Fought for democracy, not capitalists.' Other signs appealed to humanity over profits, while the metal trades banner demanded 'A Better World for the Workers ... Immediate Demand for Forty-Four

Hours per Week.' The marchers wore figure 'eights' in their hats to signify the demand for the eight-hour day. When, the following week, 570 students at Humberside Collegiate went on strike for a shorter school day and rumours spread that other high schools would strike in sympathy, few could dispute the view that the general strike was in the air. Newspapers predicted a large vote in favour of the strike. In R.C. Brown's words, 'It is going to be Winnipeg all over again. There doesn't seem to be any way out of it.'[44]

But all were not resigned to that view. Conservative labour leaders and the various levels of government were all keen to avoid such a confrontation. On the eve of the general strike convention, Tommy Church, the populist Tory mayor of Toronto met, separately, with representatives from the TDLC and the employers. Merrick was adamant; he had only responded to the mayor's invitation as a courtesy and rejected any negotiations with the Metal Trades Council. For a few days the mayor held out the promise of indirect negotiations, but it was soon apparent that it was only an attempt to buy time. Still, when the convention met on 20 May, the outcome of the mayor's efforts was not yet determined, and it was decided to adjourn until 26 May. The delay gave employers time to mull over the fact that 200 delegates representing 28,000 workers in 105 unions had responded to the convention call. There may have been opposition in the labour movement to the general strike, and certainly not all those attending would vote in favour, but its proponents had demonstrated a strong show of force.[45] When the delegates reconvened on 26 May, however, little had changed. They rejected a last-minute employers' 'offer' of a forty-eight hour week and no recognition of the Metal Trades Council, elected a strike committee of fifteen, and prepared for battle in two days' time.

Those who knew the actual vote, however, had a little extra food for thought. The motion to call a general strike had passed by 9,985 to 5,150. Delegates representing 15,550 workers had abstained! Despite strong support for the strike, the vote did not reflect a united and confident labour movement. A large number of workers would not commit themselves to the strike, knowing that a number of key unions, and leaders, were still opposed to it. Those who expressly opposed the strike were a minority, but many more were hesitant to do battle with such divided forces. The Committee of Fifteen, as it came to be known, put on a brave face and attempted to keep these figures to themselves. On the first day of the strike, however, they were released to the press by a leader of the conservative brewery workers' union.[46]

Mayor Church immediately swung back into action, organizing a round-table conference with almost anyone who would attend. Old arguments were once again exchanged, but some hope was held out. Church read a telegram from Prime Minister Borden inviting representatives of the city, the Board of Trade, the Employers' Association, and the Metal Trades Council to come to Ottawa. The general strike deadline was pushed back to 30 May, at 10:00 a.m., and a delegation of twenty-seven boarded the night train to Ottawa.[47]

Meanwhile, Toronto prepared for the general strike amidst a growing red scare. In the final months of the war, red-baiting had become commonplace in right-wing publications such as *Saturday Night*, which praised the American repression of the IWW and equated Bolshevism with German agents. Such attacks took on a nativist tinge as *Saturday Night* openly equated socialism with 'Bolshevized foreigners,' and the director of public safety, C.H. Cahan, characterized Bolsheviks as 'enemy aliens.' In Toronto, future mayor Sam McBride epitomized such sentiment by savagely red-baiting the striking civic workers in 1918 and, in December, demanding that TDLC leader and social democrat Fred Bancroft be hanged for an anti-militarist speech he had delivered in 1912. The Toronto *Telegram*, always vocal in such matters, appeared to relish the coming industrial conflict. 'Collapse of the general strike insanity will be a victory for the British, Canadian or trades union forces in the labor movement, and defeat for the Red Flag European Socialist Forces in the labor movement.' Newspapers turned to reporting the fantastic business being done in riot insurance. The *Toronto Times* carefully explained to its readers that the Committee of Fifteen was a 'soviet,'[48] and the *Financial Post* expressed the view that the 'grave menace is that labor [is] deluded by the cleverly organized underground workers who have for the time being usurped the power of the rightful leaders and have thrown off intelligent control with the idea of organizing the Trotzky [*sic*] form of government for Canada, such is now being attempted in Winnipeg and Toronto.'[49]

Less anxious observers noted other factors. The *Star* played down nativist sentiment by pointing out that all but one of the Committee of Fifteen were British- or Canadian-born. In Ottawa, Borden asked labour not to act hastily, but offered them little worth waiting for. A legislated eight-hour day, the hope of conservative labour leaders, was dismissed as beyond federal jurisdiction. Metal-trades leaders rejected pressure that the central question of hours be decided by arbitration. The strike was on.[50]

The Toronto General Strike, noted the *Star*, was general 'in name only.' The metal trades were joined by a significant number of supporters. More than 2,000 carpenters and a similar number of members of the International Ladies' Garment Workers' Union rallied to their support. The Committee of Fifteen claimed that 12,000 workers were out for the first day of the general strike.[51] But the leaders of the strike faced a dilemma. Either the strike must be generalized, or it was doomed. The next two days, Saturday and Sunday, provided a final opportunity to transform the situation to their advantage.

The general-strike convention, which reconvened Saturday night, opened with a fierce dispute over who had released the strike-vote figures to the press the previous day. The left was convinced that it had the support of the rank and file of the city's unions and demanded a new strike vote. The right aimed its fire at the Committee of Fifteen for wanting to provoke a nation-wide general strike. Finally, at 1:00 a.m. Sunday morning, TDLC president Arthur O'Leary and secretary W.J. Hevey, who were presiding over the proceedings, resigned from the convention. Socialist Tom Black and OBU proponent E.R. Bales were elected to replace them. The last façade of unity had fallen.

One final card remained to be played that night. The street-railway workers were still in session at the Star Theatre; perhaps a direct appeal over the heads of their leadership could bring them out. That afternoon, John Cottam of the carpenters' union had requested an opportunity to speak to the membership, but had been refused by the union's business agent, Joseph Gibbons. Later, as the general-strike convention was dispersing, leaders of the Metal Trades Council rushed to the street-railway-workers' meeting to appeal for their support. Gibbons stopped them at the door, while W.D. Robbins successfully appealed to the street-car workers to remain on the job. They voted three to one not to join the general strike. Later that year, in their campaign for municipal office, Gibbons and Robbins invoked the events of the night when they 'saved the Queen City from being the scene of turmoil, strike and disgraceful riots such as were witnessed in Winnipeg.'[52]

Without the support of such a large and visible bastion of labour as the street railway workers, the general strike lacked the momentum to continue. Monday morning, the numbers out on strike had grown as the marine trades joined the battle. Mayor Church estimated that 15,000 were out; the Committee of Fifteen, 17,000. But even sympathetic unions had not found it possible to come to the aid of the metal trades. Most notable in this regard were the butcher workers. Their strike early in May had been settled with the promise of a Board of Conciliation under the Industrial Disputes Investigation Act. The board, however, faced a series of unexplained delays in making its report until the crisis in Toronto had passed. The union voted unanimously to take part in the general strike but faced an overwhelming problem: should it risk the *de facto* recognition it had achieved in order to join a general strike that was clearly in trouble? The butcher workers stayed at their jobs.[53]

Monday night, the Metal Trades Council assessed the situation and determined that no more support was forthcoming. At its request, the general strike was called off. Not surprisingly, when the TDLC met the following night, recriminations flew freely. After a few references to OBU influence in the machinists' union, the metal trades came under attack for bypassing the established leadership of the labour movement. 'The metal trades have our sympathy,' claimed Robbins, 'and we'll stick to them so long as they handle their own business. But when they hand affairs over to a committee of 15, whom we don't know, then we've come to a parting of the ways.' A conservative organizer of the Canadian Brotherhood of Railway Employees claimed that 'many organizations had been unable to see why "another element" [referring to the defunct Committee of Fifteen] should have assumed control of the situation.'[54] To such individuals, the issue had become one of retaining pre-existing forms of organization in the city's labour movement, as well as their own places within it. Like the OBU, the general-strike convention, symbolized by the Committee of Fifteen, represented a challenge to the very structure of the organization that they had helped build and that sustained them in leadership. Toronto was the home, more than any other Canadian city, of a small but emerging layer of union leaders whose workplace was the Labour Temple and no longer the shop floor. By contrast, no member of the Metal Trades Council was a paid trade-union official.[55]

This is, however, only a partial explanation of the strike's failure. The uneven impact of the past five years on the city's workers had taken its toll as well. The street-railway-workers' union found itself in quite a different situation than, for instance, the machinists' or butcher workers' unions. The union had a secure collective bargaining relationship with the Toronto Railway Company, a relatively privileged position for a group of workers who lacked control over any demonstrable skill. Secondly, the street-railway workers were quite isolated from the transformations occurring in other unions. They had led a successful battle against the hiring of immigrants and women throughout the war. They had remained a remarkably homogeneous group of British- and Canadian-born men; the sort of men who responded to their country's call to arms. In June 1919, 1,300 of the 2,200 members of the union were returned soldiers. Finally, they had found in Toryism a solution to many of their immediate needs. The union's two salaried officials, Gibbons and Robbins, sat on the city council and acted in defence of working-class interests as they perceived them. With the city scheduled to take over the franchise of the street railway in 1921, there seemed little reason to question this ourse. Robbins had been proposed as deputy minister of labour and would possibly have become Ontario's first minister of labour if the Conservatives had won the 1919 provincial election. If less-conservative unions, such as the butcher workers or the Amalgamated Clothing Workers, were unwilling to risk the established bargaining relationship they had won, there was little reason to expect the street railway workers to do so. This did not, however, suggest passivity. The struggle to establish a degree of protection in the workplace through the mechanism of signed agreements had proven so laborious that, once won, the sanctity of the contract had become the guiding principle of their unionism. Two weeks after the débâcle of the general strike, their own agreement expired and they struck for twelve days to win the eight-hour day; they also assembled a crowd of 6,000 to prevent the use of strike breakers.[56]

The Metal Trades Council strike continued until late July, when William Johnston, president of the International Association of Machinists, spent a week in Toronto and persuaded the machinists to return to work on the basis of a forty-eight-hour week with no agreement on wages. The moulders, by contrast, were even less fortunate. Their international union had spent $132,000 on strike benefits in Toronto in a losing struggle for the eight-hour day. This was more than it had spent on any other local in a continent-wide campaign for the eight-hour day that bankrupted it. The fate of many who had supported the metal trades was equally uncertain. Massey-Harris, for instance, expressed less willingness to rehire strikers who had gone out in sympathy with 'the revolutionary movement' than participants in an 'ordinary strike.'[57]

Indeed this had been no ordinary strike, but had grown out of frictions very similar to those that provoked the epic struggle in Winnipeg. David Bercuson, for instance, incorrectly assumed that the Toronto struggle was primarily a minor demonstration of solidarity by a minority of Toronto workers with strikers in Winnipeg. Recent accounts by Myer Siemiatycki and Gregory Kealey more accurately reflect an understanding of the issues under dispute by the local metal workers. Nevertheless, Siemiatycki tends to dismiss the militancy displayed by

Toronto workers, considering it largely a defensive action in the face of a powerful employers' offensive. But, while the bosses were indeed unyielding, this was hardly a new stance. Rather, it was the labour movement that was attempting to seize new ground: recognition of its federation and the eight-hour day. Moreover, the tactic of a general strike represented a sharp break with the practice of craft unionism.[58] On the other hand, Kealey's important corrective to 'western exceptionalism' provides few hints as to the source of regional differences within the 'Canadian labour revolt.' Working-class supporters and opponents of One Big Union and the general strike confronted each other across Canada in the spring of 1919. Even in the West, significant segments of the labour movement hesitated to join the radical secessionists. The uneven effects of the war and its aftermath upon different groups of workers, along with an entrenched craft-union leadership (mainly resident in Toronto), largely explains such variation between and within regions of the country.[59]

The Transformation of the Labour Movement: Southern Ontario

As the industrial storm raged in Toronto, workers' struggles in other parts of the region tended to wait in abeyance. The metal trades strike, however, was not confined to Toronto. By 12 May, 800 metal workers were out in Midland, 450 in St Catharines, 250 in Welland, and hundreds more in Kingston and Ottawa.[60] But Hamilton did not join the strike, and events in Brantford revealed the mood of another important segment of the labour movement. More than 1,000 members of the local Brantford metal-trades unions had given their employers, particularly the large farm-equipment manufacturers, until 15 May to respond to their demands for an eight-hour day. However, on the eve of the strike, when the employers agreed to open negotiations, the deadline was extended. The employers dallied until 2 June, the eve of the collapse of the Toronto General Strike, when they made their final offer: a forty-eight-hour week, rather than the forty-four-hour week demanded. While this represented a slight concession in view of their refusal to budge from the existing fifty-hour week until this point, the offer was made with an eye to Toronto and some confidence that local workers would not follow their brethren into a futile conflict. The abandonment of the Toronto General Strike had made Brantford workers wary of proceeding along a parallel path.[61]

Despite the marked hesitancy of other workers to follow their counterparts in Toronto into conflict on such a scale, the issue of industrial unionism had a growing appeal among many types of unionists. As metal- building-, and marine-trades councils proliferated around the province, conservative unions had reason to fear that a wider circle of workers might come to see the One Big Union in a more favourable light. The example of luggage workers in three factories in Kitchener and Waterloo gave pause to craft unionists. The workers' initial impulse was to form a union of all the workers in the three shops, and they approached the local trades council for support. At a meeting in the local labour hall, the workers were informed that, because several AFL unions claimed jurisdiction, they would be required to join different unions. A handful of members of the Workers' International Industrial Union (WIIU; the industrial wing of the De Leonite Socialist Labor Party) objected, proposing instead an industrial union. The response of the trades-council leaders who were chairing the meeting was impolitic: they ruled any mention of industrial unionism out of order. Not surprisingly, even craft-union supporters felt the matter was being dealt with undemocratically. 'With admirable spirit,' read the WIIU report, 'in a spontaneous movement, the men in a body left the hall' and soon formed an industrial union of 250 members. It is not difficult to conclude that the insensitivity of the local leadership of the trades council had driven potential members away. In fact, it appeared that the workers had no particular interest in the WIIU *per se*, since they were soon in contact with the OBU.[62]

More evidence of the growing disenchantment with craft unionism came from the Guelph trades council. Noting the growing sentiment in favour of sympathetic strikes and the difficulty in pursuing this course 'because of the fact that there is no machinery that can make operative the full power of the labor movement in Canada,' the council proposed a major change in the structure of the organized labour movement. It rejected the notion, central to the AFL, that the right to call workers out on strike be controlled by the international craft unions. Instead, it proposed that the Trades and Labor Congress 'take immediately whatever steps may be necessary to bring into line the various interests involved: the AF of L, International Unions, and Canadian organizations, the object being to form a National Council of Labor that shall have mandatory power to take concerted power on behalf of Canadian labor, when the course of events may justify the taking of concerted action so that in all matters affecting Canadian labor the full and united strength of Canadian labor may be applied.' As well as being a rejection of craft unionism, the resolution was an unprecedented call for rapprochement with sworn enemies of the AFL – the OBU and the Canadian Federation of Labor – as well as with the British-based unions. Although it was claimed that there were five 'Reds' on the Guelph TLC, ideas dear to the socialists had swayed the majority of the central labour body in a city not hitherto known for its radical labour movement.[63]

Given developments such as these, to say nothing of events in the West, conservative labour leaders decided that blanket opposition to industrial unionism was both untenable and unnecessary. TLCC president Tom Moore attacked industrial unionists for their disloyalty (as displayed by their attraction to the OBU), but he soft-pedalled craft unionism itself. 'Closer affiliation between workers will come,' he told the carpenters' Provincial Council, 'but not by OBU, but rather by the growth of the craft unions and federated councils of closely allied trades.' Although making no proposals about the organizational metamorphosis of craft unionism, Moore was signalling the acquiescence of the TLCC leadership in the emergence of an array of federations. Moreover, there was every reason to believe that such an evolutionary change was indeed possible. Substantial building-, metal-, and marine-trades federations had emerged without the serious opposition that confronted the OBU. The carpenters' council that Moore had addressed was itself laying plans for a provincial council of building-trades unions.[64] The willingness of the internationals to countenance such discussion was in evidence in other quarters as well. The *Machinists' Monthly Journal* printed J.A. McClelland's reports on the lively discussion of industrial unionism in the Toronto IAM, as well as his plea that '[w]e must, at least, work with greater earnestness for closer affiliation; if not, the complete amalgamation of the metal trades.'[65] It appeared that unity prevailed in the labour movement; while many disparaged OBU 'destructionism,' industrial unions, through the gradual amalgamation of the crafts, appeared to be a commonly accepted goal.

Partisans of such a strategy pointed to the Niagara District Trades Federation (NDTF). Organized in August 1918, the NDTF represented workers in fourteen unions – skilled and unskilled – employed on the New Welland Canal and the Hydro-Electric Power Commission's Chippawa canal at Niagara Falls.[66] These two large construction projects gave the labour movement of the Niagara peninsula a unique character in southern Ontario. Each employed upwards of 2,000 men, mostly unskilled, immigrant workers, although a substantial number were highly skilled heavy-machinery operators. Moreover, the two groups of workers, employed in similar work and working in close proximity, but for different levels of government (the Welland Canal was a federal project, Hydro's was provincial), gave the unions both economic and political leverage. In addition, the region was seen as a potential flash-point. In 1916, when 600 unorganized labourers on the Welland Canal – 'Russians, Bulgarians, Italians and Austrians' – struck for a wage hike of five cents per hour, the federal government sent in the military. The *New York Times* reported that 'soldiers came with fixed bayonets, and most of the strikers surrendered at once. Every man was lined up and searched; then boarding houses were searched.' The government could respond in this manner, said the *Industrial Banner*, since the workers were 'without organization or votes,' noting also that the military was never used to defend workers' rights.[67]

By the end of the war, the relationship of forces had changed, and the reopening of the Welland Canal project in early 1919 provided the opportunity to put an end to the ten-hour day on both jobs. The NDTF attempted to begin negotiations with both employers in mid-March but was particularly interested in reaching an agreement for the Welland Canal workers, who were paid less than those on the Hydro project. They immediately encountered a snag when responsibility for setting fair wage schedules was volleyed back and forth between the ministers of Labour and of Railways and Canals. On 18 May, the NDTF issued an ultimatum to the Department of Railways and Canals.[68]

In the meantime, attention shifted to the Hydro workers' demand for an eight-hour day and to their strike deadline of 22 May. After intense negotiations, the NDTF leaders agreed to consider Hydro chairman Adam Beck's proposal of a basic eight-hour day with two additional hours per day at time-and-a-quarter overtime and a wage increase of at least five cents per hour. Fifteen hundred members listened sceptically to the proposal in the Niagara Falls Arena on 28 May but agreed to it when Beck personally raised the offer to time-and-a-half for overtime.[69]

Claiming victory, the NDTF aimed its sights, once again, at the federal government. Never had the fair-wage argument appeared clearer; the Department of Railways and Canals could hardly deny that the nearby Hydro canal workers were performing comparable work for substantially higher wages and with at least formal acceptance of the eight-hour day. In addition, as the contractors were working on a cost-plus basis, the issue of wages was laid squarely at the feet of the government. Still, Railways and Canals minister J.D. Reid refused to deal with the federation. The nature of the contest was dramatically revealed in August when 350 immigrant labourers – reportedly Austrians, Bulgarians, Poles, and Italians – struck for precisely that demand. Seventy special constables were sworn in by the Thorold police magistrate and issued arms, including machine guns, by the militia. As in 1916, no violence had provoked this response by the state. The strike was ended in two days as the strikers agreed to return to work pending action by the federation as a whole.[70] Few expected that a general strike on the Welland Canal could be indefinitely postponed; the strength of the Niagara District Trades Federation would soon be tested.

Less dramatically, Ontario's furniture workers reflected a similar sentiment. This was an industry that had never been successfully organized, since most of its 11,000 employees were scattered through factories in a series of cities and towns from Preston and Woodstock north to Georgian Bay. In contrast, the employers had been organized in the Furniture Manufacturers' Association since 1890.[71] J.R. Shaw, a leader of the association and the managing director of one of the most dynamic furniture firms, noted that the industry was marked by the easy entry of small competitors at the bottom and the rapid introduction of 'labour-saving devices' by the larger firms.[72] Neither of these conditions augured well for craft unionists who found themselves working for small, marginal firms under great pressure to cut costs, or for larger enterprises hoping to eliminate any need for the skills they had to sell.

In 1919 the situation altered rapidly as the result of a successful organizing drive by the carpenters' and painters' unions. In May, a leader of the Kitchener trades council reported that about half of the city's nearly 1,000 furniture workers, including all of the upholsterers, had been organized. The carpenters' union was particularly active, organizing 'mill locals' in woodworking mills and furniture factories in Woodstock, Hespeler, Kitchener, and Midland in the spring of 1919. In tacit recognition of these developments, the employers generally accepted the nine-hour day by mid-1919 without serious opposition. In Preston, where the employers in four firms had held out on this issue until June, a strike of less than two days' duration by 220 furniture workers decided the issue in favour of the unions. As late as March, few furniture workers belonged to unions; by August the industry was entirely organized.[73]

Jimmie Simpson regularly used the furniture industry as an example of the deskilling that had made craft unionism redundant. 'It would be silly,' he told the TDLC, 'to ask these men to organize upon craft or trade lines when there is no longer any need of the skill such workmen were able to sell before the machine did its work.'[74] The industry had been organized without great regard to craft differences. Almost simultaneously with the establishment of unions came regional federations of furniture workers. A new Furniture Workers' District Council of Waterloo County formed in 1919 was supplanted in 1920 by the Northern Council of Furniture Workers, as the entire region fell into line.[75]

Proof of the powerful attraction of the movement towards amalgamation came from an unlikely source: Joseph Gibbons and W.D. Robbins. On 30 May, in the midst of the preparations for the general strike, a Public Utilities Council was formed in Toronto with Gibbons as president.[76] As Robbins explained to the press, the council represented 14,000 organized workers in Toronto employed by the federal, provincial, and municipal governments: postal workers, fire fighters, hydro workers, street-railway employees, civic employees, and so on – sixteen organizations in all. In his statement to the press, however, Robbins noted that 'if anyone was to have trouble, each would have local autonomy, and it does not mean that the whole 16 would go on strike.' The *Star* recognized that the council was a conservative response to the pressure towards greater working-class unity and, on the eve of the general strike, commented that its creation 'is looked upon as auguring against [the] possibility of a tie-up in the services thus represented.'[77] Conservatives recognized the implications of amalgamation. As the structure of craft unionism was abandoned, the political traditions of craftworkers were also opened to question. In the West, for instance, industrial unionism and revolutionary socialism grew in tandem.

The One Big Union

The success of the amalgamation movement undermined the One Big Union in southern Ontario, since it appeared that there was a less-hazardous route to industrial unionism. As Simpson argued in the wake of the Calgary conference of March 1919 that laid the foundations of the OBU, the sentiment in favour of industrial unionism was understandable, but the strategy was ill-conceived. 'I am not at all surprised,' he commented, 'to see that they have made a declaration of a new type of organization. I cannot understand, however, how the breaking away from the International affiliation should be decided upon, because it is quite possible for the workers to so federate in their individual capacity as to make such an organization equally as effective as the one big union.'[78] He added that 'the evolution of the Machine in industry' had the effect of 'reducing skilled labor to merely dexterous labor,' an effect that, in turn, undermined the craft distinctions underlying the existing form of trade unionism. An evolution in the form of unionism, he argued, ought to move 'in harmony with the evolution of industry.' Consequently, the gradual fusion of craft unions was the way to proceed.

Unlike Moore, who had advocated such a course only rhetorically as a means of protecting his left flank, Simpson, now editor of the *Industrial Banner*, used the paper to make such a development a reality. As early as April 1919, the *Banner* argued that there was 'no justification for the breaking up of the International Labor movement in Canada' since the 'end which the promoters of the OBU wish to reach can be reached by the federation of the organizations in the different industries.'[79] This was not a capitulation to conservative labour leaders. 'To express opposition to the principle of the sympathetic strike,' it declared, alluding to the leadership of the TLCC and the AFL, 'is nothing less than treason to the working class, in view of the fact that employers use their right to act collectively in giving sympathetic support to those of their own organizations when they are fighting their employees.'[80] The establishment of federations of trades, added the *Banner*, represented only the first step towards a workers' movement able to undertake successful sympathetic strike action. This elaboration of a policy of the amalgamation of craft unions represented a serious obstacle to the OBU.

The majority of militants associated with the general strike, especially the revolutionary socialists who had produced the *Ontario Labor News*, took stock of the situation and accepted Simpson's assessment. Given the divisions within the city's labour movement, no 'One Big Union' was possible. A few individuals, such as Isaac Bainbridge, argued that the failure of the metal-trades strike demonstrated its necessity. And the OBU did gain some converts, particularly among members of the British-based Amalgamated Society of Carpenters who were uncomfortable in their tenuous marriage to the American-based United Brotherhood of Carpenters and Joiners. At its height in late 1919, the OBU claimed 1,100 members in Toronto.[81] But Joseph Knight, who had come from Edmonton to act as OBU organizer in eastern Canada, complained that many radicals who had expressed support for the OBU had had a change of heart. 'Many with whom I conversed with [*sic*] as possible aides,' he wrote in his report back west,

> advised me to lie low until the [TDLC] elections had taken place when Simpson and the 'progressives' would be in control. Braith-

waite, Lewis and Mellilieu assured me in stage whispers that they were in line with the OBU and after the defeat of Hevey and O'Leary they would swing the Council. The 'progressives' won and signalized their victory by a virulent attack upon the OBU in the columns of the 'Industrial Banner' edited by Simpson. Lewis turned turtle and was arded by an organizer's job for the AF of L, while Braithwaite and Mellilieu disappeared into the UFO and the Labor Party.[82]

This was no betrayal, however. Rather, the socialist militants in the TDLC had decided to stay and fight. OBU members were, as Simpson and his colleagues had predicted, isolated from the mainstream of the labour movement. By 1920, Knight bemoaned the fact that the OBU in Toronto attracted only a 'few fanatics, who know more about the political and economic conditions of Russia than Lenin and less about the situation in Toronto than a Zulu.'[83]

Outside Toronto there was a scattered interest in the One Big Union that is not accurately reflected in the dismal results achieved in the referendum on forming the OBU. Little was known about the OBU before it came under attack from such conservative opponents as the provincial executive of the International Typographical Union, which reminded members of the benefits their international provided, benefits they stood to lose.[84] The London TLC voted seventy-five to two against the OBU, while its Hamilton counterpart refused to debate the issue.[85] Even the Guelph TLC, which had proposed a 'National Council of Labor,' demurred. Council delegates probably reflected the views of countless of their brethren throughout the region when they pointed out 'that union men who had built up splendid benefits in the different crafts affiliated to the AF of L including sick and mortuary benefits and old age pensions, and had snug treasuries to back them, were not going to throw them up to take hold of something that only promised what it would do.'[86]

Personal contact with OBU organizers brought to the surface a greater measure of interest, however. In early May, for instance, the president of the Hamilton IAM Railway Lodge wrote to the OBU commenting that R.J. Johns had 'sure made some impression on the boys here' and requested more information. Interestingly, he claimed that 'we have no kick with the boys who handle our business[;] they do the best they can and of which we very much appreciate.' He added, however, that the members wanted the OBU 'so we can take in anyone and not be tied down by the AF of L.' A local of stationary firemen in Thorold wrote to the OBU also asking for information. Such examples lend credence to the claim of a London journalist that 'there seems to be more sympathy for the OBU in London than the leaders of the trades union movement like to admit.'[87]

The OBU was also able to garner support from individuals around the province who were often in a position of some influence. For instance, Arthur Skidmore declared his intention of building the OBU in Stratford. Some former Social Democrats, such as Lorne Cunningham in Guelph and Mervyn Smith in Kitchener, who opposed their party's drift towards the Independent Labor Party (ILP), were open to a secessionist movement. From Windsor, Gordon Cascaden volunteered to produce an Ontario-based paper in the interests of the OBU. Active in the Socialist Party of Canada and the Industrial Workers of the World since 1906, Cascaden was currently involved in editing the *Auto Workers' News*, published by the Automobile, Aircraft and Vehicle Workers, a left-wing industrial union based in Detroit with a handful of members in Windsor.[88]

The One Big Union potentially carried a great appeal for unskilled workers who had been overlooked by craft unionists. From Guelph, for instance, the secretary of the Federal Labor Union wrote to OBU secretary Victor Midgley in Vancouver claiming: 'We are working for the One Big Union here.' More significantly, Fred J. Flatman, president of the Hamilton General Workers Union (GWU), wrote to the OBU, informing them that '[we] are anxious to link our lot or affiliate with your movement just as soon as you are ready to consider such matters.'[89] By May, local labour leaders such as Henry George Fester were acknowledging that the GWU was making strides in the larger factories of the city. Yet Flatman was himself, in fact, more of a prize for the OBU than the relatively small band of labourers in his organization. A British-born blacksmith, Flatman had represented the ILP in the 1917 federal election and, despite his reputation as a socialist in a largely rural riding, had garnered a respectable 1,507 votes in a three-way contest. As business agent of the Amalgamated Society of Engineers (ASE), he had been behind the 1918 proposal adopted by the local Metal Trades Council to amalgamate all the metal trades in North America. Besides his key roles in the ASE and the General Workers Union, Flatman helped organize the United Textile Workers of America in the city and represented it at the 1918 convention of the Labor Educational Association.[90]

In addition to all these activities, Flatman took over the editorship of the Hamilton-based *Labor News* late in 1918, transforming a staid craft organ into a campaign vehicle for the 'new social order.' He published the new British Labour Party program and an article from the Winnipeg *Voice* strongly critical of Gompers' attacks on independent political action. In contrast to its previous defence of the wage system, the *Labor News* declared capital and labour to be natural antagonists.[91] As we shall see, the fate of the *Labor News* was determined by debates within the Hamilton ILP and Trades Council. Flatman's socialism placed him in a minority; and his growing support for industrial unionism made his position as a journalist writing on behalf of the city's labour movement tenuous. In May 1919, Flatman was ousted from his position and replaced by Walter Rollo, a central figure in both labour politics and the Hamilton TLC. The immediate effect of the *coup*, however, was to free Flatman's hand. On 22 May a new publication appeared: *The New Democracy*. It described itself as a 'Radical Labor Weekly ... (Not Endorsed by the Canadian Manufacturers Association)' and was edited by Fred Flatman.[92]

Flatman worked tirelessly to propagate a vision of a more united and inclusive labour movement. The policy of *New Democracy* was 'staunchly [to] support Trades Unionism in all its bonafide battles and [to] advocate the "linking up" of ALL Labor forces to the end of bringing into existence One Great Federated Union along the lines already marked out in Great Britain and other places.'[93] Flatman spoke to the wide sentiment in favour of amalgamation and, potentially, industrial unionism. On the strength of this and much more lively and interesting journalism than the *Labor News* was offering, *New Democracy*'s circulation soared above that of its rival. Recognizing the success of the project, and Flatman's general support for the OBU, Joseph Knight approached Flatman with a proposal to turn *New Democracy* into the eastern Canadian organ of the One Big Union. In return, the OBU agreed to take 5,000 copies a week to distribute on a much wider basis.[94]

The language of Flatman's paper reflected four years of war and the challenges faced by the labour movement: 'REAL DEMOCRACY! We've fought for it – now lets have it.'[95] It took aim at the 'Profiteers' Soviet' in Ottawa, and a 'profiteer "journalism" ... so steeped in the gentle art of camouflage and lying that it cannot give its readers a ten line truthful account of a street car collision which happens directly outside its own door.' It constructed its vision of a 'new democracy' squarely upon a vision of the intrinsic integrity and value of labour that had long motivated and guided the workers' movement: 'Labor, as we use the term, means "useful labor," socially necessary labor, such labor as that required to run railways, dig coal, keep books, till the soil, paint pictures, construct houses, build and operate automobiles, etc. When labor, which does all these things (and a million others), decides to move forward toward the ideal of production for public use instead of production for private profit, this old world will be making real social progress.'[96] While Fred Flatman was a singularly active and imaginative figure in the southern Ontario labour movement, he was not an aberration. His vision was tied to the immediate experiences and wider culture of Ontario workers in innumerable ways. His 'new democracy' represented the antithesis of kaiserism, autocracy, profiteering, and the deskilling and degradation of labour. The OBU had gained an effective ally.

Conclusion

Craft unionism was on the defensive in southern Ontario in the spring of 1919. Its alternative, however, was less clear. Around the province, federated councils of craft unions were making great headway. Moreover, their emergence had been greeted with apparent equanimity from those who might have been expected to challenge this development. Yet the defeat of the general strike in Toronto had the potential of calling this course into question. The city's Metal Trades Council epitomized this development, but had been unable to defeat an aggressive and united Employers' Association. Although the strategy would continue to have strong and articulate defenders, particularly in the *Industrial Banner*, it was, for the moment, unknown what balance sheet the labour movement would draw of the events in the provincial capital.

What of the alternative? On the 1919 Victoria Day weekend a small but important convention took place in Toronto. Representatives came from the OBU in Toronto and Hamilton, the Workers' International Industrial Union in Toronto and Kitchener, the General Workers' Union in Hamilton, and the Federal Labor Union in Guelph. Various platforms were discussed 'with much spirit and thoroughness,' but the delegates were unable to agree upon a political basis for drawing together all the secessionist currents in the province. A committee was struck 'to call at some future date a convention that would be more representative of the movement, and then do what could be done to unify the whole.'[97] As delegates left the convention, the conclusion could not have been avoided that they had lost a crucial opportunity to present a united alternative to the TLCC in southern Ontario.

The scale of this missed opportunity was evident in a tour through southern Ontario in October 1919 by William Ivens, a leader of the Winnipeg General Strike. During this tour Ivens found evidence of interest in the events in Winnipeg and a willingness to listen and consider ideas associated with the OBU. Significantly, Ivens received a warm welcome from the Toronto District Labor Council, which offered its support and money to those subject to repression in Winnipeg. Outside Toronto he caused a sensation, speaking in Brantford, Stratford, and Guelph, addressing two large meetings in the London Market Square, as well as attending a large event chaired by Mervyn Smith in Kitchener. When the Windsor trades council refused to sponsor him, a meeting was held under the auspices of the machinists' union.[98]

St Catharines and Sarnia were the scenes of major confrontations over his presence. In the former city, the mayor's campaign to keep Ivens out of the city developed into a major conflict, with both the Great War Veterans' Association (GWVA) and the Grand Army of Canada (GAC) defending Ivens' right to free speech. The meeting was finally held in the GAC hall. When the mayor appeared to explain his actions, the crowd gave 'three cheers for the NEXT LABOR MAYOR.' Despite such enthusiasm for independent political action, trades-council president Frank Greenlaw, campaigning in the provincial election, refused to be associated with Ivens and prevented his addressing the local Independent Labor Party.[99]

The GWVA, however, was not of one mind on the subject and played a major role in attempting to prevent Ivens from speaking in Sarnia. According to Gordon Cascaden, the dominance of the Imperial Oil Company in the city accounted for the difference; the president of the GWVA was a partner in a law firm associated with the oil company. As in St Catharines, the local mayor refused to allow the use of city hall for the meeting. For a week before his arrival, the local paper published front-page news items against Ivens and 'his actions in attempting Soviet rule' in Winnipeg, and a citizen's 'safety committee' was formed to prevent his entering the city. Parks were closed and signs against 'Ivens the Bolshevik' were placed in store windows asking citizens to 'Remember those who died in Flanders.' Nevertheless, with the support of the machinists, the boilermakers' union based at Imperial Oil invited Ivens to use its hall. Three thousand came to hear his message. The Safety Committee attempted to disrupt the event by hiring a band to drown out the speaker, and the electricity to the hall was twice cut. In the end, an automobile was brought into the hall to provide light. The GAC voted unanimously to invite Ivens back to address an even larger audience. For its part, the OBU concluded that Ontario was ready to explode – 'all they lack is someone to break the ice.'[100]

There was, however, no one to break the ice. By contrast with re-actions in the West, the major supporters of the OBU quickly realized that choosing such a path would plunge the Ontario labour movement into an internecine feud that they were unlikely to win. That the small secessionist currents in the region were unable to unite indicated the sectarian margins to which the OBU was confined. This should not obscure the fact that the sentiment that had led to the emergence of the OBU in western Canada was evident in southern Ontario as well. The Toronto General Strike and the emergence of trades federations revealed an impatience with craft unionism and its leaders and a will-ingness to consider a more militant strategy. Toronto Metal Trades Council vice-president John MacDonald emphasized the trajectory of the movement: 'First we struck as trades, then we have struck as a federation, but the day will come when we strike as a class.'[101] Atten-tion, for the moment, turned elsewhere. The Ontario provincial elec-tion campaign, in full swing as Ivens toured the province, gave Ontario workers an alternative means of asserting themselves as a class.

Part Two

THE POLITICAL FRONT

3 The Development of a Labourist Consensus

'In the Ballot Lies the Only Hope of the Workers'
Front-page headline, *Industrial Banner*, 1 December 1916

From the Hamilton munitions strike to the near paralysis of industrial Toronto in 1919, the conflicts that rocked southern Ontario were born of frustration and resentment at the fortunes of war: fortunes that fell unevenly upon a class-divided society. Employers' intransigence in the face of labour's demands for the eight-hour day and recognition of their unions revealed how little had been won; the Orders in Council demonstrated how much had been lost. Yet, despite devastation in Europe and creeping autocracy at home, this was an era of great promise. Mainstream religious leaders, for instance, saw 'a redemptive war,'[1] which marshalled the virtues of selflessness and sacrifice for future domestic use. Politicians' vague promises of post-war reconstruction similarly suggested that hardship would have its returns once the war no longer commanded the nation's full attention and resources.

Working-class hopes had a more concrete basis. The travails of the past few years had forged a union movement of unprecedented size and cohesion. This development was paralleled by a growing ability to articulate a class-based view of reconstruction informed by wartime conflicts. In a war fought ostensibly for democracy, the labour movement voiced a concern that the very concept of democracy would be hijacked by capitalists and politicians who had no intention of relinquishing their power. Workers' own views of democracy were, of course, complex. Often they were defined in reaction to their exclusion from wartime authority (in their dealings with the IMB, for instance), or in their opposition to the Borden government's open defence of capital (as in the prohibition of strikes). In each case, the government appeared more and more willing to intervene directly in the interests of the accumulation of capital – in popular terms, in the defence of profiteers. Consequently, the goal of working-class action was not merely the attainment of better wages and conditions, but the containment of a creeping kaiserism.[2]

In a liberal democracy, industrial action was an inappropriate, or at least insufficient, response to such a threat. Democracy applied to the political realm and particularly to the electoral system. Attention naturally turned in that direction. A handful of energetic labour propagandists argued tirelessly that independent working-class political action was necessary to safeguard and expand Canadian democracy. This chapter examines the character of this political challenge, arguing that the developing 'labourist' political movement faithfully articulated notions of democracy and progress that were widely held by the region's workers and that came to be codified in the nascent Independent Labor Party of Ontario. The remarkable success of this party, the subject of the subsequent chapter, revealed that a labourist consensus had gripped workers throughout the region. As they had on the industrial front, workers increasingly drew together as a class to confront their political opponents.

Labourism was a vague ideological current. It was, primarily, a sentiment that achieved hegemony in the regional organized labour movement in 1919, that working-class interests could be defended only by the election of workers, as workers, to public office. Its program was that of the craft-union movement. In Britain, John Saville has argued that labourism evolved in the aftermath of the defeat of Chartism as 'a theory and practice which accepted the possibility of social change within the existing framework of society.' Craig Heron's survey of Canadian labourism from its emergence in the 1880s similarly takes note of its roots in Radical Liberalism and its tenacious faith in parliamentarism. Socialists, who located the source of exploitation outside the legislatures, railed against such naïveté. It is difficult to argue with such assessments. Resolute gradualism (indeed, as Saville argues, class collaboration) defined labourism. Yet, as many contemporary socialists recognized, labourism was perhaps too weak a vessel to contain the aspirations of its adherents. There was little that was new in the wartime labourist programs; earlier manifestations, as in Ontario in 1907, were constructed on similar planks. The new ingredient was the war. The contradictions of new-found industrial muscle, expectations of 'reconstruction,' and the audacity of the 'profiteers' could push the ILP to redefine its strategies and goals. With labourism finally successful at the polls, its promise as the means to the 'new democracy' was to be tested in practice. The outcome could not be foretold. To understand the character of the developing labourist consensus in the region, we must return to the eve of the war.[3]

The Birth of a Provincial Labour Movement

For decades, unions and trades councils had debated and drafted lists of political demands. Such programs varied, but generally included amendments to factory legislation, provisions for shorter hours, improved mechanics' lien laws, improved access to education for workers' children, and electoral reforms to give workers a louder voice in the country's legislatures. The means to attain these goals proved elusive. Regular labour delegations to various levels of government were politely received and then ignored. Attempts to elect labour candidates to enact such legislation themselves repeatedly unearthed deep-seated Liberal or Conservative partisan loyalties.[4] Indeed, at least one historian considers that the Ontario working class as a whole had been 'Conservative for many years under [Premier James] Whitney,' although it should probably be added as a proviso, as Heron has argued, that workers had become deeply cynical about the political process. Industrial cities tended to vote Conservative, but voter turn-out was low and probably declining.[5] To the extent that organized labour was politically active, its world was defined by workplace and community. Trades and labour councils best reflected this focus on local issues, and municipal politics was closely watched by such bodies. But organizing to address provincial or federal concerns was a task of a much higher order. Even the Trades and Labour Congress of Canada represented little more than an annual convention, capable of passing resolutions but having little power to ensure their implementation.

On the eve of the First World War, this debility was finally overcome and a regional labour movement forged in the process. The campaign for the Workmen's Compensation Act drew together workers throughout the region and the province to a degree not achieved since the nine-hours' movement of the 1870s.[6] The issue was crucial to Ontario workers. Workplace dangers loomed large, and the common law had failed to provide protection for workers injured or killed on the job. Even if workers felt they had a good case, they had to weigh the cost and delay of litigation; the procedure was expensive and unpredictable. For employers as well, the process was becoming troublesome. Evidence suggests that the workplace was becoming more dangerous. And even as it became clearer that workers had little control over the safety

of their environment in an era of developing mass-production industries, judges and juries increasingly found for the plaintiff in such cases.
In 1910 Premier Whitney appointed Chief Justice William Meredith
to investigate a new scheme of workers' compensation.[7]

The long and successful battle to ensure the passage of legislation
forged a provincial labour movement. The campaign was led by Social
Democrat Fred Bancroft and by Joseph Gibbons, a Tory leader of the
Toronto Street Railway Employees' Union. Not only was labour politically unified in this struggle but, as Wayne Roberts has noted, the
leaders were 'buoyed by a mass movement' and 'private sessions [with
the government] were forsaken as the campaign became unequivocally
political.'[8] In contrast to later TLCC dealings with the Union government, the mobilization of as many workers as possible to ensure compliance with earlier promises was central to this struggle.

The real architect of the campaign, as well as the moving force
behind a larger and more integrated provincial labour movement, was
Joseph T. Marks. Now in his sixties, Marks had played an important
role in the Knights of Labor and had attempted to organize the Industrial Brotherhood of Canada as its successor in southwestern Ontario.[9] Despite this rich past, Marks's vision was fixed on the horizon.
In 1914, reflecting on thirty-two years in the labour movement, Marks
told a Welland audience that '[t]he golden age was not away back in
the ages, but in the future, and not in the distant future either. Evolution was getting in its work, and when the workers of the world were
united, as united they would assuredly be, they would capture the
powers of the state, for they constituted the majority, and they would
be represented in parliaments and legislatures by more of their own
class, who would legislate for the industrial emancipation of the workers
of the world.'[10] It was a vision from which he would not wander,
neither in the commitment to change through the ballot box nor in
the goal of a complete social reordering.

Marks had two instruments with which to organize workers for their
industrial emancipation: the *Industrial Banner* and the Labor Educational Association of Ontario (LEAO). Originally established under the
auspices of the London TLC in 1892, the *Banner* slowly achieved a
regional presence and remained firmly in the hands of Marks, who
relocated to Toronto in 1912. His priorities could be seen in the large
print runs supporting independent labour candidates wherever they
appeared in southern Ontario during the pre-war years. In Toronto,
the Labor Council often paid for free distribution of the *Banner* at
election time. Although subscription figures are unknown, the *Banner*

realized a $3,000 profit in 1913 and was able to send four prize-winners to Britain in its subscription contest. All indications point to a substantial base of support for the paper.[11]

The Labor Educational Association of Ontario, founded in 1902, was, in essence, a loosely organized provincial federation of labour. City trades councils and local unions were affiliated to it, and province-wide political demands were formulated at its annual conventions, but the association demanded no per-capita affiliation fees and had no paid officers. Its day-to-day functioning was in the hands of its perennial secretary-treasurer, Joe Marks, who viewed the job as a logical corollary of his work as *Banner* editor.[12] The LEAO spearheaded the campaign for the Workmen's Compensation Act. At twenty-three public meetings held around the province, Bancroft, Gibbons, Marks, and other leaders explained the issues in detail, and Marks published their speeches in the *Industrial Banner*. Throughout Ontario, 750 labour organizations, including 17 local trades councils, lent their support. Marks used these events to strengthen the provincial movement by emphasizing the role of the LEAO and its paper.[13]

Michael Piva has analysed the campaign for the Workmen's Compensation Act as peculiarly quixotic. He argues that little separated labour's and the manufacturers' positions on the matter, emphasizing that the Canadian Manufacturers' Association's 'criticisms of the legislation were not directed at the fundamental principle of compensation' and that the *Banner* 'gives quite a false impression of the severity of the conflict between capital and labour on this issue.' Rather, disagreements focused on less-substantial issues: the rate of compensation to be paid and whether workers would be required to contribute to the fund. Piva's analysis stems from a historiographical current that ascribes the main impetus of early-twentieth-century reform to capitalists who, to quote a leading member of this school, saw 'liberalism as a means of securing the existing social order'[14] by regulating 'ruthless' excesses of competition that were becoming unprofitable and potentially explosive. Certainly the final report by Meredith, which concluded with an appeal to 'the blessing of industrial peace and freedom from social unrest,'[15] supports Piva's reading of these events.

Yet this cannot fully explain the scale of conflict over the proposed legislation. Workers were naturally concerned that they could walk away empty-handed, that their common-law rights would be lost, and that, if they were injured, they would have to make do with niggardly compensation subject to technicalities in the legislation that potentially could disqualify them. Certainly the tone of CMA attacks on the draft bill could only make workers apprehensive. *Industrial Canada*, the journal of the CMA, termed the proposals 'preposterous' and proposed a reduction in the rate of compensation from a maximum of 55 per cent of the injured party's previous wage to a more 'moderate' level. The CMA also pressed to have workers pay a portion of the costs of the scheme, potentially a new and substantial tax on their wages. While the substance of the act was not, generally, in dispute, such changes promised to have a great impact on injured workers. Both the issues of who would pay the cost of industrial accidents and whether workers would be adequately protected were at the root of the conflict. Moreover, the resources the CMA threw into the fight made workers wonder what really was at stake. This was particularly the case when 250 manufacturers descended on Queen's Park in Toronto to protest the draft bill – an unusually open display of capitalist class solidarity (the *Banner* was pleased to announce that the province's factories functioned as usual in their absence).[16]

While, as Piva suggests, the CMA favoured a new compensation system, the level of class conflict was not exaggerated by the *Banner*. The Legislature passed Meredith's bill over the CMA's objections. The CMA had managed only to situate itself as the primary nemesis of working-class rights and 'common justice.' The LEAO was able to claim that the education and arousal of workers, and the expenditure of only $65.31, had defeated the CMA and its high-priced lawyers. Labour had won a political victory through its own organizations and efforts. The lesson would not be lost in the course of the war.

Democracy

Marks struggled valiantly to maintain this level of labour mobilization in the face of increasing concern with the war. Despite initial interest, his 'Provincial Publicity Campaign on Unemployment' soon collapsed. Quiescence in 1914 and 1915 was misleading and, as we have seen, economic recovery provided the occasion for major strikes before the second full year of the war drew to a close. Politically as well, the seeds of change were germinating. It was here that the *Industrial Banner* played a unique role in addressing the troublesome questions posed by the war and the events that accompanied it. Marks turned the columns of the paper to the defence of democracy, education, and workers' rights in a language that would, unamended, emerge as the official ideology of the increasingly successful labour electoral movement. Week after week, he urged a course of independent working-class political action upon his readers.

The *Banner* had been a major voice against militarism before the war but, like the organized labour movement as a whole, it was disoriented in its response to the actual conflict. Marks maintained his view of the war as the product of capitalist competition but, by March 1915, had resigned himself to the continuing conflict and begun to see within it the seed of 'salvation for the masses.' 'The war,' he suggested, 'is breaking down the lines of birth and caste, the working class is being drilled and disciplined on the battle fields of Europe; it will no longer be an undisciplined mass, and though it may to-day be fighting for its masters, it to-morrow may be in a position to assert its rights to mastery.'[17] However, by the end of that summer, the *Banner* acknowledged that there 'can be no sense in denying the fact that Organized Labor throughout the Dominion is impressed with the belief that the British Empire is fighting for the freedom of the world and the liberation of the Belgian people.'[18]

Freedom and liberation – these ideas fused with the notion that the British Empire was as close as history had come to a 'World-Wide Democracy.'[19] Such ideals also furnished a defence of working-class interests within Canada. The dominions within the Empire had come to the aid of the motherland without compulsion: such a model ought to guide the Canadian state domestically. Democracy required self-determination not only on a world scale but at home as well. It required eschewing conscription, censorship, and the expansion of state powers for use against working-class interests. A series entitled 'World Workers versus Militarism' continued to appear in the *Banner* with the implicit message that workers were fighting for democracy on several fronts.

Increasingly extravagant wartime propaganda had a contradictory effect upon the ability of the workers' movement to articulate its own agenda in the course of the war. As Peter Buitenhuis has recently documented, governments in Britain and North America mobilized the literary community in the war effort. Schools, churches, and imperialistic youth groups such as the Boy Scouts eagerly joined the recruiting effort for the crusade in Europe. In the process they added their own interpretation of its meaning for the future of Canadian society. For a broad range of activists in movements for social reform, particularly the mainstream Protestant churches, the war became, to cite Brown and Cook, 'the great patriotic challenge which would purge Canada of petty politics, materialism, and corruption,' its bright, if vague, promise captured in the title of a 1917 anthology, *The New Era in Canada*. In this particular volume, established Canadian journalists and businessmen summoned images of a reinvigorated democracy based upon 'national ideals in industry' and 'a new idea of citizenship' and rising above selfishness and patronage. The reform proposals were not radical but the rhetoric appealed to a common 'will to serve' in a new era that lay just beyond the horizon.[20] It was unnecessary for workers to slog their way through *The New Era in Canada*; in sermons, recruiting speeches, newspapers, and posters, its message bombarded Canadians.

Such propaganda did more than mobilize workers for the war effort. It validated hopes for a more secure and egalitarian society in the war's aftermath. It sharpened workers' anger at those who betrayed the ideal of service: profiteers and politicians whose selfish actions appeared indefensible in the context of a national crisis. Paul Fussell's argument that the ironic frame of mind was a product of the First World War is applicable to the home front. What were workers to make of Joseph Flavelle's call to 'send profits to the hell where they belong'? Coming from the arch-industrial-aristocrat of the Imperial Munitions Board, a man widely regarded as Canada's premier profiteer, such words dripped with hypocrisy. If a new era was to arrive, it would not be ushered in by the Flavelles of the world. The *Banner*'s declaration that only the independent activity of workers could guarantee post-war democracy had a ready audience. While John English observes that, for the 'English-Canadian elite' the 'ideology of service' served as a vindication of their right to rule, just the opposite was true for growing numbers of workers. Service and the defence of special privilege were declared incompatible.[21]

For an organized working class suspicious of militarism, support for the war effort came to be justified by the defence of democracy. By 1916, protests against property qualifications, a particularly galling obstacle to working-class political representation, grew into a significant campaign. Electors and candidates were required to own or rent property worth a specific amount in order to participate in civic elections. Not only was this viewed as a crude method of disenfranchising workers, but the rationale behind the law, that only those who held property had an interest in the community, antagonized craft workers, who viewed their skills and labour as the most useful and necessary property. The return of veterans who had risked their lives and been injured in battle but who could not exercise the franchise in municipal elections belied the claim that only those with property had a stake in the community. The *Banner*'s call to 'let the veterans vote' gained new moral weight.[22]

Other structural impediments to workers' participation in political system were also assailed. The existing structure of single-member constituencies was seen as favouring 'partyism, since minority opinions could be represented only great difficulty. Consequently, a wave of support for proportional representation accompanied moves towards independent political action. The trades councils in Toronto and Berlin carried the campaign at a municipal level, demanding the abolition of the ward system and the establishment of a commission form of government. Ironically, such measures could undermine workers' electoral weight. As Samuel P. Hayes and John C. Weaver have argued, in the cases of the United States and Canada respectively, business and professional men were behind such campaigns to wrest control of city governments from the hands of often-corrupt ward-heelers and patronage machines. In the process they undermined the community strength of unions and workers' parties, which generally were not able to mobilize a sufficiently large city-wide electorate for labour candidates. Moreover, as we have noted in our discussion of the IMB, the creation of autonomous boards to run municipal services eroded popular sovereignty. The London TLC, which had had some success in electing aldermen in working-class districts, did oppose the measure, but there was an ongoing tendency for labourists to borrow somewhat uncritically from other reform agendas.[23]

Local trades councils actively brought to light undemocratic behaviour, and the Berlin, Brantford, and London councils all fought censorship. Most noticeable in this agitation for democratic reforms was the expressed feeling that electoral reforms themselves would serve to democratize the system and give workers an adequate voice. Socialists argued that democracy was forestalled by inequality in the workplace and that the bosses' political weight stemmed from their economic power, but theirs was a faint voice. The *Industrial Banner* was clear in this regard. 'Direct legislation,' it claimed, 'could effectively fill the bill and make the people their own rulers and legislators.' On other occasions Marks argued that wars would be ended by women's suffrage, the initiative, and the referendum, and that with such measures corruption would be impossible.[24]

The faith that not only Marks but trades councils across the province placed in the reform of the electoral system was striking. It was precisely such a faith that would blossom, late in the war, into a full-blown labourist consensus. Privilege was seen as the product of a manipulated political system. The goal was to find a means whereby workers could exercise their majority in society. While it is easy to dismiss their solutions as naïve in the face of the massive economic power of Canadian capital, it is important to recognize that, when combined with the democratic rhetoric that accompanied the war and the growing disregard for democratic procedure by governments, the result was explosive. Labour's call for a wider, participatory democracy threatened a greater impact than the narrowly electoral character of its demands.

This attraction to an active notion of citizenship and natural human rights has a clear lineage running through Chartism and Gladstonian Liberalism.[25] Indeed, few elements in this reform program were alien to the Liberal reform tradition. Many of labour's demands had been articulated, in fact, by prominent Liberals in the region, such as Ontario Liberal leader Newton Rowell and Joseph E. Atkinson, publisher of the *Toronto Daily Star*. The basis for a liberal-labour current was firmly laid before the war. This was particularly the case in Toronto where an earlier Independent Labour Party supported the Liberal Party and reciprocity in the 1911 Dominion elections.[26] Such an alliance, however, encountered major obstacles after 1914. The potential Liberal side of the lib-lab equation was pulled towards an all-out support for the war effort that eclipsed concerns with specific working-class issues. Rowell and Atkinson came to support the Union government and conscription in the face of significant working-class opposition. After some searching in the wake of the Workmen's Compensation victory, Marks and the *Banner* had found the main ingredient for a campaign for political action: the defence and expansion of democracy.

Education

The labour movement was hardly unaware that, granted direct democracy and proportional representation, Canadian workers might not immediately vote in their own interests. The dead weight of 'partyism' and the power of 'the interests' were too great. Toronto labour political leader, John W. Buckley adumbrated the solution: 'education is salvation.'[27] Two aspects of this concern for education provide insight into working-class notions of knowledge and of society and were important catalysts in the development of labourism. Demands for free, compulsory, good-quality education for working-class children helped pull unions into municipal politics. Interest in their own education as adults provided a context for wide-ranging political debate.

Working-class parents naturally were concerned about what their children learned in school. Organized labour's reaction to military training in school was rooted in a belief that schools were inculcating values that were at odds with students' own interests and the well-being of working-class families. The Toronto District Labor Council's 'Educative Committee' reported in 1915 its belief that 'National Bigotry, Hero Worship and Servile Obedience are underlying principles inculcated in the children; this furnishes the right material for the workshops, etc.' At the root of this critique was a feeling that the education system, as it was constituted, represented an unwarranted intrusion into working-class life. The demand for 'efficient workers' guided the system, a fact that 'placed the matter entirely out of the parents' control.' Citing Dr Helen MacMurchy, the committee added that 'the State is the parent of the child and the parents have become but guardians.'[28] Working-class parents were forced to stand by as their children were turned into willing and obedient workers.

In 1918, an election campaign against the Conservative minister of education, Canon J.H. Cody, provided an opportunity for skilled workers to expand on this critique, arguing that the education system poorly served working-class children. Labour candidate William Varley pointed out that, despite large provincial expenditures, only a minority of the population had access to high schools and colleges. 'We are an educated people,' he added, but, 'ignorance stalks through the land. Lack of efficiency, to say nothing of dearth of culture greets us everywhere. The multitudes grow up to manhood and womanhood and live through their lives, die, never knowing the release and expression of the mind, the great doors never having been opened to them. They walk in great darkness and they know it.'[29] Others, like John T. Gunn, a leader of the electrical workers, demanded that children receive a cultural as well as a vocational education.[30]

Workers' deep faith in education combined with a high regard for the value of practical labour meant that even state-run vocational training, with all its attendant risks for unions' control of the labour market, produced 'a better citizen.' The potential inherent in the democratization of education was explained by Hamilton Social Democrat William S. Bruton. The 'monopoly of education by the ruling classes,' he argued, 'has led to the assumption that they have also a monopoly of intelligence or the ability to learn.' However, the development of modern industry had 'forced a greater distribution of education' that had revealed the intelligence of the workers as well. That this education was designed to perpetuate working-class servility, to 'prove that mastership and slavery are natural and beneficial alike to master and slave' was irrelevant, for 'thought cannot be confined.' Once stimulated, 'the workers are evolving their own ideas ... ideas that because of the fact they originate with the majority class of the race, will be pertinent for the good of the race as a whole.'[31] Demands for such things as the free distribution of school textbooks contained a democratic component that viewed equal access to the collective knowledge of society as a natural right. This view of education, however, also reflected a working-class interpretation of a positivist view of evolution that was becoming a common ideological currency. Education meant popular access to science, and hence to human progress, and was therefore basic to the social and economic development of the entire society.[32]

Such an attitude to education knew no age limits and was reflected in a long autodidactic tradition among craft workers. Ubiquitous labour forums and lectures organized by trades councils and labour parties experienced new growth with the revival of the union movement in 1916. The Brantford TLC established a People's Forum and a library in 1917, while in London, the older and rather heterogeneous Radical Club was transformed into a People's Forum more directly attuned to the labour movement. Discussion in such bodies was wide-ranging and often esoteric, reflecting a passion for the whole corpus of human knowledge. The radical tumult Gene Homel identified in the 1890s, it seems, was reborn.[33]

The questions posed by the war fuelled the intellectual ferment in workers' organizations. In addition to a haunting feeling that the war was in some way caused by 'economics,' workers were forced to contend with rapid inflation, which they traced to the protection of profiteers by the state. Self-education in the field of political economy seemed to provide the answers. The London TLC urged the city library to purchase copies of Gustavus Myers' *History of Canadian Wealth*, while the Brantford trades council requested their city's library to stock its shelves with books on 'industrial subjects.' In lectures, pamphlets, and newspaper articles, long-time London radical Harry Ashplant pursued his own battle against the 'legalization of counterfeit money,' arguing to working-class audiences that labour was exploited not in the sphere of production, as Marxists would have it, but in the sphere of exchange, by the banks' legal ability to create money not backed by gold.[34] The Social Democratic Party, of course, argued the opposite. Throughout the province, trades councils organized meetings against the high cost of living, proposing their own analyses and their own solutions to the problem – usually nationalization and price regulation.[35]

As the growing activity of the labour movement was reflected in intensified debate, these forums complemented trades councils as the focus of ideological combat. This was particularly the case in Toronto where divisions within the workers' movement were at their greatest by the end of the war. A *Saturday Night* report of Toronto's Sunday afternoon People's Forum shortly after the armistice captures the intensity of debate, albeit through an anti-radical lens. Upon completion of an address on socialist gains internationally, the audience

> went at it each in their turn. Man after man leaped to his feet and for three minutes talked as fast and loud as he could. It was oratory in sprints – a sort of relay race in which each did his utmost for the distance he had to go, and then passed on the red flag or the incendiary torch to the next. Heaven only knows where they were racing to, but they were certainly on their way ...
>
> This was really the most wonderful thing about the whole session, the way the chairman would halt young world-wreckers in full career, stay the dreadful axe in their hand, blow out the shudderful torch, and all by gravely wagging his right-hand index finger while he studied the minute hand of his watch in his left. It was a great mastery, a modern miracle of the power of mind over matter.[36]

Everywhere workers earnestly debated political questions posed by war and peace. The report of the post-war Royal Commission on Industrial Relations noted that this 'educational process' had been undertaken by workers across the country to a greater extent than by their employers, although, in the opinion of the Commissioners, 'some of the literature read may not be sound.'[37]

As class conflicts intensified at the end of the war, the adult education movement itself became a battleground. The founding of the Workers' Education Association (WEA), at least for some of the academics, such as W.L. Grant, who participated in its establishment in early 1918, was a means of challenging the 'half-baked ideas' that are 'manifest to the world in Russia to-day.' The *Toronto Daily Star* was even more forthright, claiming that the WEA 'is likely to prove a great antagonist to the possible spread of Bolshevism and other kindred revolutionary ideas.' Yet, while an attempt was clearly being made to undermine autonomous control by the working-class of its own education, the establishment of the WEA dovetailed with workers' own demands for greater knowledge. Classes reflected the lack of focus often evident in working-class self-education; the first worker-students studied the *Politics* of Aristotle, the ideas of Ruskin, political economy, banking, and political history.[38] Local labour leaders, especially James H.H. Ballantyne (who had attended Ruskin College in Britain), ran the WEA, and trades councils, whatever their political bent, lent their support.[39] Although the communists would later assail the WEA as an agency of bourgeois ideology, the more common perception was voiced by a local member of the Printing Pressmen's Union: 'knowledge,' whatever its source, 'is power.'[40]

Religion

Democracy and education proved to be two of the cornerstones of workers' political response to wartime concerns. It may well be asked if there was a third: religion. As Heron has argued, the task of determining the degree of religious motivation in working-class action is complicated by the fact that 'religious metaphors were the common coin of public discourse in Canada.' The assertion of the president of the Peterborough TLC, for instance, that 'the greatest man of all time was a carpenter,' was an affirmation of the value of manual labour in a familiar idiom. Before the war only a small group of socialists, notably the Socialist Party of North America, explicitly rejected religion.[41]

Neither references to religious themes by workers in order to legitimize activity nor participation in working-class industrial or political life by a significant group of church leaders were regular features of the southern Ontario labour movement, however. To the extent that there was a flurry of clearly religious activity, it was confined to a discernible segment of the movement. This included a small group of native-born Canadian Protestants whose radicalization had occurred within the limits of organized religion and whose theological views of a 'practical religion' sustained their political activity. James Simpson, who remained an active Methodist, dominated this current. In addition, there were a number of British immigrants whose commitment to socialism had been forged in the context of the moral and religious sentiments of what Stanley Pierson has labelled the 'ethical socialism' of the British Independent Labour Party. In fact, a significant number of socialists in southern Ontario had been activists in the British ILP, including John W. Buckley and Rose Hodgson in Toronto and Samuel Lawrence in Hamilton.[42]

In the course of the First World War, the adherence of these individuals to mainstream Protestantism was severely tested. The Methodist synthesis of militarism and social reform identified by Michael Bliss and William H. Magney was alien to the workers' movement's response to the war. As early as October 1914, a correspondent wrote to the *Industrial Banner* attacking the clergy's capitulation to militarism. Criticisms that churches had been transformed into 'political cockpits' for militarism and the re-election of Tories were plentiful, and many labour figures publicly disavowed organized religion.[43] Labour activist Minnie Singer explained her decision to a London audience in 1919:

> Mrs. Singer showed how in Toronto the churches had been thrown open to Union Government candidates in the general election, and this oftimes in localities where Labor was not even able to secure a hall, and on the Sunday before the election she told her husband if the pastor preached for Union Government that day I would get up and walk out of the church in protest. It would have been the last time I would have gone out of that church too. This declaration brought down a great round of applause. She claimed nothing could change her faith in God, but she could not go to church and listen to a man who was not sincere in the Gospel he preached.[44]

In a similar vein, a motion for the Brantford trades council to oppose military training in schools in 1917 was passed on the basis that 'It is not Christ-like to foster militarism and a spirit of hatred in our Children.'

Religious sentiments led a layer of working-class activists to seek an alternate outlook. One was available in the Christian Socialist Federation, which sprang to life in Toronto. The merging of Marxist and Christian traditions was reflected in the titles of Christian Socialist lectures: 'The Bible and Surplus Value' and 'The Reign of the Working Class Foretold in Scripture.' Within a few months, the west end branch had seventy active members and organizing was underway in the east end. In Richard Allen's terms such a movement would fall within the bounds of the 'radical' wing of the social gospel, although such a typology fails to recognize its distinctive working-class roots and the extent to which it drew upon the ethical values of organized labour.[45]

The same is true of the establishment in 1915 of the Church of the Social Revolution in Toronto. 'All workingmen who were brought up to the good old-fashioned ideas which used to obtain in Canada a few years ago,' it was suggested, 'before we had boy scouts, holy Christian wars, etc., etc., will find something in the atmosphere and conduct of this little red church to their satisfaction.' Pastor W.E.S. James expressed the language of the social gospel in his belief that Christianity 'should deal with every-day social problems and seek to understand the needs of men and women and discuss the great social questions that press for solution.' Its regular Sunday-evening liturgy differed little from orthodox Protestantism: music, prayer, Bible reading, and the sermon. The character of the sermons, however, reflected the social concerns and the wide interest in self-education of the audience. The pastor and guest speakers spoke on 'The Labour Legislation of Moses,' 'Economic Causes of the Present War,' 'Amos, the Religious Revolutionist,' 'The Bible and the Land Question,' and 'Spiritual versus Mental Hypothesis of Phenomena.' A special evening on the world's religions demonstrated by the use of lantern slides 'the parallels in the Immaculate Birth, Temptation, Baptism, and Crucifixion Symbols in the Various Religions.'[46] Doctrinal differences had little place in a movement dedicated to a wider solidarity.

Who was attracted to Christian Socialism? Almost all were British- or Canadian-born skilled Protestant workers; most seemed to have been members of the Social Democratic Party. In the summer of 1915, a picnic co-sponsored by the Women's Social Democratic League and the Christian Socialist Federation attracted 350 participants. Only rarely did the SDP's non-British members take part in such activities. Moreover, the movement was generally confined to Toronto and, briefly, Brantford. Elsewhere such activity amounted to little more than sermons by visiting individuals such as Simpson and Fred Bancroft. In Toronto, activity of this type provided a point of intersection with other currents of social reform. Speakers included the long-time 'single taxer' W.A. Douglass and Dr Augusta Stowe-Gullen on the women's suffrage movement.[47]

By 1919, this autonomous Christian Socialist movement was moribund. The end of the war and continued debate on social issues within mainstream Protestantism had persuaded a few to refocus their attention within the established churches in the search for allies for their struggles. More significantly, the meteoric rise of the Independent Labor Party had come to monopolize the energies of many of the prime movers of Christian Socialism. The ILP now sponsored the forums, lectures, and social events that had attracted many in the course of the war and was much more successful in appealing to a wider audience. Not until 1923 and the defeat of the ILP did a similar phenomenon, A.E. Smith's Labour Church, re-emerge.[48] During the height of the post-war upsurge, the ethical socialists abandoned an expressly religious form of expression for a working-class movement that had not been attracted to Christian Socialism. The Independent Labor Party was to command a much wider audience.

Independent Political Action

After two years of war, Joseph Marks and supporters of the *Industrial Banner* believed that labour in Ontario was prepared to take a bold step forward. The Workmen's Compensation campaign had produced a real provincial movement, and industrial struggles revealed new levels of organization and combativeness that made the unions a clear pole of attraction for a wider working class. As well, the war itself had reinvigorated workers' demands for a broader democracy allowing for their full participation in political life, education, and public debate. The loyalty and habits that in the past tied workers to existing political parties were breaking down. Independent working-class political action was on the agenda.

In the summer of 1916, Marks turned the focus of his paper single-mindedly towards electoral activity. The *Industrial Banner* printed a letter from a local house painter warning that 'There is going to be a great upheaval in this country in the near future, and unless labor realizes the importance of securing the reins of government, labor is going to suffer, and suffer badly.'[49] Editorially, Marks added that it was the 'essence of absurdity' that at the very moment when workers finally were challenging their employers in the factories they still dutifully followed their bosses at the polls. This was the *Banner*'s weekly refrain throughout the fall and into 1917. The old political parties had fallen into disrepute in the eyes of Ontario's workers and a 'golden opportunity' presented itself. The old parties now represented little more than 'self-constituted patronage committees or machines that dominate them and hand out public offices and appointments to keep the party heelers and spongers in line.' If posed audaciously, a 'progressive and really democratic people's movement' – one that stood for 'real democracy' – could ignite the province.[50]

In October 1916, Marks clarified his strategic perspective. A new party must encompass a wide spectrum of political views: 'Social-Democrats, Independent Labor men, social and economic reformers, people who believe in direct legislation, proportional representation, votes for women, and the nationalization of the railroads and all the national sources of wealth.' Any political differences were dismissed as 'petty' and ought not to stand as an obstacle to parliamentary representation. Marks pointed to a recent convention in Niagara Falls that had grouped both socialist and non-socialist unionists into just such an organization. In Hamilton an Independent Labor Party had, since 1906, successfully re-elected Allan Studholme to the provincial legislature where he sat independently of the two old parties and defended labour's interests with 'a prickly class pride' and typically labourist lack of ideological originality.[51] Toronto, of course, held the key to a provincial organization. In late October, a small gathering met in the city 'to see if "something" could be started.' This group, in turn, decided to organize a larger public meeting. Marks suggested that the organizers, eleven men and one woman, were notable for their heterogeneity. In the recent past they had held 'extremely opposite' views on political action. Yet they collectively recognized that the war had created new conditions that, if approached in a united manner, could lead to electoral success. The larger meeting took place in the Labour Temple on 23 November with the president of the TDLC, plumber James Richards, in the chair and Laura Hughes acting as secretary.[52]

Despite the widely representative nature of this meeting, including single taxers, members of previous labour parties, and 'adherents of both the Grit and Tory parties who had become disgusted with their policies,' the meeting focused on a debate between socialists over the efficacy of political action on a minimum program of immediate, democratic demands. The fact that every major socialist current in the city was represented – the SDP, the Socialist Party of Canada, the Socialist Labor Party, and the Socialist Party of North America (SPNA) – testifies to a common recognition of the potential of this new movement. While some, such as the SPNA, had come to argue against the project, a large number of SDP members were interested, if not fully convinced. The SDP paper, *Canadian Forward*, expressed the sentiments of its editor, Isaac Bainbridge, who took exception to suggestions by Hughes and Marks that they should lay aside their socialism in the interests of a broader unity. Others in the SDP, represented by Mervyn Smith of Kitchener, argued that a party that was not explicitly socialist would become, in time, a 'capitalist weapon.'[53]

On the other hand, the proposition appealed to those SDPers who were well placed in the labour movement. Jimmie Simpson and AFL organizer Thomas Black, both of the SDP, argued in favour of forming a labour party. The proposed labourist platform was not socialist. It included demands for free, compulsory education, the eight-hour day, abolition of the contract system on public works, equal pay for equal work, abolition of child labour, the single tax, and greater public ownership. Most of its clauses featured demands for a wider democracy through such things as abolition of the Senate and of property qualifications, proportional representation, direct legislation through the initiative and referendum, and women's suffrage. Many in the movement, Simpson and Black among them, recognized that in the context of the war these were the issues that would mobilize the working class.[54]

In January 1917 a provisional organizing committee of twenty was chosen; it was representative of all the main political currents in the city's labour movement, with the exception of a handful of more active Tories such as Joseph Gibbons of the Street Railway Employees' Union and, on the left, those socialists who had opposed the party's inception. Notably, the new party had no political program. Although one had been tentatively proposed, it was decided to have a membership drive first and then hold a convention to decide such matters. This reflected the organizers' commitment to democratic procedure, but also a dismissal of programmatic issues within their conception of democracy. Rather than defining itself in terms of differences on political questions from the old parties, the new party proposed a different political system. While it opposed the measures taken by the Liberals and the Conservatives, it primarily rejected 'partyism' itself. The organization committee set itself the task of visiting 'the various labor organizations'[55] and recruiting supporters simply with the promise of political independence, as well as a commitment to working-class interests, which it defined as 'fairness.' In Marks's words, 'The Labor Party does not propose to beat about the bush; it means to be clear cut without any deals of any sort with the old parties or understandings with professional politicians. If a man joins the Labor Party he has got to dissociate himself from the old party affiliations and play the game square.'[56] Such a catholic conception of political action was, of course, necessary to maintain a party that contained within it radically counterposed political views. It was, along with more general working-class views of democracy and the value of labour, a defining characteristic of 'labourism' in Canada.

In April, when the 'Greater Toronto Labor Party' (GTLP) finally held its founding convention, it boasted more than seven hundred members. The convention itself was more of an inauguration than an occasion for political debate. Indeed, according to the Banner, 'perfect unanimity of sentiment and harmony ... prevailed through the various debates.' The election of officers reflected the close ties between the GTLP and the TDLC. James Richards, recently president of the trades council, was chosen as the party's president. Walter Brown, the current president, became its first vice-president. The trades council's recording secretary, T.A. Stevenson, served as treasurer. Third vice-president Laura Hughes and secretary Joseph Marks were the only two officers who were not central figures in the TDLC. The GTLP was an electoral reflection of the organized labour movement in Toronto. Local business agents took it upon themselves to collect dues for the party from new members. No other reform currents from beyond the working class were represented in any substantial way within the party.[57]

Once again, the party considered the question of a political program, but the task was abandoned with little hesitation, with the comment.

> that there is no necessity for the formation of an old-time party platform because their [sic] never was any virtue in any of them.
>
>   The [program] committee believes that performance is better than promise, and rest our claim for support of organized and unorganized labour in the general declaration that we stand for the industrial freedom of those who toil and the political liberation of those who for so long have been denied justice ...

The party's goal, the democratic attainment of 'higher forms of government,' was so deeply rooted in working-class adherence to radical traditions and day-to-day struggles that the founders felt little need to articulate its content. Direct working-class representation, of its own accord, would unfetter democracy from the constraints of the profiteers and the patronage machines. Such conceptions had a loud resonance. By September, the Greater Toronto Labor Party had 2,000 members – 80 per cent trade unionists. It had been officially endorsed by the TDLC, and it regularly was voted substantial sums of money from local unions.[58]

With the Toronto party well established, Marks and his colleagues turned their attention to the creation of a provincial organization. The *Banner* echoed the sentiment of the GTLP – 'It Is More Important to Get Together than Build Platforms'[59] – while Laura Hughes toured industrial and mining centres around the province. She had already made a reputation for herself within the organized labour movement for her speech to the Trades and Labor Congress in 1916 when she had articulately and powerfully voiced the fears of many in the audience. Pointing to her own discoveries of sweating in war industries, she posed the question of what was to follow the war. The employers and the government, she suggested, 'are now developing public opinion in favor of a system of conscription for the purpose of establishing a military system in this country at the close of the war.' The solution, she told the assembled workers, was to 'fire your boss' and undertake independent political action. In December 1916 she took this message to Hamilton, Niagara Falls, Brantford, and North Bay, and through the mining communities of northern Ontario. The spring saw her tour the south-central part of the province. The *Banner*, which always featured working-class political action on the front page, followed her tour closely.[60]

A key event in the emergence of a provincial party was the convention of the Labor Educational Association of Ontario held on 24 April. A proposal to have the LEAO declare itself a labour party failed for the second year running. But on a motion put by two Hamilton labour aldermen, the 122 delegates from around the province voted unanimously to call for the formation of an Ontario labour party. Marks immediately hit the road. He explained to audiences that the new party was necessary because the Liberals and Conservatives were controlled by the railroads, because natural resources were being handed over to private interests, and because waste and graft were rampant. News of new local labour parties, often formed, as in Brantford and South Waterloo, on the initiative of trades councils, reached the *Banner* each week.[61]

At the founding convention of the Independent Labor Party of Ontario on Dominion Day 1917, fifty delegates represented sixteen branches.[62] Again, political debate was not a major feature of the meeting. Rather than a clear political statement, the new ILP's platform was eclectic, simply incorporating whatever demands were proposed by the delegates. These centred on democratic issues such as the abolition of property qualifications, direct legislation, proportional representation, abolition of the Senate, and of appeals to the Judicial Committee of the Privy Council. Education was also important, with a demand for free textbooks and free education in all institutions supported by the government. The platform called for equal pensions for all disabled soldiers, regardless of rank, and for mothers' allowances and old-age pensions. Interestingly, the convention adopted, without much debate, a demand for public ownership of all public utilities and natural sources of wealth as well as of the banking and credit systems; support for such measures by both socialists and urban progressives contributed to their general acceptability among workers. The convention made a nod in the direction of single-taxers with a demand for the 'gradual elimination of unearned increment through increased taxation.' At the end of its platform, however, the ILP appended a statement, borrowed from the GTLP, that 'performance is better than promise,' and called for support, not on the basis of its platform, but on the more general basis of direct working-class representation, which promised 'industrial freedom for those who toil.' Developing a political program had been unproblematic because of a sentiment that it was unnecessary; it was a reinvigorated democracy that would, of its own accord, herald 'the political liberation of those who for so long have been denied justice.'[63]

The crux of this new democracy was independence from the old parties; the constitution of the ILP expressly forbade entertaining any discussion of fusion or co-operation with any party 'other than a bona fide Labor Party.' Significantly, the Social Democratic Party was recognized as a labour party, allowing its members to belong to both parties and to co-operate with the ILP in electoral campaigns. However, none of the officers of the new provincial party was an SDPer. Broom maker Walter Rollo, secretary of the Hamilton TLC, was chosen president of the ILP. He had chaired an earlier attempt to form a provincial party in 1907, and in 1914 had come within thirty-nine votes of being elected in the provincial contest in West Hamilton and joining Studholme at Queen's Park. The five vice-presidents included Laura Hughes, John McAninch of the Niagara Falls party, Dr J.E. Hett, former mayor of Kitchener, Mrs William Cassidy of the Hamilton Women's ILP, and Ernest Ingles of the International Brotherhood of Electrical Workers in London. Appropriately, Marks was given the crucial post of secretary, and his *Industrial Banner* received unanimous endorsement as the official organ of the Independent Labor Party of Ontario.[64]

The new party also exhibited from the outset a 'movement culture,'[65] expressed not only in its political conceptions but also in its forms of activity. The constitution suggested that individual branches ought not to focus exclusively on elections. Their task was to 'promote social intercourse between members and their political friends by means of entertainments, educational and literary evenings, etc.'[66] The cultural tradition of debate and working-class self-education that had been expressed in various forms in the past was finding a new and congenial focus. For many workers, ILP meetings and events would come to play a central place in their social and educational lives. For the moment, however, attention was focused on the upcoming federal election.

To the Polls: 1917

THE AIMS AND OBJECTS OF THE ILP
HOW TO FORM A LOCAL BRANCH AND GET READY FOR THE
FEDERAL ELECTIONS[67]

The headlines of the *Industrial Banner* on 24 August 1917 illustrated the dilemma facing the Independent Labor Party. With the exception of Hamilton, and perhaps Toronto and Niagara Falls, local organization was still embryonic. The 1917 elections, however, held particular promise for a new party and could not be ignored. The creation of the Union government and apparent demise of the old party system held out the potential of dissolving old partisan allegiances. On the other hand, it also created an element of confusion. Angered by the 'patronage machines,' several trades councils had demanded the creation of a 'National Government,' based on non-partisanship, to lead the country through the war.[68] Prime Minister Borden and the Union government could, plausibly, hope to appeal to precisely the same sentiment as that which had, very recently, spawned the ILP.

The immediate task was organization, and prospects were bright. The membership of a new Welland branch soared to 350. Established branches shifted into high gear. The Hamilton ILP ordered several thousand membership cards and organized visits to local unions to recruit new members.[69] As local branches applied themselves to the task of nominating candidates for the federal election, however, the façade of homogeneity evident at the founding convention and in the pages of the *Banner* showed signs of wear. In most cases, particularly where there was an entrenched labourist tradition, few problems emerged. The Hamilton ILP's two candidates, accordingly, were individuals who had severed any links to the 'old, reactionary parties': Walter Rollo and local ILP leader, plumber George C. Halcrow. Fred Flatman was nominated in the suburban riding of Wentworth. In Welland, a meeting of 150 nominated town councillor James A. Hughes, a member of the bricklayers' union and past president of the local trades council. The Greater Toronto Labor Party put forward several candidates: Scottish-born member of the Amalgamated Society of Engineers James H.H. Ballantyne, bricklayers' business agent John T. Vick, electrical worker James T. Gunn, Social Democrat and plumbers' union leader John Bruce, as well as David A. Carey, whose long career in the labour movement had involved being a district master workman in the Knights of Labor and president of the Trades and Labor Congress of Canada. Only Dr Hett of Kitchener, and Brantford's M.M. MacBride came from outside the organized labour movement to run as ILP candidates. Two socialist candidates – members of the SDP faction that had opposed establishing the ILP – ran in North Waterloo (Mervyn Smith) and South Waterloo (Lorne Cunningham).[70]

Despite the party's impressive ability to organize the nominations of a strong slate of well-known working-class figures closely associated with local trades councils around the province, political problems remained. In southern Ontario, the Tories were unable to carry off the *coup* Unionist cabinet minister Gideon Robertson had helped to engineer in North Bay with the nomination of a Unionist-labour 'win-the-war candidate.' However, Toronto ILP candidate David Carey was considered 'practically a Unionist supporter.' In fact, his nomination created something of a stir in the Toronto party, as John Buckley protested his candidacy, claiming that Carey was in line for a high-ranking patronage appointment in the federal labour department. The *Banner* avoided mentioning such controversies, but the Hamilton *Labor News*, in listing the labour candidates, admitted that it was unsure of which party or parties Carey was representing.[71]

Events in Brantford were more troubling, and there was opposition to the nomination of MacBride, a man with few labour credentials. George Keen, the secretary of both the Co-operative Union of Canada and the Brantford TLC, considered MacBride to be a 'Tory politician,' 'in' but not 'of' the ILP. There was much to this accusation. On 7 November, all three Brantford parties, the Liberals, the Conservatives, and the ILP, met to choose a Unionist candidate for the election. They were unanimous in their support of the Union government and platform, but failed to agree on a candidate, the Conservatives supporting sitting member W.F. Cockshutt, the Liberals supporting the IMB representative in the United States, Lloyd Harris, and the ILP supporting MacBride. In an interesting turn of events, the meeting passed a resolution prohibiting the nomination of a 'war profiteer' and proceeded to argue that this disqualified the Liberal nominee. Notably, Cockshutt was spared such criticism. In the vote that followed, Cockshutt and MacBride were tied with eleven votes each and eight delegates abstained. Both the Liberal *Brantford Expositor* and local farmers' leader W.C. Good thought the whole event was set up by the Conservatives with the intention of 'getting' Harris. In the end, MacBride ran under the ILP banner. But the provincial executive was forced – and not for the last time – to deal with a flagrant violation of the ILP constitution by MacBride.[72]

If a Conservative wing of the ILP was drawn towards the Unionist party, the Liberals presented no less of a challenge. As we have seen, for organized labour the 1917 election revolved around the issues of 'compulsion' and, in particular, conscription. In North Waterloo, faced with a close contest between a pro-conscriptionist Union candidate and an anti-conscriptionist Laurier Liberal, Hett decided to drop out of the race, allowing the Liberal, William D. Euler, to win. The political proximity to the Liberals of some ILPers is best seen in the riding of Temiskaming where the ILP nomination went to prominent Liberal Arthur W. Roebuck. Similarly, George N. Gordon declined a Liberal nomination in Peterborough to run for the ILP.[73]

London, however, created the greatest difficulties for the ILP in this regard. The London ILP, comprising only 'a few ardent spirits,' was unable to dissuade the trades council from endorsing the Laurier Liberal candidate, George S. Gibbons. In fact, the local TLC threw its entire weight behind his campaign, producing an elaborate *Workingman's Newsletter*. The content of this publication is fascinating in its close resemblance to ILP material. Never did it mention the Liberal Party. Rather, it focused its attention on profiteering, the high cost of living, and domestic threats to democracy, the key elements in the movement that elsewhere had built the ILP. The *Newsletter* attacked 'Borden, Kaiser Co. Limited' unsparingly for allowing the profiteers, particularly Flavelle, to grow rich from the war, for not paying equal pensions to disabled officers and enlisted men, and for the disenfranchisement of Canadian citizens of German and Austrian birth. It reflected a class-conscious outrage at 'the so-called leading ladies' of the city who were inviting the newly enfranchised working-class women of the city to 'socials and entertainments,' whereas they had always disdained their company in the past. Like the ILP around the province, the London TLC, in its support of the Liberals, asked rhetorically whether it was not a 'funny kind of logic ... that asks you to fight against Prussianism in Germany and vote for it in Canada.'[74] While only the London TLC rallied to the Liberal Party in this manner, these were attractive political positions to many workers. And it spoke to the Radical and Gladstonian tradition from which the movement's concepts of democracy had emerged. Mackenzie King expressed some hope that labour would support him and the Liberal campaign when he appealed, unsuccessfully, to TLCC officers J.C. Watters and Paddy Draper, as well as James Simpson, to speak on his election platform. The Liberal Party produced a 248-page book entitled *Who Shall Rule? The People or the Big Interests*, which detailed the Borden government's record of scandals and profiteering.[75] The content of this Liberal critique of corruption differed little from that of the labourists, although the ILP answered the question of 'Who Shall Rule?' differently, by rejecting 'partyism' and running independently. Obviously, though, political lines were blurred.

Historians have not been particularly kind to the ILP's first electoral foray. Martin Robin points to the 'manifest failure of labour's entry into independent politics'[76] in this campaign. But, considering the difficulty in establishing a clear political terrain of its own and the fact that the Liberal and Unionist parties presented relatively clear alternatives on the pressing issues of the day, the outcome gave substantial cause for hope, particularly since the Independent Labor Party was barely six months old on election day. Although only Walter Rollo of the 'straight' labourist candidates managed to retain his election deposit, ILP votes generally numbered in the thousands. Altogether, 36,359 voters can be considered to have voted for the Independent Labor Party of Ontario, or for clear labour candidates. This was a substantial sum for an initial attempt, given the Unionists' appeal to non-partisanship and the Liberal attack on privilege and 'kaiserism.' A new electoral space had opened up for the ILP, and traditional Liberalism and Conservatism had made a priority of expanding to occupy it.

To what can we attribute the ILP's real, if limited, success? Given its programmatic similarities to the other parties, the ILP's only unique contribution to the political landscape was its emphasis on working-class independence. Although individuals from beyond the organized labour movement participated in the party, it was primarily an outgrowth of local trades councils and the LEAO. A substantial minority of workers had concluded that both the old parties represented class interests in opposition to their own. Although the ILP spoke in familiar political terms, it would be unfair to suggest that it was not offering something unique. The very nature of its organization expressed a commitment to a concept of democracy unlike that of the 'old, reactionary parties.' Although the ILP reached into the arsenal of a radical past to define democracy in a rather narrow and formal manner – in terms of electoral procedures – its emergence represented something much broader. Its democracy required the regular and direct participation of the mass of working people. While the federal election was in many ways a frustrating affair, as many factors blunted the ILP's message, there were positive signs. The conditions that had given rise to the new party showed no signs of abating, and the ILP had successfully posed itself as an alternative to the old political order.

4   The Battle for Democracy[1]

The 1917 federal election was the new Independent Labor Party's most difficult wartime test. Inexperienced and generally unprepared branches relied on untested speakers and organizers to mount a campaign that, if it fell short of the hopes of some, established the party on the electoral map.[2] Given the confused political landscape and the tendency for former political alliances to manifest themselves, the ILP had done well to avoid a major crisis. Disruption caused by political differences, including M.M. MacBride's disregard for the ILP's prohibition on dealing with other political parties, was successfully evaded. The provincial executive quietly investigated and exonerated the Brantford mayor of charges of violating the party constitution. George Keen suggested that the 'elastic construction' placed on the constitution would be 'a source of great embarrassment' to the party in the future, but for the moment the issue was settled. Fortunately, few other localities offered such difficulties for the provincial party. In North Bay, the Unionist-labour candidate and Liberal Arthur Roebuck both pledged their loyalty to the ILP, while everywhere in the south ILP candidates ran 'straight' labour campaigns.[3]

The election established the party's credibility. Its failure to elect members to Parliament was easily dismissed as the product of inexperience, weak organization, and the Borden government's manipulation of the election. The Wartime Elections Act disenfranchised many foreign-born workers and gave the vote to female relatives of members of the armed forces, while the Military Voters Act allowed for soldiers' votes to be distributed to ridings across the country. Such overt gerrymandering followed by the 1918 Orders in Council made increasingly credible the ILP's central message that democracy would be in great peril if political power were left in the hands of profiteers and their parliamentary protectors. As well, growing workplace combativeness in the face of inflation and labour shortages made the ILP increasingly seem the natural voice of workers at election time.

The strength of the party's allegiance to the principle of independent political action was tested when Samuel Gompers voiced his opposition to the movement during a trip to Ottawa in the spring of 1918. Hamilton labourists, who had never wavered in their loyalty to the American Federation of Labor and its president, fumed. The *Labor News* printed the response of Harry Halford who declared that 'if I had been present I would have told him where to get off at and mind his own business.' In the Toronto District Labor Council, 'delegate after delegate' denounced the AFL president for his remarks, although only one dismissed his contribution to the trade union movement. Even such Gompers loyalists as John Flett and future TLCC president Tom Moore voiced their support for the ILP.[4] While the latter declarations may have been motivated by opportunism, the anger expressed by Hamilton unionists suggested that no contradiction existed in their minds between craft unionism and independent political action. This chapter examines the course of the ILP's growing support leading to its greatest victory, the provincial election of 1919. A year after the armistice, ILPers had few doubts: a 'new democracy' was within labour's grasp.

A Strain of Nativism

If an identifiable obstacle to working-class unity lay ahead it was a growing nativism directed primarily at 'enemy aliens' from central Europe.[5] In fact, the disenfranchising of such foreign-born workers made little difference to the ILP's electoral fortunes. These immigrants were not a part of the ILP's constituency, and no effort had been made to address them in their own languages. The general lack of interest in such workers displayed by ILP leaders (and their failure to fathom the transformation of the region's unions) can be seen in party president Walter Rollo's declaration that 'there was absolutely no danger of foreigners swamping' the union movement as they were, for the most part, 'insufficiently skilled mechanically.'[6] The ILP, like the union movement that engendered it, was defined by access to skill. Its leadership was composed of veterans of the craft-union movement rather than the new industrial unionists. Nevertheless, not all shared Rollo's views. Socialists who rejected craft unionism in favour of industrial forms accepted the corollary: a political working-class movement had little room in it for divisions along ethnic or national lines. Social Democratic events such as May Day were internationalist festivals with speeches and songs in a multitude of languages. If nativism was to be challenged in the wider movement for political action, socialists had a major role to play.

Although the growth of industrial unionism eroded the basis for exclusion, a powerful injection of nativism came from outside the labour movement. The press, politicians, and businessmen vilified 'the Hun' during the war and, as we shall see, scapegoated immigrants in a post-war 'red scare.' An official nativist campaign could only reinforce trade unionists' fears of immigrant competition. The *Industrial Banner*, for the most part, opposed such sentiments. Marks urged that immigrants be covered under Workmen's Compensation legislation, deplored press attacks on Germans in Canada, and publicized the cases of individual immigrants who had been victimized by employers and the state. Yet even the *Banner* was ambiguous. 'Unrestricted' immigration was denounced as 'The Real Menace,' and groups of foreign-born workers were attacked for entering sectors of the labour market claimed by craft unions.[7]

Nativism was not solely responsible for the ILP's lack of interest in immigrant workers. The ILP did not address its message to immigrant workers from eastern and southern Europe – very often sojourners planning to return to their homelands – for the simple reason that, unless naturalized, they could not vote. If political activity was limited to casting ballots for labour candidates, there was little reason to include them in the movement. Socialists, who perceived mass industrial activity as integral to political change, were far more likely to attempt to draw such workers into their parties. The ILP had little to say to workers outside the electoral system, and unions that included large numbers of immigrants, as in the garment industry, were relatively inactive in the ILP. The ILP's electoral focus reinforced its identification with British- and Canadian-born workers. Paradoxically, then, democratic and nativist sentiments prospered together in the final year of the war. Anti-alien rallies, such as the gathering of 10,000 in Hamilton in February 1919, were an ugly feature of the period.[8] The mobilization of immigrant workers in post-war strikes and industrial union organizing would challenge this exclusivist view of democracy, but nativism did find an echo within the movement for a working-class based democracy in the last year of the war.

A provincial by-election in Toronto in August 1918 gave the ILP an opportunity to demonstrate its growing support and reflected the character of labour's political development. Very noticeable was the voice of nativism that had entered into ILP propaganda. Locally, the backdrop to the election was set by the destruction, by a crowd of hundreds of returned soldiers, of a dozen immigrant-owned restaurants. When the Toronto *Telegram* attempted to turn such sentiment against the Greater Toronto Labor Party (GTLP), the defensive response testified to nativist sentiment. Claiming to be the 'most British Canadian political organization in the province,' it declared that 98 per cent of its members were Canadian- or British-born and none were unnaturalized immigrants from enemy countries.[9] The GTLP's election program reflected such views. It called on enemy aliens to pay sharply progressive income taxes and demanded that Canada's doors be closed to new immigrants 'until all the soldiers have returned, and all further immigration to be of friendly aliens first.'

The character of this campaign, including its nativism, was largely the product of the ILP's attempt to catch the attention of veterans returning from the battlefields of Europe. Relations with veterans were difficult, as when returned soldiers invaded the London Trades and Labor Council meeting demanding that they reverse their opposition to conscription. But, as labour repeatedly noted, most soldiers were workers, and veterans' organizations were offered seats on the London TLC while the TDLC proposed joint actions with the returned men.[10] The *Banner*'s charge that the treatment of returned soldiers was reminiscent of 'Prussian Junkerism' appealed to the veterans' frustrations with the difficulties of demobilization and the official disregard for their economic and personal travails as well as to a shared fear that democracy at home was threatened.

What had prompted the *Banner*'s polemic was the case of William Varley. A union official in the building trades before the war, the Lancashire-born Varley had joined the Canadian Expeditionary Force in the summer of 1915. After being wounded, he returned to Canada in time to speak on ILP platforms in the federal election campaign. His charges about poor treatment of returned soldiers sparked demands for an investigation from the *Globe*. Shortly afterwards, Varley was confined to the military hospital at Whitby, the consequence, it was charged, of his political activity. He was later informed that, in spite of an injury, he would not be placed on the pension list. The TDLC and the Great War Veterans' Association (GWVA) joined forces in his defence, and the GTLP ran Varley as a 'soldier-labour' candidate in the provincial election with the active support of the local GWVA in spite of the association's prohibition on political endorsements. Military imagery dominated the campaign: 'The Big Offensive Is On. Will You

Do Your Bit?' asked the *Banner* in drumming up support for the candidate.[11]

Following Varley's immigration to Canada in 1904, he had been active in the Socialist Labor Party, the dominant socialist organization of the time. His trajectory, however, had been steadily away from socialism.[12] His campaign was characterized by the articulation of the nativist fears often expressed by his veteran supporters and by a straightforward labourism. That Varley's opponent was the newly appointed Conservative minister of education and rector of Toronto's wealthy St Paul's Anglican Church, Canon J.H. Cody, allowed the labourists to expand on their ideas about education and religious hypocrisy. The bitterness of the campaign was intensified by the *Telegram*'s attack, which it later withdrew, upon Varley's war record.

Faced with Tory attacks on his education and social status, Varley responded with an appeal to the fellowship of the trenches, where one 'did not ask what your calling in life was or what church you belong to,' and a ringing call for a broad and cultured education for working-class youth. At its roots, Varley's campaign was an expression of the self-respect of his working-class constituency and a voice against the aristocratic pretensions of Cody and his Tory supporters, who belittled workers' contributions on the battlefields and in the factories.[13] ILP campaigners were satisfied with the outcome. Although Cody won handily, Varley had received 4,297 votes in an election held to acclaim the new education minister. Furthermore, with the armistice and the advent of 'reconstruction,' divisions within the working class – on the electoral front, at any rate – appeared to dissolve. During 1919, nativism ceased to be a dominant feature of labourist campaigns, particularly as ILP confidence and sentiment in favour of industrial unionism grew in tandem.

The Ontario Section of the Canadian Labor Party

Following the 1917 federal campaign the ILP was strongly placed to cultivate its base of support. Municipal elections, which followed within weeks, brought promising results. Trades councils showed increasing willingness to refer issues of political action to local ILP branches, which now numbered thirty-three around the province. Sales of the *Banner* also benefited from the party's heightened status.[14] The ILP provincial executive recognized the opportunity before the party and hoped to capitalize upon it with a membership campaign for 10,000 new members announced in March 1918. Such plans proved premature, particularly considering the demands upon the leadership of the provincial party, which was still without any paid officials, and the campaign was relaunched in August, with the goal doubled to 20,000 new members.[15]

At the same time, the provincial leadership undertook another project with the hope of broadening the basis of the political movement: the development of a formal alliance with trade-union and socialist forces. Under pressure from advocates of independent political action, the 1917 convention of the Trades and Labor Congress had passed a resolution calling for the formation of a Labour Party based on the 'British precedent' uniting 'trade unionists, socialists, fabiens [sic], co-operators and farmers.' This model was attractive not only because of the electoral success of the British Labour Party, but because the federated structure of the party permitted some direct control to trade-union leaders who did not wish to turn the movement over to 'labour politicians.' It also appealed to socialists who feared that their voice would otherwise be lost in the vagueness of labourist politics. Lacking the organization (and the will) to initiate such a party, the TLCC executive recommended the 'dominating working class political organization in each province call a conference.' Action on the resolution, of course, depended on the volition of provincial TLCC executives and labour parties across the country, and organization proceeded unevenly. In Ontario, the ILP was eager to broaden the base for independent political action, and the TLCC Ontario executive, chaired by former Hamilton alderman and local ILP treasurer, H.J. (Harry) Halford, was in full accord. The latter body issued a call for a convention in Toronto on 29 March 1918, to form a new 'Labor Party in the broadest meaning of the term.'[16]

The convention reflected the broad appeal of independent working-class political action. Almost four hundred delegates from forty-four cities, towns, and districts attended. Representation was as follows:

Trade unions	200
Independent Labor Party	100
Social Democratic Party (SDP)	56
United Farmers of Ontario (UFO)	6
Socialist Labor Party (SLP)	5
Socialist Party of North America (SPNA)	3
Co-operative societies	3
Russian Socialist Revolutionary Group	3

Jewish Socialist Labor Organization	2
Fabians	2
Re-construction Group of the Theosophical Society	1

The importance of local trades councils in the provincial labour movement was evidenced in the thirty-four delegates from fifteen such bodies (including the Toronto National Council, composed of unions that were not affiliated to the American Federation of Labor) who attended the convention. Representation at the convention demonstrates the appeal of working-class unity and the recognition of the legitimacy of socialism within the labour movement. Not only were all the significant socialist organizations directly represented, many of the trade-union delegates were also active socialists. Although the convention was initiated by the TLCC, the attendance suggests a convergence, strategically if not politically, between the ILP and the Social Democratic Party. The ILP's success in placing working-class political representation before a wide audience had posed to socialists the need to participate in the new electoral movement.

The Social Democratic Party was by far the largest socialist organization in Ontario. Formed as a result of a schism in the Socialist Party of Canada (now centred in the West), the SDP concentrated, as did its parent body, on socialist propaganda. Its paper, *Cotton's Weekly* (later *Canadian Forward*), had a circulation of about 30,000 in Canada.[17] On the eve of the war, the party had 1000 members in Toronto and a array of youth, cultural, and ethnic structures, including a Young People's Socialist League and Polish, Ukrainian, Bulgarian, and Italian locals. In its successful 1914 campaign to elect Jimmie Simpson to the city's board of control, it appealed to 'Jew and Gentile, British and Foreign Born, organized and unorganized' to support the SDP's fight for reforms and its 'ultimate aim' of 'social ownership and democratic control.'[18] Its good showing reinforced its alliance with TDLC delegates who supported independent political action. The SDP's ambivalence about electoral alliances with non-socialist workers occasionally proved disruptive, but there was a working basis of unity. Despite its anti-capitalist message, the SDP's list of immediate demands was indistinguishable from that of the future ILP. The democratization of the electoral system through widening the franchise to women and the propertyless, as well as direct legislation, was prominently featured. The SDP played a crucial role in independent electoral activity in Toronto, and the TDLC came to terms with the fact that political action required co-operation with the Social Democrats.[19]

Outside Toronto, the SDP was making significant gains in 1914. New branches were established in London, St Thomas, Ingersoll, Chatham, Windsor, and Brantford, augmenting existing locals in Hamilton, Niagara Falls, and Guelph, as well as three branches in South Waterloo. While many of the branches were small, speakers from Toronto and elsewhere addressed enthusiastic audiences at meetings and annual picnics. The Guelph SDP was able to report that 'war psychology' had not interfered with their meetings in 1916. In Toronto, three to seven hundred attended the Earlscourt SDP open-air meetings that summer. In short, the SDP was a significant force through much of the region and, as indicated by the title of Simpson's speech before the Niagara Falls branch, like everyone else pondered the crucial question: 'After the War, What?'[20]

The emergence of a provincial ILP threw the SDP into confusion. As we have seen in chapter three, the formation of a Greater Toronto Labour Party sparked a debate among socialists, including the SDP, as to whether they ought to participate in the new party. A few who were fundamentally opposed to such a strategy, notably Mervyn Smith of Kitchener, quit the SDP to join the small and isolated Socialist Labor Party. On the other hand, the rising star of labourism suggested to most SDPers that even if life as socialists might be awkward inside the ILP, beyond it lay political wilderness. As Simpson argued in the pages of *Canadian Forward*, SDP affiliation to the Labor Party 'on the same lines as' the affiliation of the socialist Independent Labour Party in Britain to the British Labour Party would allow SDPers to 'run as Labor candidates [as well as] carry on its educational work as locals of the SDP.' The TLCC proposal to establish a labour party on 'British principles' fortuitously coincided with the desire of many SDPers for an electoral united front permitting the SDP to continue to present socialist ideas. Hamilton SDP secretary W.S. Bruton articulated his support for participating in such a party in just such terms. As no socialist could give total allegiance to a non-socialist party, dissolving into the ILP was out of the question. Bruton argued, however, against 'hard and fast rules.' 'As a matter of curiosity,' he wrote,

a few months ago I linked myself up with the ILP in this city, and have attended the business meetings regularly since. I must say that I am far from favorably impressed with the calibre of the great and leading lights of that movement, and it was not long before I discovered the attitude of these great ones toward Socialism was that of more or less ignorance and decided antagonism. Nevertheless there is room for hope, and signs of intelligence to be found among the lesser lights and younger blood.[21]

By their actions, the SDP delegates who attended the convention agreed; few wished to be excluded from so promising a movement.

The breadth of the movement for political action was apparent at this convention. Unions responded enthusiastically; 'not a single industry or calling' according to the *Banner*, 'being unrepresented.' A number of centres as yet without ILP branches sent delegates. As an affirmation of its broad character, the convention unanimously elected prominent ILPer H.J. Halford chairman and SDPer Jimmie Simpson secretary. While socialists had participated in the formation of the Greater Toronto Labour Party as individuals, they were now present as direct representatives of their own parties. With the existence of a labour party, (indeed two labour parties) an accomplished fact, the task became to inject class consciousness into the movement. The ensuing debate struck at the essence of the question – were they forming an openly socialist labour party? What was most notable, and a testament to the desire not to threaten the remarkable unity that had been achieved, was the frank and open debate that took place, along with the willingness to accept wide differences of opinion. Working-class political action, socialist or not, had gained a secure foothold in Ontario's labour movement and no faction was willing to accept the political liability of threatening the unity upon which that foothold was constructed.

In keeping with the labourist sentiments about egalitarianism and the value of productive toil, the resolutions committee proposed that the party's objectives be 'To secure for the producers by hand or by brain the full fruits of their industry, and the most equitable distribution thereof.' John MacDonald noted that this was a truncated version of the platform of the British Labour Party, omitting the phrase '... upon the basis of the common ownership of the means of production and the best obtainable system of popular administration and control of each industry and service.' The Socialist Party of North America disagreed with both the resolutions committee's proposal and MacDonald, and argued for a more overt 'recognition of the class struggle with its immediate aim the abolition of the capitalist system.'

Not everyone associated independent working-class political action with socialism. Responding to MacDonald's proposal to adopt the British Labour Party's objective, Arthur Roebuck suggested that they should have as 'wide' a party as possible since their real objective was, after all, 'voting power.' Fred Flatman, obliquely referring to Roebuck's Liberal connections, suggested that the party 'erect the greatest barricade against the entrance of old line politicians' and scathingly denounced the tactics of the win-the-war crowd in the recent Dominion election. When Toronto machinist Herbert Lewis suggested that individuals who did not recognize 'class distinctions' ought to be excluded from the party, the debate reverted to the issue of the class character of Canadian society and the class basis of the labour party. London's Harry Ashplant, known for his esoteric lectures on the monetary system, attempted to draw a distinction based on the sources of income of lawyers, doctors, and ministers. James T. Gunn, who had contested York South for the ILP, 'did not want state regulation in place of capitalist regulation.' A member of the Single Tax Association articulated a non-socialist variant of the sentiment that lay behind the movement for political action.[22] '[I]t should be easy,' he argued, 'for every honest man or woman who stood for democratic ideals to enter the party.'

Joseph Marks, a champion of ILP-SDP co-operation, claimed 'he could accept every plank of the British labor party programme' but asked whether Ontario workers felt similarly. Only the adoption of the committee's report, he felt, 'would unite the entire movement in the province.' He pointed out that the differences that existed were the 'reason that the different sections such as the Socialists and the ILP were allowed to maintain their separate organizations and carry on their own especial propaganda.' The SPNA motion received only 35 votes, and a motion to adopt in full the British Labour Party's clause was defeated 129 to 69. Remarkably, although the 'entire discussion was exceedingly lively, many delegates essaying to occupy the floor at the same time ... it was entirely devoid of personalities or recriminations.' Evidence of such a spirit was reflected in the almost unanimous adoption of the final program. The new party, officially named the 'Ontario Section of the Canadian Labour Party' (Ontario CLP) in expectation of similar developments across the country, was a united electoral front in which affiliated organizations would be permitted to maintain their autonomy.[23]

The Ontario CLP quickly established a lecture bureau that reflected both the breadth of the Ontario CLP and the wide varieties of concerns of working-class audiences interested both in entertainment and self-improvement. Flora MacDonald Denison and Harriet Prenter, both active feminists, volunteered to speak on 'War and Women,' the 'History of Women's Suffrage,' and 'The Woman of Tomorrow.' Arthur

Roebuck, a supporter of a single tax, addressed 'The Land Problem,' while London socialist John F. Thomson informed listeners of the advances of the Labour parties in Britain and Australia and the Bolsheviks in Russia. James Simpson was prepared to address a long list of topics of obvious interest to working-class audiences, including the 'Evolution from Craft to Industrial Unionism,' the 'Coming of Social Democracy,' and 'Political Power and How to Use It.' Next to the pressing issue of how labour could muster its political power, the most popular topic was 'democracy.' Such a theme could encompass religious interests, such as Denison's 'The Democracy of Walt Whitman,' or Roebuck's 'The Democracy of Moses,' or, more directly, the challenge immediately confronting workers in the post-war world, as with Fred Flatman's 'Labor's Place in a World Democracy.' The range of speakers reflected the diversity of the political labour movement, including conservatives such as Joseph Gibbons, socialists Isaac Bainbridge and John MacDonald, and even Lorne Cunningham who opposed socialist co-operation with labourists. The Ontario CLP lecture bureau reflected both the diverse interests of the major figures in the province's labour movement and the pressures towards unity in the struggle for electoral success and a democratic order that included Ontario's workers.[24]

Despite such initiatives, and the spirit evident at the founding convention, the new party failed to take root. A year after the founding of the Ontario CLP, only a small proportion of eligible organizations had affiliated. MacBride had argued against ILP affiliation, in fact, on the basis that the CLP had no real existence. In part, the paucity of affiliates was due to the lack of an effective provincial secretary following Simpson's departure for a temperance lecture tour of New Zealand. Attempts to induce the farmers' movement to join forces were futile.[25] The Ontario CLP's major obstacle, however, was the ILP's success. Outside Toronto socialism was a weak force, the pressures towards labourist-socialist unity were far from strong, and the need for another labour party was simply not clear. The ILP was, for the moment, the party of Ontario's organized labour movement. The Ontario CLP would, however, have its day as the weaknesses of the ILP threatened to derail political action.

The ILP and Reconstruction

Advocates of political action recognized that the fate of their movement would be decided in the months following the armistice. Peace, everyone seemed to agree, would bring 'reconstruction.' The social order, distorted and perhaps destroyed by the war, would be rebuilt according to the will of Canadians. For organizations such as the Canadian Manufacturers' Association, reconstruction meant a rapid response to new international market relations; domestically, it meant a return to the *status quo*, aided, perhaps, by government regulation of the market. The CMA's selection of Senator Frederic Nicholls as organizer of its 'Reconstruction Committee' signalled its intentions to the country.[26] Wary of post-war demands, politicians and business were studiously vague in their promises to workers. As a Kitchener union shoemaker told the Royal Commission on Industrial Relations in 1919, workers were dissatisfied because 'they were under the impression that something was promised them but they did not know what.'[27]

Marks and the *Industrial Banner* were persistent in urging electoral action throughout the war and also regularly spoke of the post-war test of strength between the established interests and an emergent working-class movement. Given the numerical weight of the increasingly active 'democratic classes,' labourism assumed that their power could only be denied by curtailing democracy. The task, argued Marks, was straightforward: to ensure that the voice of the electorate emerged as supreme after the war. As Fred Flatman's *Labor News* noted at the war's end: 'You and us have made the world safe for democracy. Who then has a greater right than WE, meaning you and us, to interpret this meaning to the world.'[28] The consequence of labour's political activity would be not merely working-class representation, but a social revolution. The 'interests' would no longer rule.

Evolving attitudes towards the state had made political action even more imperative. As the federal state became increasingly interventionist during the war, its potential for furthering working-class interests became apparent. While trades councils had long espoused 'public ownership,' particularly of street railways and other 'natural monopolies,' wartime inflation prompted the labour movement to demand federal food and fuel controllers to manage supplies and set prices of necessary commodities. The Labor Educational Association articulated this sentiment at its 1917 convention, demanding the nationalization of war industries, banks, cold-storage warehouses, and the Canadian Pacific Railway.[29] The 'high cost of living' was cited as the reason for this agitation.

By the end of the war, labour's view of reconstruction implied a rapid expansion of state ownership, although much of that support was predicated on specifically war-related protests against profiteers' manipulation of supplies of commodities to drive up prices. From one perspective, such demands were not particularly radical, as the example of the Ontario Hydro-Electric Commission, a creation of the Conservative Whitney government, demonstrated. Yet, in the context of a reconstruction that would see a reinvigorated democracy, nationalization took on a potentially new meaning. The *Banner* proclaimed that the 'great war is shattering the sacred rights of property' (although examples were limited to the income tax and the nationalization of the railways).[30]

Nevertheless, in true labourist fashion, demands for expanded democracy and public ownership took the form of widespread sentiment rather than carefully formulated policies. Labourism did not dwell on the possibility that nationalized enterprises could still elude popular or working-class control. The Hamilton ILP, in particular, acted as an uncritical publicist for the Hydro Commission and the plans of its domineering chairman, Adam Beck, to build 'radial' electric railways. Such a view of nationalization seemed endemic to the period. Hard thinking about the nature of the state and about workers' place in the new order was rare. Given all the talk of reconstruction that had taken place, Flatman still had reason to comment that '[e]ven our Organized Labor movement has not yet attempted to formulate any policy concerning after the war problems.'[31]

This did not mean that workers' hopes lacked substance. The sense that the war was ushering in a 'broader spirit' was rooted in real wartime experiences of co-operation and organization. When Toronto Employers' Association secretary James G. Merrick suggested that wages must decline if Canada were to prosper by winning world markets, he received a lecture from the *Banner* that echoed the spirit that was to prompt the general strike movement and the growth of the ILP. 'Surely the people who talk in such a strain as this must fail to perceive that the earth moves and old things have passed away, and we stand on the threshold of a new world and at the opening up of the greatest era with which history has ever had to deal.'[32] The labourist 'new world,' it is apparent, was as much a quasi-millenarian vision as a clearly sketched strategy of social reform. A vigorous democracy and war-induced selflessness were its essential elements; together they reinforced the ILP's programmatic vagueness. Peace (and for growing numbers of workers, the ILP) made it all possible. Reconstruction had come to signal a reinvigorated and widened democracy, as well as the attainment of at least some of labour's long-standing demands.

For growing numbers of workers, the hopes and responsibility for reconstruction rested squarely upon the Independent Labor Party of

Ontario. On the eve of the armistice, the *Banner* reminded its readers that 'the only possible way' to ensure that workers' interests were safeguarded during reconstruction was 'to take the necessary steps to elect its direct representatives to the federal parliament and the provincial legislature.'[33] The Hamilton Central branch of the ILP inaugurated a campaign for a thousand new members in a month, while the few centres so far untouched by the surge of labourism, such as Windsor, finally organized ILP branches.[34] Nevertheless, the announcement of a February 1919 provincial by-election in St Catharines prompted the provincial party, again, to put a membership drive on hold and focus its resources on a single campaign.

St Catharines, a long-time Conservative stronghold, had been represented by the same Tory member for thirty years and retained by a 1,500-vote majority in 1914. Despite the nomination by the local trades council of a candidate in that election (with the tacit support of the Liberals), no independent labour candidate ran in St Catharines in the 1917 federal election and a branch of the ILP was not formed until December 1918. While the city appeared to hold little immediate promise for the ILP, the wisdom of the decision to run was soon apparent.[35]

St Catharines ILPers chose as the candidate their secretary, W.E. Longden, an unemployed machinist and returned soldier. His candidacy attracted widespread support. The *Toronto Daily Star* noted the unusual 'fuss' that was being made over the by-election, and the *Banner* proudly claimed that the campaign was not the 'joke' old party politicians had predicted. Longden faithfully presented the predominant labourist themes as they had emerged at the end of the war, concentrating on direct legislation and the nationalization of the banks. The widely noted participation of women in the campaign also reflected one of the features of post-war labourism.[36] A comment by the *Star*, however, caught the essence of the movement for electoral action: 'As in similar cases elsewhere it isn't the particular planks in the Labor platform, either good or bad, that create the issues, but something much more intangible, a feeling justified or unjustified that power hitherto has been exercised by a comparatively few men to their own advantage, and that the common people have been making a mistake not only in the class of representatives they have been sending, but in bowing the knee to inflexible idols of partisan party politics.'[37] Few commentators were more astute in their observations on the movement for labour representation, now firmly on track. Indeed, the *Banner* captured the essence of Longden's popularity by noting that neither of the old parties had a 'reconstruction policy worthy of the name.'

While the Liberals did not field a candidate, the tenor of the campaign revealed that Longden had broken with local political traditions and was not appealing to Lib-Lab sentiment. Rather, the Liberals were abiding by an agreement made by provincial party leaders not to contest by-elections during the war and demobilization.[38]

The ILP demonstrated during the campaign that it had created an effective provincial organization. Joseph Marks and Montreal-based Rose Henderson each spent more than a week in the city, and labour notables such as Tom Moore, M.M. MacBride, and Harry Halford all spoke on the ILP platform. The sole significant renegade was former painters' union business agent William Stockdale, who stumped for the Tories. For this, Stockdale was denounced around the province; even the conservative Tom Moore claimed to be 'disgusted.' Although James Watt told the TDLC that Stockdale was only doing openly what others did secretly, it is indicative of the general sentiment of the labour movement that opposition to the ILP, to the extent that it existed, was forced underground.[39] On election day Longden lost only narrowly to Conservative F.R. Parnell; the Tory majority was reduced to 174. The ILP had come close to taking St Catharines by storm. How would it fare in cities where it had an established presence?

In the wake of this by-election, ILP fortunes sky-rocketed. When the provincial party met in convention two months later, it was reported that twenty new branches had been chartered in the intervening time and fourteen more were in the process of formation. The convention witnessed the enthusiastic and open debate that had been seen at the founding of the Ontario CLP over the socialist call for the 'common ownership of industry.' Hamilton conservative ILP leader Henry George Fester stood firm: 'If you adopt that, you might just as well go over to the Social Democratic party.' Situating his objections within the mainstream of labourism, he added that 'Public ownership of public utilities is all right, but collectivism in general – no.' Harry Ashplant offered a compromise that was readily accepted by the meeting. 'Common ownership' was changed to the vaguer, but quintessentially labourist, 'democratic ownership.' Socialists considered this positively, recognizing the limits of their influence and ability to add their own content to such a formulation. Satisfied, Flatman commented that 'a rose by any other name would smell as sweet.' Another delegate responded: 'Yes, but it doesn't prick as hard.'[40] Such a ready compromise reflected both a desire for unity and an impatience with theoretical issues among ILPers.

When debate turned to the more immediate question of the tariff, though, positions threatened to harden. Yet the discussion continued to reflect an essential solidarity despite differences among delegates. The issue was forced by a protectionist government in Ottawa and the emergence of a free-trade farmers' political movement. The battle lines were drawn, as Fester pointed out, and it would be difficult to ignore what promised to be 'the chief fighting ground in the next [federal] contest.' The issue was more important than many delegates were willing to admit. As the *Star* commented, although speaker after speaker dismissed the tariff as a peripheral issue, 'it consumed much more time than any other topic.' However, even the combative MacBride attempted to calm the waters by denouncing 'the two old parties,' which 'played football' with the tariff, and workers had little interest in taking sides.[41] Finally, it was decided to hold a referendum and allow members to decide among protectionism, free trade, or neutrality. Direct democracy appeared to have won out. The ability to skirt such a potentially dangerous issue was due not only to the skill of the party leadership, but also to the nature of labourism and its views on reconstruction. As the *Banner* explained, a wider vision held the delegates together. 'It was plainly apparent that there was no division in regard to the great aim of the Labor party to primarily secure direct representation in the municipal councils, the local Legislature and the Federal Parliament, that it made very little difference to the workers whether they lived under a policy of protection or free trade. In both cases the producers were the prey of an exploiting class, and the rate of wages was the least possible minimum upon which they could possibly subsist.' Resolutions against the Orders in Council (which remained in effect despite the armistice) and in favour of the release of political prisoners and the withdrawal of troops from Russia, as well as demands for the nationalization of cold-storage and resource industries, dominated the balance of the convention. The party voted to affiliate to the Ontario Section of the Canadian Labor Party over the objection of MacBride. The re-election of the entire executive in a keen contest at the close of the convention reflected a passionate interest in the fate of the party along with a general approval of its trajectory.[42]

More significant for the direction of the ILP than the decisions taken at the convention was the 're-organization' of the *Industrial Banner*. In March 1919, the directors of the *Banner* named Jimmie Simpson associate editor along with Joe Marks. The prominent Social Democrat resigned from the staff of the *Toronto Daily Star* to dedicate himself to the new post. It was soon apparent, as Marks would later charge, that Simpson had engineered a *coup*, and the paper's editorial policy turned decisively to the left. Articles soon reflected more confidence in the face of red-baiting, greater sympathy towards the Bolshevik experiment in Soviet Russia, and a new willingness to criticize the leadership of the international unions in Canada.[43] The latter development reflected events within the industrial movement where industrial unionism, or at least the amalgamation movement, were gaining widespread support. But the new editorial policy of the *Industrial Banner* was significant for the ILP as well. As the major provincial voice of independent working-class political action, it could often set the tone for labourist politics. The defensiveness with which labour responded to nativism and red-baiting in the earlier by-elections tended to give way to a more self-confident articulation of the new democracy that an electoral break-through, as well as craft union amalgamation, promised.

Counter-revolution Checked

The delegates to the conventions of the Ontario CLP in 1918 and the ILP in 1919 no doubt felt that they were riding a historical juggernaut. Within the organized labour movement, overt opposition to inde-pendent political action appeared to have collapsed. Those few indi-viduals who failed to climb aboard the new movement were powerless to prevent its advance. Political differences among the delegates had been subordinated to a greater goal of a revived democracy with direct working-class representation. The by-election in St Catharines had demonstrated the widespread popularity of this cause. It was even pos-sible to ignore the bitter divisions in the industrial movement over the OBU and the general strike. The amalgamation movement, it seemed, had rendered the conflict between craft and industrial unionists re-dundant. Among the socialists, the current led by Simpson could claim vindication. Not only was the ILP now a force that could not be ignored, but the founding of the Ontario CLP and Simpson's ascendency at the *Banner* demonstrated the potential of the socialists to increase their weight within the political movement. No obvious barriers lay ahead.

Deeper reflection about the trade-union movement, particularly after the débâcle in Toronto, may have dispelled such optimism. Not only were conservative leaders on the Toronto District Labor Council wary of the transformation of the union movement, they were also deeply committed to the old political system. The two central figures who stood in opposition to the general strike movement, Joseph Gibbons and W.D. Robbins, were prominent Tory municipal politicians. How-ever, in contrast to the polarization that was apparent in the unions, the movement for political representation appeared indivisible. By the summer of 1919, Tory politicians within the labour movement were effectively isolated, but not until after a fiery battle in Toronto.

On 27 June 1919, conservative labour leaders in that city made their bid for support. In opposition to Simpson's *Banner* and the revolutionary-socialist *Ontario Labor News*, the first issue of the *Labor Leader* appeared. Its masthead declared its purpose: 'Canadian Labor Men and Canadian Employers should co-operate in the Interests of Canadian Industry,' and 'Canadian Labor Men should not tolerate the I.W.W. and the One Big Union, nor Bolshevism.' The new paper praised the efforts of not-yet-deposed TDLC leaders W.J. Hevey and Arthur O'Leary for their 'strenuous work' in the interest of labour peace through the tumultuous months of May and June. Labour news, as well as a report of the CCM company picnic, filled the rest of the paper. Advertisements – the mainstay of other labour papers – were few. In keeping with the tone of post-war red-baiting, indigenous sources of radicalism were denied in favour of nativist explanation. 'Canada, to-day,' it claimed, 'faces the storm of unrest blown across her border from outside, and brewed in the clouded intelligence of the Red Russian Bolshevik.' The timing of the appearance of the *Leader*, just prior to the semi-annual TDLC elections, enabled it to support for re-election the conservative officers of the TDLC 'on a Sane Platform.' They campaigned, notably, not only for the 'Men [who] bear Gompers' Standard,' but also for the recently issued Majority Report of the Royal Commission on Industrial Relations. This program for gradual reform and social peace, to which Moore had signed his name, would served as a rallying point for the labour conservatives.[44]

That five of the seven 'Provisional Directors' of the new venture were union business agents reveals that such conservatism had a strong base among individuals who depended upon the established structures of the movement for their livelihood. Essentially, however, the *Labor Leader* was the project of two labour entrepreneurs. R.J. Stevenson and W.J. Hevey, a typographer and a cigar maker respectively, had long been involved in various publishing schemes, such as a souvenir book of enlisted unionists for the London TLC in 1916 and the London Labour Day Souvenir. Until the launching of the *Leader*, Hevey also had the advertising contract for the *Industrial Banner*. He had played a major conservative role in the TDLC, as he had opposed defending Bainbridge, opposed the general strike, and refused to participate in the defence of those arrested in the Winnipeg strike.[45]

The growing isolation of Hevey and his supporters on the TDLC can be traced to strategic decisions made by the socialists on the council in the spring of 1919 not to secede from the established unions. The TDLC conservatives had to carry their campaign against the swelling tide of Toronto labour radicalism. In July, socialists won every position on the council by votes of about 170 to 145. The body was still divided, but the weight had shifted to the left. The TDLC, in the words of the *Labor Leader*, had gone 'Red.'[46] This was only the first blow against the right. On 7 August 1919, the conservatives' fate would be sealed.

At the end of regular TDLC business, Jimmie Simpson took the floor of the council and read a prepared statement. 'Information of a startling character,' he began, 'revealing acts of disloyalty to this Council and its affiliated organizations on the part of two former officers of this Council, has been imparted to a number of men in the Labor Movement of Toronto.' Simpson went on to describe an approach made by O'Leary and Hevey to the Toronto Employers' Association in the midst of the metal-trades strike 'for a secret gift' of $5,000 to establish a labour paper 'which would advance the interests of the employers.' The detailed description of the meeting added credibility to his story. The intermediary between the employers and Hevey and O'Leary had been local military commander Brigadier-General John A. Gunn. The proposal had the support of some members of the Employers' Association, particularly its president, Fred Bawden of the Bawden Tool and Machine Company. Others, including W.C. Coulter of Booth and Coulter and William Inglis, were strongly opposed. Bawden finally conceded that the news of the 'gift' would inevitably 'leak out' and the meeting ought not to deal with the issue. Others agreed. Later, however, a number of employers were canvassed individually, and cheques 'as high as $500.00' were given for the project.[47]

As Simpson concluded his speech, 'an indescribable scene ensued, such as has probably never before been witnessed since the inception of the District Labor Council.'[48] The accused denied the charges, and an investigating committee of five, mostly socialists, was chosen. Employers' denials the following day did little to detract from Simpson's charges. Bawden, Inglis, and Melville P. White of Canadian Allis-Chalmers all stated that O'Leary and Hevey had not been at the meeting in question. Simpson, however, had never claimed that they had made the appeal in person. A longer statement by Bawden (printed in the *Labor Leader*) claimed that much of what Simpson had claimed was untrue, but proceeded, in essence, to confirm the charges. He acknowledged that Gunn had approached the Employers' Association 'and urged that we subscribe to a paper intended to fight Bolshevism and the like.' While denying that any specific references to Hevey and O'Leary or to a specific sum of money had been made, he later cited Inglis as asking 'Why should we give $5,000 to Hevey?'[49] The battle escalated as Hevey and O'Leary announced that they were suing Simpson for $10,000 each.

Conservatives on the TDLC who had been quick to endorse the *Labor Leader* were by now entirely discredited. Electricians' business agent James T. Gunn jumped ship, quitting the *Labor Leader* pending the investigation. Charges against Hevey and O'Leary were laid over by the TDLC pending a legal decision in the libel suit against Simpson, but the *Labor Leader* was officially repudiated by the council. Finally, on 18 December, Hevey and O'Leary were suspended from the TDLC on a roll-call vote. Michael Piva's argument that long-standing factionalism continued to debilitate the TDLC's political initiatives in 1919 cannot be sustained. This view is in keeping with his tendency, in his book-length study of Toronto workers, to paint the events of 1919 as the last breath of a fractured and declining movement. Yet an audacious Toronto labour movement was attracting great numbers of workers into unions, both old and new. On the political front, a more stunning defeat for opponents of independent political action could scarcely have been contemplated. The *Labor Leader* was discredited, and other overt opposition by union leaders to the ILP in the fall of 1919 was inconsequential. The unity of the TDLC surpassed that of the London TLC, which repudiated the *Labor Leader* by a less convincing twenty-one to twelve.[50] Labour Tories were left without a credible voice.

The TDLC initiated a defence committee for Simpson, and the major unions in the building, metal, and garment industries, as well as Toronto ILP branches, rallied to his aid. The libel trials were a celebrated event. In the first case – O'Leary's – Simpson was on relatively shaky ground, as the former TDLC president had never had any formal connection with Hevey and Stevenson or the *Labor Leader*. The jury chose not to believe the evidence of Simpson's informant who testified in the case, and O'Leary was awarded $1,500 and costs of $900. Hevey's lawyer was I.B. Lucas, the former Conservative attorney-general of Ontario. Arthur Roebuck, acting for Simpson, brought forward a witness from the Dominion Ship Building company who had issued a cheque for $500 to the *Labor Leader* but could not tell the court why it had been issued. Presiding justice Orde, apparently joining the case for the plaintiff, interjected to tell the jury that the 'cheque might have been given for advertising or something of the kind.' James Merrick testified that Hevey's name had been mentioned at the meeting in connection with a paper opposing 'Bolshevist literature.' General Gunn, however, denied that he had been taking a proposition from Hevey to the meeting and insisted that he had been acting on his own initiative, adding that 'all is fair in love and war' and there was 'war' at the time in Winnipeg; 'there was bloodshed and people were killed.' As Roebuck argued, Hevey admitted everything except an explicit agreement that Gunn should bring the matter before the Employers' Association, but there 'must have been at least a tacit agreement between Hevey and Gunn.' The jury, unsympathetic to the argument that Hevey had sold out his former colleagues, found Simpson guilty and set damages at the sum of $4,000 and costs.[51]

Simpson's legal defeat only increased his stock within the labour movement. Within weeks he was elected to the TDLC executive committee, chosen as a TDLC delegate to the TLCC, and elected president of the Toronto ILP. The Simpson Defence Committee vowed to raise the full cost of $8,000. For the provincial ILP, the significance of these events was the continued marginalization of conservative union leaders, who were now widely seen as in the pay of the employers. In the 1919 provincial election, few Conservative unionists felt confident enough to appear on official Tory platforms, although a few spoke on behalf of the 'Independent' Adam Beck in London. Such men were fighting a strong current in favour of independent working-class political action. That the *Labor Leader* supported their cause was doubtless of little help. All came in for strong denunciation from local trades councils. For their livelihood Hevey and Stevenson could no longer rely on the local labour movement, although in 1921 they received the contract to produce the new TLCC journal despite a loud chorus of anger from southern Ontario. Their loyalty to Tom Moore and Paddy Draper had finally paid dividends.[52] In 1919, however, they could provide no effective opposition to the ILP.

Rural Allies

Labourist optimism about the coming provincial election was encouraged by events in the countryside. The entrance of the farmers into the electoral arena in their own name had been delayed until late in the war but, having arrived, they shook the rural pillars of the old political system in a manner analogous to the ILP in the cities. The United Farmers of Ontario was founded only in 1914, but its roots extend back to the Dominion Grange and the Patrons of Industry, two organizations that defended agrarian interests in the marketplace and in the legislature in the last third of the nineteenth century.[53] Indeed, remnants of the Grange survived to enter the newly formed UFO. Farmers' grievances during the war and a growing disenchantment with the existing political parties fuelled the growth of the UFO. By 1916, the organization had 200 clubs and 5,000 members; by 1919 this had soared to 1,130 clubs and 48,000 members.[54]

The farmers had, of course, specific interests and concerns, as well as a history of autonomous agrarian agitation. W.R. Young, in fact, cites '[g]rowing urban dominance [as] the ultimate cause of the unrest' in the countryside. The most obvious symptom of the growing disparity between city and farm was the depopulation of rural areas of the province. Young estimates that between 1901 and 1911 almost 200,000 people left rural southern Ontario and a further 154,000 during the following decade.[55] The lure of the city was seen as the product of 'artificial' wealth created by measures, such as the protective tariff, that impoverishing the rural areas. At risk was the survival of a way of life. The countryside, it was felt, had not shared in the general expansion of the Laurier era, and after 1914 the war had brought new opportunities and higher wages to the cities. The future was bleak, and farm leader J.J. Morrison's view of it was strongly tainted by eugenics. With the city attracting the 'cleverest and most ambitious,' the old 'pioneer stock' was being weakened by a kind of backwards evolution.[56] Certainly farmers were facing the same corporate giants as labour, and from a similarly disadvantageous position. The large farm-equipment manufacturers and milling companies symbolized an economy that had escaped the farmers' control. Nevertheless, the relationship was different. Farmers encountered these corporations in the marketplace; consequently, renewed agrarian organization first stimulated new co-operative ventures. Only in 1918 did the UFO decide electoral politics was necessary. Not least among the farmers' goals was the survival of a 'rural ethic' that, according to agrarian activist W.C. Good, rose from the 'moral discipline which comes to those engaged in the more fundamental work of production.'[57] Those who took pride in feeding the nation and shared a physiocratic notion of the source of wealth took umbrage at urbanites who dismissed them as uneducated 'yokels.' The UFO sought to restore the farmer and the countryside to their proper place.

Based on such an ethos, programmatic differences with the ILP were readily apparent for those who chose to look for them. For the most part, farmers opposed the eight-hour day, as it could only increase the attraction of the city; they also opposed the protective tariff, which the craft unions had traditionally defended. They supported prohibition. They raised few demands for social welfare legislation, and they 'vehemently opposed'[58] daylight-saving time. Yet however much the program of the UFO reflected specifically agrarian anxieties, the language of revolt closely paralleled that of labourism. The claim that millionaire profiteers were 'robbing them of representation in Parliament'[59] was axiomatic to ILPers, as was the demand for the 'conscription of wealth' before men. Although the attitude of individual ILPers to the war may have varied, few would have quarrelled with the declaration of the UFO executive in 1916: 'It is a manifest and glaring injustice that Canadian mothers should be compelled to surrender boys around whom their dearest hopes in life are centred, while plutocrats, fattening on special privileges and war business, are left in undisturbed possession of their riches.'[60] The farmers had their own fight with the Borden government when it reneged on a commitment not to conscript farm labourers, but the growing anger at the consequences of partyism and profiteering were shared by farmers and workers. Moreover, each organization saw direct legislation as revitalizing Canadian democracy, and each spoke in quasi-millennial terms of cleansing the political system. Despite their specific differences, the *Industrial Banner* praised the growing alliance of the 'forces of democracy.' Others expressed their hope that 'the two great groups of producers' could unite to challenge 'the big interests.' The strength of this sentiment was revealed in the willingness of UFO organizations across the province to disregard the *Farmers' Sun's* dismissal of the political labour movement as another urban development injurious to rural interests. Individual branches of each organization were eager to co-operate in the 1919 provincial election and did so without specific direction from their provincial leaderships, and apparently without difficulty.[61]

The ILP was, in general, very favourably disposed towards the farmers' movement, though there were pockets of suspicion. Flatman, for instance, pointed out that some farmer candidates were businessmen of some consequence. In 1919, however, such criticisms were rare as there was a reservoir of sympathy for the farmers. J.E. Hett, the former ILP candidate in Kitchener, considered that Borden treated the farmers much as Germany had Belgium. Other ILP speakers suggested that the mounting economic pressures on farmers placed them in closer sympathy with urban workers. Brantford ILPer John L. Maycock attempted to develop a theoretical basis for a farmer-labour alliance by drawing a distinction between farmers and capitalists. Farmers 'were only capitalists with respect to owning the means to labor. The other class of capitalist owned the means to escape from labor and to live by others' efforts.'[62]

Local labour parties, however, required no theoretical justification for joining with other 'producers' in the interests of 'democracy.' The joint election literature of the South Waterloo ILP and UFO in support of ILPer Karl Homuth captured a common aspiration: 'The object of these two Parties is to promote the Political, Economic, and Social interest of people who live by their labor, mental or manual, as distinguished from those who live by profit upon the labor of others.'[63] Such a blurring of social differences between workers and farmers was most often a feature of campaigns in smaller centres where weaker union traditions tipped the balance towards a self-identification as producers rather than as workers. In addition, since these branches existed in mixed urban-rural constituencies, co-operation with farmers was electorally necessary. While the provincial leadership of the ILP urged branches not to make political concessions to the UFO, such a warning appeared inconsequential in a party that was not based on clear ideological distinctions, and branches spent little time considering programmatic issues. Rather, they concentrated on selecting candidates to confront the old parties. Since the relative strength and experiences of UFO and ILP branches varied greatly, a variety of local arrangements were made. Local farmer and labour forces either agreed that the ILP would contest the provincial election and the UFO the next federal one, or a joint convention of the two parties was held. Despite the lack of a jointly organized provincial campaign, only in North Waterloo and West Lambton did candidates from the two parties oppose each other. In at least ten other ridings UFO and ILP members worked together in the interests of a democratic challenge to the old parties. In Toronto a hopeful *Industrial Banner*, based far away from the farmers' movement, reported a radically changed attitude on the part of the province's farmers to urban workers.[64] For the moment, there was little to dispel such a belief.

Towards Victory

In the summer of 1919, the Independent Labor Party savoured its accomplishments and hurried to perfect its organization. Once again, a membership drive was announced, aimed at 10,000 new members in three months. The Hamilton branches attracted 2,500 people to an ILP picnic at Wabasso Park to enjoy baseball, races, games, and a few words by James Simpson. Soon afterwards the party would face its great test. With the announcement of a 20 October provincial general election, the opportunity had finally arrived to face the electorate with a well-organized and well-prepared party. The provincial executive acted quickly to apply some of the lessons learned from past contests. Any political alliances made by branches had to be on the basis of the ILP program. Recognizing members' tendencies to overlook programmatic distinctions, the provincial executive insisted on approving the platforms of branches running joint campaigns with the United Farmers. The 1917 experience with MacBride demonstrated that local autonomy could reflect badly on the entire party.[65]   ·

The provincial election campaign soon demonstrated that others shared the ILP's estimation of its own popularity. The Liberal Party issued a pamphlet entitled 'Labor,' which endorsed many of the ILP's major planks, including a provincial minimum wage, the legislated eight-hour day, sickness and unemployment insurance, and improved protective legislation for women. These policies had been approved by the Liberal convention in June at the urging of former Temiskaming ILP candidate Arthur W. Roebuck, who continued to straddle the boundary between the two parties. The appeal of these policies was somewhat diminished by the choice of Hartley Dewart, a man without credible reform credentials, as party leader.[66] Nevertheless, if ILP support had depended entirely on its platform, the Liberals' new policies would have been a serious threat. Labourism, however, was more than a political platform. It demanded the vitalization of a political system and the defeat of partyism. The Liberals were too much a part of the discredited political structure to respond effectively to this sentiment.

The Conservatives, too, attempted to speak to labour's new-found confidence and published a pamphlet entitled, audaciously, 'What Has Been Done for Labor.' Apart from the Workmen's Compensation Act, few of their actions addressed specifically working-class concerns. Hydro, public health measures and a 'strong patriotic policy' did not add up to a coherent program attractive to workers who were not already inveterate Tories. The Conservatives considered that such a constituency remained significant, backing Samuel Landers, former editor of the *Labor News* and a garment-union leader, against the ILP in Hamilton, and Toronto Street Railway Employees' Union secretary and city controller W.D. Robbins, in Riverdale, also against a labour candidate. It was 'understood' that, if successful, a Conservative government would name Robbins the first provincial minister of labour. The Conservative running in South Waterloo attempted to cover all bases by presenting himself as a 'soldier-farmer-labour' candidate. While addressing themes such as patriotism, themes that had mobilized Tory workingmen in the past, such candidates conspicuously failed to address the sentiments that had given rise to the ILP. Importantly, the Conservatives also bore the stigma of the federal Conservatives-*cum*-Unionists who had undermined democratic structures through 'government by order in council.' Conservative leader William Hearst's attack on the ILP as a party demanding class government was dismissed on the basis of Unionist support of profiteers during the war.[67]

Despite meagre financial and organizational resources, the ILP was prepared to meet the challenge of 'the old reactionary parties.' Leading figures in the party – Joe Marks, Minnie Singer, and Mary McNab – fanned out across the province to address ILP rallies. The provincial leadership, however, played a minor role in the local battles around Ontario, and campaigns reflected the particular histories of each branch. In Toronto, where the ILP had surpassed 3,000, the strength of the socialists was apparent. At the instigation of Simpson and John MacDonald, the ILP, trade-union representatives, and the Social Democratic Party met to plan the nominating convention and campaign. The TDLC demonstrated its support for this alliance by sending delegates to the convention and donating $200 to the campaign. The Toronto ILP declared its full programmatic agreement with the Grand Army of Canada, a radical veterans' organization interested in establishing co-operative stores and factories and in political action. As an indication of the alliance's commitment to labourist-socialist co-operation, its campaign was conducted under the rubric of the Canadian Labour Party, while elsewhere in Ontario the ILP continued to hold sway. Of the three candidates – MacDonald, John W. Buckley, and John T. Vick – only the latter was not a socialist.[68] In addition, Simpson was the joint nominee of the CLP and the UFO in the mixed suburban-rural riding of York West. The contest in Riverdale riding in Toronto epitomized the perceived importance of labour, as all four candidates – J.T. Vick (ILP), Joseph McNamara (Independent), W.D. Robbins (Conservative), and George Lockhart (Socialist Labor Party) – vied for that mantle.

Hamilton labourism was of a purer variety, little influenced by socialism. Party slogans continued to reflect concerns issuing from the war. In Hamilton West, signs read: 'Your Vote for Walter Rollo is a nail in the coffin of the profiteer.' His cross-town running mate George Halcrow spoke to the veteran: 'All Workers are not Soldiers, although practically all Soldiers are Workers. Then – let us unite as workers. Vote for and elect this worker.' In St Catharines, experienced ILP campaigners published a paper: the *Daily Topic*. In Brantford, candidate MacBride stayed, barely, in line. Along with the rest of the party he denounced Liberal and Tory 'friends of labor,' but his criticisms of the old parties reflected a singular view that was, at best, only partly labourist. The Ontario Liberals, he maintained, had failed to adopt the 'great progressive policy' of Lloyd George, while he attacked the provincial Tories for failing to give full support to the schemes of Adam Beck. This was hardly a full rejection of partyism. In London, where a small ILP branch of perhaps two hundred members had broken the Liberal hold on the trades council, there was little hesitation in running local physician Hugh Stevenson against the 'Independent Conservative' Adam Beck. For one London heckler, the limitations of Beck's message in the light of an ascendant working class were easily summed up: 'You cannot eat Hydro.'[69]

Among major urban centres, only Windsor and Guelph were not contested by the ILP. While some candidates, such as Stevenson in London and MacBride in Brantford, came from outside organized labour, the ILP standard was often carried by well-known figures in the trade-union movement. In St Catharines, the trades-council president, Frank Greenlaw, was nominated. The Peterborough ILP's candidate, Thomas Tooms, presided over the local Building Trades' Council. Even where candidates had a relatively weak union background, local unions and trades councils worked in tandem with the ILP. Although local notables were occasionally elected on the basis of their experiences on municipal councils, their support for the labourist cause was strong (with the possible exception of MacBride) and the character of their support qualified them as candidates of a working-class movement. This held true for alderman Karl Homuth of Galt, president of the South Waterloo ILP as well as a superintendent at the Wool Stock Factory. Charles F. Swayze, the candidate of the Niagara Falls ILP, was in a similar position. An accountant, he had participated actively in the St. Catharines by-election and spoke in true labourist terms of having 'lit the fires of political democracy.'[70] The tendency to choose such individuals as candidates reflects not only a degree of deference to those who had electoral experience but also the relatively weak history of political involvement and skills outside the larger centres of Toronto and Hamilton. It also testifies to the attraction that the political labour movement had to reform-minded people in smaller industrial centres. Such people were, however, relatively rare in a movement that was overwhelmingly led by trade unionists and that maintained close ties with trades councils across the province. Dr Stevenson, for instance, had been nominated by a convention of the ILP and the city's unions, a convention that had taken place at the instigation of the London Trades and Labor Council.[71]

The Independent Labor Party had travelled far since the 1917 federal election. Not only had it grown considerably, into an organization with branches in almost every city and town in the province, but also it had infected urban Ontario with its view of a democratically transformed society that was, with faith and luck, only an election away. It had established an alliance – albeit a rather spontaneous and uncritical one – with the farmers' movement on the basis of a producers' democracy uniting urban and rural 'workers.' Its growing self-confidence had allowed it to reject, again not very consciously, the defensive reactions to nativism and red-baiting that had been features of earlier by-elections. In the general election, the ILP presented its positive view of an invigorated democracy and did not dwell upon the alleged threats of aliens and Bolsheviks. On 20 October 1919, Ontario's farmers and workers could claim victory in 'The Battle for Democracy.' When forty-four UFO and eleven ILP members took their places on the government side of the Legislature after the election, active labourists celebrated victory in the streets and labour temples of the province. The assumption that electoral victory equalled the advent of a 'new democracy' was about to be tested. And, as we shall see, the ILP's success was inseparable from the industrial struggle. First, however, let us examine the newest participants in this democracy: recently enfranchised working-class women.

5 The Woman Democrat[1]

The Ontario provincial election of 1919, which saw the triumph of the farmer and labour parties, was the first in which women could vote. Since labourists viewed the ballot as their primary instrument to defend democracy against partyism and special privilege, the extension of the franchise to women held special promise. Long a demand of labour political activists,[2] women's suffrage was celebrated as a first, giant step towards the 'new democracy.' Moreover, it promised to draw working-class women into the mainstream of labour electoral activity, since the fate of the Independent Labor Party now rested upon the shoulders of both the men and women of the working-class. The manner in which women were integrated into this struggle, as well as the nature and treatment of women's concerns, can tell us much about the nature of the democracy that labourists were demanding. The post-war labour revolt spread far beyond the preserves of established male-dominated unions, drawing together working-class households and communities in a broad movement for political and social reform. Potentially, women could play an active role in defining that movement's goals and character.

A study of the activities and achievements of working-class women provides important insight into gender relations within the working class, as well as a more precise understanding of the goals of the labour movement through these tumultuous years, both in the workplace and in workers' communities. This chapter argues that a working-class women's movement emerged in this period with the support of male labourists who saw women's participation as a composite part of an invigorated democracy. But, as we shall argue was the case with labourism as a whole, the movement's limited social vision precluded significant and lasting accomplishments. As labourism focused on the electoral system in isolation from sources of social inequality in the workplace, working-class women, for the most part, adopted a reform agenda without critically examining gender relations inside the household. The goal of a male family wage capable of supporting an entire household remained the ideal of the labour movement; women's economic dependence was rarely questioned. For women workers, this was doubly crippling. It provided a rationale for low pay, since women were not expected to support themselves or others, and it was used to exclude married women from the paid labour force on the grounds that they could be depriving a family of its breadwinner. The needs of the working-class family never lay far behind considerations of employment and wages. Economic independence for women, particularly during times of high unemployment, was considered by employers and trade-unionists alike to be at best frivolous and at worst a threat to the family. Women were drawn back into the household as the extraordinary economic and political conditions that had created a space for their participation in the new democracy came to an end.[3]

Historians have viewed this period as the culmination of a wave of 'maternal' or 'social' feminism whereby middle-class women sought to expand the boundaries of their maternal role through participation in the public sphere. Their reform activities represented an attempt to demonstrate that the special nurturing qualities that equipped women as mothers were applicable on a wider social stage. The plethora of organizations that attracted women in the late-nineteenth and early-twentieth centuries were not working-class in character. Their social-reform activities were directed at the working-class from the outside; the social practices of working-class and immigrant populations were implicitly the target of their moral intervention. Health, education, and temperance campaigns had as their primary object the elimination of the slum and the alteration of working-class behaviour. However, in the context of a wider labour mobilization, working-class women organized and fought for their own vision of a better society. Although that vision reflected their ongoing interaction with male labourists and socialists and with middle-class feminists, their struggle never strayed far from the needs and constraints of the working-class household.[4] Both the goals and methods of this struggle merit close attention for the light they cast on the development of Canadian feminism and for the additional insights they reveal about the character of the new democracy that was capturing the imagination of working-class Ontario.

Women in Industry

From 1916, economic recovery, labour shortages, and the decision of the Imperial Munitions Board to encourage the employment of women appeared to alter the character of women's participation in the economy and in society. The government estimated that the number of women employed in Ontario's factories and stores grew by more than 50 per cent in the two years following October 1915.[5] For the labour movement, this represented the threat of a 'dilution of labour.' The entrance of women workers into trades dominated by skilled male workers threatened to undermine the position in the labour market that the male workers had so painstakingly constructed. In Toronto, where such trends were most apparent, the trades council considered that 'it was a shrewd move on the part of the manufacturers to reduce the cost of production by pressing women into service in the manufacturing of munitions.' While the council did not demand the exclusion of women, they did try to ensure that women did not undercut men's wages by demanding that male and female munitions workers be paid equal wages. The TDLC charged that 'certain war munition factories ... were exploiting the female workers and dispensing with the services of skilled mechanics because the women were unorganized and compelled to accept a low rate of wages,'[6] and it initiated an investigation of conditions in these plants.

Relations between men and women on the shop floor are difficult to assess, but two strikes provide insight into the complexity of the issues and the range of reactions. In July 1917 moulders at the Empire Brass Works in London struck against the employment of women in the core room. The specific complaint was that the 'girls' were working in the plumbing-supplies department, an area unconnected with munitions production. Apparently the understanding reached between employers and the moulders' union was that women could be hired to work on munitions only, while men would retain their monopoly of regular work. Most remarkable in this instance was the price the men were willing to pay to exclude women from the shop floor. The union won its demand that the company purchase a core machine and discharge the women. The men were willing to allow the company to 'dilute' their labour by means of technological innovation in preference to hiring women. The strategy pursued by the union did not eliminate the threat of cheap female competition; the fired women were cast back into the reserve army of unemployed. Within four months, upon receiving a major munitions contract, Empire Brass fired the unionists and replaced them with 'girls and hunkies.'[7]

Conflicts at Willys-Overland and Russell Motor Car in Toronto, both companies controlled by T.A. Russell, represented a different response to the employment of women at lower wages. The strike of seven hundred airplane workers at Willys-Overland was provoked by the unwillingness of the company to pay union wages to the less-skilled (mostly female) specialists. In a 1917 referendum, Ontario machinists had voted overwhelmingly to admit women to union membership. In contrast to the position taken by the London moulders, the Toronto machinists' strike committee statement declared: 'We have nothing against the employment of women on the work.' The employer's response, interestingly, appealed to traditional craft union values. 'The demand issued by the union,' Russell responded, 'was that all women employees shall be paid 45 cents per hour, which is impossible owing to their being unskilled and requiring weeks of instruction before they are proficient on the class of work that has to be done.'[8] Skilled workers were adamant in their contention that they were only striking in the interests of the specialists, and with their support, the wage gap was narrowed. A further concession by the company opened the door to the advancement of women workers: 'Henceforth,' read the agreement, 'all male and female employees who are recognized as efficient machinists or toolmakers shall receive the union rate of wages for the craft.'[9]

Although the strike at Willys-Overland was settled by mid-June, conflict erupted again at the Russell Motor Car plant at the end of the month. Presumably hoping to prevent a similar agreement in that plant, Russell fired one man and two women unionists. Not only did 135 men strike for the reinstatement of all three workers, but a meeting of 1,200 machinists threatened a general strike of their craft if Russell did not back down. A week later, all three workers had their jobs back. As an organizer for the International Association of Machinists reported to the union's journal, the issue in both strikes was the right of women to join the union and receive its benefits.[10] In contrast to the outcome of the London moulders' strike, women were, however temporarily, accepted as legitimate members of the work-force and the union.

Despite the union's claims, the actions of male unionists were not entirely selfless. Minnie Singer, an officer of the women's auxiliary of the machinists' union, which aided the organization of women into the union, continued to see the maintenance of men's wages and conditions as primary. Women specialists must be organized, she argued, 'so that at any future time when the IA of M members find it necessary to make demands to better their conditions, these women will not in any way interfere with their plans.'[11] While unionists declared that the strike was 'to protect conditions for their fellow-workmen now in the trenches,' a potential conflict was apparent. 'Labor organizers,' noted the *Globe*, 'say that women show no great desire to return to domestic life.'[12]

The strikes at Willys-Overland and Russell Motor Car reflected the growing ambiguity inherent in the demand for equal pay, a demand that could be either exclusionary or the reflection of a democratic desire to overcome inequities in the labour force. The former sentiment had deeper roots, since it had long been assumed that a demand for employers to pay women 'men's' wages would dissuade them from hiring women. Conservative unions, such as the boot and shoe workers, were explicit in linking equal pay to the exclusion of women workers from more highly paid jobs that they deemed to demand greater skill.[13]

The threat of competition from women was greatest in sectors experiencing labour shortages and among men in less-skilled and less physically demanding occupations who could not easily claim that women were unable to perform the tasks associated with their jobs. The street-railway union fulfilled both these criteria, and the men fought to exclude women from the cars. In June 1918, Mark Irish reported that '[i]f the Toronto Street Railway ... put on women and the men go out, as they have threatened to do, we will in a few days have Labour endeavoring to tie up the whole City.' In defence of their jobs, the men invoked both the family wage and women's morality. Women, they argued, would accept lower wages because they did not have to support families. To supplement this argument, the union aimed their moral fire directly at the women who might take these jobs. 'One thing, moreover is sure, no self-respecting female would desire to force her way through the jam that overcrowd the cars during certain hours of the day when passengers are wedged together about as thick as herrings in a box.'[14] The union even hinted at a willingness to accept the introduction of pay-as-you-enter cars in preference to hiring women. By abolishing the position of conductor, half the jobs on street cars would be abolished. That such a permanently damaging measure was preferred to the hiring of women reveals the depth of the men's commitment to the existing division of labour. No women were hired.[15]

While the street-railway union stands out in its single-minded opposition to the employment of women, the general sentiment of the international union leaders who met in Ottawa in June 1917 to publicize their concerns about wartime labour conditions was not very different. The 'unnecessary dilution of labor by the introduction of female labor before proper steps had been taken to utilize available skilled mechanics' figured among their complaints.[16] Although the demand for equal wages for women was again made, its juxtaposition to the demand for the exclusion of women from skilled trades reinforced the fact that it was just another means to the same end.

There were, however, other voices. While many male workers looked forward to a return to the gender status quo *ante bellum* within the labour market, and middle-class observers feared for the moral survival of the nation's womanhood, working-class activists pondered the position of women in the coming 'new democracy.' Joseph Marks reflected on 'the readjustment of industrial relations between the sexes' in the columns of the *Industrial Banner*. For Marks, as for the union movement as a whole, equal wages were a necessary means of preventing 'unscrupulous employers' from using women as cheap substitutes for male workers. However, he recognized the democratic potential of the equal-wage demand and felt that the entry of women into 'a hundred avenues of trade never previously dreamed of' was an encouraging component 'in the evolution to an immensely better industrial system.' He urged his readers to recognize that they could not turn back the clock and that it would be wrong to attempt to do so. Not only would there be a dearth of male labour following the slaughter of war, 'the opportunities for marriage will be immensely contracted.' 'Many of these women will depend upon these selfsame jobs for means of earning a livelihood, to discharge them would mean to throw them out upon the street.' The solution was to organize all workers, men and women, obtain an equal franchise, and work to reduce the hours of labour for all. The organization of women into unions was the first step. 'Once united on the industrial field they would inevitably unite on the political field, and become a power irresistible in its might.'[17] The exclusion of women from employment and unions would be counterproductive for the working class as a whole.

Feminist voices bearing similar messages often received a sympathetic ear from the labour movement. In 1916, for instance, the Brantford trades council heard an articulate critique of the gender division of labour from S.W. Secord of the Equal Franchise Club. 'Women had the inherent right,' she told them, 'to labor in any field where their intelligence taught them their labor was most needed and of greatest value.' As 'conditions and modern customs' had redefined women's work so that it no longer confined them to the home, women now 'claimed the right to enter all fields of labor.' Her speech culminated in a series of demands aimed at the heart of an exclusionary labour movement: 'Women must have equality with men in labor – equal pay, equal training, equal organization.' The Brantford TLC responded enthusiastically to her appeal and voted unanimously to support her association in the struggle for an equal franchise.[18]

Suggestions that the demand for equal pay might acquire a more egalitarian character and even that the distinctions between men's and women's jobs might be blunted were being placed before apparently receptive audiences. However, women's experience in non-traditional jobs was generally too short-lived to present a serious challenge to male strongholds. The employment of women in munitions manufacture reached its peak in late 1917, after which production declined and jobs were taken by returning men. By early 1918, there were again reports of unemployment among women, although the decline in women's paid employment was uneven. Most female war workers had laboured for a handful of large employers as most of the hundreds of small munitions makers in Ontario hired few, if any, women. Well over half of the 10,000 women employed in Toronto in the metal trades at the end of the war worked for three employers: Banfield and Sons, Canadian Fairbanks-Morse, and Russell Motor Car Company.[19] Not only was women's experience of working in 'men's' jobs relatively brief, it was confined to relatively few, albeit significant, work sites.

The armistice threw women's futures in even these jobs into question. Matrons at both the Fairbanks-Morse and Russell Motor Car companies commented that few female employees were willingly quitting their jobs. Peace sent a shudder through the ranks of female munitions workers, as many of them took 'French leave' from their jobs and went in search of more secure employment; munitions-industry employers even complained about the temporary shortage of women workers. 'Munitionettes,' as they were dubbed by the press, were uncertain about their fate: 'In an interview with several of the workers the majority of the women stated they had not thought out any definite plans as to what kind of work they will take up in the future.' Some inroads women had made into 'men's' employment were not lost. Although desirable office jobs were apparently rare, bank managers turned ideological somersaults to explain why the formerly male job of teller was ideal for women, and hundreds of women maintained their jobs in the financial sector.[20] 'Taking into consideration,' commented *Saturday Night*, 'the nature of the work from the standpoint of feminine tastes and qualifications, it may be said that work in a bank offers unusual advantages; the routine work is less exhausting compared with many other fields of women's activity, for it cannot be denied that pleasant surroundings and a sheltered scene of activity mean much to a woman worker.' Less gloss was placed on growing women's employment in the expanding mass-production industries such as rubber. Kitchener, where this industry was centred, reported a chronic shortage of women workers.[21]

At the end of the war any fissures in the barriers between the types of work appropriate for men and women were rapidly repaired. The gender division of labour, weakly challenged, was reconstructed. Nevertheless, the boundaries had shifted somewhat, as new employers discovered the advantages of cheap, plentiful female workers without craft traditions. And some women were able to cling to some of the inroads they had made, particularly in clerical employment, but also in mass-production industries.

What then became of Joseph Marks's call for 'equal opportunity for all'? Primarily, he had overestimated the extent of women's participation in war industries and its impact on the gender division of labour. No concerted effort came from any quarter to defend women's rights to the jobs they had held during the war. Many unionists were pleased to see the departure of women from their industries, and the few proponents of women's employment in such sectors were powerless to act. Munitions jobs were destined to die with the armistice; the labour movement was powerless to save them even if it had wished to do so. Just as before the war, marriage and withdrawal from the paid labour market remained an alternative and escape for working women, particularly those in less remunerative occupations, and employers complained to the Royal Commission on Industrial Relations that post-war marriages had drained the female labour market. Remarkably little had changed in the life-cycle experiences of working-class women. Male-led trade unions found little reason to challenge all this. Ideas about the role of women within the working-class household had never been seriously challenged; no real options were ever posed.[22] The promise held out by Marks and Secord of a new industrial role for women soon faded.

The United Women's Educational Federation and the Women's Labor League

Although the social and material bases of the gender division of labour had withstood the challenge of the war, it would be wrong to conclude that nothing changed for working-class women. Many women had found jobs in sectors that had long been organized or where unions were enjoying the increased bargaining power that the labour shortage and booming economy provided. Moreover, supporters of industrial unionism, whether by succession or amalgamation, were committed to organizing all workers, not just skilled craftsmen. This signalled a new opportunity to organize women workers. If gendered work relations were too strong a citadel to storm, the same was not necessarily true of the organizational structures of the working class. A small cadre of women already active in working-class organizations determined that women's emancipation depended on female participation in the organizations of the working class: in unions and political parties.

Very few women were active in the labour movement in southern Ontario in the early years of the war. Even unions composed largely of women, as in the garment and shoe industries, were invariably led by men. A gendered division of tasks pervaded these unions in other ways. When the Toronto shoe workers union held its annual 'entertainment' in late 1916, the lunch was provided by the women members. Even as unionists, the tasks of women could differ little from those of a 'ladies' auxiliary.' Trades councils' efforts towards organizing women workers were, at best, desultory. In major American centres, the task of organizing women workers, abrogated by the union, was undertaken, albeit inadequately, by the middle-class women behind the National Women's Trade Union League (NWTUL). In southern Ontario, no parallel movement emerged. Although the TDLC did turn its energies towards a rather quixotic struggle to organize waitresses in 1915, the singularity of this cause underlines the labour movement's general neglect. Moreover, a social evening held by the waitresses' union with the co-operation of the TDLC revealed the extent to which the union movement lacked women activists and was insensitive to the importance of speaking to women workers as women; the event was chaired and addressed entirely by the male leaders of the local movement.[23]

In view of the haphazard record of unions in such work, the resolve of the Labor Educational Association to aim for the 'more thorough organization of women workers of the province'[24] was a sharp break with the past. But what would this mean in practice? The LEAO was, in the words of its critics, little more than a resolution-passing body. When the TLCC made a similar decision at its 1918 convention, the congress executive effectively nullified it by voting not to hire a female organizer or to send a delegate to the NWTUL. The body 'was unanimous in agreeing that in view of the small number of women workers as yet attending the conventions of the Congress and the financial status of the Congress that this is not the opportune time to establish such a permanent expenditure.'[25] For the leadership of the TLCC, little had altered in the nature of women's participation in the paid labour force that would demand a change of tack.

This was not to be the experience of the LEAO. Although slow getting off the ground (little was accomplished in the first year), the initiative was maintained by two key figures in the local labour movement: Joe

Marks and Minnie Singer. Unlike the TLCC, the LEAO had a regular voice in Marks's *Industrial Banner* and in his ubiquitous personal appearances. In June 1918, for instance, he spoke to the Earlscourt ILP for a full hour on the need to organize women. For her part, Minnie Singer was able to contribute her long experience in organizing women in the machinists' women's auxiliary, of which she was an international vice-president. In March 1919 she was named director of the LEAO's women's work. It was soon recognized that a new strategy for organizing women – one that would involve more women – was needed, and the 1919 LEAO convention established the United Women's Educational Federation of Ontario (UWEFO). A committee to draft the constitution was struck, consisting of Singer, Maud Madden of the Hamilton ILP, Mrs E. Cook, the president of the Toronto Women's Social Democratic League, Mrs Redford of the Miners' Women's Auxiliary, Lucy MacGregor of the Women's Labor League in Toronto, and Miss O'Connor of the United Textile Workers. While the group exhibited a wide political diversity, only O'Connor was unmarried and an active trade unionist. Singer primarily associated with the wives of members of the machinists' union as opposed to those young women who would have to form the backbone of any drive to organize wage-earning women. She perceived the new organization in maternalist terms, as an 'influence for the uplift of citizenship, life and labor, and the protection of motherhood, childhood and the home.' Still, the *Banner* considered Singer's role in the LEAO to be the first co-ordinated attempt to organize women workers.[26]

While the organization of the UWEFO proceeded rather slowly, the organization of women into unions was proceeding at an unprecedented pace. Unions with a large proportion of women, such as the International Ladies' Garment Workers Union and the Amalgamated Clothing Workers, grew rapidly, the latter winning the eight-hour day in Toronto during the war, an unprecedented victory. Other unions were gaining new women members as well. For instance, a large number of women joined the IAM during the Russell Motor Car strike. Most spectacular was the rapid organization of telephone operators at Bell Telephone. After years of inactivity following the 1907 defeat, a local of seven hundred was rapidly formed in Toronto in the summer of 1918. It was affiliated to the International Brotherhood of Electrical Workers (IBEW) as Local 83a; the 'a' indicating that it belonged to the 'telephone girls' section of the international union. Although such a designation suggested that the telephone operators were perhaps somewhat less than full-fledged members of the IBEW, it could not have

escaped the men's attention that they had reached an agreement with
Bell in Canada at a time when the company had successfully refused
to recognize the international union. The mass-production industries
that organized in 1919 – the meat-packers and rubber workers – included a large number of women. Even the waitresses finally achieved
some success. As early as January 1919, the Toronto local boasted
more than 150 members.[27]

The emergence of an organization specifically for working-class
women suggests that existing women's organizations were unresponsive
to their concerns. This was revealed in their rejection of the Women's
Party, whose formation in 1918 by Imperialist-minded women in the
Toronto suffrage movement provoked women in the labour movement
to articulate women's class differences. A *Banner* correspondent attending a Women's Party meeting noted that a young female factory
worker was quickly dismissed by the meeting when she raised the issue
of shorter hours for women workers. Rather, the meeting was primarily
interested in ensuring the maintenance of patriotic zeal in the post-
war period. The correspondent reminded her readers that 'those same
ladies and their friends and adherents, turned the churches into political cockpits to secure the re-election of those [Unionist] men' in the
1917 election. The new party was little more than a 'Conservative
Annex.'[28]

In fact, the unabashedly anti-labour position of the Women's Party
reveals the extent to which class issues dominated political discourse
even within the women's movement. Its major pamphlet took aim at
perceived demands for the 'control of industry by the workers' by
arguing that 'the efficient management of industry is a function calling
for specialized individual ability, for thorough training and for wide
experiences. It is a function which emphatically cannot be performed
by the rank and file of industry, either by a system of committees or
by any other system.' Appealing to smouldering wartime prejudices,
the argument continued by suggesting that any ill-conceived experiments of this nature could only mean the 'capture and conquest' of
Canadian industry 'by the highly organized and disciplined industry
of Germany.' The polemic focused on the implicit consequence of the
'new democracy': democratic control of industry by workers.

> It is outside the wage-earning hours of the day that the British[-Ca-
> nadian] workers should look for and find the complete freedom
> from restraint which would be as suicidal to introduce into industry
> itself as it would be to introduce it aboard ship. There is absolutely

nothing inconsistent with personal dignity and individual liberty in submitting to discipline and obeying instructions for a certain part of each day, provided that the individual is free to utilize his ample hours of leisure according to his own particular will.

The Women's Party was in contact with the Canadian Reconstruction Association (CRA), whose work in solving the 'labour problem' and addressing the dangers posed by the 'Bolshevik element' will be discussed in chapter seven.[29]

Working-class women active in promoting both their class and sex were well aware of the limited social composition of existing women's organizations. This manifested itself in 1919 with a debate in the ILP – first in Hamilton and then at the provincial convention – over whether women in the ILP should affiliate to the National Council of Women (NCW), a federation of women's organizations whose leadership often had close ties with the CRA and the Canadian Manufacturers' Association. Mary McNab argued that ILP women should affiliate to the NCW so that working women would be represented. Otherwise, she queried, '[w]hat do they know of the working girl?' Other delegates dismissed the council as 'practically an appendage of the Unionist party' and were decidedly less interested in constructing a cross-class women's movement.[30]

The United Women's Educational Federation, then, saw its role in distinctly class terms, as a working-class women's organization, and was described in the *Banner* as 'Labor's National Council of Women.'[31] The comparison with the NCW, however, suggests a shift in the nature of the UWEFO. Rather than being primarily concerned with the organization of waged women into unions, the latter organization defined itself as a federation of working-class women's organizations – unions with large numbers of women members, women's auxiliaries, union label leagues, women's ILP branches – organized to 'champion the cause of Labor and especially advance the interests of womanhood, childhood and the home.' Attention had turned inexorably from the workplace to the household.

The UWEFO's character was determined at its official founding in Brantford in 1920 and was reflected in its leadership. Its leaders were generally married (particularly to unionists attending the Labor Educational Association convention, which met concurrently) and were primarily interested in improving the lot of the working-class family. To this end, they developed a program focusing on the education of their children and 'the nationalization of the medical profession,' as well as continued widening of the franchise. The federation approached the provincial government with a demand for swimming pools in public schools and special programs for 'backward children.' The president of the UWEFO was Minnie Singer; the post of secretary-treasurer was held by Huldah Fester, the wife of the Hamilton TLC secretary and ILP leader. Among the provincial executive of the new organization, only Mary McNab was unmarried and an active unionist. Union organizing played a declining role in the organization's agenda. UWEFO activities on behalf of wage-earning women dwindled to urging the farmer-labour government to include domestics under the new Minimum Wage Act and the Workmen's Compensation Act.[32]

In its 1921 report to the LEAO, the UWEFO could report some growth and some experience in lobbying the Drury government and the Hamilton city council 'in favor of legislation in the direct interest of the women and children as well as the home.' There were other forces at work, as was demonstrated by increased participation from the more radical suburban branches of the Hamilton ILP, particularly from Jean Inglis and Janet Inman – participation that made the UWEFO more audacious in its demands, although it continued to focus on the well-being of the working-class household. Resolutions were passed urging that fathers of illegitimate children be made responsible for the financial costs of raising their children and that schools be made to take responsibility for the nutrition and health of the children of the unemployed. Other policies, proposed by Inman, went further in breaking with the maternalist ideology of early policies: 'Recognizing that the economic factor in women's lives is one of the most important, if not the basic one; therefore be it resolved that the trend of all education will have a direct bearing towards making women economically free.' As a declaration of a new-found gender and class radicalism, the convention moved that 'capitalism pass peacefully into oblivion.' Finally, authorities were urged to adjust the gender ratio of immigrants in order to relieve the perceived pressure on non-English women immigrants to marry early.[33]

In subsequent years, the UWEFO lost the anti-capitalist edge notable at the 1921 convention and followed the LEAO's conservative drift. At the same time, it managed to branch out from its Toronto and Hamilton base to a total of nine cities by 1924. A proposal that domestic science be taught to girls in all schools and that the meals prepared be used to feed the children of the unemployed reveals both the highly constrained view of gender roles held by the UWEFO and its continued concern for the maintenance of the working-class family in a time of growing economic distress. Moreover, its program was that of the conservative wing of the labour movement; immigration restriction was proposed as the solution to unemployment.[34]

These developments in the UWEFO reflected a growing polarization among women in the labour movement as socialist women turned instead to the Women's Labor League. Based on a similarly named movement in Britain, a WLL was formed in Toronto late in 1918 by Lucy MacGregor of the Women's Social Democratic League and Harriet Prenter of the local Political Equality League and regrouped women from socialist parties and from the left wing of the suffrage movement. Like the UWEFO, the WLL identified itself as a working-class organization; Prenter herself assailed the 'silken dames ... so occupied with "committees" and "uplifting" that they allowed the social revolution to walk right past them.'[35] Rose Hodgson, an early member of the British ILP and now secretary of the Toronto WLL, often articulated the league's views of class, gender, and political action in verse:

> When a man says, 'The women should not be allowed
> To vote on a question they don't understand,'
> Their place is at home, only men are endowed,
> With brains for to cope with the question in hand;
> And then the next day to the polling booth goes,
> (And though he's a 'laborer' and hasn't a sue [sic],)
> Marks his ballot for 'Tory' right under your nose –
> I wouldn't give much for his 'wisdom,' would you?[36]

The WLL's most audacious activity was the attempt to organize domestic servants. Armed with a small grant from the TDLC, the league set out to form a union of the most isolated workers in Toronto, determined to win an eight-hour day and a minimum wage of fifteen dollars per week. It soon recruited a hundred members and received a charter from the Hotel and Restaurant Employees' Union. Not surprisingly, the union faced insurmountable opposition, and the WLL turned its attention to legislative remedies such as limiting hours of work through amendments to the Factory Act. As a result of the campaign, Prenter and Hodgson 'came in for a great deal of abuse from the ladies of Rosedale.'[37] Again, this movement demonstrated that working-class women were at odds with the mainstream of the women's movement. An anonymous domestic, writing to the *Banner*, pointed to the importance of the work domestics did, as well as the contempt

with which they were treated, and eloquently expressed their attitude
to the limited reformism of their employers.

> How often are our mistresses to be found upon the various social
> bodies invariably expounding their views on equality! But how horri-
> fied they appear when the domestic wishes a little more time to her-
> self that she may be able to have a little pleasure and be able to
> break the monotony that there is at her work. The position of
> women at housework in times past has been more or less looked
> down upon by women in other spheres of work. She is only the
> maid, and we think there should be a change. The war has created
> more independence among women workers, as they have shown to
> the world what they can do.[38]

In 1919, the league participated in raising money for the Winnipeg
Strike Defence Fund. Despite different activities, no firm ideological
boundary separated the WLL from the UWEFO in 1919 and 1920. The
league addressed itself to 'the wives and friends of all trade unionists,'
and, at the 1919 LEAO convention, moved that 'no married woman be
permitted to have employment ... provided their husband was making
an adequate wage for the upkeep of the home.' Not only was the WLL
unwilling to challenge the family-wage ideal in the interests of women's
economic independence, the threat of unemployment and concomitant
destitution led it to demand its stringent enforcement. The WLL's interest in nominating women as movie censors and juvenile-court judges
places it within the maternal feminist current that viewed women as
moral guardians of society.[39]

However, the tension between a maternalist focus on the preservation of the existing working-class household and a more critical appraisal of gender relations was always more apparent in the WLL than
the UWEFO. When Prenter inaugurated a 'women's page' in the *Industrial Banner* in 1920, she rebelled against the notion that her task
must be to 'endlessly discuss cooking, children, church and clothes.'
Rather, such a column ought to examine the socialization of domestic
labour, wages for housework, and a critical evaluation of the 'good
works' of women's organizations: 'There are such hosts of things to
be written and talked about – the "community kitchen," – and more
scientific housekeeping generally – then the very tender subject concerning the actual money value of the work of the wife and mother in
the home – should she be paid a salary!!! – or dare we start an enquiry
as to the true meaning of some well-worn phrases, such as "the worthy

poor." How comes it that people may be worthy and poor at the same time in an up-to-date civilization?'[40] The structures of the working-class household and ideas of charity that guided many women's organizations were open to question.

Under the influence of Florence Custance, the Toronto WLL moved closer to the new Workers' Party of Canada (WPC) after 1921. The WLL also began to fight for an official place within the organized labour movement, winning the right to send delegates to the TDLC. It raised money for striking Cape Breton steelworkers and defended those arrested. On the TDLC, WLL delegates fought for the creation of a 'Council of Action' to reinvigorate the labour movement and urged the council to emphasize the organization of women. When the WLL attempted to affiliate to the TLCC, however, it was red-baited and turned away. Led by Custance, and by Harriet Prenter, who joined the Workers' Party in 1922, the WLL worked closely with the WPC on communist campaigns, as well as maintaining the support of non-communists such as Simpson. As the WLL reached out from its Toronto base, it attracted the more radical women who had participated in the UWEFO. In 1922, Prenter and Janet Inman addressed a Workers' Party public meeting on women that attracted two hundred in Hamilton. Inman, on this occasion, criticized those suffragists who 'after making a great noise about votes for women, had now retired and were very respectable lecturers on morality.' In 1924, the WLL 'established a precedent in Canada' by celebrating International Women's Day.[41]

The extent of the Women's Labor League's active participation in organizing women workers in the early 1920s is difficult to gauge. Only in a strike of chambermaids at the King Edward Hotel does the WLL appear to have played a major role. Custance downplayed the potential of this work and considered that employed women 'are continually hoping that marriage would release them from their wage-earning condition,' which made them difficult to organize. As Joan Sangster has noted, the WLL soon came to focus upon maternal issues, as most women trade-union activists concentrated their energies upon trade unions and mixed organizations like the Young Communist League. By 1924, the WLL was holding educational meetings in homes in order to 'reach the house-wives.'[42]

In September 1924, a Canadian Federation of Women's Labor Leagues was formed at a conference in London. Rose Hodgson and Florence Custance were elected president and secretary of the new body. The report of the proceedings which appeared in the *Worker*, published by the WPC, emphasized class over gender, pointing out that 'machine production has made great changes in home, family and social relationships of people.' Consequently, it did not consider the WLL movement 'a feminist one,' but rather, one formed 'for the purpose of lifting the women from their position of mental dependency to that of being co-fighters and mutual advisors with working men.' The new organization proclaimed that it intended to organize both wage-earning women into unions and the wives of organized workers into union auxiliaries: a task not very different, despite the rhetoric, from that of the UWEFO. Both the UWEFO and the more radical WLL represented the politicization of working-class women as housewives; the interests of their own gender could not be dissociated from working-class interests and the structure of the working-class household. The *Worker*'s appraisal of the WLL was at best a half-truth: 'Working women are beginning to move, and, once on the path, they sweep aside the cobwebs of tradition somewhat ruthlessly.'[43] 'Tradition' in the workplace, and in the home, was far too resilient.

ILP Women

Political action was potentially of a different order. The ballot box, it might appear, was the great equalizer. No clear traditions existed to determine the limits or character of women's participation in electoral politics. Not only had the franchise been won but long-established political allegiances were shattering under the pressure of war and reconstruction. While the gender division of labour placed women in jobs deemed marginal by craft unionists, and the demands of the household dictated that such work experiences were generally episodic, the ballot was sex-blind. Most importantly, if the project of independent working-class political action that took centre stage in the fall of 1919 was to succeed, the direct support of working-class women must be obtained. Noble statements about organizing women could be easily made and forgotten in local trades councils; but it would mean disaster on the electoral front if empty promises drove women into the arms of 'the old, reactionary parties.'

Women's suffrage was considered invaluable to working-class electoral success. The arrival at the polling booths of millions of women motivated by a maternal concern for the home and the moral and material well-being of the nation's youth and free from atavistic party allegiances could only bode well for the nascent ILP. In arguing for the extension of the franchise in the *Industrial Banner*, Marks regularly pointed to women's interest in 'industrial and moral reform' and contrasted them to 'the great army of wooden-headed males who have made the ballot a veritable farce by their partizan servility.' While Marks held that women had a natural right to the ballot (his women's column was entitled 'For Equal Citizenship'), his arguments rested upon maternalist ideology. The 'enfranchisement of the wives and mothers of the state' was seen to have a beneficial effect on 'the home and the moral welfare of the nation,' an effect that would result in 'the elevation of politics to a higher plane.'[44] Marks, in fact, had appropriated maternalist arguments in his battle against militarism. The *Banner* had defended the requirement that wives must sign a consent when their husbands volunteered for military service (a requirement that was soon dropped) in terms that reinforced established gender roles in the working-class family: 'The Good Book teaches that a man's first duty is to those of his own household, and no married man who has a home to maintain and little ones to provide for has any right to volunteer to place his life in jeopardy and deprive his wife of a husband and his little ones of the father and protector.' In fact, Marks argued, women's responsibility and concern for the private sphere promised to make them anti-capitalist electors, voting 'for the protection of personal as against property rights.'[45]

The ILP attracted a number of women activists from two quite different milieux: a handful of peace and suffrage activists, and the wives of the male ILPers. The two women on the initial seven-member provincial executive of the party were representative of each of these currents. Laura Hughes had been active on many fronts during the war, investigating the conditions of women workers for the Toronto District Labor Council, campaigning against the 'high cost of living,' and organizing women pacifists. During the winter of 1916–17, she undertook an *Industrial Banner*-sponsored tour of the province in the interests of political action and was described by the paper as the best woman platform orator in Canada. She served on the Toronto committee to draft a program for a local labour party and was selected in April 1917 as a vice-president of the Greater Toronto Labor Party. She also represented the Women's Franchise Campaign before the TDLC. Although Hughes moved to Chicago at the end of the war, women such as Rose Henderson and noted suffragist and theosophist Flora MacDonald Denison, as well as Harriet Prenter and Rose Hodgson, continued to play similar roles in building the ILP in Ontario.[46]

The other woman on the first provincial executive of the ILP represented quite a different experience. Mrs Cassidy's background was in the carpenters' women's auxiliary and Catholic service organizations.

Her husband, William, was president of the Hamilton TLC and treasurer of the local ILP. When the provincial ILP was forming in the
summer of 1917, it had been suggested by the men of the Hamilton
ILP that the women get together and form an auxiliary. As Cassidy
explained to the founding convention of the provincial party, the women
'decided as they had the vote they would run a party of their own.
The men folks had an idea that they could not make a success of it,
but now [the women] had a live organization, they were growing steadily, and, what was more, they had a good treasury.'[47] The Hamilton
Women's ILP was born, with Cassidy as its first president. Its officers
were married to the leaders of the Hamilton TLC and ILP; names such
as Rollo, Fester, and Madden – the most well known in Hamilton's
labour circles – dominated the Women's ILP. Both the Women's ILP
and the Hamilton ILP ('the men's branch') represented distinctly gendered forms of activity, each directed at defending and improving their
working-class community. While the men's organization participated
successfully in the 'public' electoral sphere, the ILP women constructed
their branch on the basis of forms of activity that had long tied together
their community of wives of local craftsmen. This entailed continuing
the 'support' activities of union auxiliaries. Members entertained
Brantford ILPers on their visit to Hamilton, raised money for a 'soldier
bed' at the sanatorium, and organized a 'sock and comforts shower for
the men overseas.'[48]

The Women's ILP, then, continued the social functions of auxiliaries
and service organizations and reflected the character of the women's
community. 'A large proportion of the meetings,' it was reported, 'partake of a social character which has a tendency to interest and enthuse
the members in the work of the organization.' 'At-homes' with card
games, musical programs, and dancing were a regular feature. Well-
established social activities, though, did not preclude pursuing a new-
found interest in self-education and political action. Rather, they
wrapped the new in an air of familiarity and turned an established
network of working-class women towards participation in the new democracy. At-homes featured speakers on a range of topics, including
a local Presbyterian minister on the achievements of the Bolsheviks,
Adam Beck on hydro radials, and Flora Denison on the history of the
women's movement. The branch participated in the activities of the
ILP as a whole, with a focus on issues perceived to affect the family
directly, such as health care. Some campaigns, such as the decision that
members bake their own bread in protest against high prices, could
hardly be described as emancipatory. The same was true of the demand

that married women be barred from employment for stealing jobs from unmarried women, a demand that also demonstrates both the divisive character of the ideology of the family wage and the importance of unmarried women's income to the family economy.[49]

Nevertheless, the Hamilton Women's ILP was serious about its participation in the electoral process, and when women were ignored in the choosing of candidates, Maud Madden voiced their anger. Male ILPers continued to view the women's branch as an auxiliary, and for the most part its activities reinforced that perception.[50] While women's new-found electoral power made it difficult to ignore their efforts, male activists found it difficult to view the women outside a dependent, familial context, even when praising their efforts: 'It would be hard to find a more untiring or devoted band of workers than the members of the ladies branch of the ILP, who to all intents are just one large family, so to speak, and the union men of the Ambitious City are to be congratulated upon the way in which their wives have joined the branch and taken an active interest in its work.'[51] In spite of such paternalism, however, it is important to recognize that the relatively static form of their activity masked important developments. As has been noted by women's historians examining quite different instances of female activism, the social character of their meetings was important, for it built upon working-class women's 'own distinctive culture and life-experiences.'[52] A substantial group of working-class women had transformed a realm available to them into a forum for discussion and education.

Initially, the Women's ILP was confined to Hamilton, but the important role played by women in the February 1919 by-election in nearby St Catharines laid the basis for its expansion. The provincial ILP's decision to send in women speakers was largely responsible for this development. Rose Henderson spent two weeks campaigning in the city and was later joined by Minnie Singer. Henderson spoke directly to the concerns of the working-class household, declaring that she knew 'from first hand work among children and their mothers, politics and government affect the home in a direct and vital way, and it is women's duty to use the ballot strenuously for the good of humanity.' She urged women to support the labour party because she had found an 'innate sympathy' in the labour movement 'on humanitarian issues.'[53]

Such an appeal struck a chord among women in St Catharines, who rapidly formed a significant political force, organizing 'serious and businesslike' meetings. The *Banner* commented that women brought their children to the Labor Committee Rooms and that women 'who never knew they could speak before a public audience had developed into telling campaign orators.' The *Toronto Daily Star* noted the 'array of baby carriages and go-carts' outside one of Rose Henderson's meetings; inside sat 'hundreds' of women. Through the campaign women undertook much of the canvassing and, on election day, arranged child-care in an effort to enable women to visit the polls. These women could take much of the credit for labour's strong showing. Organizationally, Minnie Singer ensured that the gains would not be ephemeral; she persuaded women activists to form a branch of the Women's ILP that quickly swelled to four hundred members.[54]

The well-publicized success in St Catharines and a visit by Singer soon led to the creation of a women's branch in Kitchener. Notably, the two local women who undertook the work of organization had never before spoken in public. Singer then travelled to Galt, London, and Peterborough in efforts to form women's branches, although she was only successful in Orillia. By mid-1920, Sudbury, Waterloo, and Welland women had fallen into line. At its peak, then, seven branches of the Women's ILP were affiliated to the Ontario party.[55]

The organization of separate women's branches, while a significant feature of labourist politics in Ontario, was not accepted by all potential members. Most notably, women's branches were not established in Toronto. Individual women such as Laura Hughes and Rose Hodgson played a major role in the Toronto party and the *Banner* noted a 'number' of active women at the Toronto ILP's convention in 1918. While not usually outspoken in expressing concerns of particular interest to its women members, the Toronto ILP organized a well-publicized delegation of women to Queen's Park in December 1918 demanding the right of women to sit in the Legislature and increased educational opportunities. The fact that all the women who took part in this delegation were married, and that the maternalist argument dominated their presentation, suggests that the Toronto ILP addressed a milieu similar to that of the Hamilton women's branch.[56] Moreover, women in Toronto often played an auxiliary-like role, as when the women of the Ward One ILP organized a picnic at Centre Island for the Toronto branch of the party.

Why then did some ILP women choose to establish separate branches while others eschewed this route? Hamilton was the focus of the movement to establish women's branches. Craig Heron has described that city's ILP as 'the craftsmen's party.'[57] This meant that the Hamilton ILP was not only relatively isolated from the emergence of the industrial

unionism we have seen in Toronto and more likely to be swayed by
Tory appeals favouring protectionism but also more likely to replicate
the well-established gender division between craft unions and their
auxiliaries within the realm of political action. The Hamilton ILP travelled in lock-step with the city's craft unions; small wonder, then, that
women, excluded from the latter, created their own sphere within the
former. These women could function comfortably only in separate
organizations, as they did in auxiliaries. In Toronto, industrial unionism and socialism tended to challenge these divisions, at least to the
extent that women did not feel excluded from the mixed ILP branches.
Moreover, a group of women who came to the ILP from the suffrage
and reform movements, and not from the unions' women's auxiliaries,
felt little need for separate branches.

In addition, the ILP in Toronto and elsewhere was implicitly conscious of different male and female working-class cultures and attempted to bridge this gap in the interests of political unity. The social
events organized by craft unions often reflected the gender exclusivity
of the fraternal society or barroom. Often these took the form of the
'smoker,' a males-only event featuring cigars and often a boxing bout.
This was not a place for women. The cigar, in fact, helped define male
social exclusivity. The *Banner* correspondent in Peterborough who described the cigar-produced 'smoke of militant unionism' in the local
trades council meeting could have been describing any union hall in
the province – so long as women were not present. When the Ladies
Suffrage War Auxiliary was scheduled to address the TDLC the men
obligingly stopped smoking, but when it was later proposed that smoking be banned at council meetings, it 'was pointed out that the District
Labor Council was supposed to be a democratic institution. Men came
here to give their time voluntarily to work in the interests of their
fellow-craftsmen' and ought, therefore, to enjoy the right to smoke.
As women came to play a more regular part in the TDLC, the men
were less solicitous. In 1922, a local secretary of the United Garment
Workers refused to attend council meetings due to the smoke.[58]

The ILP expressly aimed its appeal directly at women both as voters
and as members. Women were often specifically invited to ILP meetings
and social events. The latter, which were an integral part of the party's
activities, reflected a desire to attract women to the movement. Local
ILPs held regular socials during the winter and picnics in the summer.
The North Barton (near Hamilton) ILP attracted 200 to its first social,
while the Toronto and Hamilton ILP socials were often two or three
times as large. All followed a similar pattern of euchre or whist, 'light'

refreshments, songs, and dancing, with perhaps a speaker. Picnics were even grander occasions, complete with games, sports, and food – provided by the women – as well as an occasional opportunity to celebrate with the United Farmers. The 1919 ILP provincial picnic in Hamilton attracted 2,500; the following year an ILP-UFO picnic in Wentworth County saw 5,000 participants. All these events stood in sharp contrast to the regular activities of many of the craft unions in which male labour-party members also participated. While women performed gender-defined roles at these events, the ILP did allow, and invite, their participation.[59]

While maternalist ideology dominated both the UWEFO and the WLL, the political movement did attract some more radical ideas. By posing the issue in terms of 'natural rights' rather than maternalist notions, Fred Flatman's *New Democracy* helped introduce more heterodox ideas into an already active examination of women's subordination. 'Absolute sex equality,' declared the paper's first editorial,

> will be a cardinal feature of our policy, and to that end we shall advocate in season and out of season the economic freedom of the sexes, for the corner stone of our present social order and moral code is woman as 'property' – elaborately decorated and disguised though it may be.
>
> No reform will be possible till the woman will think and act for herself, assert her natural rights, work for her economic freedom and determine to abolish man's proprietorial rights over herself.
>
> The crux of the whole woman question is her economic position. As long as woman is wholly dependent upon man, so long must she submit to any laws which he might lay down, however harsh, oppressive or violent to her own aspirations, desires, needs and instincts.[60]

This extraordinary statement represents a substantial break with the dominant working-class ideology reflected in the organizations we have examined, although the short and tumultuous history of the *New Democracy* provided little opportunity for Flatman to fulfil his promise. Nevertheless, such an analysis was apparent in an inchoate form elsewhere in the ILP. The provincial program of the party demanded 'equality of opportunity for men and women, politically, socially and industrially.' 'Industrial' opportunity, in this context, was undefined, but whether or not it implied that women had an equal right to access to employment, it does suggest that others shared Flatman's view that sex inequality was rooted in a lack of 'economic freedom.' Given the concern of both men and women in the ILP with the working-class household at the expense of 'equality of opportunity for men and women,' this rather abstract formulation generally translated into demands aimed at reinforcing the working-class family. When ILP MPP Walter Rollo suggested that 'half our planks are in the interests of women and children,'[61] he was referring to legislation directed not at winning women's equality but at improving conditions in the working-class household, as well as educational improvements for workers' children.

The atrophy of the ILP, particularly following the disappointing federal election results of 1921, would alter the relationship of forces. In Hamilton, attrition reduced the number of those women who favoured separate branches. Many of the most active women, especially union activists like Mary McNab, had been unhappy with this arrangement. McNab, for instance, discouraged St Thomas women from forming a Women's ILP. Such developments moved the Hamilton Women's ILP to the left into the hands of women such as Inman and Rose Hodgson (who had moved from Toronto to Dundas).[62] In 1924 they formed a Women's Labor League. Not coincidentally, they also proposed to the 'men's branch' that they fuse into a single organization. The men debated the issue and refused! Whatever the original motivation for separate branches, it was now the craftsmen of the Hamilton ILP who were insisting on gender exclusivity.

As the wives of craftworkers who had formed the Women's ILP dropped away, remaining women in the political movement tended to choose the more radical Ontario Section of the Canadian Labor Party over the increasingly conservative and moribund ILP. Already, in 1921, the Hamilton women's branches had responded more enthusiastically than the men to the reinvigoration of the Ontario CLP. In 1924, three of four East Hamilton ILP (by then the more radical branch) delegates to the Ontario CLP were women.[63] While the nature of women's participation in the labour party did not undergo substantial change, those women who had accepted 'auxiliary' status lost interest in the political movement or followed their husbands in refusing to participate with the socialists of the Ontario CLP.

The London women's labour movement followed a trajectory somewhat different from the rest of the region, and its experience is suggestive of the different possibilities and limitations that confronted working-class women. In 1919, Singer had failed to interest women in that city in forming a Women's ILP.[64] Indeed, there was little active participation by women in the city's political labour movement. In late 1920, with the appearance of the *Herald*, a local labour paper, this began to change. Under the direction of columnist Alberta Jean Rowell, discussion in its women's page ranged far and wide. Suffrage having been won, argued Rowell, it was necessary to struggle for the 'social emancipation' of women by rejecting the 'sentimental and false ideal of womanhood' and 'separate moral codes for male and female.' Unlike many of her contemporaries, then, Rowell refused to idealize the working-class family. Rather, it was often a prison 'where the arrogant male, subject to the involuntary restraint of his over-bearing propensities, in his intercourse with his fellows in the work-a-day world gives full vent to this repressed authority on the unfortunate members of his family.' [65] Proletarian families, she argued, ought to attempt to imitate 'cultured' families where the wife was the 'comrade' of her husband. While such a view may suggest that Rowell shared a middle-class view of the relative merits of bourgeois and working-class families, her orientation to the labour movement suggests a commitment to the self-activity and liberation of working-class women. Her columns in the *Herald* pursued this discussion of 'Woman and Marriage' and even carried her contributions to the London Women's Libertarian League in favour of companionate and egalitarian marriage.[66]

The *Herald*'s women's page came to reflect Rowell's desire to spark the intellectual life of her working-class audience. She shared with readers her perceptions of Elizabeth Barrett Browning and Friedrich Nietzsche. Soon, readers were ploughing through her discussion of epicureanism and George Eliot's *Romola* (alongside, still, the activities of the Canadian Girls in Training). At election time, however, Rowell was less esoteric. She urged women to 'become class conscious' and argued that labour's anti-capitalist interests were naturally complementary to women's. 'The Labor Party,' she claimed, drawing from the reservoir of religious authority, 'is the only party built on the principles laid down by the Nazarene – equality, justice and the well-being of all.'[67]

Although the *Herald* collapsed under the weight of financial burdens and a divided labour party in late 1921, Rowell's seeds germinated with the establishment of the London Women's Labor Party in December of that year. Like earlier organizations throughout the province, it was largely composed of 'the wives, mothers, sisters and daughters of labormen,' despite the many women workers in the city's numerous light industries. Moreover, the new party's activities were consistent with those of ILP women elsewhere; besides lobbying and education, they took responsibility for organizing socials and picnics. Unlike the Women's ILPs, which had generally expired by this time, the London Women's Labor Party was drawn to the Canadian Labor Party, which was more explicitly socialist, and now more active, than the local ILP. At times, the new party was referred to as the 'Ladies' branch' of the CLP.[68] Whereas other Ontario CLP women had rejected separate branches, fearing their dismissal as 'auxiliaries,' London women were less fearful of this development and chose this structure for other reasons. The logic of Rowell's focus upon gender issues may have motivated women to organize themselves not simply to support their husband's or family's interests, but also to examine and further their own goals. None the less, the London Women's Labor Party was no more successful than the other working-class women's electoral organizations in charting an autonomous course for itself. Rather, it fulfilled the support tasks analogous to women's auxiliaries.

Conclusion

What gains had women made as a consequence of all this activity? Together, the United Women's Educational Federation, the Women's Labor League and the Women's Independent Labor Party, as well as women's participation in mixed industrial and political organizations, represent a flurry of activity spurred by both feminist and labourist activism. While maternalist arguments generally held sway, the extent of activity, as well as the optimism associated with reconstruction and the promise of a new democracy, encouraged the critical examination of gender relations by a small, but visible, minority. Yet, the various promises of industrial equality and freedom for women made little impact upon a sexual division of labour that consigned women to 'secondary' and temporary employment. Most female munitions workers found themselves out of work before the war even ended, and the unions they were able to build were, given the nature of the workforce and the established labour movement, precarious. Like the working-class movement in general in this period, women's organizing developed along parallel 'industrial' and 'political' tracks. Given the difficulties of organizing women workers, however, even the 'industrial' organizations – the UWEFO and WLL – increasingly turned to legislative relief, the fruits of which will be discussed in chapter eight. For women, the electoral movement appeared to hold the greatest promise. The 'political revolution'[69] that saw the farmers and labour form the government in October 1919, then, held particular importance for women. Before we turn to examine the record of that government, however, it is helpful to turn to developments on the 'industrial' front that shaped the context within which the UFO-ILP government functioned.

Part Three

EMPLOYERS' DEMOCRACY
OR WORKERS' DEMOCRACY?

6 Welfare Capitalism and Industrial Democracy

'A soviet of cats and mice'
Fred Flatman on the industrial council at International Harvester.[1]

A working-class vision of democracy, articulated in the demands of local labour councils and trades federations and the Independent Labor Party of Ontario did not go unchallenged. A strong and active labour movement threatened to alter permanently social and political relations in Canada and, it appeared in 1919, around the world. The revolutions in Russia and Germany were, of course, far off, although less so to bourgeois Winnipeg whose social distance from the slums of the north end was revealed in its image of a plot by alien revolutionists to overthrow the government during the general strike in that city. If such apprehensions were out of place in Winnipeg, as historians have generally concluded,[2] capitalists ought to have had little to fear in southern Ontario where the resolutely gradualist ILP dominated the political labour movement. Yet, as we shall see by their actions, businessmen were shaken by the events of the post-war period. The threat need not be a revolutionary challenge to the social system. Drastically altered business conditions represented a danger of nearly the same order for individual businessmen. Profits, and the power and authority that flowed from them, faced an uncertain future. It is hardly surprising, then, that some capitalists would respond to the new conditions of accumulation as if their world were collapsing. Most had never had to deal with a strong trade-union movement, with working-class radicals, or with representatives of labour in government. Who would have guessed, three years earlier, that they would face a general strike movement in Toronto and a farmer-labour government at Queen's Park? What if the changes that had occurred since 1916 merely indicated the course of future developments?

The crisis had several aspects. In response to chaotic post-war markets, for instance, many businessmen were willing to experiment with government regulation as a means of securing adequate markets and profits. Although business did not speak with one voice on such initiatives, the establishment of a Board of Commerce by the federal government, designed to bring some order to the marketplace, represented at least the temporary acceptance of state intervention in market relations.[3] Could similar measures quell the storm that was brewing between capital and labour? Or, if the state failed to establish a new regime of industrial relations, would one emerge directly from the post-war struggles in the workshops of southern Ontario?

The Federal State and Industrial Relations

Throughout the war, the state had intervened in conflicts between individual employers and unions with increasing regularity, but always in an ad hoc fashion, responding to crises as they developed and taking care not to change fundamentally its role in industrial relations. The Industrial Disputes Investigation Act remained the primary mechanism for such activity, particularly after munitions workers were included under its provisions. The munitions strikes of 1916 were of such a scale as to warrant the establishment of a royal commission, although it lacked the power to implement its findings. Otherwise, the federal Department of Labour intervened in disputes through 'the good offices' of fair-wage officers *cum* mediators such as E.N. Compton. Such informal trouble-shooting grew in importance as officials raced around the province hoping to head off impending battles in 1919 and 1920.[4] In 1918, the federal government expanded its powers, still in an ad hoc fashion, through Orders in Council. The Labour Appeal Board, which acted as a final court of appeal for those dissatisfied with the outcome of IDIA procedures, as strikes and lock-outs were banned, gave government bodies the power (albeit difficult to wield in practice) to determine conditions of work. The Labour Appeal Board, as we have seen, was immensely unpopular, and the department announced in April 1919 that it would be disbanded. This brief experiment in state suppression of the strike weapon was so unsuccessful and potentially explosive that even a vocally anti-union board member, British American Oil Company president S.R. Parsons, welcomed its demise.[5]

More innovative avenues were, however, being explored. In December 1917, the federal cabinet appended a 'Sub-committee on Labour Problems' to its Reconstruction and Development Committee to be chaired by Senator Gideon Robertson, minister without portfolio. Its composition ensured its prominence: Labour minister Thomas W. Crothers, University of Toronto professor of political economy R.M. MacIver, Canadian Manufacturers' Association member (and 'expert in scientific management')[6] Herbert J. Daly, Trades and Labour Congress president J.C. Watters, and Calvin Lawrence representing the railway running trades. Col. David Carnegie, ordinance adviser to the Imperial Munitions Board and an enthusiastic student of industrial relations in Britain, and electrical engineer Wills Maclachlan of the Joint Committee on Technical Organization in Toronto were among those later added. It was an impressive collection of power and expertise, although its mandate was vague. It was to study 'the social and economic conditions of the working population of Canada' and recommend ways to promote 'co-operation and harmonious relations between employer and employee.'[7]

By September 1918 the 'Labour Sub-committee,' as it was known, · turned its attention to problems of 'industrial reconstruction' and arranged a conference with the Canadian Manufacturers' Association. The danger of post-war unemployment dominated the discussion, and various measures from government employment bureaus to an 'optimism after the war' campaign were approved. It was decided to hold another conference, this time with the participation of organized labour. Did this portend the emergence of tripartite planning for reconstruction? No doubt Tom Moore, who had succeeded Watters as TLCC president and had attended the conference with the CMA, hoped that the leadership of the labour movement, which had been shut out of the wartime state bureaucracy, would be able to take its rightful place beside government and business. The fact that the Labour Sub-committee's activities had been 'entirely advisory in nature,' and that 'much of the work performed' had been 'of a confidential nature,' reveals both its lack of real power and its potential inability to address the growing and active movement for a substantive 'reconstruction.'[8]

For the moment the CMA appeared open to a new relationship with organized labour, and CMA and TLCC leaders met with the Joint Committee on Technical Organization (namely, Wills Maclachlan) to present a common set of recommendations to the Labour Sub-committee. An unwillingness to jeopardize this new-found recognition reinforced the TLCC leadership's conservatism, and the recommendations to the government consisted of those elements of the CMA's program that were not openly hostile to labour. Demands for increased spending on scientific research and surveys to determine the possibilities of import substitution, land settlement schemes, and public works projects were forwarded to the federal cabinet. A further conference on union labels was called.[9] Tripartism, particularly if limited to such narrow goals, would hardly herald the 'new democracy.'

The Labour Sub-committee's recommendation, subsequently accepted by Cabinet, for a Royal Commission on Industrial Relations to tour the country promised to provide labour with an opportunity to bring private discussions and proposals to the attention of the country. Given the government's record of inactivity, many were sceptical of such a move. The *Industrial Banner* deplored such 'harmony commissions,' which merely attempted to smooth over differences without attacking 'the roots of the system.' Toronto ILP leader J.W. Buckley expressed the same thought, wondering what evidence the commissioners could gather from workers too cowed by their bosses to express their real aspirations: 'To-day we are witnessing the struggle of the workers to attempt to lead a life not fettered by poverty in a so-called democracy in which a man's thoughts must not be uttered if they conflict with his employers.' The *Toronto Daily Star* praised the move, noting that 'extremists' on both sides decried the commission.[10] Such comments could only reinforce the feeling expressed by the *Banner* that the federal government was more interested in isolating radical labour than in solving the problems of Canadian workers.

Whatever the Borden government's intention, this was an opportunity for labour to present its case to a public forum. It represented a declaration that 'labour problems' were central to reconstruction and could not be ignored. Also, given the wide mandate of the commission to determine the causes of unrest and propose solutions, labour witnesses before the commission had a soap-box to expound on any number of issues. Newspapers regularly remarked on the eloquence with which labour witnesses presented their case (although *Saturday Night*, hoping to quash such an impression, considered that most of the 486 witnesses who eventually addressed the commission were 'cranks and dreamers'). Moreover, the TLCC leadership had the prescience to name as one of its two commissioners (besides Tom Moore) socialist electrical workers' organizer John Bruce who, although loyal to the AFL and the TLCC, was respected by labour radicals. Capital was represented by Carl Riordon and F. Pauze, both of Montreal,[11] and the 'public' by Senator Smeaton White, managing director of the Montreal *Gazette* and Conservative (and ostensibly ILP) MP Charles Harrison of North Bay. Chairing the commission was Chief Justice T.C. Mathers of Manitoba.

The mandate of the 'Mathers Commission' revealed the nature of discussions that had taken place within the Labour Sub-committee. Most significantly, the commissioners were assigned to '[i]nvestigate available data as to the progress made by established joint industrial councils in Canada, Great Britain and the United States.'[12] Such councils represented a response to demands for a wider democracy, allowing workers to participate, individually or collectively, in the day-to-day functioning of at least some aspects of the firms for which they worked. At the same time, it was a means of countering a working-class uprising with a regime of industrial relations that recognized that 'democracy' had become the byword of contemporary labour struggles. At the end of the war employers could hardly decry democracy, but they could attempt to strip it of its dangerous radical and egalitarian connotations.

Yet the nature of workers' participation was unclear. 'Industrial democracy,' as it was promoted in the United States and Britain, was a remarkably elliptical concept, since the democratic content in various 'industrial council' plans varied immensely. In the United States such bodies were not entirely new: as early as 1905, a Boston department store, Filene's, had a council that took part in managing the store medical clinic and insurance plan. Some plans were quite elaborate. John Leitch promoted schemes modelled on the United States Congress, with a bicameral legislature (foremen selecting the upper house) and a cabinet of company executives. The most famous plan, which became the model for the post-war wave of industrial representation, was established by Mackenzie King at the Rockefeller-owned Colorado Fuel and Iron Company in 1915. As the United Mine Workers' strike for company recognition escalated into armed confrontations, the Colorado National Guard set fire to the miners' tent colony, killing two women and eleven children. The 'Ludlow Massacre' became a national scandal, forcing the company to attempt to buy peace, but without, John D. Rockefeller was emphatic, recognizing the union. King's solution was an industrial council elected by the workers that would meet at regular intervals with representatives of the company to deal with issues such as wages and living and working conditions. In short, workers were given a forum in which to voice their grievances, but as individuals rather than in the collective form of a union. They did not have the 'outside' support of organizers, business agents, strike funds, and so on. This, claimed Rockefeller, was democracy, for 'it is not consistent for us as Americans to demand democracy in government and practice autocracy in industry.'[13] The language was that of James Simpson or Fred Flatman; the content, though innovative, failed to challenge the status quo. For organized workers, the 'Rockefeller Plan' carried the image of its patron.

In Britain, a different relationship of forces obtained. Unions were firmly ensconced in major industries, and the problem was to win their co-operation for the war effort and avoid interruptions in production. In 1917, the parliamentary Committee on Joint Standing Industrial Councils headed by J.H. Whitley proposed a system of national, regional, and enterprise-level committees that would include employers and, wherever possible, trade unions. Such bodies were established in a wide range of industries.[14] 'Whitley' councils represented a form of collective bargaining, legitimized by the state, that the Rockefeller scheme was established to avoid.

The Canadian Department of Labour, and particularly Gideon Robertson who succeeded Crothers as minister at the end of the war, expressed considerable interest in both types of councils and sought to initiate discussion on such methods of avoiding a major class confrontation during demobilization. As a former union executive officer, Robertson preferred the Whitley system, including its proposal that bargaining take place by sector rather than by individual enterprise.[15] He commented in February 1919 that '[w]e feel that organization by industries rather than by individual business is the correct method. Such co-operation secures better standardization of labour conditions, an advantage to all the parties in industry.'[16] The Canadian government, unlike the British, lacked either the will or the power (or both) to initiate such schemes on a large scale.

Moreover, Robertson's power in the cabinet was limited, as is demonstrated by his failure to persuade Railways and Canals minister J.D. Reid to institute the eight-hour day. The labour minister's support for co-ordinated sectoral bargaining also proved fickle. When the Toronto metal trades struck as a federation, Robertson declared that he was against bargaining by councils and urged the metal workers to reach agreements employer by employer. The social and political consequences of such a degree of working-class unity and the investment labour radicals had in its success, it would seem, had dawned on him. A conservative unionist, Robertson objected both to industrial unionism and to socialism. As a representative of the state, he hoped to prevent a major confrontation in Toronto without substantially changing the conditions of business in the city or alienating the Conservative Party's powerful backers. Nevertheless, the department had a $15,000 budget to support the industrial council movement and took credit for many of the developments that occurred along these lines. The department hired Toronto District Labor Council secretary and local ILP treasurer Thomas A. Stevenson to carry out this work.[17]

Its own rhetoric notwithstanding, the federal government refused to grant the new Federal Civil Servants' Association a Whitley council.[18] However, in July 1918, with 'great difficulties looming' among 35,000 employees on the railways, concessions on wages and the eight-hour day were followed by a meeting, arranged by Robertson, to establish the 'Railway Board of Adjustment, No. 1,' modelled on a similar body in the United States. The twelve-member board, made up of equal numbers of railway company executives and representatives of the railway brotherhoods, handled eighty-seven disputes in its first two years of operation, to the expressed satisfaction of all parties. The board's positive image with labour was reinforced when it granted the eight-hour day to Canadian Express workers after a similar IDIA board ruling had been overturned by the Labour Appeal Board.[19] This sole successful example of what amounted to a national Whitley council was the product less of the Labour Sub-committee than of the ability of the rail unions to tie up the country at a crucial juncture. For much of the labour movement, this was an example of what was possible. Yet the state was not yet moved to force its implementation on a wide scale.

The New Welfarism

As the Mathers Commission discovered when it reached southern Ontario in its cross-Canada tour in the spring of 1919, innovative measures in industrial relations were generally the result of private, not state, activity. As the product of the initiatives of individual firms, they were generally modelled on the Rockefeller Plan and provided no space for trade-union participation. The development of industrial councils was largely confined to central Canada and to firms that were simultaneously implementing other measures to ease tensions in the workplace and attempting, haphazardly, to develop a professional personnel management to undertake such tasks.

Employers were guided by an image of pre-capitalist paternalism. CMA president S.R. Parsons, after extolling the virtues of 'democracy,' yearned openly for a return to 'an attitude akin to that which prevailed in the seventeenth century when there was a glory and a pride in trade and craft.' Employers, as well as workers, recognized that deskilling and the destruction of craft skills and their replacement by repetitive and routine tasks created bored and dissatisfied workers. Goodyear

Rubber and Tire attempted to bridge the division of labour by showing its workers a film on rubber manufacture from 'the banks of the Amazon' to the final product. Borrowing a leaf from another institution of social control, the workers were required to submit an essay on the film 'written outside of factory time.' One worker commented in his paper that films 'of this nature are a blessing to the working man as they enable him to see foreign lands which could not otherwise be visited.' Some workers welcomed a diversion from the job.[20]

Generally, employers were not about to attempt to overcome the division of labour by turning back the clock or converting factory lunch-rooms into cinemas. Many felt, however, that by instituting specific measures, the edge could be removed from workers' discontent. In southern Ontario, just as in the north-eastern and midwestern United States, this became an era of 'welfare capitalism.' A wide range of measures was introduced to instil a loyalty to the firm and a degree of satisfaction with the workplace. These post-war welfare programs were notable not for their novelty but for the sheer number of companies that became involved in providing new and often elaborate services to their employees as well as for the 'democratic' gloss given to the entire movement.

In pre-war Canada, the McClary Manufacturing Company, a stove works in London, was a pioneer in developing an elaborate scheme of welfare that differed little from the wide-spread programs of 1919 and 1920. In 1882, McClary's had established an Employee Benefit Society to provide workers with sickness and death benefits. In 1910, the company turned to a more generalized welfare system, instituting a company store to sell commodities at cost, 'rest' rooms, a library, a private savings bank, a dining-room with hot meals (again at cost), and some medical care. Separate eating facilities 'with charmingly tinted and panelled walls' were provided for women workers. Welfarism also reached out of the workplace with the provision of a trained nurse to visit ill workers (potentially a strong check on absenteeism as well as on personal autonomy), and 'after-hours social functions' were organized. Workers could live in houses built by the company and sold to employees at cost. The purpose, clearly stated, was 'to form a definite link between the Company, the employees and their families.' This link was cemented by means of an employees' magazine, *McClary's Wireless*, which extolled the virtues of the company's 'Welfare Department' and informed the employees of general business trends from the employers' point of view. Its subscription price was 'Just a Plain Everyday Request.' It was the principle 'medium for taking the workmen into the confidence of the management on the subject of its policies from time to time.' It was also a means of reminding the employees that there was 'No Substitute for Personal Efficiency.' Through its 'McClarygrams' the magazine transmitted many such moralizing aphorisms.

Much of the activity was directed by the employees themselves through committees of the 'Welfare Association' using funds raised by its 'Advertising Committee,' which sold billboard space in the company's dining-room to local firms. A 'Sports Committee' organized teams for baseball, lawn bowling, and hockey, a 'Dining Room Committee' held dances, euchre parties, and noon-day concerts, showed moving pictures, and erected the Christmas tree, and the 'Gardening Committee' encouraged gardening and held two flower shows a year. A 'Safety and Sanitation Committee' represented McClary's contribution to the 'Safety First' movement, which was sweeping business as a means of reducing Workmen's Compensation assessments and as an innocuous way of developing 'the co-operative idea' while continuing to blame worker carelessness for accidents. Welfarism, suggested the *Wireless*, was greater than the sum of its parts, for 'it was not merely the name, or the department, but the spirit and deeds of helpfulness to which the spirit gives rise.' Conflict was ruled out of place at McClary's.

There were many areas of workers' participation, although democracy extended to neither investment nor production decisions, which remained in the hands of the board of directors, nor, in any meaningful way, to the shop floor, which remained, in Daniel Nelson's terms, the 'foreman's empire.' Distribution of work, the piece rates workers received, and even whether they were hired or fired remained under his control. Centralized management and professional personnel officers were unknown at McClary's. Rather than what Richard Edwards terms 'bureaucratic control,' with its job descriptions, career ladders, and seniority systems, all determined by rules and enforced by personnel managers, workers were under the immediate 'simple control' of a foreman. Motivation of workers continued to be done not through the promise of security and advancement in the firm, but by the 'drive method' of the foreman's simple exhortation to workers to work as hard as possible.[21] In contrast to the company's willingness to experiment with the carrot of welfarism, the stick, firmly in the hands of the foreman, governed the shop floor.

How did this system withstand the onslaught of wartime and postwar labour radicalism? Company officer William M. Gartshore was seen locally as a leading representative of the Canadian Manufacturers' Association. He lost a mayoralty campaign to the labour candidate in

1915, when the *Industrial Banner* reminded workers of the 'famous and long-continued' pre-war moulders' strike against his company over piece rates. At the end of the war, both the sheet-metal-workers' and the moulders' unions made inroads into the plant, although neither were able to forestall wage cuts in the early 1920s. It was in this context that *McClary's Wireless* proved particularly useful for the employer. Economic motivations for wage reductions could be 'explained' to workers and the labour force immunized against radicalism by repeated polemics against 'too much government or too much mob.' It is likely, however, that foremen and the threat of unemployment spoke with still more effective voices.[22]

Prior to the First World War, McClary's was a leader in welfarism; by 1920 Ontario's major employers were caught up in the movement and had implemented similar and even more extensive programs. All the policies that combined to form a more-or-less coherent strategy of welfare capitalism represented responses to major problems of labour control. Included in the employers' arsenal was a limited series of welfare measures that were applied unevenly at different firms in the province and became widespread in 1919 and 1920. These included benefit plans and profit sharing, which often predated the war, and pension plans, vacations with pay, cafeterias, and recreation plans, which grew increasingly popular in 1919.

Benefit plans were established in a number of large companies before the war, including Massey-Harris and Dominion Express. Such plans were popular in the United States, and Canadian branch-plants followed suit. Libby, McNeil and Libby, National Cash Register, Swift Company, International Harvester, Procter and Gamble, and Bell Telephone all had benefit plans instituted before or early in the war. In the post-war labour upsurge, major Ontario manufacturers rushed to establish plans, although there were some significant holdouts, such as Lever Brothers, Sunbeam Lamp, and Mercury Mills.[23] In the scale of the benefits the plans were generally quite similar. In the case of illness, workers were eligible, for a specified length of time, for a small weekly stipend of a quarter to half their regular wage, although the amounts rarely exceeded ten or twelve dollars a week and often were as low as five. The payments were small, but for employees faced with the total loss of income, surely welcome. For employers, benefit plans also addressed the growing problem of labour turnover, itself an expression of worker dissatisfaction. A Hamilton munitions plant hired 2,100 workers in a three-month period in 1916 in order to maintain a force of 1,500 men. According to James Merrick, the rate of turnover of 'foreign' workers at some Toronto shops was as high as 20 to 30 per cent per day! *Industrial Canada* was keen to point out that the cost of replacing and training even 'semi-skilled' workers was more than was immediately apparent.[24] Employees were required to have, depending on the plan, from six months to two years 'uninterrupted' service to be eligible for benefits.

There were other advantages for employers. Like benefit plans run by fraternal societies, there were measures to prevent fraud. Members who claimed sick benefits were liable to home visits by company nurses or 'Sick Visiting Committees.' Not only was it difficult to feign illness in order to receive benefits; a claim opened one's home life to scrutiny. Also, plans generally stipulated that no payment would be made for 'sickness directly or indirectly, or partly due to the use of alcoholic liquors as a beverage, or drugs, or to any unlawful acts, or to encounters, such as boxing, wrestling, scuffling, fooling, and the like, or for any disease resulting from immoral living.'[25] Other plans elaborated on the latter point, listing venereal diseases and their symptoms at length; Motor Products Corporation of Windsor simply stated that members would not receive benefits for 'sickness peculiarly due to sex,' while National Cash Register was content to preclude 'debauchery.' Dominion Forge and Stamping in Walkerville added that their benefits could not be used to repay 'loan sharks' or gambling debts. Recipients could also be denied payment for such infractions as 'visiting questionable places.' If successfully applied, such caveats, administered by the employer, could potentially act as a check on working-class behaviour far beyond the confines of the plant. Even complying with these conditions was no guarantee of payment, for members had no automatic claim on funds. Employers stated in writing that participation in a benefit plan implied no contract between the company and the worker.[26]

Early plans were generally non-contributory and presented as an example of employer largesse. Sir William J. Gage made a display of $5,000 to establish a benefit scheme at his publishing house. More often, however, employers decided that the plans would be more effective if workers had a 'proprietary' interest in them, thereby avoiding the demoralizing effects of charity. Moreover, as S.R. Parsons felt (quite probably mistakenly), under contributory plans there would be 'no malingering, as it was a matter of self-interest on the part of the workmen to see that their fellow workers were careful.' Contributions varied considerably from between one to six dollars a year. Contributory plans also lent themselves to employee participation, and benefit associations were often managed by workers.[27] Such bodies were precursors of more elaborate industrial councils, which administered a range of welfare measures in many companies.

A feature of such associations was the exclusion of immigrant workers, as in the case of International Harvester, or of women, as was the policy at Goodyear. Companies were primarily interested in securing the loyalty of a core of Canadian- or British-born skilled workers. A different tack was taken with immigrants and women. In the latter instance, benefit plans contrast with other elements of welfarism, which were often specifically targeted at women.[28]

A corollary of the benefit association was the commercial group-insurance plan, a type of benefit that spread rapidly after the war among companies unwilling, or too small, to establish benefit plans. In general, group insurance covered death and permanent disability with benefits increasing according to length of service. The *Financial Post*, recognizing a new opportunity for insurance companies, pointed to the 'unrest in labour circles' and argued that the plans fulfilled many of the same goals as benefit associations: 'Group insurance has been adopted by a great many firms for the purpose of reducing labor turnover, to create a spirit of co-operation between employer and worker, and to interest the man's family as well in the industry.'[29] An Ontario Department of Labour official similarly noted in 1923 that employers who had implemented group-insurance policies 'during the difficult years since 1919 regard it as an important factor in stabilizing labour and improving the general attitude of employees to their work.' The 'cost of migratory labour,' she noted, was particularly reduced.[30]

The first significant profit-sharing plan in the United States was directly related to industrial militance. Procter and Gamble introduced the scheme in 1887 after being hit by no less than fourteen strikes in a single year. The best-known plan was Henry Ford's 'five-dollar day' established in Detroit in 1914. Married male workers who proved diligent at work and convinced company 'sociological investigators' that their home life reflected habits of sobriety, cleanliness, and thrift, were paid well in excess of the general wage. In Windsor, Ford followed suit in 1915, paying four dollars per day, still substantially above the industry standard. The rate was raised to six dollars in 1919 in response to an organizing drive by the machinists' union. Although Stelco's profit-sharing scheme dated from 1913, reconstruction saw a wave of new plans. Major employers such as Willys-Overland, Imperial Oil, General Motors, and International Harvester all established profit sharing in 1919 or 1920, as did the department stores Eaton's and Simpson's. The plan established at Yale and Towne, which had a plant in St Catharines, also only included workers with ten years' service, although the requirement was dropped to five years in 1924. Profit sharing became so popular in the post-war crisis that a Brantford department store jumped on the bandwagon not by changing its employment policies, but by advertising its 1919 spring sale as 'The May Profit Sharing Event.'[31]

As the Mathers Commission determined in its examination of the plan at Procter and Gamble, profit sharing had little to do with profits. Like the well-established practice of paying bonuses, profit sharing was tied to punctuality and efficient production, although with an added ideological benefit to the employer. The firm's profitability and labour's profit shares, it was alleged, were directly linked to the effort and care expended by individual workers on the shop floor. Often payment was made in the form of shares in the company at widespread intervals to prevent turnover. Business magazines voiced some wariness about stock-distribution plans. If stock prices declined, workers would be disinclined to value such a form of remuneration. Workers might even wish to dump their stock, severing the special tie to the employer. Procter and Gamble went to great lengths to prevent this. Employees received special 'profit sharing stock,' held in trust by the company, which paid a regular dividend regardless of the profitability of the firm. As royal commissioners Tom Moore and John Bruce commented, the Procter and Gamble plan amounted to a deferred wage, withheld pending a long-term display of employee loyalty.[32]

Pension plans had been implemented by a few employers, particularly the railways, as a method of retaining long-term employees. The vast majority of Canadian workers had no access to pensions, unless they were fortunate enough to have impressed a particularly generous employer, and old age meant living on meagre savings or relying on the support of sons and daughters. Following the introduction of a pension plan by the giant meat-packer Swift's, in August 1916, the idea spread rapidly to a number of large firms. As instruments of control, pensions far surpassed earlier schemes. While a worker could hope to avoid sickness or early death, old age inexorably approached. The uncertainties of regular employment for workers past their prime enabled companies to hold advancing age over employees' heads in a systematic fashion. In order to be eligible for a pension, at least ten years of service and, more likely, twenty or twenty-five years were required. Given the rates of turnover as well as of dismissal and injury, few workers would ever qualify. Moreover, eligible pensioners required not only long service but a record of unblemished loyalty to the company. Even after retirement, Bell employees could lose their pensions for 'anything ... prejudicial to the interests of the Company.' At Canadian Westinghouse, the amount of the pension was determined by three factors: wage level, length of service, and '[t]he character and quality of that service.' Pension plans generally carried the same caveat as benefit plans, pointing out that no contract existed between the employee and the company.[33] The final decision remained, as it always had, with the employer.

Most ominously, pension plans were a weapon against strikes. To confirm this, workers did not need to peruse the rules and regulations of their plan; they needed only to remember the Grand Trunk strike of 1910 when striking workers lost their pension rights. In 1916 CPR freight handlers struck for less than a week, won a 10 per cent raise, but lost the pensions to which they had contributed.[34] Events like this, and the fear of an old age spent in penury, drove unions and labour parties to demand government old-age pensions.

Organized labour's attitude to company pensions was forcefully spelled out by the *Industrial Banner* when the Swift Company offered its scheme in 1916. Citing Upton Sinclair's dramatic portrayal of the industry in *The Jungle*, Marks questioned how many workers could meet the twenty-five year service requirement. 'Not one man nor woman out of twenty can stand the fearful pace that the packing companies with their infinitesimal division of labor, drive their employees for twenty-five years. The old-age pension announced by this company depends purely upon the good will and the whims of the company. The great mass of the men and women that might attempt to reach the prize, will be worn out and thrown on the scrap heap long before they would be entitled to it.' It was hardly a sufficient return for abandoning 'all personal independence and opportunities to drive better bargains in the sale of their labor power.'[35]

Vacations with pay were an even more elusive dream and were less popular among employers. Canadian National Carbon, the Harris Abattoir, and Western Clock all claimed to offer a week's vacation with pay after five years. A few other companies stipulated shorter periods, but the list of major employers not doing so included some 'welfare' firms active in other areas such as British American Oil, Lever Brothers, Sunbeam, and General Motors. The report of an advisory committee to the federal cabinet on such matters in Toronto left little room for doubt: 'No instance was observed where day workers or piece workers received holidays with pay.' At Plymouth Cordage in Welland, for instance, only office workers received vacation with pay. This was the case despite the premonition of an American official of the company that 'With labor crying for democracy, capital must go part way or face revolution.'[36]

Benefit plans, profit sharing, and pensions did not promise a fast return on investment and were matched by more visible displays of concern for workers' well being. Companies competed with each other in finding exactly those measures that could, in a cost-effective manner, convince workers of the good intentions of their bosses. Various means were found to assist employees, from McClary's tradition of sending flowers to ill workers to American Cyanamid's practice of giving financial or legal advice to its workers in Niagara Falls. Goodyear Rubber and Tire offered a home-locating service.[37]

Most common were plant cafeterias, offering cheap meals or free coffee and tea. In some instances, these would consist of little more than a canteen operated by the YMCA. The Rudd Paper Box Company provided tea and soup to its workers for a token three cents. At the Massey-Harris cafeteria, 'a good dinner may be secured for 25 or 30 cents, a sixty-five-cent meal at the works being better than that which is to be secured at a down-town restaurant at $1.65.' At the new Canadian General Electric Plant in Toronto, which boasted that '[e]very convenience has been furnished for the employees,' the cafeteria was offered as a prime example. Wrigley's boasted that it employed a professional dietitian. With an eye to industrial-relations trends, and to marketing, McClary's responded by advertising its fully equipped factory kitchens to other employers as 'man power re-creating Welfare Kitchen[s].' Their advertisements added that their 'experience in welfare work' was similarly available to clients.[38]

Dining-rooms offered other possibilities. They provided a space for employees to enjoy the piano or even establish a company orchestra. Sunbeam Lamp workers could not only dance to the company orchestra at lunch time but also compete in Charleston contests. Evening dances and drama and glee clubs abounded. As a variation on a theme, and perhaps reflecting the ethnic background of the workers, Canadian Shredded Wheat in Niagara Falls had a highland band. At the least, the dining-rooms were the venue for 'Card Parties,' as in the case of Canada Cement. In the summer, activity moved outside in the form of the ubiquitous company picnic, a less-innovative extra, but now touted as an opportunity for 'cooperation.' At the same time, regular company-based sporting events, which had declined during the war, were heartily endorsed. The fact that even the smaller firms had 'athletic clubs' suggests that they tapped a real interest among workers. For employers, the clubs both reinforced an identification with the firm (in industrial leagues especially, they were representing the company) and ensured that workers' leisure time was spent in healthy and moral pursuits. For those not athletically inclined, companies encouraged gardening by providing land for plots and by holding contests. Much the same kind of thinking was behind the company libraries that were established in several plants, including McClary's, Canadian Kodak, and Consumers' Gas. Neilson's dairy had a branch of the public library. Stuart Brandes has noted that, in the United States, the 'objectives of company libraries flavored the holdings.' No doubt the same held true in Canada. Companies exhibited a profound interest in their employees' leisure activities, apparently fearing that the combined evils of drink and trade unionism would affect workers in their off-hours. In 1919, the manager of industrial relations at International Harvester, for instance, felt motivated to undertake a 'systematic inquiry' of how workers spent their free time.[39]

If the plant dining-room was most often the physical manifestation of the 'new welfarism,' a few companies were prepared to go further to house their various activities. The model was the E.W. Gillett Company's $100,000 four-storey 'welfare building' built solely for the 'comfort and enjoyment' of its three hundred Toronto employees. The food products company was particularly proud of the main floor clubroom. 'The most exclusive club could scarcely show a more luxurious lounge than this with its comfortable chairs, its pretty wicker tables, its decorative plants and its general air of spaciousness and brightness. A piano and Victrola are provided and a supply of the latest periodicals is to be found on the tables. Just outside the clubroom is a smoking salon for male employees, with similar comfortable equipment.' On the floor above was the cafeteria, with potted plants, canary birds 'in large brass cages,' and goldfish. An experienced dietitian supervised the meals, which were provided at the minimal price of twenty-five cents. The third and fourth floors contained separate facilities for men and women. Other firms had similar structures, such as the Dominion Rubber building in Port Dalhousie and the recreation building of Plymouth Cordage in Welland.[40]

The Gillett building was run by a joint management-worker 'Gillett Club' to which workers were automatically recruited after thirty days' employment and for which twenty-five cents a month was deducted from their pay. The amount might be small, but, as with contributory benefit or pension plans, it established a proprietary interest. Workers throughout the region found themselves members of the McClary Welfare Association, the Royalite Club (at Imperial Oil), the Goodyear Recreation Club, the Congasco Club (at Consumers' Gas), the Lever Brothers Progress Club, and the Canada Cement Company Club. As a reward for service, older employees could join the Westinghouse Veteran Employees Club (to 'foster a fraternal and co-operative spirit') and partake of their regular banquets, or could wear the Goodyear 'Service-Pin' and claim membership in the Service-Pin Association as a sign of long-term loyalty.[41] All were recreation clubs, organizing sports and entertainments under the watchful gaze of the company.

Employee Representation

Industrial councils, modelled on the Rockefeller plan, were often not much more than this. Many appeared to be little more than a concoction of company recreation clubs and democratic rhetoric. As the Social Service Council of Canada noted in its 1921 survey of 'co-management schemes' across the country, the activities of industrial councils (or, more simply, 'shop committees') 'are largely restricted to working conditions, health, safety, recreation, education and other phases of so-called welfare work.' They also found, however, that the committees could act as a 'clearing house for grievances,' paving the way for smoother industrial relations. Councils were primarily established by large employers committed, for the moment, to welfarism: Swift, Imperial Oil, Massey-Harris, International Harvester, Procter and Gamble, Gutta Percha Rubber, Gray-Dort, British American Oil, Bell Telephone, Canadian Consolidated Rubber, American Cyanamid, and Yale and Towne. All these were instituted in the short period from 1917 to 1920. American branch-plants were particularly active in the movement, often swept in by such activities at u.s. plants encouraged by the National War Labor Board; but the fact that Canadian firms in the same industries, as well as relatively autonomous Canadian subsidiaries, adopted similar schemes suggests that they were perceived to be appropriate to Canadian conditions as well.[42]

The number of such plans in operation in the early 1920s is difficult to establish because the boundary was so vague between glorified recreation clubs and councils that dealt with a wide range of workers' concerns emanating from the shop floor.[43] Councils tended to be established in mass-production or continuous-process industries with large 'semi-skilled' work-forces. Although such employers benefited from relatively weak traditions of craft control, they also had to contend with the problems this created. In capital-intensive industries with integrated production where bottle-necks easily occurred, management found it necessary to initiate a relationship with the workers in the interests of production. Particularly in industries such as meat-packing, where industrial unionism raised its head, small groups of workers could cause major disruptions. Here industrial councils had more on their agendas than gardening contests.

Running welfare programs came under the purview of all industrial councils. The council at International Harvester, for instance, concerned itself with trying to regulate the lunch-time rush at the plant cafeteria, planning sports contests, and discussing the reliability of civic streetcar service to the plant. Massey-Harris management similarly pushed its industrial council to play an active role in organizing recreation. Such activities led machinists' leader J.A. McClelland to perceive only a change in nomenclature from 'welfare committee' to 'joint council' since the latter had acquired a 'bad odor.' Such would certainly seem to be the case of councils such as the one operating at American Cyanamid 'at which all topics except wages, hours and policy are discussed.'[44] Here the term 'industrial council' gave only a democratic gloss to what was considered by many a paternalistic institution.

Most of these firms, however, hoped to accomplish something more by instituting industrial councils. They were interested in a form of negotiation with their employees that would fulfil two functions: improve production and forestall unionism. At International Harvester, 'Errors in Manufacturing' and 'Employes Stopping Work before the Whistle Blows' were items for discussion on the council. The Swift Company's council had standing committees specifically to adjust 'disputed plant rulings' and 'changes in working conditions.' Thomas Findlay, president of Massey-Harris, explained to the Mathers Commission that the council functioned to deal with workers' grievances and to provide a separate means of circumventing the control exercised by foremen. 'Now if he has complaints or suggestions regarding his treatment or the conditions, he can get past his foreman and can get help before this council ... and we provide here for the protection of the workman that does that.' The Massey-Harris council also functioned as a means to attempt to solicit from workers suggestions on improving production methods, although this proved unsuccessful. More significantly, the industrial council approved the rules of the company's Toronto factory in 1919, a procedure of potential benefit to the employer, since it could help to bring petty difficulties to management's attention, encourage compliance with the rules, and enlist employee participation in policing the shop floor.[45]

Were the councils effective on these scores? Whether they improved production is difficult to determine; probably not even the plant managers knew. More evidence exists to suggest that they prevented strikes, if not unionization. In May 1920 Massey-Harris workers striking against an 'incompetent' foreman were convinced to return to work pending an investigation by the industrial council, which, after deliberating, decided in favour of retaining the foreman. The real test came, however, on the 'ticklish matter of wages,' particularly when employers began cutting wages in 1921. The worker representatives at International Harvester spent 'five full days in investigating the company books' and determined that a wage reduction was justified. A jubilant Canadian Manufacturers' Association declared that works councils allowed wage cuts to be made 'with less trouble and bitterness' than would otherwise be the case.[46]

Were industrial councils, then, nothing but company unions – a mere façade incapable of defending workers? There are indications to that effect. When the Armour Packing Company in Hamilton was struck, the company signed an agreement with the worker representatives of the plant 'Conference Board' for an increase of wages much smaller than was being demanded. When the strike was later called off, union members were not taken back. In this case, the council had been used to break the strike, much in the manner of a company union. Company unions such as the Brotherhood of Dominion Express Employees were recognized as such and were unpopular. When the Avon Hosiery Company in Stratford tried to establish one in 1920 and held an election for an executive committee, the women simply returned blank or mutilated ballots.[47]

What is most interesting, and a sign of the employers' awareness that this was not the time to transgress the rules of formal democracy, was the extent to which the movement was encased in democratic forms. In their rhetoric, industrial councils epitomized constitutional democracy. As the Rev. Dr Strachan, the employee manager at Imperial Oil, explained, 'the object is to give every employee the feeling that he has the same rights in the institution as the highest executive.' As in many 'democratic' systems, though, 'feeling' and substance were not necessarily identical. The most striking evidence of employers' attempts to demonstrate their democratic intentions was the reliance on the rule of law, laid out in formal constitutions. Invariably such constitutions contained a preamble declaring the desire to establish a 'durable basis of mutual understanding and confidence' based on 'frank discussion.' Voting procedures and rules of order were all carefully outlined (generally excluding unnaturalized immigrants) and, as councils had equal representation from management and workers, the means of settling tied votes was outlined. In the case of some less elaborate council schemes, such as at British American Oil, the company president served as arbitrator. At Gutta Percha Rubber such a provision was considered 'not necessary' by the management. Generally, however, there was an implicit recognition that such an arrangement would undermine any impression that the council was a neutral forum. The Swift Company simply stated that if agreement could not be reached 'the management and employees are at liberty to take such action outside of the Plan as they may think desirable.' The Massey-Harris and International Harvester plans went further, stipulating that irresolvable disputes *may* be submitted to independent arbitration. In any case, this happened rarely, if at all. As Bruce Scott has noted, however, at Massey-Harris 'management's policy was never to win votes numerically, but to prepare and control the monthly meetings so that split votes on crucial issues were impossible or at least highly improbable.'[48] In the end, the relationship of power could not be completely obscured. The company, after all, ran the plant. In the final analysis, the council could only be advisory.

All the work of establishing welfarism and industrial councils, of course, would be wasted if workers were unaware of such activity. The solution to this problem was the employee magazine. Such periodicals proliferated after the war; in most cases they were launched in 1919. Published by the company, or in some instances by the industrial council (although invariably edited by management), magazines such as the *Willys-Overland Starter*, the *Plymouth Cordage Notes*, the *Blue Bell* (Bell Telephone), *At Kodak Heights*, CCM *Plant News*, *Dunlop Rubber Factory News*, the *Teller* (Sterling Bank), *Stelco News*, *Neilson News*, *General Matters* (General Motors), and *Tick Tock* (Western Clock) all attempted, to cite the National Industrial Conference Board in the United States, 'to widen human contacts within the organization and to stimulate the growth of a spirit of co-operation.'[49] This purpose was expressed in the titles of the *Goodyear Clan*, the *Studebaker Co-operator* and the Mortimer Company's *Ourselves*. Only the name of Hamilton's Cosmos Imperial Company's magazine, the *Fabricator*, appeared poorly calculated to inspire the employees' confidence

Although appearing in different formats and with varying degrees of regularity (the *Neilson News* was 'Issued Once in a While – Sometimes Oftener') there was a remarkable similarity in style. Most importantly, magazines gave information about welfare benefits and covered the various recreational activities organized by the company or the industrial council. Editors were careful to avoid appearing as mere propagandists extolling the virtues of the employer and were more interested, as Canada Cement executives suggested, in establishing an *'esprit de corps.'* A single sixteen-page issue of the *Fabricator*, for instance, contained information on the company insurance plan, the library, a request for comments on the lunch-room, and an article urging workers to make use of the Home Nursing Class being offered to company employees. It was also keenly interested in the personal touch and reinforced the 'family' feeling by printing pictures of employees' grandchildren under the title 'Imperial's Grandchildren.' Birth, marriage, and death notices were also, as with most such magazines, a regular feature. Company sports were reported in full, and general interest articles, such as a piece on the care of feet and the notes of a former employee's travels in Europe, made up the balance of the publication. Companies recognized that the effort would be wasted if the magazine was not read by employees, so general-interest articles and gossip were given significant space. There seemed to be little fear that some comments might be considered personal: 'We notice,' remarked the *Wingfoot Clan* to its 2,700 readers, 'that Elsie Green is stepping out with Eddie Jones, the Sheik of the fourth floor. Some Class, Elsie.' Editors apparently had difficulty treading the fine line inherent in the suggestion made by the federal Department of Labour in its pamphlet 'Employees' Magazines in Canada' that the 'tone of these papers is democratic; never paternalistic.'[50]

As the National Industrial Conference Board noted in surveying American employee magazines, it was impossible to measure their effectiveness with any precision. In Canada, too, it is difficult to determine the extent to which workers identified with the ersatz democracy propagated by such journals. To be recognized in the 'Who's Who' column of *At Kodak Heights* ('Edited and Published by the Employees of the Canadian Kodak Co. Limited, Toronto') was no doubt gratifying, and those who took part in the company masquerade dances, sleigh rides, and hockey games reported in the same issue would certainly evince some interest. But the reminder that workers who waste time when out of sight of the foreman falsely 'believe that they are getting away with something,' but are, in fact, hurting themselves 'and will never be promoted,' could not but remind workers of the relationship of power at the plant and the purpose of the magazine. Even those magazines that presented themselves as the bulletins of industrial councils, such as at Massey-Harris and International Harvester, regularly reminded workers of the virtues of hard work. Employee magazines were expensive to produce. Imperial Oil calculated that their cost was sixteen cents a copy for their monthly publication.[51] Employers recognized it as a business proposition; no doubt workers did as well.

The greatest permanent effect of all this activity may have been on the companies themselves. Welfarism, and particularly employee magazines, required administrative personnel. As Sanford M. Jacoby has noted, 'new' welfare work in 1919 and 1920 drew together a variety of measures into a coherent program to be 'implemented *en bloc*' by a personnel department capable, at least in theory, of overriding the individual authority of the foreman. Consequently, employment, service, co-operative, welfare, personnel, industrial relations, or education departments were created in firms around the province. Such professional personnel management was concentrated in larger firms with diverse welfare programs. Its impact on the shop-floor regimen was, at the time, generally limited. Foremen at Goodyear and McClary's, for instance, retained control of dismissing workers, although International Harvester had removed this right from assistant foremen and at British American Oil such actions could be reviewed by the industrial council.[52]

In the long run, though, a tension had been set up between foremen and centralized management. Already the *Financial Post* had printed American material on the 'Scientific Handling of Labor,' while *Industrial Canada* had defended the expansion of the role of personnel managers over foremen. For their part, personnel managers organized to further their nascent profession, forming the Employment Managers' Association of Toronto in late 1919.[53] The basis for a transition from simple to bureaucratic control of the labour force had been laid, even if its immediate impact was limited – the 'foreman's empire' was not shaken, but the battle lines were drawn.

Resistance

What did workers think of all this activity ostensibly on their behalf? Margaret McCallum, for instance, implicitly accepts the claims of employers' magazines and personnel managers in assuming that such measures played an important role in the 'continued business dominance' that marked the 1920s. But did workers accept them as acceptable alternatives to unionism? Did they believe the rhetoric of 'democracy' in which they were delivered? Answering these questions requires an examination of their role within the specific crisis of post-war Ontario, where employers scrambled to counter demands for industrial unions and an expanded democracy. The concentration of these efforts in the two years following the armistice (at least until the emergence of the CIO in the 1930s) is not clear from McCallum's otherwise useful overview, for it was only at this moment when working-class organization, industrially and politically, threatened to evade the bounds of the individual firm.[54] How did workers respond to employers' attempts to de-organize them as a class?

In most cases, southern Ontario workers appeared to respond pragmatically, partaking of those activities, such as sports, that attracted them. Organized labour was, of course, opposed to activities designed to exclude unions. Hamilton labour leader Henry George Fester was hardly impressed that International Harvester held joint 'conferences of three cats and three white mice.' Unorganized workers did, on occasion, continue their fight to organize unions despite, and perhaps against, welfarism and industrial councils. The welfare system at Kitchener's Canadian Consolidated Felt Company (a subsidiary of the rubber company by the same name that held a 'virtual monopoly' of the Canadian footwear industry) was established in the midst of an organizing drive by the Boot and Shoe Workers' Union early in 1918. In response to the firing of six women unionists, a major but ultimately unsuccessful strike was called by the normally passive union.[55] Despite its range of welfare schemes and the establishment of an industrial council, Canadian Consolidated became the focus of organized labour's anger. Delegates from the union explained to the convention of the Labor Educational Association of Ontario, 'how it [the company] was posing as a philanthropist institution by providing its employes with singing clubs and so-called welfare work, in fact with everything but living wages.'[56] The complaint not only struck at the low wages other commentators had observed, but also at working-class pride. Unionists often pointed out that welfarism would be unnecessary if they had sufficient wages to buy the services the companies were offering. When this group of workers had the opportunity, they preferred to organize independently of the company.

The royal commission of 1919 also attempted to discern workers' feelings about welfare schemes and industrial councils. In their tour from west to east, the first substantial industrial council they encountered was at the Imperial Oil plant at Sarnia. Conflicts at the refinery were rapidly coming to a head, creating conditions that enabled the commission to make an unusually thorough and revealing investigation. Representatives of various currents in the dispute were anxious to present their case. Workers with opposing views on the industrial council and on trade unionism gave evidence, as did management: there were a dozen witnesses in all. What transpired permits a rare glimpse of the conflicts engendering, and engendered by, industrial councils.

The concatenation of company and union initiatives indicates the extent to which 'employee representation' was a response to trade unionism. Union organization had proceeded slowly at the refinery, although the masons had been organized for some time. In 1918, the tide began to turn with the emergence of a pipefitters' union. Then, in December, in a 'sudden' move, the company distributed ballots for the election of representatives to a council. The management appears to have made little advance preparation for a joint council. In the course of distributing the ballots, the plan 'was kind of explained to the men in an off-hand sort of way'[57] by the foremen or superintendents.

For three months, little more was heard regarding the industrial council, but as a new Federal Labor Union for the unskilled rallied hundreds to its ranks, the first meeting of the joint council occurred in March 1919. The Sarnia trades-council president noted that Imperial Oil acted extremely slowly 'until they found out that we were organizing men, and they have been holding meetings every day since then, trying to head it off.' The company executive denied such a motive, claiming that it was unnecessary as the plant had been strike-free throughout its twenty-one-year history.[58]

The Imperial Oil scheme's 'off-hand' nature contrasts with the one at International Harvester, which was presented to the workers for approval before being implemented; as well it reflects less concern with formal 'constitutionalism' than other plans, although there was talk of a 'bill of rights' for its workers. This consisted of 'the British-born right of any man to freedom of contract'; that is, the open shop. At the same time, the company announced a range of welfare provisions, including life insurance, pensions, and sick benefits, followed by a 10 to 15 per cent wage hike. The purpose of all this activity was explained to be 'purely a policy of business administration to promote continuity of effort and permanence of employment.'[59] When asked about the expense involved, the assistant to the president of Imperial Oil replied that they expected to be 'profited by it.'

Were the company's expectations fulfilled? The employment manager told the commission that the rate of turnover had already been substantially reduced. Given the brief history of the plan, however, such a judgment was at best premature and likely an exercise in professional self-justification. Other indications were that the changes tended to exacerbate antagonisms at the refinery. At least one worker felt that the joint council was itself the main contributor to unrest since it was widely perceived that it was only initiated in order 'to buck the unions.' Several employees described the council as powerless and incapable of offering them protection. As management was to admit before the commission, the joint council was only advisory; the company retained all its original powers.[60]

The council was closely identified with the company. 'The general feeling among the workmen,' it was claimed, 'is that the men who are on it [the council] are representing the company and not the men.' The initiative was solely that of the company, and the agents for disseminating information regarding it were the workers' own supervisors. Furthermore, there were charges made that one unionist who had been elected to the council was dismissed a week before the initial meeting despite 'four or five years' of service with the company. Whatever the merits of the scheme, one witness commented that if 'you want a fair-minded ballot on it, you must take the men away from the environments of the company.' Reinforcing this feeling was the foremen's persistent authority on the shop floor. The company had no general wage scale. Rather the foremen retained the power to hire, fire, and determine the rates of pay. Several argued that whatever gains had been achieved were due to collective pressure exerted through their union.'[61]

The paternalism inherent in the Imperial Oil welfare and representation plans also came under attack. Referring to the welfare provisions, one worker complained: 'the majority of them [the employees] say that they have to die before they get anything,' and he expressed the wish that they would be given the extra cash outright, so they could buy their own insurance. Another said that they would rather deal with the company through a union, even if they could not win comparable benefits, simply because they objected to being at the mercy of their employers. As a closing comment, one witness pointed to the high profits of Imperial Oil and asked: 'Tell me how much did the worker get of that?' The question was, of course, rhetorical since no answer was possible; the company did not open its books to the employees' representatives on the industrial council.[62] Imperial Oil had failed to convince all its workers of its interest in 'co-operation.'

That the industrial council scheme was effectively rejected by the work-force at the refinery was demonstrated during a mass meeting at city hall shortly before the arrival of the royal commission. A federation representing the various unions at the plant called the meeting, which attracted about half the 1,400 employees. At issue was the question of whether a demand for a general increase in the rates of pay should be directed through the industrial council or through the unions. Only seven votes out of between five and seven hundred supported the industrial council – in spite of the presence of nine or ten members of the council! This description was corroborated by a supporter of the scheme who had attended the meeting.[63]

None the less, the Rev. Dr Daniel Strachan, the Presbyterian minister from Toronto's wealthy Rosedale district who had recently become Imperial Oil's 'assistant to the President for Industrial Relations,' claimed 'that is not history – it is largely fictitious.' Tom Moore, noting that Strachan had not been present, asked how he knew this, but received an evasive answer. A union witness, on the other hand, was able to describe rather fully the manner in which the meeting was organized.[64] No one else denied that the industrial council scheme had been decisively rejected by a well-attended meeting of the oil company's employees.

Imperial Oil's plans had, nevertheless, supporters among the workers. Above all, the welfare provisions that accompanied its announcement were welcomed by many. A member of the joint council, who told the commission that it was 'a scheme in the right direction,' claimed that 'the majority of men seem to appreciate it for the simple reason that if they get sick they get benefits.' Yet council members' support for the scheme went beyond its welfare measures. As Bruce Scott suggested in his study of the council at Massey-Harris, those employees who supported the body and participated in it tended to be those who had the greatest loyalty to the company from the outset. Such a sentiment was revealed when Tom Moore asked an employee member of the Imperial Oil council whether workers would 'feel freer in employment' if the government provided such benefits? The witness disagreed, concluding that 'there might be an idea, of course that when a person gets up in years, they would dispense with his services in order to get out of paying these benefits; that might be the case with some companies, but I don't think so with this company.' Such a statement of faith never emanated from opponents of the scheme. Indeed, one council member felt that he was considered a 'sucker' by the majority of employees, and that most of the workers he represented were 'strongly' against the scheme. He explained that for real protection a union was required. Another council member agreed. One-half to three-quarters of the plant's workers had already expressed their agreement by signing union cards.[65]

Apart from details of the various welfare measures and councils, the Mathers Commission learned little more as it examined similar schemes. Company officers, and occasionally employee representatives, came to defend the plans, unionists to denounce them. Only because the Imperial Oil plan had been examined at a moment of conflict had a wider picture, one that included a spectrum of workers, emerged. What appears clear is that in the tumultuous spring of 1919 workers did not equate industrial representation with 'democracy.' Given the events in Sarnia, and the level of union organization throughout the region, the evidence of an employee representative on the International Harvester council appears credible. 'Emphatically, yes,' he answered when asked if unrest existed, and added that it went far beyond the organized workers. The joint council scheme, he told the commissioners, was 'working out as far at it goes. 'I think it is a step in the right direction, for this reason, that under the old system the petty tyrannies that might exist in the shop can be ventilated now. Under the old system the foreman was a little god, a little kaiser, in his own department; nobody dared to brook [sic] his authority.'[66] Workers, then, had something real to gain from the council. For great numbers of Ontario workers, however, this was already insufficient. As the commission was told, the council was not the vehicle to win such demands as the eight-hour day: 'Its functions are more of an advisory character.' In 1919, Ontario workers were not content to be advisers; following the defeats of the early 1920s, they might be. Welfarism and industrial representation were preferable to destitution and petty tyrannies, and such schemes persisted. For the labour movement, however, they did not represent democracy.[67]

An Experiment in Whitleyism

In the Toronto building trades, the Mathers Commission encountered one plan that was qualitatively different from the others. In March 1919, acting on the initiative of the Labour Sub-committee, Wills Maclachlan and E.N. Compton had convened a meeting of the Toronto Builders' Exchange, unaffiliated master contractors, and the nineteen unions of the local Building Trades League. By the end of the month, the parties had adopted a draft constitution for what amounted to a

Whitley council in the city's building industry. As the past president of the Builders' Exchange told the commission, 'the aims and objects are to harmonize and standardize the conditions of contracting and employment in the Toronto Building trades and so secure the largest possible measure of joint action between employers and employees.'[68] Although the rhetoric was similar to that voiced by proponents of Rockefeller-style councils, there was a difference. The workers were to be represented through their own unions. They would be free to organize independently, to raise strike funds and to debate policy collectively. As noted in chapter two, the summer of 1919 saw the movement of the Toronto building-trades unions in the direction of an industrial union. They declared their intention of demanding 'One Big Agreement' in the next round of bargaining, raised a common strike fund, and empowered a single steward on job sites to represent all the unions. No doubt the attainment of a Whitley council reinforced this movement. They had won the right to meet together, as a federation, with the employers. Building Trades League president John Doggett was 'elated,' commenting that '[i]t means a new era in industry.' For militants, industrial unionism appeared the next logical step.

Why did employers agree to a development that appeared to reinforce the collective strength of the unions? Most obviously, because of the strength of the unions themselves, particularly in the face of contractors' hopes to take advantage of a building boom that followed the wartime depression in the industry.[69] The unions affiliated to the league had a total of 7,400 members and felt confident enough to press forward towards their goal of winning a five-day week. Employers could hardly hope to outflank the unions by establishing industrial councils that failed to recognize the workers' organizations. Moreover, the nature of the industry, with a large number of contractors of greatly varying sizes, effectively precluded the development of welfarism. The uneven application of such measures, inevitable given the limited resources of smaller employers, would most likely increase conflict rather than ameliorate it. In addition, the establishment of the joint council under government auspices was the first step in an ongoing recognition that the disorganized nature of the industry required the imposition of order from the outside. Otherwise, minor conflicts, perhaps with a single union or contractor, regularly threatened to escalate out of control. In a period of rising demands for democracy and growing industrial unionism, Whitleyism appeared the best response to a markedly unstable industry – given the strength of trade unionism.

These conditions were not unique to Toronto, and the idea soon spread to other cities. In Hamilton, the local builders' exchange was less than enthusiastic. With the city's Building Trades Council united in its demand for a 'blanket agreement' that would cover all trades, the employers, led by Joseph M. Pigott, recognized that Whitleyism would only reinforce the workers' unity. The contractors held firm, and the unions finally withdrew their demands for closed shops as well as a blanket agreement in exchange for the establishment of a joint council.[70] For the workers this was an inauspicious beginning, but they had calculated that Whitleyism would place them in a more advantageous position to raise these issues in the future.

Nationally, the Association of Canadian Building and Construction Industries was formed in 1919 as an employers' organization hoping to encompass the builders' exchanges across the country. Given the examples of Toronto and Hamilton, as well as Ottawa and London, the Labour Sub-committee saw the possibility of a national Whitley council. In May 1920, on the invitation of the new national employers' association, a 'harmonious' meeting was held in Hamilton with the international unions in the building trades to form the National Joint Conference Board of the Building and Construction Industry: in other words, a national Whitley council. This represented a significant breakthrough for Whitleyism and a victory for the leadership of the TLCC and the international unions, whose credibility had been challenged by radicals in the movement. Tom Moore, who co-chaired the meeting along with an employer representative, explained the new system of industrial relations: 'Affiliated organizations and established industrial councils would be encouraged to refer to this national council such matters as they could not adjust locally without a strike or lockout course. This national body would also undertake to present to the government such measures as may be requested by both groups. Other matters, such as the improvement of conditions as related to technical education, apprenticeship system, movement of labor, also would come under the board.' Unions had won, it appeared, genuine collective bargaining on a national scale in the building trades.[71]

Socialists remained sceptical. Fred Flatman printed G.D.H. Cole's critique of Whitleyism in Britain, noting that the 'control of industry rests on the economic power of those who control it; and only a shifting of the balance of economic forces will alter this control.' Jimmie Simpson's *Industrial Banner* echoed these sentiments, suggesting that there 'is a suspicion in the minds of the workers that such schemes are merely designed to perpetuate the old social and economic order.' Socialist commentators were not alone in their observations. Mackenzie King, writing to John D. Rockefeller, praised Whitleyism for precisely the reason socialists objected. British trade unions, he wrote while on tour to that country, 'for the most part are inclined to be conservative in their methods, largely because of the relations which they have established with employers' associations, which permit of frequent conference and joint dealings.' For the established leadership of Canadian unions, and for trade unionists generally, it was also difficult to ignore that such schemes were premised on the recognition of their organizations, a victory in itself. If regional or national councils could be established, it would be a boon to poorly organized areas and advance the cause of unionism. If there were dangers, they paled beside the immediate advantages. Compared to Rockefeller-type councils, or worse, the 'autocratic control of industry by capital alone,' Whitleyism represented, as a commentator on overseas developments argued in the *Banner*, 'the first attempt to reorganize British industry on such democratic lines.'[72] In the battle for democracy, this represented, however imperfectly, a voice for workers within their industries. In Canada, the example of the building trades demonstrated that democracy grew from power. Through building strong and enduring unions, building-trades workers had won the right to be heard.

Nationally, the post-war uprising had enabled labour to speak through its representatives to the Mathers Commission, explaining the sources of workers' discontent and their opinions of the solutions offered. In their reports, the commissioners were divided. The majority, including the union members, proposed a range of legislative reforms including unemployment insurance, old-age pensions, minimum wages for women and unskilled workers, and the eight-hour day. They praised the development of industrial councils, claiming that there was a place for both the Rockefeller and Whitley models. Commissioners White and Pauze, in their minority report, condoned only the former.[73] Labour had won a propaganda victory by having a number of its major demands accepted by a royal commission. Moreover, an even greater opportunity awaited. The federal government soon announced that a National Industrial Conference, with union, government, and 'public' representatives, would be held in Ottawa to debate the questions that confronted industrial Canada. Combined with the electoral victory in Ontario, labour's voice could not be stifled. Employers responded with their own versions of 'democracy,' but the battle, as yet, was undecided.

7 In Defence of Capital

For labourists who had long railed against such impediments to democracy as an appointed upper house and patronage-riddled partyism, the federal government's choice of venue for the National Industrial Conference rang with symbolic justice. For six stormy days in September 1919, Canada's senators were displaced from the Red Chamber by the direct representatives of organized capitalists and workers. If not for the fact that the conference had only advisory powers, it might have appeared that the parliamentary veneer had fallen; the real political power and opposition of the country had taken their places on opposite sides of the house. The tendency of employers' delegates to refer to their executive committee as a 'cabinet' suggests that the parallels were apparent not only in the minds of workers.[1]

The Borden government's decision to hold the conference was the product of labour's vastly increased industrial and political weight and, as such, represented a significant achievement for the workers' movement. Given such a highly visible forum in which to espouse and explain working-class demands, the labour conventions of the Treaty of Versailles and the recommendations of the Royal Commission on Industrial Relations could not easily be ignored by government. Never had organized labour attained such recognition from the federal government. Did these actions signify the intention of the federal state to inaugurate a new tripartite regime of industrial relations in which organized workers and employers, as well as the state, were to play ongoing roles to which they could all agree? Or was this merely another ad hoc response to increasingly open class struggles? In fact, this was very much the subject of the National Industrial Conference. Segments of capital, labour, and the federal state were apparently committed to establishing such a regime. Whether they would be successful was in doubt, but the conference was itself a promising step in that direction.

Employers' Organizations and Strategies

Officially, the conference, like the Mathers Commission before it, was the child of the Borden government's Labour Sub-committee. The initial impetus for the conference, however, came from a section of capital. Shortly before the armistice, the Canadian Industrial Reconstruction Association (CIRA) proposed that a conference of delegates chosen by the government, 'representing all interests in Canada,' including organized labour and farmers, be called 'to develop common sympathies and person [sic] relations' with which to confront the period of reconstruction. Recognizing the degree to which the political parties had fallen into discredit, the association's plan was explicitly formulated in such a manner as to minimize 'any suspicion of personal or party motives.'[2]

The CIRA, established in early 1918 from the remains of an earlier protectionist business organization, was a body of large capitalists who, unlike most members of the Canadian Manufacturers' Association (CMA), had the resources and foresight to consider the consequences of postwar conflicts in the longer run. The choice of Canadian Pacific Railway president Sir Thomas Shaughnessy as honorary president and the attempt to draft Sir Edmund Walker of the Bank of Commerce as its president suggests that from the outset the CIRA hoped to represent the highest echelons of Canadian business. Its Central (i.e., Ontario) District Committee lived up to this image, being composed of many business figures who had figured or soon would figure prominently in both industrial conflicts and welfarism: William Gartshore of McClary Manufacturing, Harry Cockshutt of the Brantford agricultural implement company, Frederic Nicholls of the Canadian General Electric and Allis-Chalmers combine, Thomas Findlay of Massey-Harris, and T.A. Russell of Willys-Overland, among others. As Tom Traves has commented, the Canadian Reconstruction Association (CRA, as the CIRA was renamed in late 1918) 'did not have to cater to the smaller businessmen who numerically dominated the CMA and demanded a much more narrowly defined and combative approach to the rights of property.'[3] In short, the CRA was better placed to consider capitalist class interests as a whole than were smaller businessmen whose vision, of necessity, did not extend far beyond their own industrial trenches.

Through its energetic president, Sir John Willison, the CRA sought to assume the position of the voice of Canada's industrial statesmen. Among the CRA's first pamphlets was a speech by Willison, entitled 'A

National Policy,' in which he sought to stir his audience to an appreciation of the dangers and challenges facing post-war Canada. The tone was reminiscent of military speeches: preparedness for peace was as necessary as it had been for war. Rhetorically, Willison spoke not in terms of class, but of nation; not of profits, but of 'stable foundations [for] a greater and happier Canada.' The gist of the pamphlet's message was that a nation divided could not prevail. 'It is vital,' argued Willison, '... if we are to pass safely through the period of reconstruction that good relations should exist between employers and employees.' This was not the time for a business offensive against labour, but for 'permanent councils of conciliation.' Referring to the Whitley Report in Britain and to the Rockefeller councils, he stressed that 'organized co-operation' was of national importance. Willison's reference to the great 'statesman' Samuel Gompers indicated that there was a place for trade unions in the CRA's national vision.[4]

The CRA viewed its task as multifaceted. The maintenance of tariff protection, the encouragement of scientific research, the aggressive development of world markets for Canadian products, and the re-establishment of returning soldiers all figured on its agenda. However, as Willison confided to Frank Beer in the summer of 1918, industrial conflict was the greatest threat facing post-war Canada. But a solution was at hand through co-operation with conservative union leaders. 'I am more concerned at the moment,' he declared,

> over the relations between capital and labor than over the return of the soldiers or the industrial outlook. To-day I have had a long talk to one of the sanest of the labor leaders. He is more apprehensive than we are and is convinced that his own class will suffer most if something like order and stability is not established. I tried him out with a wage board and industrial councils and we were able to agree upon a policy which carries my judgement and, I think, will carry yours when I can state the case to you. It is true, as you say, that the present machinery for adjusting disputes incites unrest and trouble.[5]

Such well-founded apprehension guided the work of the association during the first difficult year following the armistice. The events of that year did little to calm Willison's fears, and after the Ontario election he still felt that '[i]f we lose Labor the industrial system of this country cannot survive.' The CRA was guided by Willison's feeling that to fight labour openly would be 'suicide.'[6]

Despite some interest in the CRA's proposal for an industrial conference, the federal government was not, initially, willing to risk placing itself in the midst of class battles by initiating a conference of capital and labour. The matter, then, was temporarily laid to rest. The explosive spring of 1919 and the problem of the fate of the Mathers Commission recommendations, however, forced the cabinet to reassess its attitude. In the closing speech from the throne on 7 July, the government, '[h]aving regard to the necessity of avoiding industrial disturbance,' called the conference to commence on 15 September.[7]

Invitations to the conference, as well as the agenda, were left largely in the hands of the CMA and the TLCC, who chose seventy-two and seventy-nine delegates respectively. A further thirty members of a 'third group' named by Gideon Robertson included the members of the Labour Sub-committee and the Mathers Commission, as well as various 'interested' parties such as Mackenzie King and Willison. The government's major role, besides initiating the conference, was to set the terms of the discussion. A message from the prime minister reminded delegates of the crushing federal deficit arising from the war and the importance of 'constantly increasing production' in order to win and hold world markets. Borden expressed his approval for those segments of capital and labour that were willing to co-operate, suggesting that union recognition and the promise of 'inviolate and unbroken agreements' were achievable trade-offs. Like Willison, Borden felt that an overt open-shop drive would only undermine those conservative unions that had a history of standing by their agreements. Other opening addresses were made by Mackenzie King, who repeated the themes of his recently published book, *Industry and Humanity*, that management and community were as much party to industry as capital and labour, by David Carnegie, who spoke on Whitleyism, and by Jett Lauck of the American National War Labor Board. In one way or another, all encouraged co-operation in the interest of a wider national good. To ensure that the alternative was not forgotten, the delegates were treated to a showing of the motion picture *The World Aflame*.[8]

The labour delegation at the National Industrial Conference was reminiscent of the conference of eighty international union leaders that had met in June 1917 to prepare a response to the pending introduction of conscription. No broad discussion had taken place in the labour movement in preparation for the conference and Tom Moore and Paddy Draper had carefully attempted to choose delegates in their own conservative image. Not only were the One Big Union and the Canadian Federation of Labour ignored, but socialists within the TLCC were mostly excluded by the limitation of representation to one delegate per international union. Consequently, large, militant unions such as the machinists and butcher workers were limited to a single representative. Radical Toronto machinists felt that delegates 'should have been nominated and elected in a democratic manner by the rank and file.' Both the London and Toronto trades councils echoed this sentiment, the latter passing a motion of censure.[9]

The labour delegates at Ottawa represented the 'sane' leaders Willison had referred to in his letter to Beer. If a new regime of 'cooperation' was to emerge, it would be with this segment of the labour movement at the expense of the radicals. As a Winnipeg delegate reminded the employers present, 'you have here to-day the moderates; you have not the extremists.' Tom Moore was explicit. The international unions, he declared, had 'stood as the bulwark' against radicalism and the OBU over the course of the past year.[10]

Unlike the CRA, most employer delegates were not at all convinced that such a new industrial relations regime was necessary or desirable. Even before the conference began Borden received comments like that from C.H. Carlisle of Goodyear Tire that it was his 'personal opinion the best method does not lie through organized labor as it operates today.'[11] The CMA's attitude was evident in the advisers it consulted. James A. Emery, counsel for the National Association of Manufacturers, was summoned from Washington. From 1903, the NAM had been identified with the open-shop movement and 'the crusade against unionism' in the United States. Emery himself was known in Canada for a 1906 speech to the Empire Club in Toronto on the 'evils of modern radicalism.'[12]

Predictably, given its identification with the NAM (the September 1919 issue of the CMA's magazine *Industrial Canada* carried the 'Declaration of Labor Principles of the National Association Of Manufacturers'), the employer delegation was willing to make few compromises. It was willing to concede a minimum wage law 'if necessary,' but only 'with respect to women and minors.' Men would have to continue to take their chances in a free labour market. On all other recommendations of the Mathers Commission the employers maintained a fierce opposition. The proposals concerning old-age pensions and sickness and unemployment insurance, the employers argued, were far too complex to be decided at the conference. Toronto garment industry employer and CMA vice-president John S. McKinnon was merely blunter than most when he launched into a tirade against international unionism and demanded to know why the company union at Dominion Express was not present. The eight-hour day, which many of the Toronto employers had successfully beat back in the spring, was naturally summarily dismissed. And, except from building-trades employers, Whitleyism received an icy reception. As the Rev. Dr Strachan told the conference, Imperial Oil had 'the right kind of collective bargaining.'[13]

Superficially, the employers' attitudes seemed to diverge from the actions of at least some industrial capitalists in establishing 'progressive' welfare and representation schemes in their own industries. The contradiction, however, was more apparent than real. Their primary concern in both areas was the containment of the developing working-class cohesion they saw around them. In general, employers were wary of appearing undemocratic and readily claimed that they accepted workers' rights to organize, to bargain collectively, and to participate in joint industrial councils. They recognized these as rights of groups of workers who worked for a single employer, not as class rights. Therefore, when considering the Mathers Commission proposal that employees have the right to collective bargaining, their position was to 'Accept so far as the plant, the individual unit of production, is concerned. Oppose, if attempt is made to extend beyond individual plant.'[14] This was essentially the attitude the Toronto Employers' Association adopted when confronted with the demands of the Metal Trades Council that its federation be recognized. Employers appreciated the power that the growing movement for industrial unionism through amalgamation of craft unions and the push for sectoral bargaining held for workers.

Their strategy at the conference was consistent with this concern. Their goal was to undermine working-class organization ideologically. The effort employers placed on denying that workers were a class, and as such had common interests, reflects their own preoccupation with a growing proletarian class consciousness. The eight-hour day, for instance, was an occupational, not a class, concern. CMA past president S.R. Parsons explained: 'In some industries men can work for long hours, in others for only short hours; and when we begin to legislate and definitely set a time for every industry in the country, I think we are making a very great mistake.' Moreover, added C.H. Carlisle, workers hardly acted as a class, and he pointed to the 'conflicting purposes and demands' of the TLCC, the Canadian Federation of Labour, and the OBU, as well as the unorganized worker who has 'the God-given right to sell his labour where he chooses.' By denying the existence of class interests and making the firm the focus of identification, employers could dismiss unions as undemocratic and uninformed interlopers. Speaking of the Imperial Oil scheme, the Rev. Dr Strachan could ask: 'Is that [scheme] not Canadian? Is it not democratic? Is that not according to the very genius of our country – that where we are dealing with our own affairs we know our own conditions better than outsiders?' Referring to unions, he claimed that a 'third party does not know the business, does not understand our business.'[15] 'Our' business was a private relationship between employer and employee; classes did not exist.

A. Monro Grier, a lawyer representing the electrical industry, denied that those seated on opposite sides of the senate chamber were in opposing camps, declaring that 'I am a labourer and have always been a labourer ...' John S. McKinnon, hoping to appeal to a common interest in rising industrial productivity, 'thought ... that this whole assembly might well rise and sing, "Blest be the tie that binds." ' Exhorting the labour delegates not to think in collective terms, Carlisle opined that '[e]xperience and history conclusively prove that great combinations or organizations whose object is selfish and personal have operated to the detriment of society.' He likened great combinations of capital or labour to the regimes of Louis XIV, Napoleon, and the Kaiser.[16]

All this represented a deeply felt individualism and faith in their own accomplishments. But, equally, it was an acknowledgment that individualist premises were being challenged by a growing working-class feeling – articulated in deed as in word – that democracy was consistent with, and even required, collective action. Unions and working-class parties, growing numbers of workers felt, were necessary to overcome the imbalance of power in the workplace and in society. In this debate, the CMA was on the defensive. The *Financial Post*'s observation that labour delegates outshone their opponents in debate was a recognition that, for the moment, capital was unable to challenge effectively the political initiative that remained with labour. It also appeared as a belated acknowledgment of the strength of working-class autodidactic traditions in political economy and public speaking. Nevertheless, they claimed, the employers had the cold, hard, economic facts on their side.[17]

A corollary to all this was the CMA's opposition to state welfarism and regulation of industrial relations. Trying to turn labourist arguments that the Grits and Tories were the defenders of capitalist privilege against the employee delegates, employer John R. Shaw expressed a general opposition to 'labour' laws, asking, '[w]hy should we have class legislation in this country?' Not only would social legislation increase the cost of labour, but also labour legislation, and particularly the official recognition of unions through Whitley councils, would encourage working-class self-identification and make it difficult to roll back the organizational gains of labour during the expected industrial depression. Such tripartite schemes were inconsistent with the CMA's attempt to atomize the working class by stubbornly refusing to recognize interests beyond the level of the individual firm. From this perspective, Whitleyism was particularly to be discouraged. The CMA had responded immediately to the publication of the Whitley Report in Britain, declaring that such a plan was impractical in a large and decentralized country such as Canada. And it blocked any attempt by the government to hold a second National Industrial Conference in the future. The regularization of such an institution could only serve as a highly visible forum for labour's demands and provide a focus for national working-class organizing. The TLCC leadership, enthralled with such high-level recognition, dedicated itself to this project, but with little success.[18]

The CMA's role at the conference only fixed the association more firmly in the eyes of the labour movement as the general staff of reactionary business. The lessons of the pre-war workmen's compensation campaign had been reinforced. As R.H. Hessel of the London TLC had told the Mathers Commission, 'Statements have been freely made among the workers that they think it is a condition brought about by the Manufacturers Association, as a general thing – that they have brought pressure to bear upon these people [local manufacturers] not to give way to their workers.' The praise the Toronto CMA chairman heaped on the local Employers' Association confirmed labour's view of the association. And the CMA's denunciation of the labour clauses of the Treaty of Versailles placed it in opposition to what the labour movement had come to consider as a key aspect of the Allies' victory.[19]

Moreover, the CMA had been busy. Like labour, capitalists were organizing at an extraordinary pace. The association moved outside its traditional Toronto-Hamilton base and established branches in Brantford, Niagara Falls, Ottawa, London, Peterborough, Windsor, and Owen Sound, as well as a large regional branch in South Waterloo and Kitchener as part of a provincial division of the CMA. Much of this activity went on outside the CMA as well, as a number of new provincial and national employers' associations were formed in various industries. Such organizations were concerned with volatile trade conditions, but no less with labour relations.[20]

The CMA was not entirely unwilling to take a conciliatory stance – on its own terms – and was effusive in its praise of Hamilton employers who had participated in a 'roundtable' discussion at the request of local labour leaders. In February 1919, six employers from Canada Steel Goods, Canadian Westinghouse, Stelco, International Harvester, Dominion Steel Foundries and Frost Steel and Wire met with an equal number of leaders of the local trades council. The event was particularly gratifying to employers. Because the meeting was private, labour leaders were given no platform to speak to a wider audience and the discussion that took place appears to have been on the employers' terms. According to the Hamilton *Spectator*, 'it was clearly evidenced to those present that the interests of capital and labor are identical and each cannot get along without the other.' Employers were able to push their 'Made-in-Canada' campaign and were open to the suggestion made by the labour representatives 'that a closer co-operation between employer and employe should be arranged for by having the management give direct personal assistance in adjusting difficulties in their own plant.'[21] Such a vague proposal was unobjectionable, particularly as it accepted the individual firm as the appropriate level for co-operation. Much of the discussion dealt with the problem of employment for returned soldiers and 'for civilians with families,' a concern both parties could share. This was the type of co-operation the CMA could accept. Safe topics were discussed, without the threat of broadening the level of working-class organization or of a state-initiated attempt to institutionalize the process in a manner that would make it difficult to curtail the discussions if they got out of hand. The CMA's Labour Committee proposed this as a model for other branches to follow.[22] Growing working-class radicalism and CMA belligerence, however, undermined any such movement.

Business was not unanimous in its support of the CMA's strategy. The association's most vocal opponent was Col. J.B. Maclean and his *Financial Post*. On 1 June 1918, in a front-page article entitled 'Canadian Manufacturers Most Unpopular Body throughout All Canada,' the *Post* started a campaign to oust the existing leadership of the CMA, arguing that 'the stupid, pin-headed management' of the association by a 'small clique' in Toronto had alienated potential allies across Canada. What was needed, Maclean proposed, was 'a $50,000 manager' to lead the CMA in working 'in unity with the press of the country, with farmers, trade unions, and various journals.' Two years later, the *Post* was repeating the same charges. 'The fact that the Canadian Manufacturers' Association is regarded as an enemy of labor is unfortunate. This attitude can be regarded as a consequence of the activities of a small group of pinheads in the organization who, led by S.R. Parsons, have

been campaigning against Labor at a time when it is generally recognized today that the old-fashioned unions with their conservative
leaders are the main bulwark against the efforts of the doctrines of
Bolshevism.'[23] Parsons, in particular, was accused of unnecessarily isolating the CMA through his widely reported polemics against the Methodist Church and its recent social-gospel-inspired call for a 'complete
social reconstruction.' Furthermore, claimed the *Post*, the CMA's obstinacy on the eight-hour day and its attack on recipients of Workmen's
Compensation as 'shirkers' only provided labour with ammunition. A
campaign organized by former CMA leader G.M. Murray for a boycott
by business advertisers of anti-protectionist newspapers was widely
viewed as a serious error in judgment, opening manufacturers to the
charge of manipulating the press.[24] Parsons and the CMA leadership
only seemed to bring trouble onto the heads of all capitalists. As an
alternative, Maclean proposed that manufacturers avoid unnecessarily
antagonizing labour and reach a *modus vivendi* with 'the safe and sane
element in Canadian labor' represented by Tom Moore and Paddy
Draper. As the 'Canadian Newspaper for Investors,' the *Financial Post*
could (like the CRA) view developments somewhat more dispassionately
than the small capitalists embroiled in direct conflict with increasingly
assertive unions.[25]

To a great extent, the *Financial Post*'s pro-unionism was simply hum-
bug. It dismissed labour demands for the eight-hour day as 'illogical'
in much the same spirit as the CMA and lambasted Adam Beck for his
capitulation to workers on the Hydro Chippawa project. The *Post*'s
primary concern, which it voiced early in its battle against Parsons *et
al.*, was the fear that the CMA was contributing to the unpopularity of
the tariff.[26] Simultaneously defending protectionism and attacking
workers and farmers was, in a word, impolitic. In a candid moment,
the *Post* admitted that it shared the CMA's goals in both realms and
merely objected to combining them. '[T]he little group in the CMA
headed by S.R. Parsons persists in the ... policy of making the Association the chief media for fighting labor – instead of delegating that
job to some different organization like the Employers' Association.'[27]
Particularly given the new-found political strength of farmers and
workers, pursuing the same open-shop course as the NAM south of the
border would only undermine the position of protected employers.
The CMA implicitly recognized this by avoiding a declared open shop
drive, but in all other respects followed the 'labour principles' of its
American colleagues.

Although Maclean and the CRA shared a common strategic perspective on the major issues of the day, tactical differences separated them. In Willison's eyes, Maclean was 'an ill-conditioned animal and wholly without capacity for team play.' As a polemicist, he lacked the qualities of industrial statesmanship, particularly in the remarks he directed towards the Canadian Manufacturers' Association. The CRA never openly attacked the CMA, although its existence was an implied criticism of the CMA. Like the *Financial Post*, the CRA set itself the task of supporting conservatives and isolating socialists within the labour • movement. Consequently, CRA pamphlets praised responsible unions, welfarism, and co-operation (including Whitleyism), and Willison toured the country calling for better relations with union leaders. At the same time, the CRA published 250,000 copies of a leaflet summarizing the 'salient features' of a United States Senate Committee report on 'German propaganda and Bolshevism under the title 'Bolshevism: The Lesson for Canada.' It also distributed 30,000 copies of an article entitled 'Bolshevism – The Poison of Production,' which described the 'menace' of the 'extravagant doctrine' and concluded with the essence of the CRA's message: 'The salvation of the future is not to be found in conflict between classes, but in the closer association of all elements.' In its campaign of 'counter-propaganda' against the revolutionary left, the CRA sought the advice and co-operation of others engaged in the task, such as Col. E.J. Chambers, the chief press censor.[28]

The CRA's work, however, went beyond propaganda. Its covert projects were even more revealing of the deep concerns of large capital regarding the inroads being made by radicals in the labour movement. In the first such venture, the CRA reached an agreement with Adanac Films and the Canadian Pacific Railway to produce an anti-Bolshevik film that was released in late 1919 under the title *The Great Shadow*. The melodrama depicted honest unionists being led astray by a foreign Bolshevik with terrible consequences – mayhem and the death of an innocent child. The *Industrial Banner* found the theme an insult to workers. 'An interesting feature of this Canadian production is the low appraisal set on the intelligence of the workers, who oscillate to this side and that side according to the appeal made to them.' To the CRA, the 'outside agitator' was as real a threat as it was to the CMA. *Saturday Night* and the Toronto *Telegram* were highly impressed, the latter proclaiming it a masterpiece. To ensure that the message would not be lost, several Toronto employers provided their employees with free admission tickets.[29]

More serious for the labour movement was the decision of Willison and a handful of other CRA figures (not even everyone on the General

Committee of the association was privy to such dealings) to spend $50,000 'in the hope of getting a satisfactory judgement at the Dominion Trades and Labor Congress ... in Hamilton' in September 1919. The CRA's intermediary in this matter was George Pierce of the Montreal-based *Canadian Railroader*, a magazine associated with conservative leaders of the running-trades unions. Pierce encouraged the CRA's work of buying the decisions of the TLCC by reminding Willison of the 'impatient and radical element' within the Independent Labor Party of Ontario.[30]

Although this 'special project' has been described elsewhere by Tom Traves, the question of the actual disposition of the money remains a mystery. The transfer of an identical sum from President Allen E. Barker of the Brotherhood of Maintenance of Way Employees to Paddy Draper 'to be used in combatting the One Big Union movement in Canada' raises one possibility. The matter came to light when Barker was charged with embezzling more than $220,000 from his organization, all of which (with the exception of a $50,000 cheque made out to P.M. Draper) went to purchase real estate in Detroit in the name of Barker and his wife. For his part, Draper was unapologetic, declaring that he had: 'documents showing that the instructions were carried out to his [Barker's] satisfaction. I am not in a position to talk as to the people to whom the money was given. I simply acted as an agent in handling it and my transactions in that capacity were accounted for and acknowledged. I acted privately and not as secretary of the Trades and Labor Congress.'[31] Draper successfully blocked demands that the issue be investigated by the TLCC, arguing that it was a matter only for the Maintenance of Way Employees. Nor is it clear whether the money was legally (as Barker claimed) or illegally taken from the Brotherhood, or whether it was funds from the CRA or the railroads 'laundered' through the union. The conservative Maintenance of Way employees played a major part in the 1919 TLCC convention by sending an exceptionally large number of delegates to the Hamilton convention: ninety-seven, as compared to twenty-nine in 1918 and twenty-four in 1920.[32] However, as the OBU had already left the TLCC, the outcome of the deliberations was not in serious doubt.

The labour movement faced the forces of capital on many fronts. Besides the CMA, the CRA, and industry-based employers' organizations, unions confronted city-wide employers' associations, most visibly in Hamilton in 1916 and Toronto in 1919. There were tactical differences to be sure, as the CMA and the employers' associations were more interested in a show-down with organized labour than Maclean or Willison, who both felt that the time was not propitious. As representatives of large industrial or financial capital, they enjoyed the luxury of long-term planning. An economic depression, which loomed on the horizon, would take care of the unions by swamping the labour market. The revolutionary left, however, was a problem of a different nature. It was possible that it might even gain ground as the conservative labour leadership lost credibility over its inability to capitalize on wartime and post-war organizational gains. Large capital, then, aimed its guns at the left of the labour movement.

Despite this, capital showed only rhetorical interest in innovations such as Whitleyism, which would institutionalize a bargaining relationship with organized labour on a broad scale. Even for the CRA, co-operation meant clandestine deals with conservative leaders or secret support for conservative labour papers, as the *New Democracy* had become by the time Willison recommended it to Hamilton employers in 1920. Even the CRA was wary of lending the labour movement credibility by entering into a sustained open dialogue with conservative labour about the nature of reconstruction and the road ahead. By late 1919, Willison told Flavelle that he had become convinced that the 'ideal form of industrial organization is ... the plant council which brings employers and workers close together,' and that, whatever road is taken, 'there should be no joint management by representatives of capital and labour. Management must be free and independent if the best results are to be secured.' Moreover, he confessed, 'the interference of Government in industry' made him increasingly 'uneasy.' Indeed, from the outset the CRA's activities were meant to forestall state intervention in industrial relations. On this score the CRA differed little from the CMA. As the crisis passed after 1920, Willison and the CRA were quick to pack up their operations and end their attempts to woo the eager forces of conservative labour.[33] In the end, none of these capitalist organizations carried through on their vague promises of co-operation. Such plans died with the National Industrial Conference.

The Joint Council in the Building Trades

Developments in the building trades contrasted sharply with this picture. Were employers in this industry convinced by the arguments in favour of a new industrial relations regime, or was their acceptance of a Whitley council only a tactical response to changed conditions, as was the rhetoric of the CRA? An examination of the history of the building trades in the two major centres where councils were established, Toronto and Hamilton, provides an interesting insight into the motives of both employers and workers in the industry. In Toronto particularly, the Building Trades League tended to view the Joint Council as a move towards the recognition of an industrial union in the industry. The first step in this direction would be the acceptance of a 'blanket agreement' covering all of the 7,400 workers in the Toronto building trades. The employers refused even to discuss such a measure.[34]

More inviting from the employers vantage point was the prospect of using the Joint Council as a means of disciplining militant or radical unions. This was apparent from the outset, as the painters' union strove to obtain a major improvement in hours and wages just as the Toronto council was being organized. The master painters' main bargaining chip when confronted with a strike of four hundred painters was to threaten to withdraw their support for the Joint Council. In Hamilton, under the adept leadership of Joseph M. Pigott, the contractors were forthright in their use of Whitleyism in such a manner. Indeed, abandonment of their demands for a blanket agreement was the condition upon which Hamilton unions achieved a Joint Council. Nevertheless, this still did not win them recognition. The employers continued to use the council, or more accurately, the promise of the council, as a means of curtailing wage demands. In early 1920, with inflation still soaring, several unions put forward their demands for wage increases, and a small number broke ranks and struck to protest delays in the formation of the council. The contractors then accused the Building Trades League of bad faith and boycotted the Joint Council until all the workers had returned to the job. By mid-1920, still with only the promise of the Joint Council (it had not yet met), the employers had won the open shop and the rejection of a blanket agreement and had seriously split the Building Trades League.[35]

Finally, in July 1920, following a visit by Gideon Robertson and the 'reorganization' of the Building Trades League, the Joint Council met. Impressed by developments in the Toronto Building Trades League, particularly the joint steward system and the league's commitment to organizing all building trades workers, the Hamilton Building Trades Council committed itself to supporting the unskilled hod carriers and building laborers who were not recognized by the contractors. Although the unions 'used up a lot of stationery in requesting a meeting of the industrial council' on this matter, they were effectively stonewalled. The hod carriers were a new union in Hamilton organized in late 1919 by leaders of the local trades council in order to prevent unskilled building-trades workers from falling into the clutches of the

One Big Union. By October 1919 the local had received its charter and boasted one hundred members; by spring, that number had increased fivefold. Rapid recruitment, however, failed to sway the contractors, who repeatedly refused to deal with the new union, until a three-week strike in July 1920 forced them to agree to refer the matter to the Joint Council. There, through a strategy of delay, the contractors prevented any decisions from being made until the onset of the economic depression. In July 1921, Pigott could claim 'that 1,500 men had answered his ad for laborers at 40 cents an hour and that he could have employed any number at 35 cents.' The Hamilton Building Trades League had organized and backed the hod carriers, but had been outmanoeuvred through the employers' use of the Joint Council.[36]

If the unions were keen to include the least-skilled workers under the terms of the Joint Council, the employers were determined that the most-skilled should not escape its determinations. The bricklayers had a tradition of holding themselves aloof from the rest of the building trades, confident in their own skill and long enjoying the highest wages in the industry. In 1921, as the Joint Council agreed to utilize the IDIA to resolve its deadlock over wages, the employers were adamant that the bricklayers' wages be included in its considerations, although the union protested loudly, demanding the right to negotiate separately. The employers were counting on the other building trades unions to moderate the bricklayers' demands in the interest of maintaining a united front. The tactic appears to have worked, as Hamilton bricklayers who had enjoyed parity with Toronto settled for a lower rate.[37] Dealings with the lathers' union further demonstrated the potential of the Joint Council as a means of disciplining an individual union. In September 1920 the union fined a contractor ten dollars for employing non-union men on lathing in violation of their agreement. The Joint Council upheld the fine, but the contractor refused to pay. When the lathers struck to enforce the fine, the Joint Council reversed its original decision and unanimously agreed that the union was in the wrong. The union members of the Joint Council had joined with the employers in order to maintain peace in the industry and to maintain the council.[38]

By 1921, the end of economic prosperity threatened the Joint Council movement, and a guerrilla war was developing in Hamilton as contractors implemented wage reductions unevenly and unions struck the worst perpetrators. Walk-outs included about a fifth of the building-trades workers in the city; many more were rendered idle by unemployment. In Toronto, when painters struck sites with non-union workers, the employers simply refused to deal with the matter in the Joint

Council and threatened a lock-out of all union painters. Sympathetic strike action became increasingly difficult as employers threatened to abandon the Joint Council in retaliation for any such action. Moreover, having agreed to have all contracts expire at the end of a calendar year (a stipulation of the employers for accepting the Joint Council), the unions were faced with a major strike in mid-winter at the depths of the building cycle.[39]

Having humbled two of the strongest unions, the Toronto Builders' Exchange was now in a position to enforce wage cuts through the Joint Council. The union delegates accepted a 10 per cent wage cut, which was, in turn, rejected by the members; in the end, wages were cut unilaterally by the employers without the unions' feeling confident enough to strike. Employers had hoped that the union delegates would convince workers to accept the cuts, but the results were the same. Discovering that the existence of the Joint Council was no guarantee of collective bargaining, carpenter John Doggett, long an advocate of the body, felt betrayed. Speaking of Robertson's role in all this, he declared that the government as well was trying to 'freeze out the building trades.' In 1922, the Builders' Exchange again cut wages. Plasterers, sheet-metal workers, painters, and carpenters all struck against their contractors, but with generally poor results. Some of the stronger unions of skilled craftsmen, such as the bricklayers, reached compromises. Less skilled workers, such as plasterers' helpers, were ignored, undermining the declared hopes of the Building Trades League of uniting all workers on building sites in Toronto.[40] It came as little surprise that the Joint Council voted to disband in early 1923. In the eyes of the employers its function was over. For unions it offered little protection.

In the context of wage cuts, the meeting of the short-lived National Joint Conference Board of the Building and Construction Industries in January 1922 could not escape a discussion of 'basic principles.' The contractors placed on the table a proposal calling for wage reductions and a national open shop with a ban on sympathetic strikes. The unions refused to sign their own death warrant, and the meeting adjourned 'to meet again at the call of the chair.' Ten days later the Association of Canadian Building and Construction Industries held its national convention in Hamilton and determined to deal with 'actual employees' rather than with unions through their business agents. Further, it resolved 'that in our industry we have found Joint Industrial Councils tend only to cause dissension rather than cure it, and therefore such Councils should not be continued.'[41] For employers, the advantages of councils failed to outweigh the opportunity provided by the post-war depression. Employers felt confident that they could bring order to the industry on their own terms by smashing the unions.

The Limits of Welfarism

By 1921, there was little to show for the work started by the Labour Sub-committee only three years earlier. A February 1921 Conference on Industrial Relations, organized by the Department of Labour, reflected the existing relationship in the country's major industries; only the employers were represented, as labour was not asked to participate. Implicitly recognizing that the CMA was not to be the vehicle of innovation in industrial relations, invitations were sent only to the large firms that had established industrial councils in their plants. The meeting brought few innovations from the employment managers in attendance, but it did signal a significant shift in their concerns. The main opposition to the establishment of industrial councils had ceased to be the organized labour movement, although the vice-president of Gray-Dort Motors in Chatham noted, this was still a factor. Instead, discussion turned to the role of foremen. George Valentine noted that the appointment of 'a slave driver' had provoked a strike in one department at Massey-Harris, adding that 'every Company is, so to speak, at the mercy of its foremen or its agents or those who administer its policy.' The official in charge of industrial relations at Canadian Consolidated Rubber agreed: 'if industrial councils are not useful for any other purpose than to make bigger men out of your foremen, they will have done much in that way alone.' F.J. Gernandt of International Harvester was even more blunt, declaring that, after substantial experience with industrial councils, his company's foremen and assistant foremen still 'need enlightening.'[42]

These comments are significant, for they suggest that employers felt less threatened by organized labour and that the innovations they had undertaken since the war had brought them face to face with a somewhat different problem. The 'empires' that foremen had built on the shop floor had proved a major hindrance to management plans in the fields of welfarism and production. If a plot was being hatched at this meeting, it was directed less against workers than against foremen. The threat from the former had subsided, but the crisis had thrown up a layer of employment professionals who now felt compelled to secure their positions, and it was now necessary to strip foremen of their power and centralize control in the administrative office. Professional self-interest and the recognition by employers that real problems of labour control existed beyond the immediate threat of a strike explain why structures established to repel labour militancy in 1919 and 1920 persisted through the decade. Richard Edwards and Sanford Jacoby have argued that the emergence of 'bureaucratic control' through 'company rules' or 'company policy' emanating from the firm's administration would eventually displace the direct power of the foreman, at least in the largest enterprises. No doubt the eventual establishment of stable industrial unions in the 1940s and the attainment of collective agreements with grievance procedures that largely curtailed foremen's powers played a key part in this development. As Daniel Nelson has argued, however, welfarism had important consequences in 'the evolution of managerial technique.' The struggle was to be a long one, but the first front was soon opened. By 1921, as the Conference on Industrial Relations demonstrated, the battle between the new personnel bureaucrats and foremen was engaged.[43]

As had happened with the ringing pronouncements of the Canadian Reconstruction Association, or the image of a new era of industrial relations heralded by the National Industrial Conference, the reality behind the rhetoric of welfare capitalism was soon revealed. Surveys of welfare capitalism in Canada tend to accept employer and labour department propaganda at face value.[44] A study of Toronto by the federal government's Committee on Industrial Fatigue in December 1920, however, revealed that the practice of welfarism hardly measured up to the picture presented by manufacturers. Measures were introduced piecemeal 'without any clear purpose in view' other than 'preventing discontent.' Innovations were discarded when they failed to appear profitable. 'No firm in Toronto,' for instance, 'has both systematic job analysis and compulsory medical examination.' No production workers in the city received holidays with pay, despite company propaganda. Lavatories, although increasingly plentiful, were generally in a 'deplorable' condition. In 'a few instances' dressing rooms or lockers were adequate, but they rarely surpassed the minimum requirements under the Factory Act, and medical facilities, often publicized by the companies, rarely surpassed the requirements under the Workmen's Compensation Act. It is important to appreciate that the authors had a purpose in mind other than simply reporting on the state of welfarism in Toronto. 'Good working conditions ...,' suggested the report, 'can be accurately determined by science ...' with the help of 'expert advice.' Employment professionals had found yet another platform. Nevertheless, the report does reveal that to a great extent welfare measures were a temporary response to a crisis in indusial relations and that in many instances employers' claims exaggerated the extent of their innovations.[45]

The same conclusions can be drawn from the Ontario Department of Labour's 1926 Survey of Industrial Welfare. The department received replies from 81 per cent of the 360 firms it investigated. The aggregate results appear impressive. The 'onward march of industrial progress' was apparently evidenced by the 'many excellent schemes' employers had introduced. Of the firms surveyed, 36 per cent (with 55 per cent of the employees) had cafeterias, 41 per cent (with 75 per cent of employees) had organized recreation, 20 per cent (with 56 per cent of employees) had pension plans, and so on. Yet the figures were misleading. Twelve of the sixty-one firms claiming to offer pensions had 'no definite pension plan,' recreation often amounted to little more than the 'annual picnic outing,' and, as the Committee on Industrial Fatigue had suggested, it was unlikely that many of the 117,402 workers employed by companies claiming to provide holidays with pay ever enjoyed such a benefit. While many individual welfare measures were retained in some form, the one measure designed to draw them together, the employee magazine, was in decline. At least five major firms had ceased to publish them: Dunlop Tire and Rubber, Procter and Gamble, Steel Company of Canada, Dominion Chain, and American Cyanamid.[46] In some cases the decline of industrial militancy in the 1920s removed the impetus behind such measures; in others, it seemed simply too expensive to continue such programs in tougher economic times. The extreme case was Gray-Dort Motors. The plant closed in the mid-1920s, spelling the end of the industrial council as well as of local unions that had survived the introduction of welfarism and the company's use of stool-pigeons to single out union leaders to be fired.[47] Welfarism had not been a mirage, but it seemed so by the mid-1920s. Employers continued to sing its praises, but few concrete benefits for their employees remained.

The Exhaustion of Militancy

Following the National Industrial Conference, it was clear that any permanent gains for labour would be made through political action or through strikes rather than by means of tripartite co-operation. Electoral and industrial action were not mutually exclusive and no truce was to be found on the trade union front in 1920. Outside Toronto, in fact, there were more strikes and more striker-days 'lost' than the previous year. The differences, however, were important. Following their major defeat in Toronto, the metal trades were relatively quiescent. Many of the days lost in the industry in 1920 were the product of unfinished battles of the previous year, particularly on the part of the moulders. Only one major offensive was launched by the vanguard force of post-war militancy, the machinists. In May 1920, 675 workers struck Nicholl's Canadian General Electric plant in Peterborough in an attempt to regain some control over the craft. As the *Peterborough Review* paraphrased machinist leader Harry Harper, 'During the war the machinists had thrown down the barriers of their trade in order to speed up the delivery of munitions and help the Allies, but since then they had a hard fight to return to the pre-war conditions with respect to the trade.'[48] As a sign of what was to follow, the strike collapsed after fifty-five days. Even this strike, a defensive reaction to deskilling, differed from the battles of the previous year. In 1919, metal-trades workers had fought not just for the eight-hour day, but, implicitly, for a new social order that Marks and Flatman had termed the 'new democracy.' David Montgomery has noted this feature of post-war contests throughout the continent.[49] Each battle demonstrated militancy and the potential for industrial organization. Through its growing trades federations, labour was showing itself as a self-confident class able to present its own, albeit inchoate, program for reconstruction. However, there were too few victories in 1919 to nurture such optimism.

Strikes did not seem to threaten to widen into class battles in 1920 as they had in 1919. There would be no repeat of the Toronto General Strike, nor even of the 1919 Windsor street-railway strike where local authorities, distrusting the police who refused to guarantee the defence of strike breakers, called in the army to patrol the city's streets. On that occasion, the Windsor trades-council president threatened a general strike; no such calls seemed appropriate the following year.[50] Employer intransigence at any hint of class-wide activity, either through trades amalgamation or through tripartite ventures, cast workers back into individual disputes of individual crafts against employers often themselves grouped into employers' associations.

Working-class militancy had not been entirely defeated and the strikes of 1920 did represent attempts by unions to gain new ground. The 2,000 members of the Niagara District Trades Federation who struck the Hydro Chippawa project in an attempt to gain a 'straight' eight-hour day were striving for an unprecedented concession for work of this type. Newly organized sectors in mass-production industries were similarly attempting to entrench their organizations and win their first real gains in the face of welfarism and unrestrained foremen. Four hundred and forty-six rubber workers, more than half of them women, struck the Gutta Percha Rubber Company in Toronto for four weeks to demand wage increases and the abolition of the newly imposed 'team system' for piece workers.[51] Both these strikes ended in failure; 1920 was a year of defeat.

The street railways symbolized workers' frustrations. In Toronto, on the strength of having won their strike in the wake of the defeat of the metal-trades strike in 1919, the street-railway union put forward its demand: an astounding wage increase from fifty-five to eighty-five cents per hour. The *Financial Post* and *Saturday Night* scoffed at the idea of paying unskilled workers craft wages. As the *Globe* commented, the 'demands of the street railway men surprised the officials of other trades unions who had regarded the union as conservative.' In a curious fashion, however, the union's conservatism came back to haunt it. Choosing a like-minded individual to represent it on an IDIA board of conciliation, the union's nominee, bricklayer John T. Vick, was apparently convinced by the employer's argument that the Toronto Railway Company could not pay the increase and that such a wage would undermine the proposed muncipalization of the road in 1921. The IDIA board unanimously recommended that no wage increase at all be awarded. Following a final attempt by E.N. Compton to avert a strike (the Department of Labour's role in industrial relations had not changed despite two years of debate), the men struck for four days and won a small raise. The London street-railway union, with a tradition of much lower pay and of radical leadership, fared no better. The company claimed to be unable to pay any more and, through the intervention of ILP MPP Hugh Stevenson, the workers were convinced to return to work with no increase in pay. Neither the workers themselves nor the provincial government (either through the Legislature or the Railway and Municipal Board) could overcome employer intransigence.[52]

While the frustrating conflicts of 1920 did little to further the workers' cause, they did embolden the region's employers. In 1921, employers declared war on precisely those sectors that had made the greatest breakthroughs in the course of the war and the post-war economic boom. The building trades were but one example. The radical butcherworkers' union was defeated in a strike of 1,700 workers against the 'big five' Toronto meat-packing firms, which diverted their production to other cities. Although workers retained the guarantee of forty hours' work per week through slow production periods, the union was unable to win a signed agreement. The international union itself played a large part in the defeat. In an attempt to drive out radicals, it demanded that Louis Braithwaite be replaced as local business agent and eventually imposed its own appointee on the local. When the local ceased remitting its dues in protest, it was expelled. With the strikers, thus weakened, the meat-packing firms delivered the death blow.[53]

Less dramatically, the Amalgamated Clothing Workers union was forced into a major battle to defend its weak flank: Hamilton. Ostensibly in opposition to wage cuts, the Hamilton ACWA strike was widely seen as provoked by an attempt by some employers to abandon the arbitration system established in 1919 (1917 in Toronto) and to reinstitute the open shop. Eleven hundred workers, 70 per cent of them women, struck and were able to preserve the union but not their wage rates. Nevertheless, the battle in Hamilton encouraged Toronto employers to sign a three-year agreement with the ACWA in 1922 on the basis of the forty-four-hour week, the maintenance of the arbitration system, and '1919 wages.' Employers, however, maintained the battle by contracting non-union shops to fill orders. In part, the union's relative success was due to its real ability to stabilize the industry. As minor disputes grew in the Toronto garment factories in 1924, the ACWA warned shop chairmen against stoppages and, on more than one occasion, ordered workers to return to work.[54] A combination of militancy and self-restraint were the hallmarks of the *modus vivendi* reached with the employers.

A corollary to the growing self-confidence of employers, and also to the red scare, was the willingness of both the federal and provincial governments to use police rather than mediators to intervene in conflicts. This is not to suggest that the police had been inactive throughout the post-war crisis, only that their activity had generally been covert in nature. As Barbara Roberts has documented, immigrants 'considered undesirable on the basis of their political beliefs and activities'[55] were deported from Canada with increasing regularity. By 1921, however, police activity moved increasingly into the open. A large show of force that in 1919 might have aggravated workers' resentment became a useful tactic against an increasingly demoralized labour movement. When three hundred members of the papermakers and other unions struck the Beaver Board Company at Thorold in order to prevent wage cuts and the open shop, they were surprised to find themselves facing the combined forces of armed private detectives, seventy members of the Royal Canadian Mounted Police, and the Ontario

Provincial Police. Such an operation was unprecedented in strikes in southern Ontario. It was even more remarkable given the lack of provocation. When the OPP inspector arrived at the scene, he was able to write to his superintendent that '[w]hen we arrived we found everything very quiet, no trouble whatever.' The federal government also intervened by preventing union officers involved in the strike against the company's Tonawanda plant across the Niagara River from entering Canada to assist with the strike.[56]

Provincial attorney-general W.E. Raney, who had ordered in the OPP, had reason to fear violence, although not at the hands of the unionists. From the outset of the strike, armed company guards from the Washington Detective Agency illegally roamed the streets of Thorold 'menacing ... peaceful workmen.'[57] Department of Labour correspondence reveals that the strike was largely a cover for a police operation against immigrant communities. A local official agreed that it 'was a very wise move of the Department at Ottawa in sending in the RNWMP force into the district, as the district has been badly in need for some time of being straightened up on account of the brothels and booze shops. What the outcome of the strike will be is impossible to say at the present time, but under existing conditions the company has the best chance of maintaining their rights. From conversation I have had with the Union representatives we do not anticipate trouble of any kind.'[58] Whether or not it was their original intention, the lack of 'trouble' at the plant freed the police to busy themselves in raiding immigrant working-class communities and arresting people for violations of the Ontario Temperance Act and various other – usually minor – infractions. Only seven arrests were made at the picket lines, all under the Vagrancy Act, for 'using improper language toward the [strikebreaking] workers, calling them "rats," etc.' Strike leaders were cowed and responded to the armed force and red-baiting by claiming that any danger of Bolshevism came only from 'foreign laborers.' The ambivalence and defensiveness of the strike leaders was apparent from their attempt to address immigrant workers in their own languages while, at the same time, declaring that they were 'glad, personally and collectively, that the Provincial Police are cleaning up the foreign section of the Thorold Township.' However, even TLCC leaders viewed the whole operation as a means of intimidating workers in a region of the province that, since the war, through conflicts against Hydro and the contractors on the Welland Canal, had established itself as a centre of militancy.[59] The intervention of police from all levels of government signalled that reconstruction was over. The freedom of action won by workers during the war and its aftermath would no longer be countenanced.

Three further conflicts defined the world of industrial class relations that emerged in the 1920s. The first of these was the final chapter in the labour movement's ongoing battle to enforce fair wages on government works. As unemployment soared in late 1920, the federal government announced that it had contracted to complete the construction of two unfinished ships at the Dominion Shipbuilding yards in Toronto. Workers' enthusiasm, however, collapsed with the announcement that wages would be 20 per cent below the 'prevailing rate'; a strike began even before construction commenced. The Toronto District Labor Council and the Grand Army of United Veterans led the campaign to restore the Fair Wage Schedule, charging the Department of Soldiers' Civil Re-establishment with supplying strikebreakers. Eventually they arranged for Mackenzie King, T.A. Crerar, and the sole Ontario ILP MP, Angus McDonald, to attempt to mediate the dispute and raise it in the House of Commons. Reinvigorated by the re-establishment of the Metal Trades Council, the TDLC once again considered a city-wide general strike. The implication of events since 1919, however, were not lost on either the striking workers or the TDLC delegates. The federal government ignored the labour movement with little consequence, a reminder of the days of the Imperial Munitions Board – and of how little had been won.[60]

In the context of declining worker militancy, the 1921 strike by the International Typographical Union (ITU) and the allied printing trades was a peculiar anomaly. Quiescent in the midst of major battles in 1919, always willing to defy general strike movements in the name of the sanctity of contract, the ITU entered into a life-and-death confrontation in the depth of the post-war depression. The 2,300 printing-trades workers who struck for the eight-hour day account for more than two-thirds of the striker days lost in the region for 1921, and 85 per cent in 1922. The union confronted the recently reorganized Toronto Typothetae, an employers' association committed to the open shop. As part of a continent-wide struggle for the forty-four hour week in the printing trades, central Canada, and particularly Toronto, became a major battleground. In an understatement, the historian of the union, Sally F. Zerker, notes that the Toronto unions 'failed to make a realistic appraisal of the relative strengths in the contest.' The strike was called off by the international union in 1924 against the wishes of the Toronto local. By that time, more than 600,000 striker days had been lost in southern Ontario. Erstwhile allies from the social-gospel-dominated Methodist Church and the provincial government had fallen by the wayside and supported the anti-union Typothetae. The only explanation of the major strategical error made by the printing trades was a fateful overconfidence in craft, as opposed to class, solidarity. Such a battle, if it had been faced in 1919, stood every chance of success. As part of a wider strike movement for the eight-hour day, the support of the large and powerful ITU would have immensely strengthened the metal trades' struggle for precisely the same goal. The conservative ITU's principle of always respecting existing agreements made a battle on favourable terrain impossible. This principle was maintained, in part, by a confidence that the well-organized printing trades could win, on their own, concessions that had eluded upstart unions. Their defeat spelt the end of the eight-hour movement, the demand that defined the struggles of 1919.[61]

The third conflict occurred on the railways. The thorough organization of the railway unions and their official recognition through the Railway Board of Adjustment No. 1, made them a formidable force. Their achievement of the eight-hour day reinforced their self-confidence and, by 1918, established the railway unions as a model to others of what could be won. South of the border, all this was called into question in 1922 as 400,000 railway shop craft workers struck to defend their wartime gains.[62] Unpromising developments in the United States made Canadian union leaders nervous about following their lead. Yet, by 1922, it was abundantly clear that if the ceaseless round of wage cuts and union busting were to be stopped, the railway shop crafts would have to play a major role. In July 1921, the employers demanded a 12 per cent wage cut, to which the unions agreed in exchange for the preservation of rules and working conditions. When further wage cuts were proposed in 1922, the shop crafts hesitated and, through a complex series of IDIA boards, attempted to delay their implementation while watching events in the United States. The railway companies, however, cut wages in violation of the IDIA and, when they could delay no more, the Canadian union leaders accepted the wage cuts. The outcome, to be sure, was not predetermined. At one point the unions had a 97 per cent strike vote and were possibly in a stronger position than their American counterparts. Nevertheless, the last bastion had fallen without a battle; the fate of the labour movement was sealed. For radicals in the labour movement, this failure to seize the 'opportune moment' characterized the timidity of the labour leadership and its inability to secure what had been won in better times.[63]

In March 1919, Fred Flatman had argued that the period was characterized by a 'reconstruction' of the ruling class. In alliance with conservative union leaders, intellectuals, the petty bourgeoisie, and organized farmers, the capitalist state was becoming actively interventionist, and nationalizations that failed to challenge existing social relations would become the order of the day. 'Owing to [the] mood of the working class,' he claimed, 'it is evident the capitalist class had reached the pass where it has to tread with caution. The ground under its feet is very slippery. Something must be done to control this working class, to appease it, to tame it, to cool its revolutionary ardor. The capitalist politicians have responded to their comrades' call to save Canadian capitalism by fleeing into the arms of "State Capitalism." '64

By 1922, it was obvious that Flatman was wrong. Yet he had accurately captured the spirit of CRA propaganda and the vision of the Labour Sub-committee. Moreover, his analysis was consistent with the establishment of the Mathers Commission and the National Industrial Conference. Yet Canadian capital had rejected this path. There was a 'reconstruction of the ruling class,' but on its own terms, without a new relationship with conservative labour and without the institutionalization of state intervention that it had opposed from the start. Flatman may have foreseen developments well into the future, but for the moment capital looked backwards and, with the end of economic prosperity, was aware that it already had the necessary arsenal with which to confront labour. If a new state-directed industrial-relations regime was to emerge, or if innovative social legislation was to be passed to ameliorate many of the inequities that lay at the root of the social crisis, it seemed that it would emanate from the Ontario Legislature at Queen's Park. Here the Independent Labor Party shared power on the government benches. The promise of a new industrial union movement was soon exhausted, but all was not necessarily lost. If the old order was to be challenged and a new democracy created, labourism suggested, it would be from the halls of legislative power. The ball was in the ILP's court.

8 Labourism Tested

'... it was a government composed of workers from the cities and workers from the farms. It was a political revolution!'

Toronto labour election manifesto, 1923[1]

The Ontario election of 1919 was a momentous event in the province's history as labourism and the agrarian revolt together claimed victory on behalf of the province's 'producing classes.' It was a victory rooted in five years of war and social dislocation, of struggle for democracy and against profiteers. It was a means of declaring that those who toiled on the farms and in the factories and fought in the trenches were willing and prepared to ensure that their needs would not be forgotten in the post-war reconstruction. In the cities, it was also the culmination of a decades-long struggle to redistribute the fruits of industrial development. Less than three years old, the Independent Labor Party rode the crest of working-class anger at the old social order and its hollow democracy. By 1919, seventy-eight branches of the party had been established around the province, and local membership drives counted new recruits in the hundreds. The strength of this movement was dramatically reflected in the election results. It was, as the *Globe* described it, a 'political revolution.'[2]

Given the magnitude of the popular rejection of the established parties, and of partyism, it is notable that this popular uprising has received sustained attention only from historians of farmer protest.[3] Their focus on national and western manifestations of agrarian radicalism, aided by the relatively rapid and permanent demise of the United Farmers of Ontario, has left the myth of an innate Ontario conservatism relatively intact. Consequently, Peter Oliver can effectively ignore the massive class conflicts that lay behind the defeat of the Hearst government in 1919. The popular anger and hopes embodied in the farmer and labour movements, he suggests, did not defeat the Tories. Rather 'the fatal wound was self-inflicted.' Conservative collapse was due, above all else, to the weak and indecisive leadership of Sir William Hearst. Although Oliver grudgingly concedes that '[g]eneral strikes and red scares did not leave Ontario entirely unscathed,' he struggles to impose an artificial homogeneity on the province, describing it as 'conservative to the core.'[4] Missing from this explanation is the mass sentiment for class-based political representation that gave birth to both the UFO and the ILP and that sustained their impressive growth. In diverse studies, Craig Heron, Charles Johnston, Michael Piva, Martin Robin, and Brian Tennyson have all drawn attention to the dramatic rise of farmer and labour political movements and popular anger at the old parties to explain the Tories' defeat in 1919.[5] The UFO, now solidly in favour of electoral action, had grown to 48,000 members in more than a thousand clubs, while in the cities the handful of adherents to the old political parties within the mushrooming union movement had been marginalized. Furthermore, much of the confusion and factionalism within the Liberal and Conservative parties was rooted in their inability to respond to the new economic and social pressures that gave rise to the UFO and the ILP.[6] Weak leadership within the established parties cannot explain the massive revulsion in both rural and urban Ontario against political parties long mired in patronage and profiteering. The old parties could not respond to the mass democratic sentiment because they were, in large part, its targets.

Labourism's meteoric rise was matched by its demise. This chapter examines not only the collapse of the ILP, but also the disappearance of labourism as a political current. Junior partner in the farmer-labour government, the ILP was not in a position to impose its policies. More damaging, however, was the growing recognition by ILP supporters that their party had no coherent program of its own for which to fight. Labourism had never explicitly defined the character of the new democracy other than as an escape from the control of the old parties, which 'merely represent the special interests which have permitted profiteering and exploitation of the people for their own benefit.'[7] The ILP had gone far without an explicit agenda; once elected, labourist legislators would have a difficult time setting their own course. Labourism suffered a setback because of the relationship of forces within the Drury government; it collapsed because expectations of a new society emerging automatically on the heels of electoral victory by the producers proved wrong. The paucity of the farmer-labour legislative record, as far as labour was concerned, is striking. The demands of the 'industrial' movement were buried under farmer opposition and labourist uncertainty of how to address them in the 'political' arena. Interestingly, legislative attention came to focus on the working-class family and the status of women's paid labour. This was insufficient to sustain the enthusiasm of 1919. Chastened and shrinking, the forces of working-class political action turned away from the vagaries of labourism and towards various streams of socialism.

Labourism Triumphant

On 20 October 1919 the twenty-three candidates of the Independent Labor Party received 124,564 votes; eleven were elected. Together with the forty-five members elected by the United Farmers, the forces of the 'new democracy' barely held power. The Liberals held their own with twenty-nine seats while the Conservatives were reduced to only twenty-five. The ILP led the count in city after city. In the labourist bastion of Hamilton the ILP candidates swept the polls. George Halcrow overwhelmed the 'Conservative-labour' candidate, Samuel Landers, by 16,012 votes to 8,424, the largest majority in the province, while Walter Rollo topped the combined totals of Liberal and Conservative ballots by almost 3,000 votes. In the Niagara peninsula, ILP candidates Charles Swayze in Niagara Falls and Frank Greenlaw in St Catharines won substantial victories in three-way contests. In South Brant, Brantford mayor M.M. MacBride won handily, while ILPer Karl Homuth carried South Waterloo, including the industrial centres of Galt, Preston, and Hespeler. In Peterborough, a large procession wheeled MPP-elect Thomas Tooms, president of the local Building Trades Council, through the city to celebrate his somewhat narrower victory.[8] ILP campaigns similarly delivered the smaller centres of St Thomas and Woodstock to allied UFO candidates, although, in the latter instance, the rural vote was insufficient to carry the seat. ILP candidate Hugh Stevenson convincingly defeated 'Hydro Czar' Adam Beck in London, one of the few two-way contests in urban Ontario. Although Beck was credited with contributing to the downfall of the Hearst government by opposing Hearst's leadership and running as an 'Independent Conservative,' his reputed 'almost fanatical following'[9] was insufficient to return him to Queen's Park in the face of an insurgent political labour movement. In the north, the ILP won the Fort William and Kenora ridings, while the strength of the movement was symbolized by the defeat of Premier Hearst himself by the ILP in Sault Ste Marie.

The provincial ILP, however, was still barely two years old, and its fortunes continued to be rooted in the strength of local labour movements and, particularly, local trades councils. Variations in industrial development and union activity were reflected in the election returns. In eastern Ontario the labour movement was weak and the ILP won no seats. The Windsor trades council, more closely tied to the Detroit Federation of Labor than to the Ontario labour movement, had considered forming an ILP only in early 1919. The weak Stratford ILP was unable to draw many votes for the UFO candidate, and the Guelph ILP 'existed only in name'[10] and did not contest the election. In North Waterloo, the ILP faced opposition from both the UFO and the Socialist Labor Party, finishing second amidst six candidates.

The uneven development of the ILP across the province gave little cause for concern. The party had scored major victories in most cities and, in view of its rapid growth, could expect the future to take care of itself. It was difficult to be as sanguine about Toronto, where the four ILP candidates had all been defeated. The Liberals were the main benefactors of the collapse of Tory Toronto. Undoubtedly the ILP did not expect to make great breakthroughs in the financial and commercial capital of the province, a city with an economic and social structure hardly conducive to the development of a relatively homogeneous labourism. And, while the trades council had rallied behind a left-wing leadership, the débâcle of the general strike did little to unite working-class Toronto around a common vision. Among the ILP candidates were two symbols of militant labour: James Simpson and John MacDonald. Both received significant numbers of votes (Simpson got 8,323 and MacDonald 6,457) but were swamped in the large urban ridings. In Riverdale, John Vick placed third in a close three-way contest among 'labour' candidates of various political stripes. John W. Buckley failed to make an impact in the wealthier riding of North-East Toronto. Together, the four had received 23,563 votes: a disappointing but hardly insignificant showing.

Overall, ILPers were delighted at the results. The Hamilton ILP immediately announced a campaign to triple its membership to 3,000, Welland ILPers began a search for 1,000 new members, and the provincial party soon declared its goal: one hundred new branches and 50,000 new members. The prospects appeared limitless. By the time of the provincial ILP convention in April 1920, branches had been established in the few cities, such as Windsor and Oshawa, that had been missed in earlier waves of organizing, and southern Ontario labourists could take heart at the success of their Temiskaming comrades in the election of ILP candidate Angus McDonald to the federal Parliament.[11]

The summer of 1920 was a time of celebration. Organizationally the party was in fine shape. Steady growth reinforced a sense of confidence, even a kind of evolutionary predestination. The forces of democracy had planted secure roots in Ontario, and the outlook was bright. Party pamphlets with such titles as 'Mr. Workingman, Listen' and 'The Need for a Labor Party' were printed and sold around the province. Thousands wore red-on-white ILP pins on their lapels or affixed ILP stickers to the backs of letters, reminding recipients that 'Every Vote for Labor is a Vote for Democracy.' Most popular were the picnics held around the province that summer, often in conjunction with the UFO or, as in Woodstock, with the Great War Veterans' Association as well.[12] The highlight was the ILP provincial picnic held in Wabasso Park in Hamilton on 21 August. A.W. Mance from the *Industrial Banner*, Premier Drury, George Halcrow, and Walter Rollo defended the record of the farmer-labour government and spoke with optimism of the future. That future, however, depended upon the ability to transform popular support into palpable gains inside and outside the provincial parliament.

Workers and Farmers in the Legislature

Following the provincial election, the future of the ILP was in the hands of the eleven members of the party's caucus. Most had a long history in the labour movement, but they were not representative of the radicalism that was emerging in many of the province's unions. The electoral failure of the Toronto ILP contributed to the conservative character of the caucus, as did the tendency of some ILP branches to select members already experienced in municipal office, such as Brantford mayor Malcolm M. MacBride and London ex-mayor Hugh Stevenson. Surveying the new labour caucus, *Maclean's* magazine considered Peterborough MPP Thomas Tooms as 'the most radical perhaps in the Labor party.' Yet it would become apparent that Tooms, a supporter of the single tax, was no more able to provide a coherent conception of the ILP's role in the provincial parliament than were his colleagues. Although there was some truth in the Socialist Labor Party's claim that the ILP 'has about one hundred immediate demands,'[13] the reference to the party's program was misleading. The inclusive yet inchoate character of the program was the product of a widespread belief that, freed from the grip of the 'special interests' and partyism, labour MPPs could directly represent the interests of the province's workers. As Walter Rollo explained: 'Trade unionists had spent much time and money holding conventions, passing resolutions and sending deputations to wait on the legislators. Now labor had at Toronto thirteen resolutions dressed up in clothes [including sympathetic UFO members] who were in a position to do something.'[14] Carefully worded programs were superfluous now that labour was present to speak for itself in an invigorated democracy.

Great accomplishments were expected of labour's parliamentary representatives, but there was little to guide them. It quickly became clear that the differences that would inevitably arise given the lack of programmatic focus and the character of the caucus could emerge as personal animosities. The presence of M.M. MacBride ('Me-Me MacBride' as he was christened by the Labor News[15]) in the caucus guaranteed that they would. MacBride's style of political discourse was highly personalized and, despite his avowed allegiance to the labour movement, his highest praise went to renegade Tory Adam Beck, while his colourful red-baiting regularly found its target in Jimmie Simpson. MacBride had also discovered in the storm following his manoeuvres with Conservatives and Unionist Liberals in 1917 that he could defy the provincial ILP with impunity. He had never hidden his contempt for socialism, he deplored class struggle, and he was fully convinced that 'capitalists are just 'folks''' who could be convinced of the justice of labour's cause through reasonable argument. He considered himself eminently qualified to play the role of intermediary. In the spring of 1919 he settled a strike at the Verity Plow Company and took credit for persuading Beck to concede to workers' demands for the eight-hour day on the Hydro Chippawa project. In the latter instance the facts were somewhat at variance with MacBride's claims, as Beck had threatened to resign if not given a free hand in the matter. MacBride carefully cultivated a paternal relationship with Brantford unionists and helped in winning the eight-hour day on civic works.[16]

MacBride's running feud with Simpson appears to have stemmed from the founding convention of the Ontario Section of the Canadian Labor Party which he perceived as an attempt by socialists and anti-protectionists to take over the political labour movement. Adding fuel to the fire was MacBride's perception that Simpson was the contagion that would transmit the Toronto metal-trades strike to Brantford where MacBride was anxiously trying to prevent similar developments in the local agricultural implements industry and was convinced that he could personally mediate a settlement. The matter was brought to a head when the Brantford trades council invited Simpson to the city while MacBride's ILP passed motions in opposition. MacBride's actions at a Metal Trades Council meeting reveal that much of his blustering against Simpson was an attempt to isolate local union militants as a means of achieving a settlement. MacBride demanded to know who present recognized the Union Jack as their emblem and who stood by the Red Flag. The weak and somewhat abashed socialist contingent was unable to regain the offensive. As the local paper commented, the 'meeting turned out as a decided check to certain radical elements,' and a major strike was avoided without any concessions on the part of the employers.[17]

Any misgivings the provincial ILP had concerning MacBride's election were borne out at the first meeting of the ILP MPPs. After helping to produce a joint legislative program with the UFO, MacBride bolted an ILP caucus meeting, citing the failure of the ILP to fight for a legislated eight-hour day. It emerged that MacBride's real complaint was that the ILP would not have a hand in naming cabinet ministers. Confirming MacBride's fears, Premier Drury passed him over when he named two ILP ministers, Walter Rollo in labour and Harry Mills in mines. Although MacBride was lured back to the party, *Maclean's* magazine commented in an appraisal of Labour minister Walter Rollo's performance that this 'writer has talked with Mayor MacBride of Brantford, and knows what would have been done had he been minister,' adding that MacBride 'is not cursed with that so prevalent quality of modesty.' MacBride, of course, denied such ambitions and, in response, drew upon his surest form of defence. He attacked Simpson, who had defended the pact with the UFO, for acting as a 'mouthpiece' for Drury. Throughout, MacBride took care to retain the backing of the Brantford ILP, returning to the city to solicit its explicit support for his actions.[18]

The ILP caucus received little respite from MacBride as events appeared to repeat themselves in January 1920. Playing upon George Halcrow's criticisms of the government's refusal to make commitments regarding labour legislation, MacBride persuaded Halcrow, Greenlaw, Swayze, and Riverdale 'Independent-Soldier' member Joseph McNamara to discuss forming a rump-ILP caucus entirely independent from the UFO. As he had two months previously, though, MacBride subsequently concluded that his future lay in the ILP and, with caucus leader Walter Rollo, he issued a vacuous joint statement claiming 'that the difficulties have been more in the nature of misunderstanding than differences of policy.' MacBride weakly explained that he could support the government, but not 'Druryism.' It was now apparent that the Brantford mayor (he was re-elected for 1920) would exploit schisms in the caucus when they arose. The tensions inherent in supporting a government dominated by farmers with little regard for workers' demands for the eight-hour day and increased spending on projects such as hydro radials promised to provide many such opportunities for MacBride.

Hamilton MPP George Halcrow's differences with the caucus were more principled. Support for the government, he argued, could only be conditional upon its support of workers, and attempts to impose party discipline for political expediency smacked of 'partyism.' His public declaration that Beck would have been a better premier than Drury signalled trouble for the caucus and party. For the moment, however, reconciliation was possible, and MacBride persuaded the Brantford ILP to pass a motion of praise for the caucus. A caucus statement that it would introduce legislation if the Drury cabinet was inactive created the impression of cohesion and purpose, and the ILP MPPs set their sights on a Mothers' Allowance Act and amendments to the Workmen's Compensation Act.[19]

The fate of the labour caucus was, of course, intricately entwined with that of the United Farmers. Having formed a governing alliance with the UFO, the ILP was naturally constrained by priorities established by the farmers, by its openness to innovative social reforms, and by its attitude to experimentation with the political structure of the province. As the initial confrontation over the eight-hour day revealed, farmer and labour legislators had quite different goals, regardless of their common dedication to a reinvigorated democracy. The ILP leadership and caucus seem to have had few illusions that they would be able to influence the UFO on the eight-hour day and never made the issue a precondition for the alliance. The inability of MacBride and Mc-Namara to embarrass the ILP on this issue suggests a general acknowledgment that the UFO, fearing a continued rural exodus to more attractive working conditions in the cities and an increase in farm labour costs, would not be moved. Cabinet and caucus documentation is scarce, but there seems little reason to challenge Premier Drury's contention that he had 'little trouble maintaining harmony' between the farmer and labour members of his government.[20] This appears to be true despite other sources of friction. Labour interest in state ownership, and particularly in Beck's grandiose plans for the Hydro Commission, were not shared by most farmers.[21] Not only would electric 'radial' railways linking urban centres be of little use to them, but Ontario farmers shared a fundamental economic liberalism, rooted in their historic Liberalism and reinforced by a *petit-bourgeois* suspicion of an interventionist state. Farmers were interested in freeing the market from the unfair influences of monopolies and the tariff, not in adding a new constraint. While the ILP never articulated a clear alternative to economic liberalism, its view of reconstruction had a place for state activity. Such a farmer-dominated government 'pledged to economy, if not parsimony,'[22] would not adopt the more statist, and more expensive, elements of the ILP program – large-scale public works and welfare measures such as old-age pensions.

In any case, ILP support had not been built upon well-defined policies. Labourism, after all, had seen 'no justice' in 'old-time party platforms,' and ILP legislators felt little pressure to implement specific measures. Yet, however vague, ILP supporters expected the promise of a 'higher form of government' and a new democracy to be fulfilled. On this score, the differences with the farmers appeared minor. Each decried patronage and partyism; each had elected its direct representatives to the legislature. The United Farmers, however, were deeply torn over the depth of their challenge to the existing political system. As happened with their counterparts in the Progressive Party nationally, two distinct wings emerged. One current, strongest in the United Farmers of Alberta, sought the replacement of geographical constituencies with a system of occupational representation or 'group government' and the abandonment of many parliamentary traditions. E.C. Drury, however, stood staunchly in the other camp of 'crypto-Liberals,' as W.L. Morton aptly dubbed them for their ideological proximity to the Liberal Party. Drury, in fact, had been nominated as a Liberal in the 1917 federal election and, in 1921, seriously considered an offer by Mackenzie King to join a Liberal-Progressive federal cabinet.[23]

For agrarian activists like Drury, the decision to turn to political action was as much the product of a feeling of betrayal at the hands of the Liberal Party and its defence of the tariff-protected interests as it was a rejection of liberalism. Although Morton equated this current with the 'Manitobans,' David Laycock appropriately points to the UFO as best illustrating the quasi-liberal ideal type.[24] The differences between the two currents emerged most sharply in the 'broadening-out' controversy in Ontario. From the inception of the UFO-ILP government, Drury sought to 'broaden out' the UFO into a multi-class people's party with representation from urban reformers. He hoped to create, in effect, a new Liberal Party purged of the entrenched and corrupting business interests. As Charles Johnston notes, Drury was 'a creature of parliamentary orthodoxy,'[25] and such a project posed no threat to the party system. Drury's plans came under constant fire from many in the UFO, particularly J.J. Morrison. Indeed, Drury's memory of cordial relations with the ILP was possibly formed in contrast to the turbulence that he faced in his own organization. Neither Morrison nor W.C. Good formulated as coherent a theory of government as Henry Wise Wood or William Irvine in Alberta, however, and Drury maintained his control of the UFO caucus.[26]

While the details of the debate in the UFO do not concern us here, the consequences are important. Drury's ability to curtail the experimentation by the UFO's radical democrats (to use Laycock's term) narrowed the options for the ILP caucus. As long as parliamentary traditions persisted and the UFO was subject to defeat by a vote of non-confidence, the ILP had to choose between supporting the farmers or abdicating to the old parties. There was little room to manoeuvre. It is noteworthy, though, that the ILP never entered the broadening-out debate. Whatever sympathy ILPers felt for other reform currents, their movement was defined as specifically working class; merger was never proposed.

Drury's orthodoxy, however, did not entirely preclude political reform. While Drury rejected proposals for direct democracy as injurious to parliamentary government, he was open to some form of transferable vote. The report of a Special Legislative Committee on Proportional Representation in 1921 proposed, as an experiment, that a few multi-member constituencies be established.[27] Despite the fact that any electoral reform would draw attention to the great overrepresentation of rural votes (the UFO had won 40 per cent of the seats with only 22 per cent of the provincial vote), the government accepted and fought for the report. In fact, Tory opposition to the measure dragged the Legislature to a halt in 1923, and the government withdrew the bill on the eve of dissolution.[28] However meagre the proposed reform, the farmer-labour government could be seen as being defeated in the battle for a wider democracy.

What, then, did the Drury government accomplish? The abolition of property qualifications and the establishment of a provincial savings bank were pointed to with some pride by the ILP, as were the increased benefits under the Workmen's Compensation Act. Although Drury was later to claim that 'we enacted a program of social legislation [such] as Ontario and indeed all Canada and North America had never seen, or perhaps thought possible,'[29] the record was, in fact, very much in keeping with progressive reform throughout the continent. Mothers' allowances, minimum wages for women, a higher school leaving age, and reforms dealing with adoption and with the responsibilities of unmarried parents were the major pieces of legislation. Measures to ameliorate and regulate the workplace and home lives of working-class women figure prominently in this list. It is therefore worthwhile examining more closely the fate of the 'woman democrat' to gain an insight into the character and limits of labourist reform.

Protective Legislation

As we have seen in chapter five, the various promises of industrial equality and freedom for women made little impact upon a sexual division of labour that consigned women to 'secondary' and temporary employment. For working-class men and women, the demands of the household and the family wage took priority. The Drury government was active in defending this ideal. New protective legislation, such as the minimum wage for women and the mothers' allowance, was neither innovative – factory acts dating from the 1880s 'protected' women from long hours and night work – nor emancipatory. Women's reproductive role and assumed moral vulnerability were the prime concerns of these legislators. Such a perception could and did disqualify women from particular jobs as well as reinforce the argument that women's proper place was at home within the context of the family. As Alice Kessler-Harris points out, whatever genuine concern lay behind these measures, 'there was ideological danger in asserting women's weakness.'[30] Proponents of such legislation perceived women as incapable of defending themselves against employers and as needing the protection that could be offered by the state. Needless to say, such a view of women workers hardly commended them to male trade unionists as reliable or powerful allies.

The Drury government was quick to recognize the path of least resistance (a trail already broken by several governments in the West) and created a Minimum Wage Board to set minimum rates for women by district and industry. The ILP caucus, eager to find 'labour' legislation acceptable to its farmer allies, grabbed at the measure. George Halcrow even described it as more important than the long-sought eight-hour day. The process was speeded by the fact that the previous Conservative government had already considered such legislation.[31]

If the minimum wage was designed to protect the most defenceless workers, it became evident that this category could include not only women but also unskilled male workers, whose wages plummeted after

1920. When the Drury government cut the wages of its own labourers to thirty cents an hour, the Hamilton ILP responded by unanimously urging the Ontario ILP to demand a minimum wage for all workers, regardless of sex. The Hamilton TLC agreed, arguing that such legislation was necessary to enable unskilled men to earn a family wage.[32] It fell to Jimmie Simpson to express traditional union opposition to this policy. '[W]hile a minimum rate was good for certain classes of labor,' he argued, 'it was not good for others. For the defenceless workers it was fine, but where strong organizations were to be contended with it did not meet with favor as the men could realize more through their organizations than the board might be willing to award them.'[33] Simpson persuaded the ILP convention to demand that the Minimum Wage Board could intervene only on the request of a particular group of workers. Unionized workers were guarding their autonomy and freedom of action against quasi-judicial interference in the bargaining system. The issue was not entirely one of gender. The Ontario executive of the TLCC followed a similar logic in demanding a minimum wage for youth, regardless of sex. The ILP came to draw its major distinction between organized (or organizable) skilled workers and all others. Its demand included 'unskilled' labour in general, including immigrants. Proposals to include not just boys but unskilled men under the act represented a significant shift. The goal of forming industrial unions that included skilled and unskilled workers, including women, had been all but abandoned.[34]

The consequences of a minimum wage for women were recognized by women on the left-wing of the labour movement. For socialists such as Rose Henderson, working-class self-activity, not reliance on protective legislation, was the answer. In 1924, the TDLC, in conjunction with the Toronto Women's Labor League, organized a public meeting with Minimum Wage Board chairman J.W. McMillan, who was challenged to defend the low minimum rates being established by the board. Defending rates of just $12.50 a week, McMillan provoked the audience by attacking the 'unreasonable' demands 'of the impossible radical worker.' In reply, women from the audience pointed out that such a rate did not provide economic independence for women or allow them to maintain their dependents, that it was unenforced among the immigrant work-force, and that the minimum wage had a tendency to become the maximum. The *Worker* reported: 'When asked what the girls could do to get wages higher than the minimum Dr. McMillan was not prepared to answer. The girls, without hesitation, replied, "organize."'[35]

The very existence of such protective legislation for women, how-ever, shifted the political terrain. Whatever qualms women had about the legislation, it was a *fait accompli*. Proposing its repeal seemed a step backwards, and demanding the extension of the act to cover men was unlikely to succeed given the unpopularity of the measure among unionists and the rapidly declining weight of the labour movement in any case. Consequently, working-class women's organizations, partic-ularly the WLL, found themselves drawn into repeated conflicts over board decisions, as was seen in the mass meeting with McMillan. By 1924, the focus had shifted to attempting to provoke the board into action to enforce its own decisions.[36] The low minimum rates set by the board were a constant irritant to wage-earning women and their defenders.

The board's rationale for setting such low rates was defended by H.G. Fester, now 'Labour' representative on the Minimum Wage Board. Fester argued that raising the minimum would throw women's jobs into jeopardy by making it more profitable to hire men whose wages were not protected by legislation. Cases existed, he claimed, 'where, when women's salaries were increased to a living wage, they were dis-charged and men given the places at a smaller rate.' Such a statement, in itself, however, does not prove that such protective legislation ac-tually disadvantaged women in the labour market. It must be viewed as an excuse on the part of an ineffective labour figure for his inability or unwillingness to challenge the assumptions and practices of the ma-jority of the board. In fact the women covered by the board's decisions were not in competition with a significant number of men. Most de-cisions covered 'women's jobs,' and rates were substantially lower than those being received by men.[37]

The other major piece of protective legislation passed by the farmer-labour government was even more explicitly designed to maintain ex-isting gender relationships. The mothers' allowance for widows with children was meant to address a real problem. The carnage of the war and of the shop floor had left an increasing number of women strug-gling to care for themselves and their children without the pretence of access to a male family wage. Reformers of all stripes welcomed the measure, including Henderson. Minnie Singer was among the first appointed to the provincial Mothers' Allowance Commission. In fact, given the level of unanimity on the issue, the niggardly response by the government is remarkable. 'Mothers' pensions' were initially given only to women with more than one child and not to women deserted by their husbands. Demands quickly spread for the extension of the mothers' allowance to mothers with one child and to incapacitated and deserted mothers, and for increases in payments.[38]

While providing much-needed relief to some single mothers, the act did little to improve women's position within the labour market. An *Industrial Banner* cartoon depicting the mothers' pension plank of the ILP program shows a woman looking at a notice posted at a factory. It reads:

Notice
Widows
With Dependent
Children
No Longer Needed
To Work Here.
GOVERNMENT
PENSIONS
Will Enable Them
To Devote Themselves
To Their Homes and
Little Ones.

A child is tugging at her skirt saying: 'Come on home mother, and look after us. You don't have to work in the factory now.' The caption reads: 'A "Sign" of the Times (Soon)'[39] Mother's allowances could do more than maintain women and children from a real threat of destitution. They could also preserve the domestic ideal from a challenge rooted in the fact that access to the family wage was beyond the grasp of a growing number of families without a male breadwinner. While the state assumed some social responsibility for the care of children, the perception of the domestic sphere as women's proper domain was reiterated. The legislation also provided the means to ensure that the presumed moral character of the nuclear family was maintained. Not only was the wife penalized by the husband's desertion, the commission that administered the act investigated recipients and discontinued allowances 'where the mothers proved to be immoral, cruel or improvident, as the allowance is considered a salary from the government to enable the mother to make good citizens of her children.'[40] Mothers were not only subject to repressive state intervention, their reproductive capabilities were reified by legislation that considered them solely as child-rearers without autonomous rights of their own.

In the face of a significant mobilization by working-class women, the labour movement, including the ILP, broke reluctantly, and unevenly, with the dominant perceptions of woman's sphere, perceptions that were deeply rooted in a concept of the family. This is hardly surprising, as few commentators, even the most imaginative, critically examined the nature of the household economy. Consequently the working-class women's movement was unaware of the contradictions it faced in demanding equal economic and political opportunities at the same time as it defended men's right to a 'family wage' and its own protection through legislation that reinforced images of women's innate powerlessness. Individuals caught glimpses of the ideological tangle the movement faced, but they were unable to articulate a coherent alternative. Moreover, working-class women were confronted on a daily basis with the apparently inexorable demands of the household economy. When the survival of their family was at stake in the bleak days following the collapse of the wartime boom, few women or men could see far beyond the hope that the male breadwinner would be able to produce a pay packet. The wife's task of maintaining a household on an insufficient or non-existent wage was difficult enough; the possibility of a radical re-ordering of the working-class economy and household seemed remote. The obstacles were too great.

The Limits of Labourism

As the fate of the 'woman democrat' demonstrated, political advances for working-class women, particularly in the paid labour force, depended on both ideology and economic strength. This was true, of course, for the ILP in its relationship with the workers' movement as a whole. Any material gains for workers required that the ILP clearly define its objective, win the acquiescence of the farmers' movement through argument or external pressure, and overcome the hostility of the business community. The party had demonstrated little ability to achieve any of these goals. Most specifically, there had been little recognition that its ability to fulfil even the vague promises of labourism was dependent upon a vital and active union movement. This connection was tenuous in the ideology of a workers' movement that made no explicit connection between the 'economic' and the 'political.' In the context of working-class advance on both these fronts, few problems might arise. The same was not true if workers looked to the government to defend union gains.

While intrigues in the provincial parliament did not seem to have shaken labourism's hold on Ontario's workers, a new round of class conflict might do so. The ILP's mandate was vague in its details, but clear in its intent. Workers looked to their MPPs to deprive employers of the political props that protected them in confrontations with workers. It was to be a major strike that signalled the beginning of the end of an uncritical acceptance of labourism by workers. Having won an eight-hour day, of sorts, from the Hydro-Electric Commission in 1919, the Niagara District Trades Federation (NDTF) set its sights on the abolition of compulsory overtime on the Chippawa project. A year earlier Beck had presented himself as the workers' comrade, 'destroying property of the corporations and creating wealth for the people.' In 1920, he eschewed the rhetoric and dug in his heels; workers would work straight ten-hour days with no overtime pay. The ILP caucus was wedged between two considerable forces: one of the strongest trades federations in the province and Ontario's most skilled manipulator of public support, Adam Beck.[41]

The ILP caucus moved quickly, proposing an IDIA board of inquiry. Beck refused. As the 2,000 Hydro workers threatened to quit work, the region's two labour MPPs, along with MacBride, rushed to Niagara Falls to argue against a strike, requesting that the NDTF leave the matter in their hands. The workers were urged 'to play Labor's game by staying on the job and not allowing the capitalistic element to lock out thousands and starve Labor into servitude.' After some speeches accusing Beck of 'trying to be a kaiser,' the workers agreed to let the caucus deal with the Hydro Commission.[42] Besides trying to avoid a showdown, the Labor MPPs demonstrated that they had more faith in their own abilities than in the strength of the unions. They soon discovered how little influence they had over Beck and the Hydro Commission and had to content themselves with the establishment of a legislative committee to investigate conditions on the project. Their powerlessness in that forum was publicly displayed.

On 20 May 1920, the same day Hydro extended the workday to ten hours, the five-member legislative committee was established. No doubt due to his well-advertised mediation skills, MacBride was named as its sole ILP member. Hearings started immediately in Niagara Falls, and the extent of anger against Beck's attitude and the ten-hour day were evident. Fred Flatman, who had been ousted from the *New Democracy* and was now working as a blacksmith on the project, articulated the popular view that the government had a particular responsibility to its own workers. 'We take the stand ... that if the people of the province employ their own labour they should be model employers of labour.' The appointment of the committee did not defuse the conflict, and the government and the ILP caucus could not easily duck responsibility for its outcome. Predictably, the committee recommended the only potentially acceptable compromise, the maintenance of the eight-hour day with two hours of overtime. The scale of wages was considered comparable to that paid elsewhere (although, inexplicably, 'skilled labour in factories is receiving a somewhat higher scale'), and living conditions were 'fairly satisfactory.' To this somewhat vapid report, MacBride appended his own 'observations' supporting the recommendations, praising Beck and the project, and hoping that the municipalities purchasing hydro power could be forthcoming with more money for the workers. Of the four parties represented on the committee, it was W.H. Casselman of the UFO who had the least sympathy for the workers. In a sharply worded dissenting statement he decried the eight-hour day as 'a vicious principle.'[43] At a crucial juncture, the UFO demonstrated that it would actively oppose labour on the economic front.

The majority report was, however uninspired, a rebuke of Beck's implementation of the ten-hour day. Unfortunately, the government was unwilling to challenge the devolution of its authority by exercising direct control over the Hydro Commission. Walter Rollo defended this position: 'The Government is not the commission and the commission is not the Government'; and he cited Beck's often-repeated threat to resign if the boundary between the two was breached. Local ILP MPP Charles Swayze went so far as to defend the autonomy of the Hydro Commission from legislative control with democratic rhetoric. He praised Drury for having 'refused to dictate to the Hydro.' Its parliamentary card trumped, the NDTF had little choice but to strike if it wished to defend the eight-hour day. On 16 June the 2,000 workers did just that. At a mass meeting of Hydro workers, Tom Moore placed the blame squarely on the Drury government, which had been 'shirking responsibility' for the growing conflict. Nineteen days later, having won only token concessions, the unions narrowly voted to abandon the fight and return to work. At the annual Trades and Labor Congress convention, Rollo defended himself by claiming that any other course would have led to the resignation of the Hydro chairman and the collapse of the government. Moore's retort that it would be better to lose Beck than the eight-hour day was enthusiastically received by the convention.[44]

A single-minded commitment to the politics of coalition with the UFO was not the only source of the self-defeating behaviour of the ILP caucus. A profound ambiguity regarding public ownership, and hydro in particular, led them into still more trouble. In its fight for local enabling by-laws, the provincial labour movement had elevated the fight for hydro radial railways to overwhelming symbolic significance. UFO opposition, whatever its source, was seen as a rejection of a key element of reconstruction. In sharp contrast with the arms-length relationship the ILP MPPs had supported in the course of the fight over the return to the ten-hour day, the Drury government acted quickly to foil Beck's radial plans. Drury's appointment of a royal commission to investigate the feasibility of the project was denounced by George Halcrow. The ILP caucus as a whole scrambled for safe ground, declaring itself in favour of both the royal commission (to please the UFO) and of hydro radials (to please the ILP membership).[45]

The caucus and, by extension, the provincial ILP were now in serious trouble. They had failed to defend either Hydro workers against the Hydro Commission or the Hydro Commission against the UFO. They were also publicly split. The stage was set for MacBride to strike a decisive blow by leaving the caucus. (Driving him out of the party proved to be a longer and even more disagreeable task.)[46] At long last, the ILP leadership was moved to to rethink the functioning of the caucus. A joint executive and caucus resolution was adopted stating that, while maintaining the alliance with the farmers, the ILP 'shall emphasize its distinction as a separate political unit in the Legislature.' To demonstrate its independence from the cabinet, the caucus replaced Rollo with Halcrow as house leader. The meeting also established, again for the first time, a list of demands on the Drury government: unemployment relief, old-age pensions, and improvements in the Mothers' Allowance Act, demands that were to be dealt with in the coming session. Finally, in a move that reflected both a growing red scare and the ILP's vulnerability to rising discontent within its ranks, the meeting resolved that 'extremists' – referring to a minority of revolutionary socialists – should 'decline nomination to executive positions within the party.'[47]

MacBride's departure brought little relief to the caucus. The 1921 provincial ILP convention called on the caucus to account for its inaction. The Minimum Wage Board, which had been one of labour's 'gains' in the coalition, was criticized for its approval of low wage rates. The issue of prohibition was only narrowly ducked as the convention tabled a demand that Attorney-General W.E. Raney be forced to resign because his conduct in attempting to enforce the law was 'unbecoming that of a democratic government.'[48] But keen to preserve unity, and without having posed a coherent alternate strategy or leadership, the convention returned the provincial executive of the party to office.

The prospect of a federal election in 1921 produced another set of problems for the ILP. A debate on the tariff first emerged at the 1920 ILP convention, which, after reaffirming the alliance with the UFO, managed to hammer out a policy favouring the 'gradual elimination of import duties on all necessities of life.' The *Industrial Banner* explained that the tenor of the convention revealed that 'in the opinion of the delegates there were reconstruction problems that overshadowed the tariff altogether.'[49] Thomas Tooms suggested that the tariff question was 'a twaddle,' as workers suffered the same destitution and poverty in high-tariff countries as they did in low-tariff ones. Speaking as a Hamilton ILP delegate to the convention, however, Rollo told the delegates to 'quit dreaming' and predicted that 'not one of our labor candidates could run on a free trade platform and have a chance to win a single seat in Ontario.' Given the large number of branch-plants of American firms in Hamilton whose existence was due to the tariff barrier, it was hardly surprising that the Hamilton ILP was committed to protectionism. It dismissed the ILP convention as 'none too representative' and, with the support of both Hamilton labour papers, the *Labor News* and the *New Democracy*, campaigned to have the party reverse its decision. Hamilton ILPers did not, in fact, deny that the tariff had been misused to enrich the few and, as democrats, they opposed this. The solution, as they saw it, was the establishment of a 'nonpartisan, non-political commission' that would set the tariff 'scientifically.' They were convinced that such a body could produce a tariff structure 'which would prove acceptable to the farmers, manufacturers and workers.' Democracy, and reason, in short, could solve the problem; no fundamental social cleavage stood in the way of obtaining a 'happy medium.'[50]

The potential for political disaster began to present itself, for an issue had arisen in which Hamilton workers apparently felt that they had more in common with their own protected employers than with the Independent Labor Party. Obviously this did not augur well for the future of independent working-class political action or for the continued development of the class solidarity that had spawned it. Hamilton's labourists, effectively unchallenged by local socialists, could not accept Simpson's view that the tariff was 'a bogey issue,' one that diverted workers from 'the real source of economic servitude [which] lies in the private ownership of natural resources and the machinery of production and distribution.' The Hamilton ILP demanded, and got, a special provincial convention to reverse the decision before the 1921 federal election. Protectionism, in the guise of a 'nonpartisan tariff commission,' became provincial party policy. However, from London, the *Herald* downplayed the issue, asking 'Is the tariff some new kind of breakfast food ... that it is held as so efficacious in the cure of our economic ills?'[51] ILPers could speak with little conviction on what was emerging as the central issue of the election.

The federal election was little short of a disaster for the ILP. Of eighteen candidates (some nominated jointly with the UFO), it elected no new members to Parliament; only Temiskaming member Angus McDonald was returned. In its key centre of Hamilton, ILP candidates E.J. Etherington and Thomas J. O'Heir ran strongly, but were defeated by Conservatives. While improving its showing, the ILP failed to make a breakthrough in Waterloo North, despite running former Kitchener mayor and regional ILP vice-president Dr John E. Hett. The newly reorganized branch in Brantford (finally without MacBride) placed former collegiate principal A.W. Burt in the field on a free-trade platform. The candidate ran third, failing to win any polls in Brantford, but taking several in surrounding rural areas. In spite of a strong showing, ILP candidate returned soldier Edwin J. Lovelace failed to win Lincoln, which included St Catharines. Although Lovelace had been active in the ILP and had edited its 1919 election paper, the *Daily Topic*, his candidacy signalled the revival of a Lib-Lab tradition in the city. He had attended the local Liberal convention, and the Liberals had endorsed him. On the eve of the election, ILP vice-president Mary McNab had refused to share a platform in St Catharines with Toronto Liberal candidate James Murdock in support of Lovelace.[52] Labourism was in trouble.

A smug *Labor Leader* considered that the ILP had botched the federal election by having no coherent statement on the tariff. That the tariff could dominate the election, however, was itself a sign of labourism's weakness and the tarnished image of the new democracy. The ILP's manifesto, calling on workers to 'Vote for your civil rights and against repression,' and to 'Vote for the toilers and against the drones,' attempted to refocus workers' attention on the fight for democracy and the dignity of labour. The impact of such appeals was waning. Most seriously, the leadership of the TLCC, namely Moore and Draper, announced their defection from the movement for independent political action by producing a questionnaire for candidates as was the tradition in the American Federation of Labor. The TLCC had re-embarked on the search for 'friends of labour' among the old parties. The move was widely condemned by unionists, but a giant step away from the aims of the ILP had been taken.[53]

The poor showing in the cities came as a shock to ILP leaders. Active membership had been declining, but for an electoral organization such as the ILP it was not unusual for members to fall away between elections only to be drawn back in the next campaign. In 1921 they stayed at home, demoralized by the failures of the Drury government and defeats on the industrial front that undermined their vision of the working class as an agent for social reconstruction. The most astute leaders of the political labour movement, particularly former members of the Social Democratic Party, had foreseen the crisis. Their solution lay in broadening the bases of political action organizationally and refining it programmatically. Their mechanism would be the Ontario Section of the Canadian Labor Party.[54] The labourist consensus was about to fracture.

Labourism Superseded

The re-emergence of the Ontario CLP promised to change the character of labour politics in the province. By 1921, the crisis in the ILP had convinced socialists looking for a mechanism to further political action outside the confines of labourism to attempt to breathe life into the organization, which had been inactive since its establishment. With only forty-five delegates, the 1921 Ontario CLP convention was much smaller than the founding meeting three years earlier. Few delegates came from outside Toronto, Hamilton, or London; none came from the north. Executive elections established the Ontario CLP to the left of the ILP. Metal-trades leader Harry Kerwin defeated H.J. Halford for the presidency, while Simpson was re-elected secretary. Mary McNab was elected vice-president. The executive included socialists from London (J.F. Thomson and E.A. Pocock) and Toronto (James Scott and Lucy MacGregor).

The relaunching of the Ontario CLP infuriated ILP loyalists. The ILP provincial executive publicly reiterated its position as the dominant labour party in the province, while a Hamilton ILPer described the event as 'the biggest "red" meeting that he ever was at.' The ILP legislative caucus, which had not been represented at the convention, was similarly dismissive of the Ontario CLP's claims.[55] Nevertheless, an alternative organization that combined the impulse towards labour political representation with an implicit critique of the faltering ILP had the potential to draw increasing numbers to its ranks. Still, the Ontario CLP had not adopted an explicitly socialist platform in 1918 and, in

1921, it was still measured in its criticisms of the ILP as it tried to avoid an open split.

Events in London revealed both the earnest desire of Ontario CLP leaders to maintain a united front with the ILP and the logic of the party's separate existence. The local labour movement was evenly divided between partisans and opponents of independent political action, and only in 1919 had the London ILP convinced the trades council to join it in forming a Labor Representation Committee (LRC) to contest elections. Success in the provincial election strengthened the hands of J.F. Thomson and William G. Tite, the central advocates of electoral action.[56] By late 1920, somewhat later than the rest of the province, these developments culminated in a blossoming of working-class educational and political life in London. A London Labor Forum, sponsored by the London LRC, was established in October and soon became a centre of public discussion with speakers from various currents in the farmer and labour political movements. Conservatives were less enthusiastic about this development, and in early 1921 the trades council debated whether to secede from the Labor Forum to protest a socialist speaker. The centrepiece of this political opening for the left was a weekly labour paper, the *Herald*, which appeared in September 1920 and won the endorsements of the London, Stratford, St Thomas, Guelph, and Brantford trades councils.[57] Its lively columns supported public ownership, low tariffs, and political action. Harry Ashplant contributed a regular column on 'Impure Currency' (i.e., paper money), and international news told of achievements in Australia and Britain. Most importantly for the local political movement, 10,000 copies of the *Herald* were produced in support of municipal LRC candidates in December 1920.[58]

The excitement did not last long. The hold on power by labourists and socialists was always tenuous and, in the January 1921 elections (following Ashplant's disastrous campaign for mayor), conservatives swept the offices of the London TLC. In their efforts to rid the council of 'reds,' an appeal was made to the AFL that the charter of the Federal Labor Union, whose leaders included Thomson and Arthur Mould, be lifted. In 1923, in a move aimed against the Labor Party, the London TLC forbade any of its officers to appear on political platforms. Ironically, the carpenters, machinists, and stovemounters took advantage of the measure to demand that the TLC secretary and treasurer be ejected from the council for having appeared on Tory platforms. In the end, Paddy Draper intervened in the name of the TLCC to save the local conservatives from being hoist with their own petard.[59]

The defection of the London TLC thrust political action back into the hands of the rather inactive London ILP. Weakened provincially and active only as a means to re-elect two rather ineffectual labour aldermen, the local party was moribund. Consequently, the LRC, re-named the London Labor Party and now accepting individual memberships, requested recognition as a Canadian Labor Party branch in the autumn of 1921. The Ontario CLP executive refused, reiterating its position that the CLP was a united front of the ILP and socialist, farmer, and trade-union organizations. It was not in competition with the ILP. Those who wished to join as individuals, they declared, must join the ILP. While the effort to form a new labour party based on individual membership and to the left of the ILP was, for the moment, on hold, it was the remnants of the London Labor Party that ran the 1921 federal election campaign of Arthur Mould.[60]

The main impetus for expanding the role of the Ontario CLP came from Toronto where, in 1919, socialists initiated the establishment of a branch of the Ontario CLP, under the presidency of left-wing SDPer John MacDonald, to contest the municipal election. The Toronto ILP and the trades council, as well as a substantial number of local unions, participated. The effort was not particularly successful, and by 1921 the *Labor Leader* could jibe that Simpson was the sole surviving member of the Toronto CLP. The effort reflected a wide desire in the city for greater working-class unity on a program to the left of the provincial ILP. The project soon took the form of a Labor Representation Committee which did not, for the moment, claim any connection with the inactive Ontario CLP. The Toronto LRC's real inauguration was in the 1921 federal election. The candidates were all socialists of one stripe or another: James Simpson, John Bruce, Harriet Prenter, and Harry Kerwin. All had long histories in the political labour movement and now represented the current that had come to dominate the local trades council. The *Labor Leader*'s dismissal of the LRC as a 'Committee of Red Dictators' was unable to prevent the TDLC from granting the campaign $300.[61] The candidates received 9,360 votes. While their radicalism did not lose them votes, independent political action, this time of a socialist character, had once again failed to make an impact on Toronto. Nevertheless, a break with the programmatic vagueness of labourism had been made. Renamed the Labor Representation Political Association (LRPA), it presented a united front for electoral activity with at least thirty local affiliates by the 1923 provincial election. The strength of socialism in Toronto was reflected in the extremely representative character of the LRPA and in its willingness to accept the leadership of socialists. From the revolutionary socialist Workers' Party and the Women's Labor League on the left to the moulders and street-railway workers on the right, the LRPA represented an unlikely spectrum of political allies who were committed to the preservation of working-class representation at Queen's Park. The *Labor Leader*, true to its nativism, commented on the participation of a large number of 'men and women of Eastern and Central European origin' not previously active in the electoral movement. The Toronto ILP appeared satisfied with the developments and contributed generously to the LRPA.[62]

The vibrant working-class autodidactic culture associated with labour's strong post-war presence in Toronto similarly flourished in the first years of the 1920s. The weekly Sunday meetings of the Toronto ILP Forum were the cornerstone of this tradition. Week after week, Forum attendance averaged 800; a total of 15,000 each season. Fifteen hundred packed the hall for Scottish Labour MP Neal MacLean and 1,200 heard William Z. Foster, known to Canadian workers for organizing in the Chicago stockyards and for the massive 1919 American steel strike. More than 2,000 heard French socialist Jean Longuet. Working-class tastes in education remained eclectic. In the 1921–2 session, Chief F. Loft spoke on 'Unrest among the Indians,' Bishop Francis Michael Fallon on separate schools, John G. O'Donoghue on 'Appeals to the Privy Council,' and Professor J.W. Bridges on the 'Psychological Analysis of Personality.' Revolutionary socialists and conservatives were all welcomed on the platform. For workers interested in a broad political education, this was the best show in the province, and one that always included a singalong from ILP song sheets with the lyrics to 'Onward Faithful Comrades' (to the tune of 'Onward Christian Soldiers'), 'Toilers Arise,' 'The Red Flag,' and 'The Internationale.' The meetings did not go unnoticed outside the labour movement. At the insistence of the *Telegram*, J.A. Dale was refused promotion at the University of Toronto for chairing the Forum with guest speaker Scott Nearing.

It was fitting that the Toronto ILP Forum hosted the symbolic split between revolutionary and reform socialism. On 28 January 1921, speaking of the need to build the Third International, John MacDonald declared the ILP 'moribund' and announced his intention of building a party of socialism. The following week, James Simpson declared his ground. He stood for reformism in the tradition of the British Labour Party. Notably, however, MacDonald and Simpson would continue to co-operate in the LRPA and the Ontario CLP, and both would appear again at the Toronto ILP Forum.[63]

By 1922, the growing rejection of labourism as a political current was apparent to Ontario CLP supporters, who sought to rescue political action from the sinking ship of the ILP. In the aftermath of the ILP's disastrous showing in the 1921 federal election, the Ontario CLP could report growth, a notable achievement in the context of falling trade-union membership. With fifteen new affiliates, including several local labour councils, the total affiliated membership approached 40,000. At the urging of the London Labor Party, the convention that year decided to establish CLP branches based on individual membership, placing the Ontario CLP directly in competition with the ILP for members. The wording of the resolution, although attempting to smooth relations between the organizations, left little doubt that the two parties represented distinct alternatives in the political labour movement: 'It shall be expressly understood in the charter given [local Ontario CLP branches] that they are not in conflict with local ILP's except in friendly rivalry to build up the labor movement.'[64]

Around the province the debate opened. Joseph Marks, the moving spirit of the ILP, declared that the Ontario CLP was unrepresentative of labour. In Hamilton, both the trades council and the majority of the ILP stood true to their original conceptions of labourism despite a direct appeal by Ontario CLP president Harry Kerwin. In London, there was little opposition from the remnants of the ILP to joining, and a second branch of the London Labor Party was formed for approximately one hundred individual members who did not already belong through their affiliated organizations. In Toronto, where socialists had always played a significant role in the ILP, the LRPA already represented the goals of the Ontario CLP. Revolutionary socialists, such as William Moriarty, were critical of the 'evasions' in the LRPA's federal election manifesto and its attempt to ascribe the economic crisis to the war rather than to capitalism. Still, Moriarty and his newly founded Workers' Party of Canada (WPC) affiliated, as did the British-based Amalgamated Society of Carpenters, the Canadian Electrical Trades Union, and the Amalgamated Clothing Workers, all engaged in bitter jurisdictional disputes with the international unions that formed the bulk of the Ontario CLP union base.[65]

Only six years after the founding of the Independent Labor Party of Ontario, and less than four years after the election of the farmer-labour government of E.C. Drury, the province's political labour movement had undergone a startling metamorphosis. Socialism had displaced labourism. The 1922 ILP convention had seen the censuring of MPPs Homuth and Swayze for their voting records, and of Tooms for appearing on a Liberal platform. None had appeared to face the charges. Not surprisingly, an air of doom hung over the 1923 convention of the ILP. Confronting a provincial election, the small gathering of only nineteen delegates from a mere twelve branches (even though the party still claimed sixty-six branches) reopened the bitter debate over its relationship with the United Farmers. The main resolution, that the ILP participate in no government 'unless the Labor Party is sufficiently strong to form a government,' was defeated and the alliance with the UFO reaffirmed. A sign of the ILP's increasing isolation was the decision of the Labor Educational Association, which had sponsored the party's founding convention in 1917, to turn to the American Federation of Labor's 'non-partisan' approach. A month before the 1923 election the association approached all candidates with a questionnaire, declaring that it would support candidates who favoured legislation for the eight-hour day and wage hikes for workers on provincial contracts.[66]

The 1923 convention of the Ontario Section of the Canadian Labor Party, in contrast, outlined an election platform that focused on the failures of the provincial government to respond to working-class demands. The Drury government's failure to pay union wages, the niggardly levels of women's minimum wages and mothers' allowances, and the failure to improve the Factory Act suggested that, while not explicitly socialist, the Ontario CLP stood for a coherent series of reforms that were of greater significance than participation in a coalition government. With the failure of labourism and the ILP, the banner of independent political action had been picked up by the socialists, both reformist and revolutionary, who guided the Ontario CLP. The appeal of the Ontario CLP, in contrast to that of the ILP, was evident over the course of the next year, as thirty-eight new affiliates were gained. More than one hundred delegates attended the 1924 convention. And its message contrasted sharply with the language of the ILP. Whereas labourism had traced workers' powerlessness to electoral exclusion, the CLP spoke more broadly of a ruling class based on capitalist social relations and private property. The program of the Ontario CLP, however, did not speak of a revolutionary assault on capitalist power, and the participation by the communists of the Workers' Party of Canada, though substantial, was not overwhelming. Rather, this was an electoral united front with reformist socialists like Jimmie Simpson, Arthur Mould, and Hamilton alderman Sam Lawrence. The Ontario CLP continued to model itself on the British Labour Party and to applaud its electoral victories.

Electorally, the Ontario CLP had few prospects, given the devastating experience of the ILP. Moreover, an explicitly left-wing political movement was unlikely to be able to recreate the unity of 1919, a unity that had been predicated on the lack of a political program by the ILP. Independent working-class political action had come to be identified with socialists, and its non-socialist form – labourism – had disappeared from the electoral landscape and from within the labour movement.

Central to the future of this movement was the affiliation of the Workers' Party of Canada to the Ontario CLP. The WPC, which included several of the key militants in the Toronto labour movement from the days of the 1919 general strike, had emerged as the most substantial revolutionary current in Ontario, although this status was still challenged in the west by the One Big Union.[67] The Workers' Party best articulated socialists' desire to bridge the gap between industrial and political action that had been a defining characteristic of labourism. The distinction between labourism and the reformist social democracy represented within the CLP was effectively drawn by the paper of the WPC when it contrasted the activities of James Woodsworth in the federal House of Commons with those of the provincial ILP caucus. Although critical of Woodsworth, the *Worker* praised his effective use of Parliament to 'focus attention on the issues of the mass struggles outside of parliament ... and so perhaps force whatever concessions possible from the capitalist class.' The ILP, in contrast, had failed to direct the industrial militancy of 1919 and 1920 towards attainable political goals. The legislative caucus, argued the *Worker*, was directly responsible for the demoralization of its working-class supporters. 'One does not expect Rollo, Halcrow and their fellows, to have any sense of the international interests of the working class or of the developing social revolution, but, even from them, one does at least look for some clear-cut declaration and activity in the problems of unemployment, wage cuts, etc.'[68] Erstwhile ILP members and voters had foreseen a social revolution of sorts that would follow an electoral breakthrough; their assessment of the record of the ILP and its legislative caucus could not have been very much different.

Defeat

In the 1923 provincial election there was no *Industrial Banner* to rally the province's working-class voters. Simpson had never given it the attention it required to thrive (as Marks caustically reminded the labour movement), and it was published only monthly from June 1921 until its demise early the following year. Faced with a hostile London trades council no longer willing to cover its debts, the *Herald* fared no better. Independent working-class political action had no voice, and the actions of the labour MPPs failed to speak for themselves. While the alliance with the UFO had survived widespread criticism from the trade-union movement, it was severely shaken in 1923 by a growing tendency for the UFO simply to ignore a weakened ILP. The first sign of dissension came in South Wellington where, citing the failure of Guelph voters to support their candidate in 1921, the UFO reneged on an agreement to support an ILP candidate in the provincial election. In St Catharines, the UFO failed to show at a joint nominating convention, instead sending a message that it disapproved of Frank Greenlaw's lukewarm support of the government and of Attorney-General Raney's temperance enforcement and intended to nominate its own candidate. In Peterborough West, Thomas Tooms similarly lost UFO support.[69]

Difficulties also came from within the ILP. In early 1922, Halcrow's attacks on the government and, by implication, the ILP cabinet ministers led the Labor group to renounce him as caucus leader. A year later he refused to accept the party's renomination if it implied that he was committed to supporting the alliance with the UFO. When the Hamilton ILP, by a two to one majority, accepted the alliance, Halcrow left the meeting determined to run as an independent. The city's ILP was divided over whether to oppose him. Moreover, trade-union conservatives had regained their initiative. Not only was the LEAO distancing itself from the ILP but, contrary to the policy of supporting the ILP that had been announced in the *Canadian Congress Journal*, Tom Moore endorsed MacBride, who was also running as an independent. Nor was there any help from the Liberals as there had been in St Catharines in 1921; Liberal candidates opposed the ILP in all contests in southern Ontario except South Waterloo.

In Toronto, the LRPA manifesto exemplified the Ontario CLP's labourist roots and socialist trajectory. While delivering a ringing denunciation of capitalism and a call for a 'New Social Order,' the LRPA uncritically lauded the rather meagre record of the Drury government.[70] The LRPA's remarkable choice of candidates revealed similarly incongruous thinking. In South-West Toronto the standard was carried by revolutionary socialists Malcolm Bruce and John MacDonald. In Riverdale, carpenter Alex Lyon, a former OBUer and current Workers' Party member, was nominated. In South-East Toronto, the candidates were John G. O'Donoghue, who had been censured in 1919 for his support of Adam Beck, and James T. Gunn of the Canadian Federation of Labour, in the eyes of the *Financial Post*, a safe and sane unionist.[71]

Given the disintegration of labourism as a political current in Ontario, the ILP was fortunate to survive the provincial election with two and, shortly thereafter, three members. Peter Heenan was re-elected by acclamation in Kenora and was joined by a new member and fellow railroader, John F. Callan, who narrowly won the neighbouring riding of Rainy River. In South Waterloo, Karl Homuth was eventually returned to Queen's Park in a 1924 election held due to voting irregularities.[72] In all, seventeen labour candidates received 34,561 votes, a loss of 90,000 labour electors in less than four years. The record of the UFO-ILP government, combined with defeats on the industrial front, undermined the working-class self-confidence and vision that had originally propelled the ILP to Queen's Park. Growing apathy was reflected in reduced voter turn-out. In twenty-two ridings contested by the ILP in 1919 (Kenora was not counted) 352,342 voters went to the polls; in 1923 the number had declined to 258,174. Almost 100,000 voters stayed home. In London, where Adam Beck received four times the vote of ILP incumbent Hugh Stevenson, the turn-out was only 63 per cent of that of 1919. In Hamilton, Halcrow (unopposed, as it turned out, by the ILP) and Rollo each placed third in the polls, as did Tooms in Peterborough and Greenlaw in St Catharines. The results in some northern ridings were less humiliating, but the ILP still lagged far behind the front runners. In Toronto, interestingly, the left-wing candidates in the west end retained the traditional labour vote, while O'Donoghue and Gunn fared very poorly in South-East Toronto, with less than a thousand votes each.

At Queen's Park, the ILP caucus soon disappeared. Callan did not survive the next election, while Heenan and Homuth soon returned to the folds of the Liberal and Conservative parties. The old order was firmly re-established, and the collective memory of a province governed by the direct representatives of the producers began to fade. The death of the new democracy on the electoral front was complete, and the obituary was suitably written by its main enemy from within the labour movement, the *Labor Leader*. Under the heading 'The End of Ontario's Experiment in Class Government,' the *Leader* celebrated the return of democracy as it conceived it. That it shared the views of business in this regard was evident in its vision of the future: 'We feel safe in saying that during the next four years Ontario will feel more secure and business generally will feel more confident with the old party back in

Queen's Park.'[73] The legacy of a labourist presence in government was minimal. No new industrial-relations regime emerged; it had hardly been considered. The provincial government appeared content to allow Ottawa to extinguish the sparks of confrontation in the ad hoc manner it had adopted since Mackenzie King's tenure in the Department of Labour. Neither the UFO nor the ILP caucus displayed much interest in becoming a party to industrial conflicts, which, they apparently felt, could only undermine their increasingly tenuous electoral bases. New social legislation in the form of a Minimum Wage Act for women and a Mothers' Allowance Act had been passed. Improvements were made to the Workmen's Compensation Act, and the franchise in municipal elections was extended. These were, from one point of view, solid achievements; labourism had never specifically promised more. Yet it had implied a great deal more. The ILP's 1923 election campaign struck no chord of working-class rebellion; its promise had faded in the wake of defeated strikes and dashed hopes for an ethical political system that could advance the dignity and well-being of labour. Less than a decade after Sarajevo, the 'new democracy' was a dim memory.

Conclusion: Real Democracy[1]

Through the war and its aftermath Ontario workers had constructed a vision of democracy that was in constant tension with that of their bosses. This vision lacked clarity, perhaps, to the ongoing frustration of socialists who struggled valiantly to bring it into focus. But in the 1919 provincial election, and in the amalgamation movement and incipient industrial unionism, a notion of democracy defined in collective terms was taking shape. It was a democracy that challenged class distinctions in Canadian society. Of necessity, it incorporated notions of economic and social justice absent from what revolutionary socialists readily decried as 'the sham democracy of capitalism.'[2] It was not confined to a minority of radicals. Even conservative unionists, such as AFL organizer John Flett, implicitly challenged the idea that democracy could be won in the 'political' sphere alone without the achievement by workers of economic rights as well. As he told a St Catharines audience, 'During the Great War, the young men of the nation went out and fought courageously, and won enduring fame for the nation, and today the nation says: "Yes, you fought for democracy, but really we have no work to give you," or if they have a job to hand out, it's at starvation wages.'[3] Workers' livelihoods could not easily be separated from the issue of democracy. In labourist terms, though, democracy need not require the demise of capitalism; it merely necessitated the elimination of the 'profiteer' – the capitalist under the protection of the politicians of the old, corrupt political parties. By the time Flett spoke in late 1921, however, it was apparent to growing numbers of activists that labourism had proven incapable of inaugurating the new democracy either in terms of a more accessible, direct electoral system or in terms of material benefits for the province's workers. Two years of government by the 'producers' of the countryside and the city had brought few gains.

Militant unionism had been the fuel that fired working-class confidence and prepared the ground for independent political action. Yet labourism held no solution for the difficult problem of transforming collective working-class power in the economic sphere into political power. In the West, the general strike became the means by which to bridge the economic and political spheres; radicals had hoped that the exercise of workers' industrial power would provoke a political crisis. Labourism's fidelity to the rules of liberal democracy, however, demanded the strict separation of the two spheres. In fact, labourists viewed their democratic task as that of rescuing the legislature from the economic influence of the profiteers. Their image of an untainted political realm did not allow them to countenance combining their electoral weight with industrial pressure as a means of winning new ground. Instead, the fate of labourism rested on the integrity and skill of its eleven members in the provincial parliament. The union movement received little political help from Queen's Park (as in the case of the Hydro workers), and the caucus squandered the support of the working-class movement which spawned it. Each reached an inglorious end.

Socialism did not share labourism's overwhelming confidence in the legislature. The boundary between labourism and socialism was not fixed and, as we have seen, the political complexion of labourism varied considerably from one ILP branch to another and fused with socialism in the Ontario Section of the Canadian Labor Party. The manifest failure of the labourist caucus at Queen's Park had tilted the balance towards the latter, and labourism disappeared from the political landscape of the 1920s. What, then, of socialism? Its fate reveals much about the consequences of the events this study has considered. In spite of its success in Toronto and particularly on the trades council where conservatives had been stymied by the *Labor Leader* affair, socialism had no organizational presence between the effective demise of the Social Democratic Party in 1919 and the emergence of the Workers' Party of Canada (WPC) in 1921. The only exceptions were organizations such as the One Big Union or the Socialist Labor Party, which, for different reasons, placed themselves outside the mainstream of the labour movement and had little effect on its direction.

At its first public conference in December 1921, the Workers' Party attracted a substantial number of the best-known radical labour leaders in the city and the region: Alex Lyon, J.E. Dobbs, Harriet Prenter, Arthur Skidmore, Fred Peel, John MacDonald, William Moriarty, Florence Custance.[4] The WPC was securely rooted in the events of the post-war upsurge. Its acceptance by the Ontario CLP as an affiliate was, above all, a recognition that it was a legitimate current within the labour movement. Despite the WPC's late arrival on the political scene, it embodied what radicals had been proposing through 1919 and 1920. Tim Buck's response to a Windsor correspondent's request for information on the WPC reads much like the socialist proposals in 1919, or the TDLC's 1920 resolutions calling for industrial unionism and autonomy for Canadian locals:

> As you will see by the Program, our policy is to build up a left-wing movement throughout the existing trade unions, so as to propagate the idea of amalgamation of craft unions into powerful industrial organizations, to help in every possible way to build up a mass labor Party on a federated basis similar to the British Labor Party so as to abtain [sic] unity of working class political action, support to all real organizational efforts to organize the unorganized workers, with the end always in view of a powerful virile labor movement that will be able to challenge the present rulers of society for supremacy.[5]

In short, support for the new Workers' Party was consistent with the thinking of many of the left-wing veterans of 1919. By the spring of 1919, the revolutionary socialists behind the *Ontario Labor News* had already rejected the secessionist movement for the future communist strategy of 'boring from within' the existing unions to win them to industrial unionism and socialism.

Although the new party embodied the aspirations of a significant number of workers from the 1919–20 upsurge, this was insufficient to propel it to prominence. In 1919 socialists had been checked by the success of the ILP and in the early 1920s by its failure. The WPC was formed in the midst of political and industrial defeats, hardly an auspicious beginning for a new party, regardless of its character. As a consequence of the defeats, the political space that the Rev. William Ivens had found in his 1919 tour of Ontario had inexorably closed. Then, the working class had appeared to labourists and socialists alike as the prime agency of social change. Defeats had dulled that vision. Democracy as defined by the authors of the growing red scare now excluded radicalism and with it any independent political role for the workers' movement. The affinity of the WPC to the Russian Revolution and its success in drawing together immigrant radicals enabled conservative opponents to draw on nativist sentiment to isolate the new party. In the London trades council, conservative Fred Young announced that there were two opposing forces in the world: British and Bolshevik. The *Labor Leader* denounced the 'Reds' as being in the pay of Moscow and ran lurid stories about Welland 'Russian Reds' threatening church-goers with death.[6]

Red-baiting was hardly an innovation, as the *Financial Post, Saturday Night*, the *Labor Leader*, and the Toronto *Telegram* had amply demonstrated. Moreover, nativist sentiments had been weakly challenged in the working-class upsurge, and with a contracting labour market nativism again became a powerful instrument with which to isolate radicals. The WPC's internationalism ran afoul of a concept of 'British Democracy' that the ILP had used rather than challenged. From the Toronto Board of Trade to the TLCC executive, demands for the 'Canadianization' of immigrants reflected both a fear of the 'foreigner' and an equation between southern and eastern Europeans and Bolshevism. Directed against an organization that challenged the credentials of 'British democracy' and contained an absolute majority of non-Anglo-Celtic members, it was a powerful charge. In 1918 the Greater Toronto Labor Party had defended itself by claiming that it was 98 per cent British-Canadian. The WPC could make no such claim, being largely composed of Finnish, Jewish, Ukrainian, and Russian immigrants, and it was by no means disposed to passivity in the face of nativist attacks.[7]

Economic depression, the firing of militants, and the WPC's commitment to organizing the working class as a whole led the party to concentrate much of its efforts on organizing the unemployed. In Hamilton and Toronto, large and militant Unemployed Associations were formed at the initiative of the WPC. They pointed to capitalism as the source of joblessness and demanded 'work or full maintenance.'[8] The Hamilton Trades and Labor Council maintained its distance from a movement it considered too radical, while the TDLC lent its support in spite of some reservations. To those open to a nativist attack on the radicals, however, these attempts to organize an immigrant underclass socially distinct from conservative craft unionists placed the WPC beyond the pale of respectability. With its repeated references to Russia, the new party appeared strange to many Canadians not used to judging by standards other than British; it could not escape an image as 'foreign' and therefore undemocratic.

Although the Workers' Party had succeeded in establishing a space for itself, the death of the new democracy was by now obvious. Only those whose birthplace, politics, and respectable jobs corresponded to conservative notions of democracy gained admittance to the emerging polity. A wider definition of democracy had obtained in 1919, but the

WPC arrived on the scene too late to benefit from its promise. Revolutionary socialism had had a substantial presence in 1919, but such support did not accrue to any organized working-class party. The narrow political culture of the 1920s accepted few newcomers. With the defeat of labourism, the WPC stood as the only organized force potentially blocking a return to the political hegemony of the Liberals and Conservatives. The exhaustion of working-class militancy and the Workers' Party's excommunication as an 'alien enemy' of Canadian democracy effectively isolated the new party. Socialism, including revolutionary socialism, would have a permanent place in Ontario political life, but in the 1920s only at the margins.

Workers in southern Ontario saw a new political world open and then close in the decade after 1914. The labour movement entered the war with its own critique of militarism and autocracy, a critique that could be mobilized at home as well as abroad. The successful campaign for workmen's compensation gave labour both the provincial organization and the confidence to press its concerns collectively, and a specifically working-class view of democracy led increasing numbers into unions during the war and into large and militant strikes. Government and business accusations that such workers were acting disloyally, as in the Hamilton munitions strike, were readily dismissed. Was it not loyal to uphold fairness and democracy against autocracy on whatever front?

However, workers' views of democracy were not entirely autonomous. Whatever measures they were willing to take through their unions to defend their crafts and their wages in their workplaces, most workers shared the notion that permanent change must come through an electoral process. In 1919 Ontario workers swept onto the electoral stage. Like the organized farmers, workers grew to see the Liberals and Conservatives as merely patronage machines blocking the course of democracy. As a solution, they proposed new, although hardly innovative, electoral mechanisms: the initiative, referendum and recall, the abolition of appointed offices, and proportional representation. Workers built upon established traditions of working-class self-education to attempt to prepare themselves to enter this political stage and to run the government in the interests of all rather than simply in the interests of the politicians and profiteers. The movement gave impetus to working-class women, who found a congenial arena in which to put forward their own demands and constructed organizations that linked the characteristics of labourism with those of their own community. Such women took an active role in the struggle for the new democracy, albeit in a gendered manner that, like labourism itself, failed to address the roots of inequality. On the basis of such a wide mobilization, the Independent Labor Party and the Canadian Labor Party openly identified themselves as parties of the labour movement. Less often did they fully consider the consequences of entering the political arena as a class rather than as individuals.

For decades, labourists had attempted to build a movement independent of partyism, but broad support had eluded them. Finally, with their creation of a successful political movement and collective massive entrance into electoral politics as a class, they had achieved a break with individualist notions of democracy, provoking the Liberals and Conservatives to attack the ILP as the harbinger of 'class legislation.' But the experience of the war had reinforced an understanding that workers had been excluded from power and had to organize to gain effective representation. Through their unions, a segment of skilled workers had long recognized that collective action was necessary if they were to be heard on the shop floor. During the war, much larger numbers of workers applied the same conclusion to electoral action. The transition, however, was a difficult one. The rules of collective action in the workplace, although disputed, were well established. The defence of craft autonomy and living standards through the threat of a strike was a familiar experience. But what would workers do in government? The ILP responded vaguely, not only because they were afraid of shattering the unique working-class electoral alliance of labourists, socialists, single-taxers, suffragists, and other reformers, but also because they honestly did not know. Their critique of the 'old reactionary parties' had concentrated on their corrupt manipulation of the electoral system. The ILP could be more honest and more democratic, but that did not provide much of a guideline for legislative action.

Moreover, action might unravel the unity so painfully constructed. Socialists particularly were wary of being seen as the source of disunity in such a successful electoral movement. Having pushed for the organization of the Ontario Section of the Canadian Labor Party in 1918, they were loath to force an explicitly socialist program on it, and they all but abandoned such ideas until the ILP had demonstrably run out of steam. Instead, they inadvertently reinforced the division between electoral and industrial action by concentrating most of their energies on the latter. The collective impulse in the hands of socialists was focused on the formation of militant industrial unions, or at least trades federations, and attempts to refine local trades councils into centres of working-class political life. The results were impressive and surpassed the ethnically limited solidarity of labourism by drawing in immigrant workers.

Capital and the state responded on several fronts. The initial repressive response, characterized by well-established practices of firing union militants and hiring strike-breakers or, on the federal level, by Orders in Council under the War Measures Act, proved generally ineffective, and 'co-operation' gained prominence. This did not mean that repressive tactics were abandoned. The War Measures Act stayed in place, and amendments to the Immigration Act, as well as the passage of the infamous Section 98 of the Criminal Code, provided powerful weapons with which to fight 'sedition.'[9] Such new measures involved labelling their targets as subversives or aliens. The state would uphold British justice; but, by definition, not all were entitled to its benefits. In May 1921, in sharp contrast to police restraint in 1919, mounted Toronto police charged a meeting in front of city hall organized by the local unemployed association. Their victims were those excluded from the democracy of the 1920s: radicals, the unemployed, and immigrants.[10]

Measures directed against independent political action were more subtle. A 1920 amendment to the Dominion Elections Act forbade any 'unincorporated company or association,' (i.e., a trade union) from contributing to an electoral campaign. Also in 1920, president D.B. Hanna of the Canadian National Railway issued an order forbidding any employee of the CNR from running for political office. In November 1920, the effect of the Hanna Order was driven home: Toronto labour candidate James Higgins was fired from his job at the CNR's Leaside shops for violating the order. A single political appointee of the federal government could, at a stroke, abolish the political rights of 85,000 workers. While Higgins was eventually rehired, the federal government's defence of the order signalled the closure of the post-war debate on democratic reform.[11]

The response of business is particularly interesting because of its attempt to reconcile two objectives. Businessmen wished to limit the state's activity because they were afraid official recognition of the claims of labour would legitimize its presence as a class. Although it was difficult to attack conciliatory efforts such as the National Industrial Conference, the Canadian Manufacturers' Association and eventually business as a whole were resolute in their refusal to allow a tendency towards treating labour as a class to continue. At the same time, larger firms were wary of running afoul of the post-war crusade for democracy. Therefore, as business responded to working-class militancy by a wide range of elaborate (if often jerry-built) ameliorative programs, it took great effort to clothe them in the vestments of democracy. The pinnacle of such measures was company unionism, reflagged as industrial representation or even industrial democracy. On a national level, business spokespersons such as Willison or Maclean strove to convince employers not to challenge directly workers' goal of a post-war democratic reconstruction of Canadian society, but to direct it towards a less dangerous end. Business and conservative labour, they argued, shared a conception of democracy that would exclude those who challenged the status quo. By the mid-1920s, however, such rhetoric was rare. Capital confidently focused on defeating the organizations of the working class, both industrial and political. That accomplished, promises of a new relationship through industrial councils or tripartism were no longer necessary.

For the labour movement, time had run out. The opportunity to impose its concepts of democracy had been lost, as a demoralized and demobilized working class lost faith in its own transforming power. If democracy is defined, in part, as mass participation in deciding social priorities and direction, the post-war uprising in Ontario qualifies as a unique democratic moment in our history. It was an imperfect moment, however, as labourism had no ready solutions to workers' lack of power, and the undercurrent of nativism survived to return with a vengeance in the 1920s. Nevertheless, a massive, popular, debate on the nature and direction of Canadian society raised a host of possible futures. Parallel movements on the 'economic' and 'political' fronts repeatedly promised (or threatened) to fuse into a movement against capitalism. The new democracy, however, was soon stifled. In 1923 the Hamilton-based *New Democracy* abandoned its roots and changed its name to the *Canadian Labor World*. The editor's explanation of the move exemplifies the political culture of the 1920s and serves as a fitting epitaph for the 'new democracy.'

> And we knew all the time that the name 'New Democracy' did not stand for the best ideals of labor. There is really no such thing as a 'new' democracy. Christ gave us the real democracy, the real key to success and lasting peace. That was 'real' democracy. What was meant by 'New Democracy' as it originally stood at the head of this publication when the 'Reds' owned and controlled it, was the destruction by force of the present ideals of civilization and placing the national utilities and resources in the hands of the red-eyed and cov-

etous element that hated to earn its bread by the honest sweat of its brow.[12]

Such 'real' democracy had little room for dissent; the 'new democracy' had been built upon it.

Appendix: Strikes and Lock-outs

Regional* Strikes and Lock-outs: 1914–24

Strike Totals: 1914–24

Year	Strikes	Strikers	Days lost
1914	21	1,287	49,508
1915	16	1,085	25,255
1916	50	5,825	77,020
1917	43	6,299	53,604
1918	56	9,155	121,635
1919	109	35,770	852,235
1920	113	14,095	202,837
1921	61	8,224	478,964
1922	33	1,846	318,200
1923	23	1,055	141,560
1924	21	2,367	17,280

*Bounded on the west by Windsor, on the east by Peterborough, and on the north by the Georgian Bay ports

Toronto Strike Totals: 1914–24

Year	Strikes	Strikers	Days lost
1914	8	470	32,350
1915	10	554	20,846
1916	10	953	6,413
1917	15	4,286	29,858
1918	23	6,823	88,636
1919	30	27,855	723,379
1920	32	5,214	55,858
1921	17	4,023	344,792
1922	15	1,408	295,768
1923	12	351	128,197
1924	12	2,126	13,369

Region* Outside Toronto Strike Totals: 1914–24

Year	Strikes	Strikers	Days lost
1914	13	817	17,158
1915	6	531	4,409
1916	40	4,872	70,607
1917	28	2,013	23,748
1918	33	3,332	32,999
1919	79	7,915	128,856
1920	81	8,881	146,979
1921	44	4,201	134,172
1922	18	438	22,432
1923	11	704	13,363
1924	9	241	3,911

*Bounded on the west by Windsor, on the east by Peterborough, and on the north by the Georgian Bay ports

Separate Fronts: Conflict by Industry, 1914–24

Cigar Makers' Strike Totals: 1914–24

Year	Strikes	Strikers	Days lost
1914	0	0	0
1915	0	0	0
1916	6	1,098	17,846
1917	2	380	7,223
1918	4	435	30,972
1919	3	142	6,150
1920	3	582	3,538
1921	2	350	1,750
1922	0	0	0
1923	0	0	0
1924	0	0	0

Metal Trades' Strikes Totals: 1914–24

Year	Strikes	Strikers	Days lost
1914	4	240	2,756
1915	3	360	3,654
1916	14	2,748	38,970
1917	19	1,680	17,892
1918	13	2,127	32,876
1919	18	7,962	522,042
1920	28	2,412	63,349
1921	6	141	8,419
1922	3	36	460
1923	4	190	1,010
1924	2	25	865

Marine Trades' Strike Totals: 1914–24

Year	Strikes	Strikers	Days lost
1914	0	0	0
1915	0	0	0
1916	1	0	0
1917	0	0	0
1918	3	461	5,440
1919	8	2,922	53,892
1920	1	10	200
1921	1	0	0
1922	0	0	0
1923	0	0	0
1924	0	0	0

Niagara and Chippawa Canal Workers' Strike Totals: 1914–24

Year	Strikes	Strikers	Days lost
1914	0	0	0
1915	0	0	0
1916	1	300	300
1917	0	0	0
1918	0	0	0
1919	2	1,550	16,525
1920	2	2,034	38,204
1921	0	0	0
1922	2	40	240
1923	1	23	828
1924	0	0	0

Building Trades' Strike Totals: 1914–24

Year	Strikes	Strikers	Days lost
1914	11	827	29,212
1915	2	311	18,631
1916	7	158	3,344
1917	5	478	7,210
1918	11	284	4,011
1919	18	3,344	29,101
1920	31	3,105	43,986
1921	18	1,382	60,493
1922	11	1,055	32,870
1923	4	459	2,724
1924	7	270	3,628

Printing Trades' Strike Totals: 1914–24

Year	Strikes	Strikers	Days lost
1914	0	0	0
1915	0	0	0
1916	1	0	0
1917	0	0	0
1918	0	0	0
1919	2	14	106
1920	4	220	586
1921	5	2,317	332,394
1922	0	0	271,273
1923	0	0	5,799
1924	0	0	0

Garment and Textile Trades' Strike Totals: 1914–24

Year	Strikes	Strikers	Days lost
1914	3	185	16,350
1915	4	122	1,686
1916	2	70	1,125
1917	6	295	2,714
1918	5	346	18,766
1919	7	2,822	120,211
1920	14	619	11,831
1921	9	1,525	27,764
1922	6	207	5,285
1923	11	194	126,474
1924	7	114	762

SOURCES: Compiled from National Archives of Canada, RG 27, Department of Labour, Strike and Lock-out files; local newspapers; and labour papers

Notes

Abbreviations

AO   Archives of Ontario
Building Industries Conference   Joint Conference of the Building and
   Construction Industries in Canada. Held in Ottawa, May 3–6, 1921
CAR   *Canadian Annual Review*
CCJ   *Canadian Congress Journal*
CIRA   Canadian Industrial Reconstruction Association
CMA   Canadian Manufactures' Association
CRA   Canadian Reconstruction Association
FP   *Financial Post*
IB   *Industrial Banner*
IC   *Industrial Canada*
ILP   Independent Labor Party
'IR Information'   'Industrial Relations Information Obtained from Firms
   Visited'
LG   *Labour Gazette*
LL   *Labour Leader*
LN   *Labor News*
LOC   *Labour Organization in Canada*
London TLC   London Trades and Labor Council
MMJ   *Machinists' Monthly Journal*
MTL   Metropolitan Toronto Library
NA   National Archives of Canada
ND   *New Democracy*
NIC, *Proceedings*   *National Industrial Conference of Dominion and Provincial*
   Governments with Representative Employers and Labour Men, on the Subjects of
   Industrial Relations and Labour Laws, and for the Consideration of the Labour
   Features of the Treaty of Peace (Ottawa, 15–20 Sept. 1919)

OBU   One Big Union
OBU Bulletin   One Big Union Bulletin
OLN   Ontario Labor News
OPP   Ontario Provincial Police
PAM   Provincial Archives of Manitoba
PC   Privy Council
RCIR   Royal Commission on Industrial Relations
SN   Saturday Night
Star   Toronto Daily Star
TDLC   Toronto District Labor Council
TLCC   Trades and Labor Congress of Canada
UBC   University of British Columbia Special Collections
UWO   University of Western Ontario, Regional Collection

Introduction

1 Cited in James E. Cronin, 'Labor Insurgency and Class Formation:
  Comparative Perspectives on the Crisis of 1917–1920 in Europe,' in
  James E. Cronin and Carmen Sirianni, *Work, Community, and Power: The
  Experience of Labor in Europe and America, 1900–1925* (Philadelphia
  1983), 23. The literature on radical working-class movements in this
  period is vast, but see particularly Charles Maier, *Recasting Bourgeois
  Europe* (Princeton 1975), Charles L. Bertrand, ed., *Revolutionary Situa-
  tions in Europe, 1917–1922* (Montreal 1977), James Hinton, *The First
  Shop Stewards' Movement* (London 1973), Gwyn A. Williams, *Proletarian
  Order* (London 1975), Larry Peterson, 'The One Big Union in Inter-
  national Perspective: Revolutionary Industrial Unionism 1900–1925,'
  Labour / Le Travailleur 7 (Spring 1981), and David Montgomery, *The
  Fall of the House of Labor* (Cambridge 1987).
2 See David Jay Bercuson, *Confrontation at Winnipeg: Labour, Industrial
  Relations, and the General Strike* (Montreal 1974; rev. ed. 1990), and his
  Fools and Wise Men: The Rise and Fall of the One Big Union (Toronto
  1978), D.C. Masters, *The Winnipeg General Strike* (Toronto 1950), A.
  Ross McCormack, *Reformers, Rebels, and Revolutionaries: The Western Canadian Radical Movements, 1899–1919* (Toronto 1977), Carlos A.
  Schwantes *Radical Heritage: Labor, Socialism, and Reform in Washington
  and British Columbia, 1885–1917* (Vancouver 1979). Similarly, general
  surveys of Canadian labour history deal with the post-war explosion
  under the rubric of the 'western revolt,' as in the cases of both Desmond Morton with Terry Copp, *Working People: An Illustrated History of
  the Canadian Labour Movement* (Ottawa rev. ed. 1984), and Stuart Mar-

shall Jamieson, *Times of Trouble: Labour Unrest and Industrial Conflict in Canada* (Ottawa 1968).

3 Bercuson, *Confrontation at Winnipeg* (rev. ed.), 196–205, and his 'Labour Radicalism and the Western Industrial Frontier: 1897–1919, '*Canadian Historical Review* 58 (Jan. 1977)

4 Gregory S. Kealey, '1919: The Canadian Labour Revolt,' *Labour / Le Travail* 13 (Spring 1984)

5 See Bercuson, *Confrontation at Winnipeg* (rev. ed.), 196–205, for an extensive list of offenders.

6 Craig Heron and Bryan D. Palmer, 'Through the Prism of the Strike: Industrial Conflict in Southern Ontario, 1901–1914,' *Canadian Historical Review* 58 (Dec. 1977), 425. For the subsequent period, see Appendix.

7 However, see Nolan Reilly, 'The General Strike in Amherst, Nova Scotia, 1919,' in *Acadiensis* 9 (Spring 1980).

8 The best explanation of the character of urban, industrial development in this region in the nineteenth century is John McCallum, *Unequal Beginnings: Agriculture and Economic Development in Quebec and Ontario until 1870* (Toronto 1980). In *Urban Development in South-Central Ontario* (1955; Ottawa 1983), geographer Jacob Spelt has demonstrated that the development of Toronto was not at the expense of other industrial centres within relatively close proximity to the provincial capital. Similarly, Ian Drummond also notes the geographically dispersed nature of industrial development in *Progress without Planning: The Economic History of Ontario from Confederation to the Second World War* (Toronto 1987).

9 For a discussion of labourism consistent with my usage of the term, see Craig Heron, 'Labourism and the Canadian Working Class,' *Labour / Le Travail* 13 (Spring 1984).

10 The best survey of such conflicts with the state in the West remains Jamieson, *Times of Trouble*.

11 Karl Marx, *Capital*, 3 vols (Moscow 1954), vol. 1, 505

12 Ellen Meiksins Wood, 'The Separation of the Economic and the Political in Capitalism,' *New Left Review*, 127 (May-June 1981), 67

13 Myer Siemiatycki, 'Labour Contained: The Defeat of a Rank and File Workers' Movement in Canada, 1914–1921' (PhD diss., York University 1986). Through neglecting the connection between working-class industrial and political action, Siemiatycki perpetuates the assumptions of southern Ontario conservatism inherent in the works of Desmond Morton and David Bercuson, of which he is so critical. Like Bercuson, Siemiatycki is unjustified in accusing Kealey of suggesting that a 'uni-

form' working-class militancy emerged in 1919.

14 In particular, Peter Oliver challenges the existence of a significant radical heritage in Ontario in this period. See my discussion in ch. 8.

1 Workers, Unions, and War

1 *Journal of Electrical Workers and Operators* 23 (Oct. 1924), 712

2 *IB*, 5 Mar. 1920; this pamphlet was written by Rose Henderson, see Queen's University Archives, Andrew Glen Papers, box 1, file 5, 'Literature Report,' 15 Oct. 1921.

3 *IB*, 10 Sept. 1915

4 On the 'community accent' of the Toronto labour movement, see D. Wayne Roberts, 'Studies in the Toronto Labour Movement, 1896–1914' (PhD diss., University of Toronto 1978). On the eclipse of the local entrepreneur and the growing role of Toronto see Thomas William Acheson, 'The Social Origins of Canadian Industrialism: A Study in the Structure of Entrepreneurship' (PhD diss., University of Toronto 1971), ch. 4.

5 For an example of the use of the concept of 'negotiated response,' see Sarah Eisenstein, *Give Us Bread but Give Us Roses: Working Women's Consciousness in the United States, 1890 to the First World War* (London 1983).

6 These include Joseph Marks, Luke H. Gibbons, John A. Flett, and D.A. Carey. Gregory S. Kealey and Bryan D. Palmer, *Dreaming of What Might Be: The Knights of Labor in Ontario, 1880–1920* (Cambridge 1982), 80, 89, 131; *Brantford Expositor*, 28 July 1917; *MMJ*, 27 (Apr. 1915); NA, RG27, Dept of Labour, vol. 3126, file 36, 'Album of Labor Leaders ... 1909'

7 Kealey and Palmer, *Dreaming*, 277–329

8 Ibid., esp. 369–375; Gregory S. Kealey, *Toronto Workers Respond to Industrial Capitalism, 1867–1892* (Toronto 1980); Bryan D. Palmer, *A Culture in Conflict: Skilled Workers and Industrial Capitalism in Hamilton, Ontario 1860–1914* (Montreal 1979)

9 Robert H. Babcock, *Gompers in Canada: A Study of American Continentalism before the First World War* (Toronto 1974), ch. 4

10 Craig Heron and Bryan D. Palmer, 'Through the Prism of the Strike: Industrial Conflict in Southern Ontario, 1901–14,' *Canadian Historical Review* 58 (Dec. 1977). See also David Montgomery, *Workers' Control in America* (Cambridge 1979), 91–112.

11 Ian M. Drummond, *Progress without Planning: The Economic History of Ontario from Confederation to the Second World War* (Toronto 1987), 105,

132, 167. For the opposing view on the 'Great Depression' see H.A. Innis, *Essays in Canadian Economic History* (Toronto 1956), 108–22; W.A. Mackintosh, *The Economic Background of Dominion-Provincial Relations* (1939; Toronto 1964), 51; M.C. Urquhart and K.A.H. Buckley, *Historical Statistics of Canada* (Cambridge 1965), 463; Robert Craig Brown and Ramsay Cook, *Canada 1896–1921: A Nation Transformed* (Toronto 1974), 86.

12 David S. Landes, *The Unbound Prometheus* (Cambridge 1969), 231–358; Ernest Mandel, *Late Capitalism* (London 1975), 120; Craig Heron, 'The Second Industrial Revolution in Canada, 1890–1930,' in Deian R. Hopkin and Gregory S. Kealey, eds, *Class Community and the Labour Movement: Wales and Canada, 1850–1930* (Aberystwyth 1989)

13 Drummond, *Progress without Planning*, 110

14 Craig Heron, *Working in Steel: The Early Years in Canada, 1883–1935* (Toronto 1988); Daniel Nelson, *Managers and Workers: Origins of the New Factory System in the United States, 1880–1920* (Madison 1975)

15 A.E. Epp, 'Cooperation Among Capitalists: The Canadian Merger Movement, 1909–1913' (PhD diss., Johns Hopkins University 1973); Tom Traves, *The State and Enterprise: Canadian Manufacturers and the Federal Government, 1917–1931* (Toronto 1979), 5; J.C. Weldon, 'Consolidations in Canadian Industry, 1900–1948' in L.A. Skeoch, ed., *Restrictive Trade Practices in Canada* (Toronto 1966); Drummond, *Progress without Planning*, ch. 7; Michael Bliss, *Northern Enterprise: Five Centuries of Canadian Business* (Toronto 1987), ch. 12; Bryan D. Palmer, *Working Class Experience: The Rise and Reconstitution of Canadian Labour, 1800–1980* (Toronto 1983), 137

16 Craig Heron, 'Working-Class Hamilton, 1895–1930' (PhD diss., Dalhousie University 1981), 81; Michael J. Piva, *The Condition of the Working Class in Toronto – 1900–1921* (Ottawa 1979), 170

17 Heron, *Working in Steel*, 79; On sojourning, see Robert F. Harney, 'Men without Women: Italian Migrants in Canada, 1885–1930,' *Canadian Ethnic Studies* 1 (1979), and his 'Montreal's King of Italian Labour: A Case Study in Padronism,' *Labour / Le Travailleur* 5 (1979); also, John Bodnar, *The Transplanted: A History of Immigrants in Urban America* (Bloomington Ind. 1985), 1–84.

18 John E. Zucchi, *Italians in Toronto: Development of a National Identity, 1875–1935* (Montreal 1988), 44; *Census of Canada*, 1921, II, tables 38, 50

19 *MMJ*, 26 (June 1914), 602; Canada, Dept of Labour, *LOC* (1914), 214 and (1915), 209; *LG* 14 (Feb. 1914), 881. For instance, the large Massey-Harris works in Toronto and Brantford suffered as European or-

ders were lost in the conflict. In Hamilton, International Harvester, which had previously employed 3,000 workers, was temporarily closed, and major firms such as Canadian Westinghouse, Otis-Fensom Elevator, and National Steel Car were all working shorter hours, or with greatly reduced work-forces. *MMJ* 26 (July 1914), 700, (Oct. 1914) 990. In Welland, unemployed immigrants marched for food, while in Peterborough, the TLC organized a concert to raise money for unemployed workers, whether unionists or not; Fern A. Sayles, *Welland Workers Make History* (Welland 1963), 59; *IB*, 13 Feb., 22 May 1914.

20 *LOC* (1914), 19; Samuel Gompers, *Seventy Years of Life and Labor: An Autobiography*, 2 vols (1925; New York 1967), vol. 2, ch. 37; *CAR* (1917), 417; TLCC, *Proceedings* (1914), 15

21 Thomas P. Socknat, *Witness against War: Pacifism in Canada 1900–1945* (Toronto 1987); *IB*, 2 Jan. 1914; UWO, London TLC, *Minutes*, 21 Jan. 1914; NA, MG28, I44, TDLC, *Minutes*, 20 Apr. 1916; *IB*, 16 Oct., 27 Nov. 1914, 14 and 21 Apr., 24 Nov. 1916; TDLC, *Minutes*, 19 Apr. 1917; *Brantford Expositor*, 5 Apr. 1917

22 *IB*, 10 Mar. 1916

23 *IB*, 11 Sept. 1914. The military was asked to participate in the 1915 London Labour Day parade, *IB*, 11 June 1915.

24 *IB*, 18 Feb. 1916

25 Barbara M. Wilson, *Ontario and the First World War* (Toronto 1977), xx

26 TDLC, *Minutes*, 5 Aug. 1915; *IB*, 11, 18, and 25 Sept. 1914

27 *IB*, 16 Oct. 1914

28 *LG*, 14 (Aug. 1915), 154; *IB*, 23 July 1915

29 *IB*, 23 July 1915

30 Roberts, 'Studies in the Toronto Labour Movement' 416; *IB*, 9 Jan., 14 Aug., 13 Nov. 1914, 12 Mar. 1915. The SDP manifesto is in *IB*, 28 Aug. 1914.

31 UWO, Arthur Mould Papers, 'Reminiscences of Arthur Mould,' 60–61

32 *IB*, 5 Mar. 1915

33 *IB*, 22 Jan. 1915

34 Sixty per cent of IMB orders were placed in Ontario. NA, MG30, A16, J.W. Flavelle Papers, vol. 18, file 182, 'Memo Showing Geographical Location and Percentages of Workpeople Employed on Munitions'; to the new IMB, dispersal of production across Canada was considered a weakness of the Shell Committee; Michael Bliss, *A Canadian Millionaire: The Life and Business Times of Sir Joseph Flavelle, Bart.* (Toronto 1978), 249.

35 For example, the Toronto Boot and Shoe Workers' Union, *IB*, 16 Oct. 1914

36 *IB*, 29 Jan., 26 Mar., 17 Sept. 1915; *MMJ* 17 (Mar. 1915), 262–3, 271

37 *IB*, 24 Sept. 1915

38 Heron, 'Working-Class Hamilton,' 503; John C. Weaver, 'Elitism and the Corporate Ideal: Businessmen and Boosters in Canadian Civic Reform, 1890–1920,' in A.R. McCormack and Ian Macpherson, eds, *Cities in the West* (Ottawa 1975); H.V. Nelles and Christopher Armstrong, 'The Great Fight for Clean Government,' *Urban History Review* 2 (1976)

39 For formation and membership of the IMB, see Peter Rider, 'The Industrial Munitions Board and Its Relationship to Government, Business and Labour, 1914–20' (PhD diss., University of Toronto 1974). In *A Canadian Millionaire*, Bliss emphasizes the degree of personal control Flavelle exercised over the board. Through the British Labour Party leader the executive of the TLCC also appealed to the British government; UWO, London TLC, *Minutes*, 1 Mar. 1916, and David J. Bercuson, 'Organized Labour and the Industrial Munitions Board,' *Relations industrielles* 28 (July 1973).

40 TLCC, *Proceedings* (1915), 50–1; NA, Flavelle Papers, vol. 2, file 11, Gerald H. Brown to Flavelle, 25 Jan. 1916; *MMJ* 17 (Mar. 1915), 271

41 Epp, 'Cooperation among Capitalists,' 687–700. For Nicholls' views from an earlier period, see Ross Harkness, *J.E. Atkinson of the Star* (Toronto 1963) 37, and Michael Bliss, *A Living Profit: Studies in the Social History of Canadian Business, 1883–1911* (Toronto 1974), 60, 92–3; *MMJ* 27 (Mar. 1915), 271.

42 NA, Flavelle Papers, vol. 2, file 11, Gerald Brown to Flavelle, 25 Jan. 1916

43 Ibid, Brown to Flavelle, 16 Feb. 1916; Bliss, *A Canadian Millionaire*, 305

44 *Amalgamated Sheet Metal Workers Journal* 21 (Feb. 1916), 45

45 See Paul Craven, *'An Impartial Umpire': Industrial Relations and the Canadian State 1900–1911* (Toronto 1980), ch. 9; *IB*, 14 Apr. 1916.

46 TLCC, *Proceedings* (1916), 26–27, 156–61; NA, RG6, E, Dept of the Secretary of State, Chief Press Censor, vol. 528, file 170-G-1, clipping, *Ottawa Journal*, 10 Dec. 1915, and E.J. Chambers to Crate, 11 Dec. 1915

47 NA, Flavelle Papers, vol. 2, file 11, Brown to Flavelle, 16 Feb. 1916; H.H. Macrae to Gerald Brown, 31 Jan. 1916; James Somerville to Flavelle, 20 Mar. 1916, and Nicholls to Flavelle, 24 Mar. 1916; IAM, District Lodge 46 to Flavelle, 20 Mar. 1916; *IB*, 28 Jan., 18 Feb., 31 Mar. 1916; *MMJ* 28 (May 1916), 484

48 *MMJ* 28 (May 1916), 492

49 NA, Flavelle Papers, vol. 2, file 11, Thomas Findlay to Thomas W. Crothers, 31 Mar. 1916; Basil Magor to Flavelle, 7 June 1916

50 *MMJ* 28 (July 1916), 677

51 Myer Siemiatycki, 'Munitions and Labour Militancy: The 1916 Hamilton Machinists' Strike,' *Labour / Le Travailleur* 3 (1978)

52 *IB*, 16 June 1916

53 NA, Flavelle Papers, vol. 2, file 11, Gerald Brown to Flavelle, 7 June 1916

54 *IB*, 17 Sept. 1915

55 NA, Flavelle Papers, vol. 2, file 11, Brown to Flavelle, 7 June 1916

56 *IB*, 14 Mar. 1919

57 Canada, Dept of Labour, *Report on Organization in Industry, Commerce and the Professions in Canada*, 1921, 38; Bliss, *A Living Profit*, 93

58 NA, Chief Press Censor, vol. 528, file 170-G-1, Chambers to C.L. Clarke, 12 June 1916 and passim, particularly Joseph Marks to E.J. Boag, 21 June 1916 and Samuel L. Landers to Chambers, 4 July and 7 July 1916; *IB*, 28 July 1916

59 Hamilton *Spectator*, 12 June 1916

60 *IB*, 16 June 1916

61 *MMJ* 28 (June 1916), 608

62 *LG* 16 (July 1916), 1398; *IC* (June 1916), 170, (July 1916), 394; *FP*, 9 Sept. 1916

63 Bercuson, 'Organized Labour,' 607; NA, Flavelle Papers, vol. 6, file 64, Flavelle to Col. H.M. Elliot, 8 Dec. 1915

64 NA, Flavelle Papers, vol. 38, file 'Irish, Mark H., 1915–1918,' Flavelle to Irish, 21 Feb. 1917

65 Bliss, *A Canadian Millionaire*, 265, 324

66 TLCC, *Proceedings* (1917), 20–2; *LOC* (1916), 36; NA, Flavelle Papers, vol. 38, file 'Irish, Mark H., 1915-1918,' 21 Feb. 1917

67 On labour and conscription generally, see Martin Robin, 'Registration, Conscription and Independent Labour Politics, 1916–1917,' *Canadian Historical Review* 47 (June 1966).

68 TLCC, *Proceedings* (1917), 22; *IC*, Dec. 1916, 926

69 *LOC* (1916), 47; the annual TLCC convention took place in Vancouver in 1915 and in Toronto in 1916.

70 TLCC, *Proceedings* (1917), 36–40

71 NA, MG26, H, Robert L. Borden Papers, RLB Series, file 1419, TLCC, 'Pronouncement of Organized Labor in Canada on War Problems,' 11 June 1917; this statement is also to be found in NA, Flavelle Papers, vol. 6, file 64.

72 Ibid.

73 NA, Borden Papers, RLB Series, file 1419, Flavelle to Borden, 7 June 1917

74 NA, Flavelle Papers, vol. 6, file 64, Mark H. Irish to Flavelle, 15 June 1917

75 NA, Borden Papers, RLB Series, file 1419, T.W. Crothers to Borden, 9 June 1917; NA, Flavelle Papers, vol. 6, file 64, 'Summary of Replies to Chairman's Circular of June 11–17'

76 Margaret Prang, *N.W. Rowell: Ontario Nationalist* (Toronto 1975), 232–4; *IB*, 18 and 25 Jan. 1918

77 NA, Borden Papers, OC Series, vol. 505, Memorandum of Conferences between Representatives of Labour and the War Committee, Jan. 1918, 6

78 Prang, *N.W. Rowell*, 233

79 NA, Borden Papers, OC Series, vol. 505, Memorandum of Conferences between Representatives of Labour and the War Committee, Jan. 1918, 7

80 There is a large literature on American labour and the state in the First World War. See particularly Gwendolyn Mink, *Old Labor and New Immigrants in American Political Development: Union, Party, and State, 1875–1920* (Ithaca, NY 1986), ch. 7; Valerie Jean Conner, *The National War Labor Board: Stability, Social Justice, and the Voluntary State in World War I* (Chapel Hill, NC 1983); James Weinstein, *The Corporate Ideal in the Liberal State, 1900–1918* (Boston 1968), 214–54; Christopher L. Tomlins, *The State and the Unions: Labor Relations, Law, and the Organized Labor Movement, 1880–1960* (Cambridge 1985), 74–82; Philip S. Foner, *History of the Labor Movement in the United States*, vol. 7, *Labor and World War I* (New York 1987).

81 AO, RG7, Ministry of Labour, Series II-1, Office of the Deputy Minister, box 2, 'Jan. 31, 1918'; NA, Borden Papers, OC Series, vol. 488, 'Report of Special Committee to examine into the National War Organization developed by the United States Government for dealing with Industrial, Commercial and Labour Problems,' and vol. 505, 'Visit of Samuel Gompers to Ottawa'; NA, Dept of Labour,vol. 3135, file 161, Samuel Gompers, 'Labour and the War,' 6; James Foy, 'Gideon D. Robertson, Conservative Minister of Labor, 1917–1921' (MA thesis, University of Ottawa 1972), 51

82 AO, Ministry of Labour, Series II-1, box 2, 'Jan. 31, 1918'; *IB*, 19 Apr. 1918; NA, MG27, II, D13, Newton Wesley Rowell Papers, vol. 4, file 20, Rowell to Borden, 24 Apr. 1918

83 The Labour Sub-committee was established by Order in Council PC 3466 in Dec. 1917 and turned into a tripartite body by PC 1034 the

following May; *LG* 18 (Aug. 1918), 619.

84 NA, Borden Papers, OC Series, vol. 557, Report of Labour Sub-committee of Reconstruction and Development Committee, 9 Sept. 1918; NA, Borden Papers, RLB Series, file 527, Labour Sub-committee, Reconstruction and Development Committee, 9 Sept. 1918

85 NA, Flavelle Papers, vol. 38, file: 'Irish, Mark H., 1918–19, 1924,' Irish to Flavelle, 6 June 1918

86 PC 1743

87 On York Knitting Mills see NA, Dept of Labour, vol. 308, file 18(55); *IB*, 28 June 1918; on Kitchener see UWO, London TLC, *Minutes*, 20 Feb. 1918; Ontario Provincial Council, United Brotherhood of Carpenters and Joiners, *Proceedings* (1918), 17; *IB*, 6 Sept. 1918, 29 Nov. 1918; TLCC, *Proceedings* (1918), 154; NA, Dept of Labour, vol. 318, file 19(358). On the IMB see NA, Flavelle Papers, vol. 38, file: 'Irish, Mark H., 1918–19, 1924' Irish to Flavelle, 26 Sept. 1918; NA, CMA Papers, vol. 11, Executive Council Minutes, 14 Nov. 1918.

88 *Advance*, 30 Aug. 1918. These were Orders in Council PC 905, PC 915, PC 1832, PC 2299, and PC 2384; *CAR* (1918), 491; Social Service Council of Canada, *Co-Management Experiments in Canadian Industry*, Jan. 1921, 8; *LG* 21 (Feb. 1921), 275, (Mar. 1921), 501; *LL*, 12 Nov. 1920.

89 PC 2525

90 *OLN*, 1 May 1919

91 For clothing workers see Amalgamated Clothing Workers of America, *Proceedings* (1919), 122; *Advance*, 12 Oct. 1917, 18 Jan. 1918; NA, Dept of Labour, vol. 316, file 19(254), and *ND*, 25 Dec. 1919. For street-railway workers see NA, Flavelle Papers, vol. 38, file: 'Irish, Mark H., 1915–1918,' Irish to Flavelle, 10, 11, and 13 July 1917, and file: 'Irish, Mark H., 1918–19, 1924,' Irish to Edward FitzGerald, 28 June 1918; *IB*, 17 May, 20 Sept. 1918; UWO, London TLC, *Minutes*, 21 Mar., 18 Apr. 1917; *Brantford Expositor*, 14 Apr. 1917; *LG* 17 (Apr. 1917), 269.

92 *IC* (July 1915), 303; *LG* 15 (July 1915), 85; *IB*, 20 Aug. 1915

2 Beyond Craft Unionism: The Post-war Industrial Challenge

1 *Star*, 17 May 1919. Brown used this analogy again, at a large demonstration at the provincial parliament, promising: 'We will give them a little Winnipegitis,' *Mail and Empire*, 19 May 1919.

2 See Appendix.

3 *IB*, 12 Apr., 22 Nov. 1918; *LG* 19 (Jan. 1919), 51–2

4 D. Wayne Roberts, 'Studies in the Toronto Labour Movement, 1896–1914' (PhD diss., University of Toronto 1978), 119, 123; Wayne Roberts, 'Toronto Metal Workers and the Second Industrial Revolution, 1889–1914,' *Labour / Le Travailleur* 6 (Autumn 1980), 70–1; Craig Heron, 'The Crisis of the Craftsman: Hamilton's Metal Workers in the Early Twentieth Century,' *Labour / Le Travailleur* 6 (Autumn 1980); NA, Dept of Labour vol. 306, files 17(56A), 17(57A), and 17(66), vol. 308, files 18(79) and 18(80); *IB*, 10 and 17 May, 7 June 1918

5 NA, Dept of Labour, vol. 310, file 18(173); *IB*, 10 May, 14 and 28 June, 5, 12 and 19 July, 16 Aug. 1918

6 David J. Bercuson, *Fools and Wise Men: The Rise and Fall of the One Big Union* (Toronto 1978)

7 See *IB*, 22 Feb. 1918, regarding 'Real Democracy's Coming Triumph: A World-Wide Labor Movement Will Enforce Universal Peace,' and 22 Mar. 1918, that Canadian workers are 'Democracy's First Real Line of Defence'

8 *IB*, 8 Nov. 1918

9 NA, MG28, I44, TDLC, *Minutes*, 6 June 1918; NA, MG30, A15, George Keen Papers, vol. 3, file: Brantford Trades and Labor Council Correspondence, 1917, Keen to C.J. Doherty, 26 Oct. 1917; NA, RG6, E, Chief Press Censor, vol. 604, file 279-7, part 1, Ernest J. Chambers to Thomas Mulvey, 3 Nov. 1917, Col. H.J. Grassett to Chambers, 4 Dec. 1917; NA, MG26, H, Robert L. Borden Papers, OC Series, vol. 519, C.H. Cahan to Minister of Justice, 22 Oct. 1918, and vol. 559, 'Memorandum for Solicitor General,' 20 June 1919; *Brantford Expositor*, 25 Oct. 1917; *Star*, 23 Nov. 1917; Toronto *Telegram*, 1 Mar. 1918; *IB*, 14 June 1918

10 Forty-four socialists were arrested in Toronto that night. AO, RG23, OPP, E-30, file 1.6, James P. Smith to Joseph E. Rogers, 29 Dec. 1918; Ian Angus, *Canadian Bolsheviks: The Early Years of the Communist Party of Canada* (Montreal 1981), 29

11 TDLC, *Minutes*, 17 Apr. 1919; *Star*, 20 Jan. 1919; the Labour Appeal Board was abolished by Order in Council, 1 May 1919, *LG* 19 (May 1919), 555.

12 Michael Piva, 'The Toronto District Labour Council and Independent Political Action: Factionalism and Frustration, 1900–1921' *Labour / Le Travailleur* 4 (1979)

13 *Star*, 18 Nov. 1918

14 *IB*, 29 Nov., 13 and 27 Dec. 1918; *Star*, 20 Dec. 1918; TDLC, *Minutes*, 17 Nov., 5 Dec. 1918

15 *Star*, 17 Jan. 1919; TDLC, *Minutes*, 2 and 16 Jan., 6 Feb. 1919; *IB*, 24 Jan. 1919

16 *IB*, 27 Dec. 1918, 3 Jan. 1919; *Star*, 20 and 31 Dec. 1918, 1 Jan. 1919. For comments of the magistrate who sentenced Skidmore see *Star*, 14 Jan. 1919.

17 *Star*, 9 and 16 Jan. 1919; Angus, *Canadian Bolsheviks*, 30–2

18 *Star*, 10 and 13 Jan. 1919; NA, Chief Press Censor, vol. 605, file 279-7-7, clipping, nd, 'Extremists at Toronto Heckled Labor President'

19 See for instance testimony to the Royal Commission on Industrial Relations, 2823–4, 2877.

20 *IB*, 22 Jan. 1915, 11 Jan. 1918, 4 Apr. 1919

21 *Toronto World*, 13 June 1918; NA, Dept of Labour, file 18(84); *Star*, 5 Apr. 1919

22 See Roberts, 'Studies in the Toronto Labour Movement,' 118–21; *LG* 19 (Jan. 1919), 51–2, *Star*, 5, 29, and 30 Apr. 1919; *Globe*, 29 Apr. 1919.

23 TDLC, *Minutes*, 18 July 1918, 5 Dec. 1918; *IB*, 27 Dec. 1918; *Star*, 31 Dec. 1918

24 Report from the Employers' Detective Agency of IAM meeting of 25 Jan. 1919, Queen's University Archives, Andrew Glen Papers, box 1, file 3; NA, Dept of Labour, vol. 160, file 611.21, J.A. Young to Robertson, 25 Jan. 1919

25 UBC, VF213, One Big Union, Referendum Results; PAM, OBU Papers, D. Sime, ASE Local 1189, to F.W. Welsh, 3 Apr. 1919, and J.G. Robinson, ASE Local 1188, to Midgley, 27 Apr. 1919, J. Ferguson, ASE District Council, to Midgley, 22 Apr. 1919, and R.B. Russell to Midgley, 1 May 1919; *Globe*, 1 and 3 May 1919; *IB*, 14 Nov. 1919; *OLN*, 1 May 1919; *LL*, 11 July 1919

26 *Toronto World*, 20 May 1919

27 *OLN*, 1 May 1919; PAM, OBU Papers, Johns to Midgley, 7 May 1919

28 *IB*, 7 June 1918, 17 and 31 Jan., 7 Mar., 9 May 1919; *Plumbers, Gas and Steam Fitters' Journal* (Chicago) 23 (June 1918), 18, and 24 (Jan. 1919), 14, (Feb. 1919), 13, (Apr. 1919), 14, (May 1919), 20; *MMJ* 31 (Feb. 1919), 133–4, (Apr. 1919), 330, (June 1919), 552; *SN*, 5 Oct. 1918; *Mail and Empire*, 6 May 1919; *OLN*, 15 May 1919; United Brotherhood of Carpenters and Joiners, Provincial Council, *Proceedings* (1919), 410–11; NA, Dept of Labour, vol. 313, files 19(137) and 19(147A), vol. 315, file 19(207), and vol. 316, file 9(229)

29 *IB*, 14 Mar. 1919

30 *Globe*, 29 Apr. 1919; *Star*, 17 May 1919

31 *Globe*, 19 May 1919

32 *LL*, 11 July 1919; NA, Dept of Labour, file 19(262); *IB*, 16 Aug., 11 Oct., 18 Oct., 15 Nov. 1918, 31 Jan., 7 Mar., 3 Oct., 7 Nov. 1919, 9 Jan. 1920; TDLC, *Minutes*, 22 Jan. 1920; *LOC* (1919), 106; on the 1907 defeat see Joan Sangster, 'The 1907 Bell Telephone Strike: Organizing Women Workers,' *Labour / Le Travailleur* 3 (1978).

33 *IB*, 9 May 1919; *Star*, 22 and 30 May, 11 June 1919

34 See David Brody, *The Butcher Workmen: A Study in Unionization* (Cambridge 1964); J.T. Montague, 'Trade Unionism in the Canadian Meatpacking Industry' (PhD diss., University of Toronto 1950), 31–2; G.S. Bains, 'The United Packinghouse, Food and Allied Workers' (MA thesis, University of Manitoba 1964), 60–1; Canada, RCIR, *Evidence*, 2871; PAM, MG10, A14/1, R.B. Russell Papers, Cassidy to Russell, 13 Apr. 1919; Toronto *Telegram*, 5 May 1919; *Star*, 5 and 19 May 1919; *Toronto World*, 9 May 1919; *IB*, 9 May 1919; *Globe*, 5, 6, and 7 May 1919.

35 *Toronto World*, 20 May 1919; *Star*, 2 and 22 May 1919

36 NA, MG28, I230, CMA, 'Minutes, Labour Committee Appointed by the Toronto Branch Executive,' 12 Aug. 1918; The *Labor Leader* made the same observation a year later; see *LL*, 18 July 1919.

37 See all Toronto daily newspapers, 30 Apr. 1919; Roberts, 'Toronto Metal Workers' 71; the federation consisted of twelve crafts, *IB*, 14 Mar. 1919; *Globe*, 29 Apr., 2 May 1919; *Star*, 3, 27, and 31 May, 5 June 1919; *Telegram*, 28 Apr. 1919.

38 *Star*, 2 May 1919; *OLN*, 15 May 1919

39 *Star*, 14 May 1919

40 Roberts, 'Studies in the Toronto Labour Movement,' 178–9; *IB*, 11 Dec. 1914, 4 Jan., 1 Feb. 1918, 3 Jan. 1919; TLCC, *Proceedings* (1916), 167; *Brantford Expositor*, 25 May 1917; NA, MG30, D29, John S. Willison Papers, vol. 23, folder 174, clipping, 'Canadian Severity to Bolshevism: Demonstration in Toronto'

41 *Globe*, 14 May 1919; *Star*, 14 May 1919; *OLN*, 15 May 1919. For a comment on the situation in Toronto at this moment by an AFL organizer see Duke University, Frank Morrison Letterbooks, vol. 509, 628–32, William Varley to Frank Morrison, 14 May 1919. This reference is courtesy of David Frank.

42 *Toronto World*, 16 and 22 May 1919; *Globe*, 19 May 1919; *Star*, 15 and 16 May 1919; *Telegram*, 19 May 1919

43 *Telegram*, 6 May 1919; *Star*, 7 May 1919

44 *Toronto World*, 16 and 20 May 1919; *Mail and Empire*, 17 and 19 May 1919; *Star*, 7 May 1919. On the student strike, see *Toronto World*, 22 May 1919; *Star*, 20 and 21 May 1919.

45 Star, 21 May 1919

46 *Star*, 27 and 30 May 1919

47 *Star*, 28 May 1919. For the proceedings of the mayor's conference see NA, Borden Papers, OC Series, vol. 564.

48 SN, 13 Apr., 31 Aug., 28 Sept., 7 Dec. 1918; NA, Borden Papers, OC Series, vol. 519, C.H. Cahan to C.J. Doherty, 14 Sept. 1918; *IB*, 19 July 1918; *Star*, 28 Nov., 3 Dec. 1918; *Telegram*, 30 May 1919; *Globe*, 30 May 1919; *Toronto Times*, 30 May 1919

49 *FP*, 31 May 1919

50 *Star*, 30 May 1919

51 *Star*, 31 May 1919

52 *Star*, 2 June 1919; *LL*, 26 Dec. 1919

53 NA, Borden Papers, OC Series, vol. 564, Church to Borden, 2 June 1919; *Star*, 31 May, 2 June 1919

54 *Star*, 6 June 1919

55 *Star*, 30 Apr. 1919; David Montgomery, 'New Tendencies in Union Struggles and Strategies in Europe and the United States, 1916–1922,' in J.E. Cronin and C. Sirianni, eds, *Work, Community, and Power: The Experience of Labor in Europe and America, 1900–1925* (Philadelphia 1983); David Brody, 'Career Leadership and American Trade Unionism,' in F.C. Jaher, ed., *The Age of Industrialism in America* (New York 1968)

56 *Globe*, 25 June 1919. On hiring women, see *IB*, 17 and 24 May, 20 Sept. 1918 and NA, MG30, A16, J.W. Flavelle Papers, vol. 38, Irish to E. FitzGerald, 28 June 1918. On Robbins, see *IB*, 11 Dec. 1914; *Star*, 6 May 1919; *LL*, 19 Sept. 1919. On the 1919 strike see NA, Dept of Labour, vol. 315, file 19(222). For an analysis of the ACWA in this period see Steve Fraser, 'Dress Rehearsal for the New Deal: Shop-Floor Insurgents, Political Elites, and Industrial Democracy in the Amalgamated Clothing Workers,' in M.H. Frisch and D.J. Walkowitz, eds, *Working-Class America* (Urbana, Ill. 1983).

57 *Star*, 4 June, 28 July 1919; *Toronto World*, 28 July 1919; International Moulders' Union, *Proceedings* (1923); NA, MG 28, I256, International Moulders' Union, Executive Board, *Minutes*, 8–24 Apr. 1921 (microfilm copies)

58 David Bercuson, *Confrontation at Winnipeg: Labour, Industrial Relations, and the General Strike* (Montreal 1974), 155; Myer Siemiatycki, 'Labour Contained: The Defeat of a Rank and file Movement in Canada, 1914–1921' (PhD diss., York University 1986), ch. 6; Michael Bliss, *A Living Profit: Studies in the Social History of Canadian Business: 1883–1911* (Toronto 1974), ch. 4

59 Gregory S. Kealey, '1919: The Canadian Labour Revolt,' *Labour / Le*

Travail 13 (Spring 1984); Bercuson, *Fools and Wise Men*, 131–2

60 *Telegram*, 12 May 1919; *ND*, 29 May 1919

61 *Brantford Expositor*, 14, 15, 22, 27, and 28 May, 3, 14, and 20 June 1919

62 *Industrial Union News*, 10 May 1919; PAM, OBU Papers, Adam Schippling to Midgley, 28 Dec. 1919

63 *Brantford Expositor*, 26 June 1919; *LL*, 27 June 1919; *IB*, 18 July 1919; PAM, OBU Papers, Edward G. Hill to Midgley, 15 May 1919

64 United Brotherhood of Carpenters and Joiners, Ontario Provincial Council, *Proceedings* (1919), 34, 10–11

65 *MMJ* 31 (Feb. 1919), 133–4, (June 1919), 552

66 *IB*, 17 July 1914; *Star*, 23 May 1919; AO, RG18, B-60, 'Inquiry into Wages and Living Conditions of the Men Employed by the Hydro-Electric Power Commission at the Queenston-Chippawa Development (1920),' 1

67 NA, Dept of Labour, vol. 93, file 424.01:7, part IV, clipping, 'Soldiers Guard Canal: Austrian Strikers on Welland Work Are Cowed by Bayonets,' *New York Times* [incorrectly dated]; *IB*, 12 and 19 May 1916

68 *IB*, 2 May 1919; NA, Dept of Labour, vol. 94, file 424.01:7, part V, George Pay to G.D. Robertson, 18 May 1919

69 *Star*, 20, 22, and 29 May 1919

70 NA, Dept of Labour, vol. 94, file 424.01:7, part V, W.D. Killins and E. McG. Quirk to F.A. Acland, 16 July 1919, G.D. Robertson to J.D. Reid, 31 July 1919 and Memorandum, 'Re Welland Canal' nd, and Deputy Minister of Militia and Defence to G.D. Robertson, 9 Aug. 1919; vol. 2272, file 19(309)

71 *Star*, 28 Mar. 1919; Canada, Dept of Labour, *Report on Organization in Industry, Commerce and the Professions in Canada*, 1921, 15

72 *IC*, Jan. 1918, 1280–2

73 Canada, RCIR, *Evidence*, 2610; United Brotherhood of Carpenters and Joiners, Provincial Council, *Proceedings* (1919), 6 and 10; NA, Dept of Labour, vol. 316, file 19(246); *IB*, 14 July 1919, 13 Feb. 1920

74 *IB*, 27 Aug. 1920

75 *London Free Press*, 5 July 1920; *IB*, 1 Oct. 1920

76 *LOC* (1919), 139

77 *Star*, 31 May 1919

78 *Star*, 15 Mar. 1919

79 *IB*, 25 Apr. 1919

80 *IB*, 6 June 1919

81 *ND*, 31 July, 21 Aug. 1919; *OBU Bulletin*, 1 Nov. 1919; *People's Cause*, 27 Apr. 1926

82 UBC, VF213, OBU, 'Report of Proceedings, First Semi-Annual Con-

vention of the OBU,' Report of J.R. Knight
83 UBC, Mine-Mill Papers, box 160, folder 8, Report to General Executive Board, 20 Apr. to 7 May 1920
84 *Star*, 28 and 29 Apr. 1919
85 UWO, London TLC, *Minutes*, 7 May 1919; *LN*, 9 May 1919
86 *IB*, 16 May 1919
87 PAM, OBU Papers, Harry Ram to Midgley, 2 May 1919; John Nicol to Midgley, 13 May 1919; Verne De Witt Rowell to Midgley, 17 Apr. 1919
88 Ibid., R.B. Russell to Midgley, 24 Apr. 1919, W.T. Walton to Midgley, nd; G. Cascaden to Midgley, 26 May 1919; PAM, Russell Papers, box 3, file 7, A. Skidmore to Russell, 15 Apr. 1919; *IB*, 19 June 1914; *Canadian Forward* 10 Dec. 1917, 24 Mar. 1918; *LN*, 30 Nov. 1917, 3 May 1918; *LOC* (1920), 294
89 PAM, OBU Papers, Edward G. Hill to Midgley, 26 Apr. 1919; F.J. Flatman to Midgley, 22 Apr. 1919
90 Canada, RCIR, *Evidence*, 2410; *IB*, 30 Nov., 7 Dec. 1917, 12 Apr., 31 May, 14 June 1918; *LN*, 30 Nov. 1917
91 *LN*, 5 Apr., 17 May, 28 June, 9 and 23 Aug. 1918
92 *ND*, 16 June 1919
93 *ND*, 10 July 1919
94 *ND*, 28 Aug. 1919; UBC, VF213, OBU Convention, *Proceedings*, 26 Jan. 1920, 'Report of Executive Officer J.R. Knight'
95 *ND*, 10 July 1919
96 *ND*, 17 July 1919
97 *Industrial Union News*, 21 June 1919; *ND*, 26 June 1919
98 TDLC, *Minutes*, 16 Oct. 1919. The TDLC had participated in organizing the tour, *OBU Bulletin*, 18 and 25 Oct. 1919; *LL*, 10 and 17 Oct. 1919.
99 *OBU Bulletin*, 11 Oct. 1919
100 *ND*, 23 Oct. 1919; *OBU Bulletin*, 18 and 25 Oct. 1919
101 *Star*, 2 May 1919

3 The Development of a Labourist Consensus

1 *Christian Guardian*, 12 Dec. 1917, cited in Michael Bliss, 'The Methodist Church and World War I,' *Canadian Historical Review* 49 (Sept. 1968), 221
2 This language was evident, for instance, in a strike at the Canada Cycle and Motor Company, *IB*, 22 Feb. 1918.
3 John Saville, 'The Ideology of Labourism,' in Robert Benewick, R.N.

Berki, and Bhikhu Parekh, eds, *Knowledge and Belief in Politics* (London 1973); Craig Heron, 'Labourism and the Canadian Working Class,' *Labour / Le Travail* 13 (Spring 1984); Martin Robin, *Radical Politics and Canadian Labour* (Kingston 1968); Suzanne Morton, 'Labourism and Economic Action: The Halifax Shipyards Strike of 1920,' *Labour / Le Travail* 22 (Fall 1988), and for a study of this tradition in Britain, David Howell, *British Workers and the Independent Labour Party, 1888–1906* (Manchester 1983)

4 Gregory S. Kealey and Bryan D. Palmer, *Dreaming of What Might Be: The Knights of Labor in Ontario, 1880–1900* (Cambridge 1982), 204–76. All three of the 'Labour' members of the federal Parliament elected early in the twentieth century drifted to the Liberal caucus; A.R. McCormack, 'Arthur Puttee and the Liberal Party: 1899–1904,' *Canadian Historical Review* 51 (June 1970), and A.R. McCormack, *Reformers, Rebels, and Revolutionaries: The Western Canadian Radical Movement, 1899–1919* (Toronto 1977); Robin, *Radical Politics*, ch. 5.

5 Brian D. Tennyson, 'Premier Hearst: The War and Votes for Women,' *Ontario History* 52 (Sept. 1965), 121; see also Michael J. Piva, 'Workers and Tories: The Collapse of the Conservative party in Urban Ontario, 1908–1919,' *Urban History Review* 76 (Feb. 1977), and Craig Heron, 'Working-Class Hamilton, 1895–1930' (PhD diss., Dalhousie University 1981), ch. 8.

6 John Battye, 'The Nine Hour Pioneers: The Genesis of the Canadian Labour Movement,' *Labour / Le Travailleur* 4 (1979); Bryan D. Palmer, *A Culture in Conflict: Skilled Workers and Industrial Capitalism in Hamilton, Ontario, 1860–1914* (Montreal 1979), ch. 5

7 Michael J. Piva, 'The Workmen's Compensation Movement in Ontario,' *Ontario History* 67 (Mar. 1975), 39–41; R.C.B. Risk, '"This Nuisance of Litigation": The Origins of Workers' Compensation in Ontario,' in David H. Flaherty, ed., *Essays in the History of Canadian Law*, vol. 2 (Toronto 1983), 432

8 D. Wayne Roberts, 'Studies in the Toronto Labour Movement, 1896–1914' (PhD diss. University of Toronto, 1978), 403–8

9 Kealey and Palmer, *Dreaming*, 80, 89, 308–10; *LL*, 9 May 1924

10 *IB*, 24 Apr. 1914

11 In 1915, the London TLC ordered 5,000 copies of the *Banner* for the municipal election campaign. The 1914 contest winner had a choice of $500 or an automobile. That year, the *Banner* acquired its own printing press to serve hundreds of new subscribers through the region, *IB*, 23 Jan., 6 Mar., 22 and 29 May, 3 July, 4 Sept., 25 Dec. 1914; NA, MG28, I44, TDLC, *Minutes*, 17 Dec. 1914; UWO, London TLC,

'TLC Election Committee,' *Minutes*, 21 Nov. 1915.

12 For a history of the *Banner* and of the LEAO by Marks, see 'James Simpson Makes Uncalled for Attack on Joe Marks,' 1 Mar. 1922, TDLC, *Minutes*, 21 Sept. 1922; also, *IB*, 27 Mar. 1914. The first issue of the *Banner* after it moved to Toronto in 1912 was 25,000 according to Ron Verzuh, *Radical Rag: The Pioneer Labour Press in Canada* (Ottawa 1988) 98. Verzuh gives a misleading account of the relationship between the *Banner* and the LEAO.

13 NA, MG31, B8, John W. Bruce Papers, vol. 1, Bruce interviewed by Don Montgomery, Mar. 1965, part 5, 15

14 Piva, 'Workmen's Compensation,' 49, 56; James Weinstein, *The Corporate Ideal in the Liberal State, 1900–1918* (Boston 1968), xiii

15 Cited in Risk, '"Nuisance of Litigation,"' 463

16 *IC* (Feb. 1914), 909, 919; *IB*, 23 Jan., 12 Mar. 1914; Risk, '"Nuisance of Litigation,"' 468; TLCC, *Proceedings* (1914), 59–76

17 *IB*, 12 Mar. 1915

18 *IB*, 10 Sept. 1915

19 *IB*, 2 July 1915

20 R. Matthew Bray, '"Fighting as an Ally": The English-Canadian Patriotic Response to the Great War,' *Canadian Historical Review* 61 (1980); Peter Buitenhuis, *The Great War of Words: British, American and Canadian Propaganda and Fiction, 1914–1933* (Vancouver 1987); Alan R. Young, '"We Throw the Torch": Canadian Memorials of the Great War and the Mythology of Heroic Sacrifice,' *Journal of Canadian Studies* 24 (Winter 1989–90); Robert Craig Brown and Ramsay Cook, *Canada 1896–1921: A Nation Transformed* (Toronto 1974), 294–5; Richard Allen, *The Social Passion: Religion and Social Reform in Canada 1914–1928* (Toronto 1973); Bliss, 'The Methodist Church and World War I'; J.O. Miller, ed., *The New Era in Canada* (Toronto 1917)

21 Paul Fussell, *The Great War and Modern Memory* (Oxford 1975), 35; Flavelle, cited in Michael Bliss, *A Canadian Millionaire: The Life and Business Times of Sir Joseph Flavelle, Bart., 1858–1939* (Toronto 1978), 295. Bliss acquits Flavelle of wrongdoing, although the high profits Flavelle made on volume during the war sufficed to create a perception of him as a profiteer among workers who did not share his capitalist mores. Moreover, that the war was 'especially fertile in rumor and legend' (Fussell, *The Great War*, 115) no doubt encouraged such scandals; John English, *The Decline of Politics: The Conservatives and the Party System, 1901–1920* (Toronto 1977), 106–22.

22 *IB*, 24 Mar., 19 June, 4 Dec. 1914, 15 Jan., 22 Oct. 1915, 16 Jan., 4 Feb. 1916

23 Samuel P. Hays, 'The Politics of Reform in Municipal Government in the Progressive Era,' *Pacific Northwest Quarterly* 55 (Oct. 1964) and his 'The Changing Structure of the City in Industrial America,' *Journal of Urban History* 1 (Nov. 1974); Weinstein, *Corporate Ideal*, ch. 4; John C. Weaver, 'Elitism and the Corporate Ideal: Businessmen and Boosters in Canadian Civic Reform, 1890–1920,' in A.R. McCormack and Ian Macpherson, eds, *Cities in the West* (Ottawa 1975), and John C. Weaver, '"Tomorrow's Metropolis" Revisited: A Critical Assessment of Urban Reform in Canada, 1890–1920,' in Gilbert A. Stelter and Alan F.J. Artibise, eds, *The Canadian City: Essays in Urban History* (Toronto 1977). The critique of this literature by H.V. Nelles and Christopher Armstrong in 'The Great Fight for Clean Government,' *Urban History Review* 2 (1976) demonstrates working-class disorientation in the face of municipal reform, more than undermining Weaver's thesis of business impetus behind reform; *IB*, 30 Jan., 4 Dec. 1914, 8 Mar. 1918; UWO, London TLC, *Minutes*, 18 Nov. 1914.

24 *IB*, 16 Oct. 1914, 5 Feb., 2 July 1915, 26 May 1916; *Brantford Expositor*, 23 Nov. 1916; UWO, London TLC, *Minutes*, 5 July 1916

25 See Heron, 'Labourism.'

26 See Margaret Prang, *N.W. Rowell: Ontario Nationalist* (Toronto 1975), and Ross Harkness, *J.E. Atkinson of the Star* (Toronto 1963); Roberts, 'Studies in the Toronto Labour Movement,' 417, provides a more substantial discussion of such partisan allegiances than does Michael J. Piva in 'The Toronto District Labour Council and Independent Political Action: Factionalism and Frustration, 1900–1921,' *Labour / Le Travailleur* 4 (1979).

27 *IB*, 22 Nov. 1918

28 TDLC, *Minutes*, 16 Sept. 1915

29 *IB*, 12 July 1918

30 *Toronto Star*, 13 Jan. 1919

31 *IB*, 15 Nov. 1918; *LN*, 12 July 1918

32 UWO, London TLC, *Minutes*, 21 Jan. 1914; *IB*, 2 Jan., 20 Nov. 1914, 15 Jan., 12 Feb., 28 May 1915; Mark Pittenger, 'Evolution, "Women's Nature" and American Socialism, 1900–1915,' in *Radical History Review* 36 (Sept. 1986)

33 Gene Howard Homel, '"Fading Beams of the Nineteenth Century": Radicalism and Early Socialism in Canada's 1890s,' *Labour / Le Travailleur* 5 (Spring 1980), 24–5; *Brantford Expositor*, 18 Oct. 1917; UWO, Arthur Mould Papers, 'Reminiscences of Arthur Mould' 62; UWO, London TLC, *Minutes* 1 Sept. 1920

34 UWO, London TLC, *Minutes*, 4 Mar. 1914; *Brantford Expositor*, 15

Feb. 1917; University of Toronto, Rare Book Library, Kenny Collection, Harry B. Ashplant, 'Karl Marx's Theory of Exchange: A Criticism of Political Economy'; *IB*, 30 July 1915; Canada, RCIR, *Evidence*, 2231–42; and Ashplant's regular column in the (London) *Herald*

35 For example, in Toronto, *IB*, 20 Oct. 1916, 1 Dec. 1916; in London, *Advertiser*, 24 Aug. 1916

36 The reporter, writing under the pseudonym 'P.O'D.,' was Peter Donovan; *SN*, 11 Jan. 1919; 18 Sept. 1920.

37 Canada, RCIR, *Report*, 6

38 W.L. Grant, 'The Education of the Workingman,' *Queen's Quarterly* 27 (Oct. 1919); *Star*, 26 Nov. 1918

39 *CAR* (1918), 330; TDLC, *Minutes*, 15 Aug. 1918, 20 Nov. 1919, 6 Jan. 1921; UWO, Mould Papers, 'Report of Organizational Meeting of W.E.A., June 5, 1923'; *CCJ*, 2 (June 1923), 251; Hamilton Public Library, Hamilton Central ILP branch, *Minutes*, 26 Sept. 1924; *MMJ*, 36 (Nov. 1924), 563–4, (Dec. 1924), 607–8; Ian Radforth and Joan Sangster, '"A Link between Labour and Learning": The Workers Educational Association in Ontario, 1917–1951,' *Labour / Le Travailleur* 8/9 (Autumn/Spring 1981–2). On Ballantyne, see AO, RG7, Ministry of Labour, XV-1, vol. 5; *IB*, 14 Oct. 1921; *LL*, 14 Oct. 1921.

40 *MMJ*, 36 (Nov. 1924), 607–8; *Justice*, 28 Nov. 1924

41 Heron, 'Labourism,' 64; Ontario Provincial Council, United Brotherhood of Carpenters and Joiners, *Proceedings* (1920), 3–4; Ian Angus, *Canadian Bolsheviks: The Early Years of the Communist Party of Canada* (Montreal 1981), 43

42 Stanley Pierson, *Marxism and the Origins of British Socialism: The Struggle for a New Consciousness* (Ithaca, NY 1973); see also Stephen Yeo, 'A New Life: The Religion of Socialism in Britain, 1883–1896,' *History Workshop* 4 (Autumn 1977); John M. McMenemy, 'Lion in a Den of Daniels: A Study of Sam Lawrence, Labour in Politics' (MA thesis, McMaster University 1965), 8–9; MTL, John Warburton Buckley Papers, Scrapbooks, vol. 1; *IB*, 25 Apr. 1919; *IB*, 25 Apr. 1919.

43 Bliss, 'Methodist Church and World War I,' 213; William H. Magney, 'The Methodist Church and the National Gospel,' United Church *Bulletin* 20 (1968); Edward A. Christie, 'The Presbyterian Church in Canada and Its Official Attitude towards Public Affairs and Social Problems, 1875–1925' (MA thesis, University of Toronto 1955), 306; *IB*, 9 Oct. 1914

44 *IB*, 2 May 1919

45 Allen, *Social Passion*, 17

46 *IB*, 12 Mar., 1 Oct. 1915

47 *IB*, 22 May, 6 Nov. 1914, 12 Mar., 11 June, 28 May 1915. On Douglass, see Ramsay Cook, *The Regenerators: Social Criticism in Late Victorian English Canada* (Toronto 1985), 115, 122, 202, and Homel, '"Fading Beams,"' 24–5.

48 Queen's University Archives, Collection 2137, Andrew Glen Papers, box 2, file 8, Glen to A.E. Smith, 12 Feb. 1923, and box 2, file 9, Glen to William Irvine, 15 Apr. 1923; *LL*, 13 Apr. 1923; TDLC, *Minutes*, 18 Oct. 1923

49 *IB*, 18 Aug. 1916

50 *IB*, 8 Sept., 3 Nov. 1916

51 Heron, 'Working-Class Hamilton,' 607

52 *IB*, 3 Nov., 1 Dec. 1916

53 *Canadian Forward*, 2 Dec. 1916

54 On Black see TDLC, *Minutes*, 21 May 1914; *IB*, 26 June 1914, 12 Nov., 17 Dec. 1915, 23 June, 29 Sept., 1 Dec. 1916; *LOC* (1915), 180.

55 *IB*, 19 Jan. 1917

56 *IB*, 26 Jan. 1917

57 *IB*, 20 and 27 Apr. 1917

58 TDLC, *Minutes*, 1 Feb. 1917; *IB*, 27 Apr., 17 Aug., 26 Oct. 1917

59 *IB*, 23 Feb., 16 and 30 Mar. 1917

60 *IB*, 10 Nov., 15 and 22 Dec. 1916, 5, 12, and 19 Jan., 30 Mar. 1917; *Brantford Expositor*, 22 Dec. 1916; Fern A. Sayles, *Welland Workers Make History* (Welland 1963), 80

61 *IB*, 20 and 27 Apr., 11 and 18 May, 1 June 1917; *LG* (June 1917), 491–2

62 The branches present were: Cobalt, North Bay, Norwood, Toronto, Kingston, Niagara Falls, Port Colborne, Welland, Thorold, Chippawa, Hamilton, Brantford, Guelph, Kitchener, London, as well as a recently organized women's branch from Hamilton.

63 *LOC* (1917), 40–1; *IB*, 6 July 1917

64 AO, MU2518, Arthur W. Roebuck Papers, file 'Elections, 1917: Federal – Temiskaming,' 'The Independent Labor Party – Declaration of Principles, Platform and Constitution'; J.L. Rutledge, 'The Birth of a Labor Party,' *Maclean's*, 33 (Jan. 1920), 22; Jacqueline F. Cahan, 'A Survey of the Political Activities of the Ontario Labor Movement, 1850–1935' (MA thesis, University of Toronto 1945)

65 For a discussion of the concept of 'movement culture,' see Lawrence Goodwyn, *The Populist Moment: A Short History of the Agrarian Revolt in America* (Oxford 1978), ch. 2, and 293–310; Kealey and Palmer, *Dreaming*, ch. 8.

66 *IB*, 13 July 1917

67 *IB*, 24 Aug. 1917
68 For instance, the Brantford TLC voted unanimously for such a government; *Brantford Expositor*, 18 Jan. 1917.
69 *IB*, 17 Aug., 19 Oct., 9 Nov., 1917; *LN*, 2 Nov. 1917
70 *LN*, 26 Oct., 23 Nov. 1917; *IB*, 9 Jan., 6 Mar. 1914, 28 Sept., 16 and 23 Nov. 1917; Sayles, *Welland Workers*, 80–1; *Brantford Expositor*, 28 July 1917; Kealey and Palmer, *Dreaming*, 31; Morrison Mann Mac-Bride was a Brantford alderman and an employing printer at the MacBride Printing Company, *Expositor*, 26 Dec. 1916, 6 Jan. 1917.
71 *IB*, 9 and 23 Nov. 1917; *LN*, 2 and 23 Nov., 7 and 14 Dec. 1917; *CAR* (1917), 623; NA, MG27, II, D13, Newton Wesley Rowell Papers, vol. 3, file 17, Rowell to Borden, 17 Oct. 1917, and vol. 4, file 18, Rowell [?] to Borden, 1 Nov. 1917
72 NA, MG30, A15, George Keen Papers, vol. 3, file: 'Brantford Trades and Labor Council Correspondence, 1917,' letter, A.J. Kite, nd; *Brantford Expositor*, 8, 9, and 16 Nov. 1917, *LN*, 23 Nov. 1917
73 AO, MU2457, Roebuck Papers, Roebuck to Mrs Hector Prenter, 24 Nov. 1917; NA, Rowell Papers, vol. 4, file 19, F.L. Hutchinson to Rowell, 10 Nov. 1917, and file 18, George N. Gordon to Rowell, 10 Nov. 1917. Unlike Roebuck, the provincial ILP appears not to have had any dealings with Gordon and he was not endorsed by Rollo as an official labour candidate.
74 *Workingman's Newsletter*, 13 Dec. 1917; see also Gibbon's address to the London TLC asking for its support; UWO, London TLC, *Minutes*, 17 Oct. 1917.
75 NA, MG26, J1, W.L. Mackenzie King Papers, vol. 36, King to Draper, 10 Dec. 1917; Draper to King, 12 Dec. 1917; vol. 37, King to James Simpson, 10 Dec. 1917; *IB*, 22 Mar. 1918; Canadian Liberal party, *Who Shall Rule? The People or the Big Interests* (Ottawa 1917)
76 Martin Robin, 'Registration, Conscription, and Independent Labour Politics, 1916–1917,' *Canadian Historical Review* 47 (June 1966)

4 The Battle for Democracy

1 *IB*, 17 Oct. 1919
2 Marks considered the results disappointing, *IB*, 25 Jan. 1918.
3 *LN*, 23 Nov., 7 and 14 Dec. 1917; *Brantford Expositor*, 22 Nov. 1917; Margaret Prang, *N.W. Rowell: Ontario Nationalist* (Toronto 1975), 223
4 *LN*, 3 May 1918; *IB*, 10 and 24 May, 27 Sept. 1918, 10 Jan. 1919; *Star*, 14 Feb. 1919; Robert H. Babcock, *Gompers in Canada: A Study in American Continentalism before the First World War* (Toronto 1974), 158,

179; Canada, RCIR, *Evidence*, 2391

5 Howard Palmer, *Patterns of Prejudice: A History of Nativism in Alberta* (Toronto 1982), 5–15; John Higham, *Strangers in the Land: Patterns of American Nativism, 1860–1925* (1955; New Brunswick, NJ 1988); Frances Swyripa and John Herd Thompson, *Loyalties in Conflict: Ukrainians in Canada during the Great War* (Edmonton 1983)

6 E.g., *IB*, 16 Apr. 1915, 28 Apr. 1916

7 *IB*, 3 and 17 July, 11 Sept., 9 Oct. 1914, 12 Feb. 1915

8 Craig Heron, *Working in Steel: The Early Years in Canada, 1883–1935* (Toronto 1988), 85

9 *Star*, 3 Aug. 1918; *IB*, 16 Aug. 1918; Desmond Morton and Glenn Wright, *Winning the Second Battle: Canadian Veterans and the Return to Civilian Life, 1915–1930* (Toronto 1987), 120–1

10 *IB*, 5 Jan., 20 Apr. 1917; *LOC* (1917), 41–2; *London Free Press*, 7 June 1917; *Brantford Expositor*, 7 June 1917; UWO, London TLC, *Minutes*, 16 Aug. 1916; NA, MG28, I22, TDLC, *Minutes*, 7 Feb. 1918

11 *IB*, 29 Jan., 6 Aug. 1915, 25 Jan., 15 and 22 Feb., 8 Mar., 12 and 26 July, 9 Aug. 1918; *LOC* (1914), 187; Ontario, 'Report of the Bureau of Labour' (1914), 150; TDLC, *Minutes*, 7 Feb., 21 Feb. 1918; UWO, London TLC, *Minutes*, 20 Feb. 1918

12 *Canadian Forward*, 24 June 1918; *IB*, 5 Apr. 1918; *LN*, 5 Apr. 1918; *ND*, 28 Aug. 1919

13 *IB*, 16 and 23 Aug. 1918

14 *IB*, 28 Dec. 1917; 11, 18, and 25 Jan 1918; *LN*, 8 Mar. 1918

15 *IB*, 8 Mar., 5 and 18 Apr., 16 Aug. 1918; *LN*, 29 Mar., 5 Apr. 1918

16 TLCC, *Proceedings* (1917), 43–4, and (1918), 42–3; *LN*, 15 Mar. 1918

17 Ross McCormack discusses the focus of pre-war socialist parties on propaganda in *Reformers, Rebels, and Revolutionaries: The Western Canadian Radical Movement, 1899–1919* (Toronto 1977), 68–76. On the schism see also Norman Penner, *The Canadian Left: A Critical Analysis* (Scarborough 1977), 46–52.

18 TDLC, *Minutes*, 4 June 1914; D. Wayne Roberts, 'Studies in the Toronto Labour Movement, 1896–1914' (PhD diss., University of Toronto 1978), 421–2; Gene Howard Homel, 'James Simpson and the Origins of Canadian Social Democracy' (PhD diss., University of Toronto 1978); *IB*, 2 Jan. 1914

19 *IB*, 10 and 24 Apr. 1914, 18 and 25 Aug. 1916, 20 Apr. 1917; TDLC, *Minutes*, 16 Apr. 1914

20 *IB*, 17 July, 14 and 28 Aug. 1914, 20 Aug. 1915, 21 Apr., 28 July, 4 Aug. 1916

21 *Canadian Forward*, 10 Mar. 1918; *LN*, 19 July 1918

22 On the single tax, see Allen Mills, 'Single Tax, Socialism and the Independent Labour Party of Manitoba: The Political Ideas of F.J. Dixon and S.J. Farmer,' *Labour / Le Travailleur* 5 (Spring 1980), and Ramsay Cook, 'Henry George and the Poverty of Canadian Progress,' in Canadian Historical Association, *Historical Papers / Communications historiques* 1977.

23 *LN*, 5 Apr. 1918; *IB*, 5 Apr. 1918; TLCC, *Proceedings* (1918), 42–6; MTL, John Warburton Buckley Papers, 'John W. Buckley, Reminiscences,' Scrapbook, vol. 7, 21

24 The list of speakers was regularly printed in the *Industrial Banner*; the most complete of these appeared 31 Jan. 1919.

25 United Brotherhood of Carpenters and Joiners, *Proceedings of the Ontario Provincial Council* (1918), 29–30; *IB*, 5 July 1918, 28 Mar., 25 Apr. 1919; *Star*, 19 Apr. 1919; *LN*, 25 Apr. 1919. Contact with the United Farmers was maintained through W.C. Good, *IB*, 21 Mar. 1919.

26 *Star*, 9 Nov. 1918; The CMA and reconstruction are discussed later, but see Tom Traves, *The State and Enterprise: Canadian Manufacturers and the Federal Government, 1917–1931* (Toronto 1979), 10, 90–4, and Mark Cox, 'Innovation Denied: The Board of Commerce of Canada and the Problem of Expert Authority, 1919–1920,' in Peter Baskerville, ed., *Canadian Papers in Business History* 1 (1989).

27 Canada, RCIR, *Evidence*, 2602

28 *IB*, 21 July 1916; *LN*, 15 Nov. 1918

29 For examples of labour support for public ownership see *IB*, 12 June, 25 Dec. 1914, 12 Mar., 26 Mar., 30 July 1915, 15 Sept. 1916, 17 Nov. 1916, 1 Feb. 1918; UWO, London TLC, *Minutes*, 15 Dec. 1915; *Brantford Expositor*, 23 Nov. 1916, 25 May, 4 Oct. 1917; TDLC, *Minutes*, 27 May 1917; NA, MG30, A15, George Keen Papers, vol. 3, file: 'Brantford Trades and Labour Council Correspondence, 1917,' Keen to P.M. Draper, 4 Oct. 1917. For a list of IMB-owned 'national plants' see NA, MG30, A16, J.W. Flavelle Papers, vol. 15, file 162.

30 *IB*, 2 Aug. 1918

31 *LN*, 29 Nov. 1918

32 *IB*, 6 Dec. 1918

33 *IB*, 1 Nov. 1918

34 *IB*, 27 Dec. 1918; 10 Jan., 7 and 21 Feb., 28 Mar. 1919; *LN*, 24 and 31 Jan., 14 Feb. 1919; Francis Graham Stevens, 'A History of Radical Political Movements in Essex County and Windsor, 1919–1945' (MA thesis, University of Western Ontario 1948), 53; J. Douglas Sammons, 'Desperate Union: Co-operation between the United Farmers of On-

tario and the Independent Labour Party in the Ontario Election of 1919' (MA thesis, University of Waterloo 1973), 126

35 *IB*, 1 May, 5 and 19 June 1914, 24 Jan. 1919; *LG*, 14 (June 1914) 1420

36 *LN*, 20 Dec. 1918; *IB*, 27 Dec. 1918, 3, 10, and 24 Jan., 14 Feb. 1919; *Star*, 11 and 13 Feb. 1919

37 *Star*, 13 Feb. 1919

38 *IB*, 17 Jan. 1919; *CAR* (1917), 644; *Star*, 11 Feb. 1919

39 *IB*, 10 Jan., 21 Feb., 19 Dec. 1919; *Star*, 11, 14, and 21 Feb. 1919; *LN*, 21 Feb. 1919; TDLC, *Minutes*, 20 Feb. 1919; *Painter and Decorator* (Lafayette, Ind.) 34 (Feb. and Mar. 1920), 71

40 *IB*, 25 Apr., 9 May 1919; *LN*, 25 Apr., 9 May 1919

41 *Star*, 19 Apr. 1919

42 *IB*, 25 Apr. 1919

43 *Star*, 26 Feb. 1919; *IB*, 7, 21, and 28 Mar., 4 Apr. 1919; 'James Simpson Makes Uncalled for Attack on Joe Marks,' in TDLC, *Minutes*, 21 Sept. 1922. Ron Verzuh is incorrect in assuming Simpson took over the paper on Marks's death, *Radical Rag: The Pioneer Labour Press in Canada* (Ottawa 1988), 98; see, TLCC. *Proceedings* (1924), 145; NA, RG27, Dept of Labour, vol. 3130, file 89, 'Report 9th Annual Convention of the ILP,' 1926.

44 *LL*, 27 June, 4 and 11 July 1919.

45 *LL*, 4 June 1920; UWO, London TLC, *Minutes*, 16 Aug., 4 Oct. 1916, 17 Jan., 4 Feb., 18 Apr. 1917, 6 Feb. 1918, 19 Feb., 6 Mar. 1919; TLCC, *Proceedings* (1916), 9; *Star*, 22 Nov. 1918, 20 June 1919

46 *IB*, 25 July 1919; *LL*, 18 and 25 July 1919

47 NA, MG28, I44, TDLC, *Minutes*, 7 Aug. 1919; *IB*, 15 Aug. 1919; *LL*, 8 Aug. 1919

48 *IB*, 15 Aug. 1919

49 *LL*, 15 Aug. 1919

50 *IB*, 15 Aug. 1919; TDLC, *Minutes*, 3 Oct., 6 Nov., 4 and 18 Dec. 1919 Michael Piva, 'The Toronto District Labour Council and Independent Political Action: Factionalism and Frustration, 1900–1921,' *Labour / Le Travailleur* 4 (1979) and his *The Condition of the Working-Class in Toronto, 1900–1921* (Ottawa 1979), 143–4

51 *IB*, 14 May, 4 June, 13 Aug. 1920; *LL*, 7 May, 4 June 1920

52 TDLC, *Minutes*, 6 June 1919, 5 Aug. 1920, 3 Nov. 1921; *LL*, 6, 13, and 22 Aug. 1920, 14 and 21 Oct. 1921, 9 Feb. 1923, 23 Oct. 1925; *IB*, 19 and 26 Dec. 1919, 23 July, 10 Sept. 1920; UWO, London TLC, *Minutes*, 2 Nov. 1919, 6 Apr. 1921; TLCC Executive Council, *Minutes*, 27 Aug. 1921, 11 Jan. 1922

53 S.E.D. Shortt, 'Social Change and Political Crisis in Rural Ontario: The Patrons of Industry, 1889–1896,' in D. Swainson, ed., *Oliver Mowat's Ontario* (Toronto 1972); Russell Hann, *Some Historical Perspectives on Canadian Agrarian Movements* (Toronto 1971); L.A. Wood, *A History of the Farmers' Movements in Canada* (1924; Toronto 1975); Ramsay Cook, 'Tillers and Toilers: The Rise and Fall of Populism in Canada in the 1890s,' in Canadian Historical Association, *Historical Papers / Communications historiques*, 1984

54 Jean MacLeod, 'The United Farmer Movement in Ontario, 1914–1943' (MA thesis, Queen's University 1958), 34

55 W.R. Young, 'Conscription, Rural Depopulation, and the Farmers of Ontario, 1917–19,' *Canadian Historical Review* 53 (Sept. 1972), 318, 319

56 Morrison cited in Charles M. Johnston, *E.C. Drury: Agrarian Idealist* (Toronto 1986), 47

57 Ibid., 27

58 MacLeod, 'United Farmer Movement,' 69. See also Johnston, *E.C. Drury*, ch. 5, Wood, *History of the Farmers' Movements*, ch. 23, and W.L. Morton, *The Progressive Party in Canada* (Toronto 1950), 71.

59 *Weekly Sun*, 3 July 1918, cited in F.J.K. Griezic, '"Power to the People": The Beginning of Agrarian Revolt in Ontario, The Manitoulin By-Election, October 24, 1918,' *Ontario History* 69 (Mar. 1977), 40

60 Cited in Brian D. Tennyson, 'The Ontario General Election of 1919: The Beginnings of Agrarian Revolt,' *Journal of Canadian Studies* 4 (Feb. 1969), 28, and in Griezic, '"Power to the People,"' 36

61 Margaret J. Watson, 'The United Farmers of Ontario and Political Co-operation with the Independent Labour Party, 1919–1923' (Unpublished research paper, York University 1984), 15

62 Sammons, 'Desperate Union,' 128; *ND*, 26 June 1919; *IB*, 18 Apr. 1919; *Brantford Expositor*, 11 Oct. 1919

63 Leaflet, 'The Independent Labor Party of South Waterloo Working in Conjunction with the United Farmers of South Waterloo,' in Sammons, 'Desperate Union,' App. III

64 *IB*, 8 Aug. 1919

65 *LN*, 8, 15 and 22 Aug. 1919; *IB*, 22 Aug., 3 Oct. 1919

66 AO, Ontario Provincial Liberal Party, 'Labor' (1919); Peter Oliver, *G. Howard Ferguson, Ontario Tory* (Toronto 1977), 87; Prang, *N.W. Rowell*, 310–17

67 AO, Ontario Conservative Party, 'What Has Been Done for Labor' (1919); *LL*, 15 Aug., 10 Oct. 1919; *ND*, 9 Oct. 1919; *LN*, 17 Oct.

1919; *CAR* (1919), 659; NA, MG26, H, Robert L. Borden Papers, OC Series, vol. 570, Foster to Borden, 11 Oct. 1919, and Yates to Borden, 14 Oct. 1919

68 *IB*, 1 and 29 Aug., 12 Sept. 1919; Canada, RCIR, *Evidence*, 2947; Morton and Wright deal with radical veterans' organizations such as the GAC and the Grand Army of United Veterans in a somewhat cursory manner, see *Winning the Second Battle*, 119, 127, 129, 180; *LOC* (1916), 163; *IB*, 21 July 1916, 21 Feb. 1919; TDLC, *Minutes*, 27 Feb. 1919. Vick was in the anti-prohibitionist Liberty League, which was opposed by SDPers such as Simpson, *LN*, 5 Sept. 1919; Gerald A. Hallowell, *Prohibition in Ontario, 1919–1923* (Ottawa 1972), 66–7.

69 *IB*, 10 Oct. 1919; *LL*, 17 and 24 Oct. 1919; *Brantford Expositor*, 15 Oct. 1919.

70 *Star*, 13 and 14 Feb. 1919; *LOC* (1919), 138; *IB*, 25 Jan. 1918, 21 Feb. 1919; *Parliamentary Guide* (1920), 301–2; *Brantford Expositor*, 25 Aug. 1919

71 UWO, London TLC, *Minutes*, 1 Oct. 1919; *LL*, 3 Oct. 1919

5 The Woman Democrat

1 This was the title of the short-lived women's column of the *Industrial Banner*, starting 11 June 1920.

2 Hamilton labour member Allan Studholme was a lone voice for women's suffrage in the provincial legislature; Craig Heron, 'Working-Class Hamilton, 1895–1930' (PhD diss., Dalhousie University 1981), 613.

3 The significance of the 'family wage' has been the subject of an important historical debate. See Jane Humphries, 'Class Struggle and the Persistence of the Working-Class Family,' *Cambridge Journal of Economics* 1 (1977), and her 'The Working-Class Family, Women's Liberation, and Class Struggle: The Case of Nine-teenth Century British History,' *Review of Radical Political Economics* 1 (Fall 1977), Hilary Land, 'The Family Wage,' *Feminist Review* 6 (1980), Martha May, 'The Historical Problem of the Family Wage: The Ford Motor Company and the Five Dollar Day,' *Feminist Studies*, 8 (Summer 1982), Michele Barrett and Mary McIntosh, 'The "Family Wage": Some Problems for Socialists and Feminists,' *Capital and Class* 11 (Summer 1980), and their *Women's Oppression Today: Problems in Marxist Feminist Analysis* (London 1980), and Johanna Brenner and Maria Ramas, 'Rethinking Women's Oppression,' *New Left Review* 144 (Mar.-Apr. 1984); Bettina Bradbury, 'Women's History and Working-Class History,' *Labour / Le Travail* 19 (Spring 1987).

4 Linda Kealey, ed., *A Not Unreasonable Claim: Women and Reform in Canada, 1880s–1920s* (Toronto 1979). Carol Lee Bacchi, *Liberation Deferred? The Ideas of the English-Canadian Suffragists, 1877–1918* (Toronto 1983), and Joan Sangster, *Dreams of Equality: Women on the Canadian Left, 1920–1950* (Toronto 1989), provide greater focus on working-class women.

5 The number grew to 81,029. According to the census of 1911, 154,878 women were 'gainfully employed' in Ontario. This grew to 195,106 in 1921; AO, RG7, Series 2: 1, box 1, Dept of Labour, Deputy Minister, General Subject Files, file: 'Hours of Labour'; *Census of Canada*, 1911, vol. 6, table 5, 162 and 1921, vol. 4, table 4, 214. There were 35,000 women munitions workers in Canada by 1917; David Carnegie, *The History of Munitions Supply in Canada, 1914–1918* (London 1925), 254. Also on women in the First World War, see Ceta Ramkhalawansingh, 'Women during the Great War,' in Janice Acton, Penny Goldsmith, and Bonnie Shepard, eds, *Women at Work, 1850–1930* (Toronto 1974), and Enid M. Price, 'Changes in the Industrial Occupations of Women in the Environment of Montreal during the Period of the War, 1914–1918' (MA thesis, McGill University 1919).

6 NA, MG28, I44, TDLC, *Minutes*, 18 May, 1 June 1916, TDLC Circular dated 11 June 1917, included in *Minutes* of 19 June 1917; TLCC, *Proceedings* (1917), 32; *IB*, 26 May, 24 Nov. 1916

7 *International Molders' Journal* (Cincinnati) 53 (Nov. 1917), 811; NA, RG27, Dept of Labour, vol. 306, file 17(65); UWO, London TLC, *Minutes*, 1 Aug., 5 Dec. 1917

8 *MMJ* 29 (Apr. 1917), 371; *Star*, 13 June 1918

9 *Toronto World*, 13 June 1918; *Globe*, 18 June 1918

10 NA, RG27, Dept of Labour, vol. 308, file 18(87); *Globe*, 8 and 15 July 1918; *Toronto World*, 11 July 1918; *Mail and Empire*, 9 July 1918; *Toronto News*, 9 July 1918; *IB*, 28 June, 19 July 1918; *MMJ* 30 (Oct. 1918), 925

11 *MMJ* 30 (Mar. 1918), 209. The international president of the Women's Auxiliary was, in fact, hired by the IAM to organize women working in machine shops, *MMJ* 30 (Feb. 1918), 161-2.

12 *Globe*, 15 June 1918

13 *Shoe Workers' Journal* (Boston) 18 (July 1917), 71; *IB*, 6 Sept. 1918

14 NA, MG30, A16, J.W. Flavelle Papers, vol. 38, file: 'Irish, Mark H., 1918–19, 1924,' Irish to Edward FitzGerald, 28 June 1918

15 *IB*, 17 May 1918. Women were hired in Kingston, *Star*, 30 Jan. 1919;

Barbara Wilson, ed., *Ontario and the First World War: A Collection of Documents* (Toronto 1977), 140–4

16 TLCC, *Proceedings* (1917), 32; see also *LOC* (1917), 36–9, and TDLC, *Minutes*, 19 June 1917.

17 *IB*, 28 Jan. 1916

18 *Brantford Expositor*, 7 Dec. 1916.

19 Women's Department, CRA, 'What Shall I Do Now? How to Work for Canada in Peace' (Toronto, 7 July 1919), 10; *Report of the Women's War Conference* 35; *FP*, 19 Oct. 1918; *LG* 18 (Sept. 1918), 690; *Star*, 14 and 27 Nov. 1918

20 *Star*, 14 Nov. 1918, 24 Feb., 31 Mar. 1919

21 *SN*, 8 Nov. 1919; NA, RG27, Dept. of Labour, vol. 160, file 611.21, S.J. Welheuser to G.D. Robertson, 31 Jan. 1919

22 Canada, RCIR, *Evidence*, 2625. For a thoughtful discussion of the role of marriage in defining the work experience of working-class women see Sarah Eisenstein, *Give Us Bread but Give Us Roses: Working Women's Consciousness in the United States, 1890 to the First World War* (London 1983), esp. 113–45; also Veronica Strong-Boag, *The New Day Recalled: Lives of Girls and Women in English Canada, 1919–1939* (Toronto 1988).

23 *IB*, 8 Jan., 16 and 23 Apr., 8 Oct., 7 Dec. 1915, 30 June, 8 Dec. 1916, 1 Aug. 1919; Nancy Schrom Dye, *As Equals and As Sisters: Feminism, Unionism and the Women's Trade Union League of New York* (Columbia, Mo. 1980); and Colette A. Hyman, 'Labor Organizing and Female Institution-Building: The Chicago Women's Trade Union League, 1904–1924,' in Ruth Milkman, ed., *Women, Work and Protest: A Century of U.S. Women's Labor History* (Boston 1985); TDLC, *Minutes*, 7 Jan., 20 May 1915, 20 Apr., 4 May 1916, 7 Feb. 1918, and 17 Mar. 1921; NA, MG28, I103, TLCC Executive Council, *Minutes*, 25 Nov. 1918; UWO, London TLC, *Minutes*, 15 May 1918

24 *IB*, 31 May 1918; *LG*, 18 (June 1918), 461

25 TLCC Executive Council, *Minutes*, 25 Nov. 1918

26 *MMJ* 27 (Sept. 1915), 847; *IB*, 7 and 21 Mar. 1919, 21 May 1920; *LN*, 30 May 1919

27 Joan Sangster 'The 1907 Bell Telephone Strike: Organizing Women Workers,' *Labour / Le Travailleur* 3 (1978); Toronto *Telegram*, 9 Sept. 1918; *IB*, 19 July, 16 Aug., 27 Sept., 11 Oct. 1918, 31 Jan., 7 Mar. 1919. In Jan. 1919, the local was still growing, *IB*, 31 Jan. 1919; *Star*, 9 Jan. 1919.

28 *IB*, 22 Nov. 1918; Bacchi, *Liberation Deferred?*, 129–31

29 NA, MG26, H1, Borden Papers, RLB Series, file 1, 'The Women's

Party: The Woman's Programme for the War and After' (1918); NA, MG30, D29, John Stephen Willison Papers, vol. 26, folder 195, Mrs J. Campbell MacIver to Willison, 2 Dec. 1918

30 Veronica Strong-Boag, *The Parliament of Women: The National Council of Women of Canada, 1893–1929* (Ottawa 1976), esp. 364–71; Mary McNab was the former business agent of the Amalgamated Clothing Workers, as well as organizer (along with Fred Flatman) of the United Textile Workers in Hamilton, *Star*, 19 Apr. 1919; *LN*, 27 Sept. 1918, 25 Apr. 1919; *Advance* (New York), 27 Apr., 15 June, 21 Sept. 1917; *IB*, 31 May, 11 Oct. 1918

31 *IB*, 7 May, 9 July 1920

32 *IB*, 9 July 1920; *LOC* (1920), 104; *Herald* (London), 11 Nov. 1920

33 *IB*, 27 May, 3 June 1921

34 *LL*, 30 May 1924; *Canadian Labor World*, 27 Nov. 1924

35 *IB*, 15 Mar. 1918, 14 Nov. 1919; Joan Sangster, 'The Communist Party and the Woman Question, 1922–1929,' *Labour / Le Travail* 15 (Spring 1985)

36 *IB*, 6 Sept. 1918

37 *Star*, 6 and 20 Mar. 1919; *IB*, 7 and 14 Nov. 1919; *LOC* (1919), 106; TDLC, *Minutes*, 17 Feb. 1921

38 *IB*, 20 June 1919

39 *IB*, 30 May 1919, 25 June 1920; TDLC, *Minutes*, 6 Feb. 1920

40 *IB*, 11 June 1920; Bacchi's dismissal of Prenter for failing to challenge class privilege would appear to be misplaced given her activity in the labour movement, her decision to join the nascent Workers' Party, and these articles in the *Industrial Banner*; Bacchi, *Liberation Deferred?*, 123.

41 TDLC, *Minutes*, 15 June 1922, 5 and 19 Apr., 19 July, 16 Aug., 6 Dec. 1923; NA, RG27, Dept of Labour, vol. 3130, file 89, Third National Convention, Workers' Party of Canada, 18 Apr. 1924, 'Report of Secretary at Annual Meeting of Toronto Women's Labor League, 18 Apr. 1924'; *MMJ* 35 (Dec. 1923), 575; *LL*, 13 Jan. 1922, 26 June, 19 Sept. 1924; TLCC, *Proceedings* (1923), 131–2; *Workers' Guard*, 17 Dec. 1921; *IB*, 27 Jan. 1922; *Worker*, 1 June 1922; *LOC* (1924), 264; NA, MG28, IV, 4, Communist Party of Canada Papers, vol. 14, file 'Third National Convention 18–20 Apr. 1924, Toronto: Resolution on Women's Work, Report, 1924'

42 *Worker*, 10 Jan. 1925; *People's Cause*, 20 Apr. 1925; *LL*, 19 Sept. 1924; Sangster, 'The Communist Party and the Woman Question,' 33; NA, MG28, IV, 4, Communist Party of Canada Papers, vol. 14, file 'Third

National Convention 18–20 Apr. 1924, Toronto: Resolution on Women's Work, Report, 1924'

43 *Worker*, 25 Oct. 1924

44 *IB*, 12 June, 27 Nov. 1914, 1 Jan. 1915

45 *IB*, 25 Dec. 1914, 17 Sept. 1915, 1 Dec. 1916

46 TDLC, *Minutes*, 18 Nov. 1915, 15 Feb. 1917; TLCC, *Proceedings* (1916), 126–7, (1917), 137–8; Frances H. Early, 'The Historic Roots of the Women's Peace Movement in North America,' *Canadian Women Studies* 7 (Winter 1986), 45; Thomas Socknat, 'Canada's Liberal Pacifists and the Great War,' *Journal of Canadian Studies* 18 (1983–4); *IB*, 26 Nov. 1915, 20 Oct., 10 and 24 Nov., 8, 15 and 22 Dec. 1916, 5, 12, 19, and 26 Jan., 30 Mar., 19 Oct., 9 Nov. 1917; *Brantford Expositor*, 22 Dec. 1916; *LN*, 19 Oct. 1917

47 Mrs Cassidy died in 1918; *IB*, 6 July 1917, 22 Mar. 1918; *LN*, 5 July 1918.

48 *LN*, 15 and 29 Mar. 1918; *IB*, 3 May, 2 and 30 Aug. 1918, 4 June 1920

49 *IB*, 1 Feb., 3 May, 7 June 1918, 5 Dec. 1919; *LN*, 12 Apr., 17 May 1918, 14 and 28 Feb., 14 and 28 Mar. 1919; *LL*, 9 Jan., 7 May, 11 and 18 June 1920, 21 Jan., 4 Feb. 1921

50 *LN*, 12 and 19 Dec. 1921. When the East Hamilton Women's ILP was formed the *Banner* declared it a second ILP 'women's auxiliary.' *IB*, 7 Feb. 1919

51 *IB*, 2 Aug. 1918

52 Milkman, ed., *Women, Work and Protest*, xiii

53 *IB*, 14 Feb. 1919; *Star*, 11 Feb. 1919

54 *IB*, 17 and 24 Jan., 14 and 21 Feb., 14 Mar. 1919; *Star*, 11 Feb. 1919; *MMJ* 31 (Mar. 1919), 246

55 *MMJ* 31 (Apr. 1919), 326; *Plumbers, Gas and Steam Fitters' Journal* (Chicago) 24 (Apr. 1919), 14; *IB*, 14 Mar., 4 Apr., 2 and 9 May, 24 Nov. 1919, 23 Jan., 27 Feb., 9 July 1920; *LN*, 7 May 1920. The branches were Hamilton, Mount Hamilton, St Catharines, Orillia, Kitchener, Welland, and Waterloo, *IB*, 4 June, 9 July 1920.

56 *Star*, 11 Dec. 1918, *IB*, 15 Nov., 13 Dec. 1918, 20 Dec. 1922

57 Heron, 'Working-Class Hamilton,' ch. 7

58 *IB*, 27 Nov. 1914, 26 Mar. 1915; TDLC, *Minutes*, 20 Jan. 1916, 19 Oct. 1922

59 *IB*, 8 Aug. 1919, 2 Apr. 1920; *LN*, 18 Apr., 8 Aug. 1919, 28 Jan., 27 Aug. 1920; *LL*, 25 June 1920, 8 Apr. 1921

60 *ND*, 22 May 1919

61 *IB*, 24 and 31 Oct. 1919
62 *LL*, 7 Oct. 1921
63 *LN*, 25 Apr. 1921; *LL*, 21 Mar. 1924
64 *IB*, 2 May 1919
65 *Herald*, 24 Mar. 1921
66 *Herald*, 21 Apr. 1921. Notably, there was still little discussion of birth control. See Angus McLaren and Arlene Tigar McLaren, *The Bedroom and the State: The Changing Practices and Politics of Contraception and Abortion in Canada, 1880–1980* (Toronto 1986).
67 *Herald*, 19 May, 1 Dec. 1921
68 *London Advertiser*, 20 Dec. 1921, 6 Jan. 1922; *LL*, 14 Dec. 1923; UWO, London TLC, *Minutes*, 17 Jan. 1923, 16 July 1924; NA, MG28, IV, 4, Communist Party of Canada Papers, W.T. Coughlan to Tim Buck, 16 June 1923; Canadian Labor Party, Ontario Section, 'Minutes of the Fifth Annual Convention ... Hamilton, Mar. 22nd, 1924,' in TDLC, *Minutes*, 3 Apr. 1924
69 *Globe*, 21 Oct. 1919

6 Welfare Capitalism and Industrial Democracy

1 *LN*, 28 Mar. 1919
2 D.C. Masters, *The Winnipeg General Strike* (Toronto 1950), and David Jay Bercuson, *Confrontation at Winnipeg: Labour, Industrial Relations, and the General Strike* (Montreal 1974)
3 Tom Traves, *The State and Enterprise: Canadian Manufacturers and the Federal Government, 1917–1931* (Toronto 1979), esp. 159–60
4 *IB*, 21 Apr. 1916; NA, MG28, I44, TDLC, *Minutes*, 19 Oct. 1916; TLCC, *Proceedings* (1916), 128–32, and (1917), 22–31; NA, MG30, A16, J. W. Flavelle Papers, vol. 2, file 11, Gerald H. Brown to Flavelle, 28 Jan. 1916; *Star*, 15 Mar., 7 May 1919; *Toronto Times*, 1 May 1919; *Machinists' MMJ* 30 (Nov. 1918), 1042
5 *Star*, 12 and 14 Apr., 10 May 1919; *NIC, Proceedings*, 94–6
6 *Star*, 17 Dec. 1918; also Doug Owram, *The Government Generation: Canadian Intellectuals and the State, 1900–1945* (Toronto 1986), 110, 124, 150–1
7 PC 1034, 4 May 1918, PC 415, 24 Feb. 1919, PC 551, 14 Mar. 1919; Peter E. Rider, 'The Imperial Munitions Board and Its Relationship to Government, Business and Labour, 1914–1920' (PhD diss., University of Toronto 1974), 12; NA, MG26, J1, W.L. Mackenzie King Papers, David Carnegie to King, 2 Apr. 1919; AO, MU59, Frank Beer Papers, Carnegie to Beer, 18 Mar. 1919; *IC*, Oct. 1918, 47

8 NA, MG26, H, Robert L. Borden Papers, OC Series, vol. 557, 'Report of Labour Sub-committee of Reconstruction and Development Ctte,' 9 Sept. 1918, and RLB Series, vol. 527, Labour Sub-committee, Reconstruction and Development Committee, 9 Sept. 1918; NA, MG28, I230, CMA, vol. 11, Labour Committee appointed by the Toronto Branch Executive, *Minutes*, 12 Aug. 1918, and Executive Council, *Minutes*, 12 Feb. 1914; *LG* 19 (May 1919), 562–4

9 *CAR* (1918), 558-9; *FP* 21 Dec. 1918; TLCC, *Proceedings* (1919), 32

10 NA, RG27, Dept of Labour, vol. 3754, file 610.011-(3), 'Work of Dept. Special Attention being given to matters of Labour Policy'; *LG* 19 (May 1919), 564; *IB*, 18 Apr., 9 May 1919; *Star*, 4 Apr. 1919

11 *SN*, 24 May 1919; *IB*, 18 Apr. 1919

12 Canada, RCIR, *Report of Commission*, 4

13 Stuart D. Brandes, *American Welfare Capitalism, 1880–1940* (Chicago 1970), 122, 127; James Weinstein, *The Corporate Ideal in the Liberal State, 1900–1918* (Boston 1968), 191–207; Philip S. Foner, *History of the Labor Movement in the United States*, vol. 5, *The AFL in the Progressive Era, 1910–1915* (New York 1980), 196–213

14 Canada, Dept of Labour, 'Industrial Councils: Text of Reports of Whitley Committee and of Certain Communications Relating Thereto' (Ottawa 1919); James Hinton, *The First Shop Stewards' Movement* (London 1973)

15 CMA, vol. 12, Executive Council, *Minutes*, 27 Mar., 24 Apr. 1919; *IC* (May 1919), 51; Canada, Dept of Labour, 'Joint Councils in Industry' (Ottawa 1921); James Foy, 'Gideon D. Robertson, Conservative Minister of Labour, 1917–1921' (MA thesis, University of Ottawa 1972), 18–19

16 Cited in *CAR* (1919), 503

17 NA, RG27, Dept of Labour, vol. 160, file 611.21, J.D. Reid to Robertson, 29 Jan. 1919; vol. 3754, file 610.011-(3), 'Work of Dept. Special Attention being given to matters of Labour Policy,' 10; *Star*, 27 May 1919; Harold A. Logan, *The History of Trade-Union Organization in Canada* (Chicago 1928), 292–5; TLCC, *Proceedings* (1920), 74; *IB*, 29 May 1914, 20 Apr. 1917; *LG* 21 (Mar. 1921), 485; *LL*, 1 Apr. 1921

18 *SN*, 8 Feb. 1919; *LG* 20 (Aug. 1920), 942; *CCJ*, 1 (Mar. 1922), 118; *IB*, 25 Apr. 1919; TLCC, *Proceedings* (1920), 15, 74, (1922), 122-3, (1923), 49; *LL*, 13 May 1921; *CAR* (1920), 471–2

19 *LG* 18 (Aug. 1918), 615–19, 19 (Aug. 1919), 862, 21 (Feb. 1921), 274, and (Mar. 1921), 17; *IB*, 16 Aug. 1918; *CAR* (1918), 493; NIC, *Proceedings*, 118; *LL*, 12 Nov. 1920; Social Service Council of Canada, *Co-Management Experiments in Canadian Industry*, 'Advance Copy' (Jan.

1921), 8; R.M. MacIver, 'Arbitration and Conciliation in Canada,' in
W.P.M. Kennedy, ed., *Social and Economic Conditions in the Dominion of
Canada* (Philadelphia 1923), 294; NA, RG27, Dept of Labour, vol.
311, file 19(58)

20 S.R. Parsons and James A. Emery, 'Fundamentals of Industrial Progress, Being a Reprint of Addresses Delivered at the Annual General
Meeting of the Canadian Manufacturers Association, Montreal, June
1918,' 3; *IC*, Sept. 1920, 89

21 Richard Edwards, *Contested Terrain: The Transformation of the Workplace
in the Twentieth Century* (New York 1979), ch. 2, 8; Daniel Nelson,
*Managers and Workers: Origins of the New Factory System in the United
States, 1880–1920* (Madison 1975), 43–4; Sanford M. Jacoby, *Employing
Bureaucracy: Managers, Unions, and the Transformation of Work in Ameri-
can Industry, 1900–1945* (New York 1985), ch. 1

22 Craig Heron and Bryan D. Palmer, 'Through the Prism of the Strike:
Industrial Conflict in Southern Ontario,' *Canadian Historical Review* 58
(Dec. 1977), 444; *IB*, 31 Dec. 1915; NA, RG27, Dept of Labour, vol.
320, 20(116). Information on McClary's programs is from AO, RG7,
Dept of Labour, Series 15, 4, box 3, Pamphlets, 1915–30, McClary
Manufacturing Co.; London *Advertiser*, 18 Mar., 20 Mar. 1919; UWO,
London TLC, *Minutes*, 19 Mar. 1919, 18 Jan. 1922; Canada, RCIR,
Evidence, 2105, 2157–72, 2202–11; UWO, London Chamber of Com-
merce, *Minutes* (Special Committee on Immigration), 19 Mar. 1920; *IC*
(Sept. 1920), 66, (Dec. 1920), 84, (Feb. 1921), 122; NA, MG28, I256,
International Moulders and Allied Workers Union (microfilmed cop-
ies), Executive Board Minutes, 9–21 Aug. 1920, 91; *LL*, 1 Sept. 1922;
FP, 6 Oct. 1922

23 AO, RG7, Dept of Labour, Series 15, 4, box 3, Pamphlets, 1915–30
(Bell Telephone Co. of Canada, Dominion Express Co., International
Harvester Company of Canada, Ltd, Libby, McNeil and Libby, Mas-
sey-Harris Co. Ltd, National Cash Register Company of Canada, Ltd,
Procter and Gamble Company, Swift and Co., Dominion Forge and
Stamping Co., Imperial Oil, Ltd, British American Oil Co., Goodyear
Tire and Rubber Co. of Canada Ltd, Slingsby Manufacturing Co.,
Ltd), and Series 7, 1, Research Branch, Senior Investigator, General
Files, 1923–46, file 8, 'Miss Marion Findlay's Papers – re Survey of In-
dustrial Welfare in Ontario,' and vol. 3, 'IR Information' (Lever
Brothers, Sunbeam Lamp, Mercury Mills, Beaver Board); Canada,
RCIR, *Evidence*, 2372–77, 2508–15; *IC* (Aug. 1919), 63; *LG* 19 (Aug.
1919), 863, 20 (May 1920), 498; *FP*, 8 Nov. 1919; *Sarnia Canadian Ob-
server*, 24 July 1919; David Brody, *The Butcher Workmen: A Study in*

Unionization (Cambridge, Mass. 1964), 61

24 *CAR* (1916), 385; *FP*, 2 Nov. 1918; Associate Committee on Industrial Fatigue of the Honorary Advisory Council for Scientific and Industrial Research, 'Survey of General Conditions of Industrial Hygiene in Toronto' (Ottawa 1921), 6; *IC* (Mar. 1918), 1639

25 AO, RG7, Series 15, 4, box 3 (Barber-Ellis Ltd)

26 Ibid. (National Cash Register Co. of Canada, Ltd, Dominion Forge and Stamping Co., Canadian Explosives Ltd, Barber-Ellis Ltd, W.J. Gage and Co. Ltd)

27 Ibid. (W.J. Gage and Co. Ltd, Cockshutt Plow Co., Dominion Express); *IC* (Dec. 1923), 55

28 AO, RG7, Series 15, 4, box 3 (Goodyear Tire and Rubber Co., International Harvester Co.); International Harvester allowed women to join. However, if they became pregnant they were paid fifty dollars and could no longer retain membership in the association.

29 *FP*, 17 Apr. 1920

30 Marion Findlay, 'Protection of Workers in Industry,' in Kennedy, ed., *Social and Economic Conditions*, 263

31 Brandes, *American Welfare Capitalism*, 17; Nelson, *Managers and Workers*, 105; Stephen Meyer, III, *The Five Dollar Day: Labor Management and Social Control in the Ford Motor Company, 1908–1921* (Albany, NY 1981), 95–147; *IB*, 7 May 1915, 27 Sept. 1918; *Sarnia Canadian Observer*, 12 May 1919; H. Michell, 'Profit Sharing and Producers' Co-operation in Canada,' *Queen's Quarterly* 25 (Jan. 1918), 313–17; Craig Heron, *Working in Steel: The Early Years in Canada, 1883–1935* (Toronto 1988), 101–2; *FP*, 1 Feb. 1919, 10 Apr. 1920; *LG*, 19 (Apr. 1919), 381–2, 20 (Apr. 1920), 422–3, 24 (Nov. 1924), 967; AO, RG7, Series 15, 4, box 3 (International Harvester Co., Robert Simpson Co., Yale and Towne Manufacturing Co.), and Series 7, 1, vol. 3, 'IR Information' (John Northway); *IC* (Aug. 1920), 96; *CAR* (1918), 239; *Brantford Expositor*, 2 May 1919

32 Canada, RCIR, *Evidence*, 2487–98. On stock distribution see AO, RG7, Series 7, 1, vol. 3, 'IR Information' (British American Oil, John Northway, Toronto Carpet Co., International Harvester, Steel Co. of Canada, Dominion Chain, General Motors, Canada Cement), and Series 15, 4, box 3 (Imperial Oil, International Harvester, Procter and Gamble, Yale and Towne Manufacturing Co., Goodyear Tire and Rubber Co.); *LG* 19 (July 1919), 755, 20 (Apr. 1920), 422–3; *FP*, 10 Apr. 1920, 6 Oct. 1922; *IC* (Nov. 1919), 108.

33 *IC* (Oct. 1916), 743; *LG* 16 (Sept. 1916), 1521. On pensions see AO, RG7, Series 15, 4, box 3 (Bell Telephone Co., Canadian Explosives

Ltd, Canadian Westinghouse Co., Dominion Textiles Co., Canadian Consolidated Rubber Co., Hydro-Electric Power Commission of Ontario, Libby, McNeil and Libby, Niagara Falls Power Co., Studebaker Corporation), and Series 7, 1, vol. 3, 'IR Information' (Steel Company of Canada); *IC* (Feb. 1918), 1463; *IB*, 6 Dec. 1918; *CAR* (1919), 506; Heron, *Working in Steel*, ch. 3; *FP*, 4 Jan. 1919, 28 Jan. 1922; *LG* 19 (May 1919), 502, 20 (Apr. 1920), 373–4; *LL*, 23 Jan. 1920.

34 Paul Craven, *'An Impartial Umpire': Industrial Relations and the Canadian State, 1900–11* (Toronto 1980), 348–9; *Globe*, 21 Nov. 1916

35 *IB*, 4 Aug. 1916

36 Committee on Industrial Fatigue, 'Survey ...,' 7; Brandes, *American Welfare Capitalism*, 27. On paid vacations, see AO, RG7, Series 7, 1, vol. 3, 'IR Information' (British American Oil, Canadian National Carbon, Harris Abattoir, Lever Brothers, Sunbeam Lamp, General Motors, Western Clock, Plymouth Cordage).

37 *SN*, 28 June 1919; *LL*, 1 Sept. 1922; AO, RG7, Series 7, 1, vol. 3, 'IR Information' (American Cyanamid); and Series 4: 15, 4, box 3 (McClary Manufacturing Co., Ford Motor Co., Goodyear Tire and Rubber Co.)

38 Jacoby, *Employing Bureaucracy*, 56–61; NA, Flavelle Papers, vol. 6, file 64, 'Summary of Replies to Chairman's Circular of June 11–17,' 3; *IC* (July 1918), 237, (Sept. 1918), 93, (May 1921), 108; *FP*, 8 Nov. 1918; AO, RG7, Series 7, 1, vol. 3, 'IR Information' (Wrigley's)

39 *IC* (May 1921), 108; AO, RG7, Series 7, 1, vol. 3, 'IR Information,' (Canadian Kodak, Consumers' Gas, Neilson's, John Northway, Sunbeam Lamp, Westinghouse, General Motors, Mercury Mills); Hamilton Harvester Works Industrial Council, *Bulletin* 9 (Jan. 1920), 13, 32, and 12 (Apr. 1920), 29, and 17 (Sept.–Oct. 1920), 17; Bruce Scott, 'A Place in the Sun: The Industrial Council at Massey-Harris, 1919–1929,' *Labour / Le Travailleur* 1 (1976), 162; Margaret Wade, *A Sample of Canada's Industrial Life: The McClary Manufacturing Company of London, Ont.* (London, Ont. 1921), 9; Brandes, *American Welfare Capitalism*, 61. Employers had long been concerned about workers' leisure time. See especially Roy Rosenzweig, *Eight Hours for What We Will: Workers and Leisure in an Industrial City, 1870–1920* (Cambridge 1983).

40 *IC* (Feb. 1924), 46–7; Labor Educational Association of Ontario, 'Official Annual Labor Review,' 1924, 6–7, AO, RG7, Series 7, 1, vol. 3, 'IR Information' (Gillett, Plymouth Cordage)

41 AO, RG7, Series 7, 1, vol. 3, 'IR Information' (Lever Brothers, Canada Cement), and Series 15, 4, box 3 (Canadian Westinghouse Veteran Employees' Association, Goodyear Tire and Rubber Co., McClary

Manufacturing Co.), box 4, *Congasco, Green Label* (Christmas 1928), 8, *Wingfoot Clan* 8 (Mar. 1926), 1; *IC*, (Feb. 1924), 46-47; *Sarnia Canadian Observer*, 8 Feb. 1919. The railways also participated, see Mark Rosenfeld, '"She Was a Hard Life": Work, Family, Community and Politics in the Railway Ward of Barrie Ontario, 1900–1960' (Ph.D. diss., York University 1990), ch. 5.

42 Social Service Council of Canada, *Co-Management Experiments*, 8; Norman S. Duce, 'Plant Level Labour Management Co-operation in Canada' (MBA thesis, Queen's University 1965) 14

43 According to Ontario Department of Labour researcher Marion Findlay, ten industrial council plans existed in the province in 1926: Canadian National Railways, Imperial Oil, British-American Oil, Swift Canadian, Bell Telephone, Massey-Harris, International Harvester, Merchant's Rubber, Verity Plow, and Dominion Rubber; AO, RG7, Series 7, 1, vol. 8, 'Miss Marion Findlay's Papers – re Survey of Industrial Welfare in Ontario.' Since Massey-Harris owned Verity and Merchant's and Dominion Rubber were both part of Canadian Consolidated Rubber (and, in turn, U.S. Rubber), the number drops to eight.

44 Hamilton Harvester Works Industrial Council, *Bulletin* 10 (Feb. 1920), 13, and 11 (Mar. 1920), 2; Scott, 'Place in the Sun,' 171; *MMJ* 33 (June 1921), 494; AO, RG7, Series 7, 1, vol. 3, 'IR Information' (American Cyanamid)

45 Hamilton Harvester, *Bulletin* 12 (Apr. 1920), 15, and 13 (May 1920), 10; AO, RG7, Series 15, 4, box 3 (Swift Canadian Co., Massey-Harris Co.); Canada, RCIR, *Evidence*, 2805; Scott, 'Place in the Sun,' 169–71

46 *FP*, 8 May 1920; *Canadian Machinery* 24 (30 Dec. 1920) 597–8; *Canadian Foundryman* 12 (May 1921), *LG* 21 (Aug. 1921), 978–9, (Sept. 1921), 1081; *IC* (July 1922), 157

47 NA, RG27, Dept of Labour, vol. 319, file 20(76) and vol. 323, file 20(331), W.J. Pearson to Deputy Minister of Labour, 18 Sept. 1920; *IB*, 12 Apr., 31 May, 14 June, 13 Sept. 1918; NA, Borden Papers, RLB Series, File 2739, A.R. Mosher to Borden, 2 Sept. 1918, and G.D. Robertson to Borden, 6 Sept. 1918

48 *FP*, 4 Jan. 1919; Canada, RCIR, *Evidence*, 2676; AO, RG7, Series 7, 1, vol. 8 (Gutta Percha), and Series 15, 4, box 3 (Swift Canadian Co.) Scott, 'Place in the Sun,' 163

49 National Industrial Conference Board, *Employee Magazines in the United States* (New York 1925), 3. Various employee magazines are in AO, RG7, Series 15, 4, box 4.

50 AO, RG7, Series 15, 4, box 4, *Neilson News, Fabricator* 6 (Jan. 1925),

Green Label 11 (Christmas 1928), *Wingfoot Clan* 8 (Mar. 1926), 2, and Series 7, 1, vol. 3, 'IR Information' (Canada Cement); Canada, Dept of Labour, 'Employee Magazines in Canada' (Ottawa 1921), 7

51 National Industrial Conference Board, *Employee Magazines*, 61; Hamilton Harvester Industrial Council, *Bulletin* 9 (Jan. 1920), 36; *LG* 21 (Mar. 1921), 527–8

52 Jacoby, *Employing Bureaucracy*, 196–7; Plymouth Cordage and Neilson's each had an employment department, Goodyear a service department (for employees, not customers), Studebaker a co-operative department, McClary's a welfare department, American Cyanamid a personnel department, International Harvester an industrial-relations department, and Ford, perhaps most interestingly, an education department. AO, RG7, Series 7, 1, vol. 3. 47 and Series 2, 1, Deputy Minister, General Subject Files, box 2, file, 'Reports – Employment Offices,' 'Report, Women's Dept, London Employment Bureau, Nov. 1918 – Oct. 1919,' and 'Annual Report, Niagara Falls, Ontario Government Public Employment Bureau, 31 Oct. 1919,' and Series 15, 4, box 3 (British American Oil Co., Goodyear Tire and Rubber Co.); *IC* (Apr. 1919); Canada, RCIR, *Evidence*, 2363

53 *FP*, 2 Nov. 1918, 7 Feb. 1920; *IC* (May 1920), 74–5; *LG* 20 (Jan. 1920), 3; Canada, Dept of Labour, *Report of a Conference on Industrial Relations* (Ottawa 1921), 49

54 Margaret E. McCallum, 'Corporate Welfarism in Canada, 1919–1939,' *Canadian Historical Review* 71 (Mar. 1990). Similarly, McCallum does not note the degree of resistance in the late 1930s, as councils often provided an arena for CIO organizing. See Bill Freeman, *1005: Political Life in a Union Local* (Toronto 1982), 35–6; Daniel Nelson, 'The Company Union Movement, 1900–1937: A Reexamination,' *Business History Review* 56 (Autumn 1982).

55 Canada, RCIR, *Evidence*, 2411; A. Ernest Epp, 'Cooperation among Capitalists: The Canadian Merger Movement, 1909–1913' (PhD diss., Johns Hopkins University 1973), 652–7; *IB*, 10 May 1918

56 *IB*, 31 May 1918

57 Canada, RCIR, *Evidence*, 2017, 2088

58 *Plumbers, Gas and Steam Fitters' Journal* (Chicago) 24 (May 1919), 14; *IB*, 28 June 1918. Canada, RCIR, *Evidence*, 1776, 1999, 2087

59 *LG* 19 (Jan. 1919), 46; *Sarnia Canadian Observer*, 23 May 1919

60 Canada, RCIR, *Evidence*, 2071, 2082, 2789, 2795

61 Ibid., 1999–2003, 2017, 2025, 2035–6, 2040, 2060, 2099

62 Ibid., 2036, 2064, 2072, 2075–6

63 Ibid., 1997–8, 2052

64 Ibid., 2052, 2099, 2775, 2780, 2782; *Sarnia Canadian Observer*, 8 Feb. 1919
65 Canada, RCIR, *Evidence*, 2022, 2046, 2062, 2067, 2070–2, 2092; Scott, 'Place in the Sun,' 184
66 Canada, RCIR, *Evidence*, 2328–9.
67 Ibid., 2337–8. Whether welfarism and industrial councils were successful in securing workers' allegiance has been the subject of some debate among historians. In 'The Rise and Decline of Welfare Capitalism,' in his *Workers in Industrial America* (New York 1980), David Brody criticizes Brandes and Irving Bernstein, *The Lean Years: A History of the American Worker, 1920–1933* (Boston 1960), for their adherence to the 'comforting' notion that welfarism was ephemeral and generally unsuccessful. See also Nelson, 'Company Union Movement.'
68 Canada, RCIR, *Evidence*, 2796, 2858–70, 2932–9; *Star*, 15 Mar., 17 May 1919; 4 Apr. 1919. The draft constitution appears in *LG*, 19 (Apr. 1919), 437–8; Joint Conference of the Building and Construction Industries in Canada, 3–6 May 1921, *Proceedings*, 42–3, and *Peoples' Cause* (Oct. 1927)
69 Ian M. Drummond, *Progress without Planning: The Economic History of Ontario from Confederation to the Second World War* (Toronto 1987), 151; Kenneth Buckley, *Capital Formation in Canada, 1896–1930* (1955; Toronto 1974), 59
70 *LL*, 6 and 13 Feb., 19 and 26 Mar., 2 Apr. 1920; Hamilton *Spectator*, 6 and 27 Apr. 1920; Hamilton *Herald*, 15 and 27 Apr. 1920
71 *Star*, 7 May 1919; *LL*, 28 May, 4 June 1920, 5 Aug. 1921; *LOC* (1920), 102; also see NIC, *Proceedings*, 137–8; Logan, *History of Trade-Union Organization*, 292–3; Social Service Council of Canada, *Co-Management Experiments*, 'Advance Copy,' 'Amendments.'
72 *LN*, 18 Apr. 1919; *IB*, 14 Mar., 9 May 1919; NA, King Papers, vol. 50, King to Rockefeller, 2 June 1919, 6
73 Canada, RCIR, *Report*

7 In Defence of Capital

1 Canada, NIC, *Proceedings*, 33–4; NA, MG28, I230, CMA, vol. 12, Executive Council, *Minutes*, 1 Oct. 1919, 'Report of Industrial Relations Committee'; *FP*, 27 Sept. 1919
2 NA, MG30, D29, Sir John Stephen Willison Papers, vol. 4, folder 32, Willison to R.L. Borden, 15 Oct. 1918
3 NA, MG28, I40, CRA, Canadian Home Market Association, Provisional Executive Committee, *Minutes*, 14 Mar. 1918, and CIRA, Provi-

sional Executive Committee, *Minutes*, 29 Apr. 1918, General Meeting, *Minutes*, 3 May, 11 June 1918, and Central District Committee, *Minutes*, 2 May 1918; CMA, vol. 12, Executive Council, *Minutes*, 27 Mar. 1918; Tom Traves, *The State and Enterprise: Canadian Manufacturers and the Federal Government, 1917–1931* (Toronto 1979), 18

4 NA, Willison Papers, vol. 7, folder 53, CIRA, Bulletin No. 1, 19 Aug. 1918, 20, and 'A National Policy,' 15

5 Ibid., vol. 3, folder 22, Willison to G. Frank Beer, 23 July 1918

6 Ibid., vol. 12, folder 100, Drummond to Willison, 29 May 1919, vol. 5, folder 42, Willison to W.J. Bulman, 27 Oct. 1919, vol. 35, folder 265, Willison to Major H.B. Richey, 6 May 1919

7 Ibid., vol. 4, folder 32, R.L. Borden to Willison, 25 Oct. 1918, and Willison to Borden, 26 June 1918, and vol. 5, folder 42, Willison to W.J. Bulman, 16 Oct. 1918; NA, MG31, B8, John W. Bruce Papers, vol. 1, Bruce interviewed by Don Montgomery, 30 Mar. 1965, part 2, 4–5

8 NIC, *Proceedings*, 6–28; *LL*, 19 Sept. 1919

9 NA, MG26, H, Robert L. Borden Papers, OC Series, vol. 556, Charles E. Clay to Borden, 11 Sept. 1919; *OBU Bulletin*, 20 Sept. 1919; TLCC, *Proceedings* (1919), 219; UWO, London TLC, *Minutes*, 6 Aug., 1 Oct. 1919; NA, MG28, I44, TDLC, *Minutes*, 18 Sept. 1919; *LL*, 19 Sept. 1919.

10 NIC, *Proceedings*, 86, 212

11 NA, Borden Papers, OC Series, vol. 556, C.H. Carlisle to Borden, 6 Sept. 1919; Clarence E. Bonnett, *Employers' Associations in the United States: A Study of Typical Associations* (New York 1922), 24, 74–90; *IC* (June 1917), 202–3; CMA, vol. 11, Labor Committee, *Minutes*, 1 Oct. 1918. Clare Pentland has suggested that the employer delegates expressed 'remarkably liberal views' and that 'in all probability they were unusually advanced employers,' see *A Study of the Changing Social, Economic and Political Background of the Canadian System of Industrial Relations* (Ottawa 1968), 98–9. As the analysis below suggests, particularly in contrast to the CRA and the Labour Sub-committee, this was not at all the case.

12 James Weinstein, *The Corporate Ideal in the Liberal State, 1900–1918* (Boston 1968), 15; Allen M. Wakstein, 'The National Association of Manufacturers and Labor Relations in the 1920s,' *Labor History* 10 (Spring 1969); Doug Owram, *The Government Generation: Canadian Intellectuals and the State, 1900–1945* (Toronto 1986), 50; CMA, vol. 12, Executive Council, *Minutes*, 1 Oct. 1919, 'Report of the Industrial Relations Committee'; *LG* 19 (Oct. 1919), 1173

13 *IC* (Sept. 1919), 51; CMA, vol. 12, Executive Council, *Minutes*, 1 Oct. 1919, 'Report of the Industrial Relations Committee'; NIC, *Proceedings*, 133, 147

14 CMA, vol. 12, Executive Council, *Minutes*, 1 Oct. 1919, 'Report of the Industrial Relations Committee'

15 NIC, *Proceedings*, 95, 119–120, 133

16 Ibid., 50, 89, 121

17 *FP*, 20 Sept. 1919

18 NIC, *Proceedings*, 46; *IC* (Apr. 1919), 50, (July 1921), 137; TLCC, *Proceedings* (1921), 75–7; *LL*, 1 Apr. 1921; Building Industries Conference, *Proceedings*, 7

19 Canada, RCIR, *Evidence*, 2149; *Star*, 16 May 1919; *Toronto World*, 16 May 1919; *IC* (July 1919), 209–10; CMA, vol. 12, Executive Council, *Minutes*, 27 Nov. 1919; NA, Willison Papers, vol. 33, folder 244, S.R. Parsons to Willison, 28 Jan. 1922

20 *IC* (Dec. 1918), 43, (Mar. 1919), 51, (Nov. 1919), 56–8; *LG* 19 (Aug. 1919), 924–5; CMA, vol. 12, *Minutes*, 27 Feb. 1919; Canada, Dept of Labour, *Report on Organization in Industry, Commerce and the Professions in Canada* (1921), 13–23; Building Industries Conference, *Proceedings*, 14; *IB*, 19 July 1918, 14 Nov. 1919; *LN*, 28 Mar. 1919; NA, Borden Papers, OC Series, Vol. 564, 'City Hall, Toronto, May 27th, 1919,' 2

21 CMA, vol. 17, Hamilton Branch, Executive and Recreation and Entertainment Committees, *Minutes*, 12 Feb. 1919; Hamilton *Spectator*, 18 Feb. 1919

22 CMA, vol. 12, Executive Council, *Minutes*, 27 Feb. 1919

23 *FP*, 1 June 1918, 17 Sept. 1920

24 Richard Allen, *The Social Passion: Religion and Social Reform in Canada, 1914–1928* (Toronto 1973), 71–80; *Star*, 26 Apr., 26 May 1919; Canada, RCIR, *Evidence*, 2688; NIC, *Proceedings*, 95; *FP*, 17 May, 21 June, 12 July 1919, 12 June 1920, 29 Apr. 1921; *CAR* (1920), 177; *IB*, 10 Sept. 1920

25 *FP*, 6 Sept. 1919, 17 Jan., 17 Apr. 1920, 7 Jan., 13 Sept. 1921

26 *FP*, 8 June 1918, 24 and 31 May 1919, 5 Nov. 1920, 4 June, 8 July, 16 Sept. 1921

27 *FP*, 15 May 1920

28 *FP*, 25 May 1918; NA, Willison Papers, vol. 2, folder 20, Willison to E.W. Beatty, 19 Oct. 1922, vol. 7, folder 53, CRA, 'A National Policy,' in 'Industrial Relations,' 1 Nov. 1918, and Willison, 'Bolshevism – The Poison of Production,' vol. 12, folder 100, H.R. Drummond to Willison, 25 Mar. 1920, Willison to Drummond, 29 Mar. 1920, and vol. 21, folder 156, Willison to T.P. Howard, 23 June 1920, vol. 47,

folder 322, Willison to J.E. Walsh, 19 Feb. 1919; NA, MG28, I40, CRA, Central District Committee, *Minutes*, 5 Dec. 1918; *IC* (Oct. 1918), 58; AO, CRA, 'Bolshevism: The Lesson for Canada' (Toronto, *c.* 1919); *CAR* (1919), 443; NA, RG6, E, Chief Press Censor, vol. 614, file 292, part 4, S. Roy Weaver to E.J. Chambers, 28 May 1919

29 *IB*, 3 Apr. 1920; Peter Morris, *Embattled Shadows; A History of Canadian Cinema, 1895–1939* (Montreal 1978), 64-70; NA, Willison Papers, vol. 2, folder 20, 10 Mar. 1919

30 NA, Willison Papers, vol. 5, folder 42, Willison to Bulman, 27 Oct. 1919, vol. 12, folder 100, Willison to H.R. Drummond, 29 Mar. 1920, vol. 21, folder 156, T.P. Howard to Willison, 7 July, 21 July 1919, Willison to Howard, 18 July 1919, and folder 152, Willison to Robert Hobson, 25 Sept. 1919, vol. 33, folder 253, George Pierce to Willison 15 Mar., 6 Apr. 1920, vol. 49, folder 335, Frederick Williams-Taylor to Willison, 25 June 1919; Traves, *State and Enterprise*, 26

31 NA Willison Papers, vol. 12, folder 100, Willison to Drummond, 29 Mar. 1920; Traves, *State and Enterprise*, 25–7 and his '"The Story that Couldn't Be Told": Big Business Buys the TLC,' *Ontario Report* 1 (Sept. 1976); *IB*, 23 July 1920

32 United Brotherhood of Maintenance of Way Employees and Railway Shop Laborers, *Proceedings* (1919), 43, (1922), 94–101, (1925), 93; *IB*, 23 July, 27 Aug., 17 Sept. 1920; TLCC, *Proceedings* (1918), 5–12, (1919), 8–21, (1920), 5–12, 152; *LL*, 17 Nov. 1922

33 NA, Willison Papers, vol. 7, folder 55, C.H. Carlisle to Willison, 1 May 1920, vol. 47, folder 322, J.E. Walsh to Willison, 26 Jan. 1920; Queen's University Archives, Joseph Flavelle Papers, box 5, Willison to Flavelle, 10 Oct. 1919; CRA, Annual Meeting, *Minutes*, 12 Dec. 1921

34 Canada, RCIR, *Evidence*, 2881; *IB*, 5 Mar., 16 July 1920; *LL*, 30 July, 22 and 29 Oct., 12 Nov. 1920

35 NA, RG27, Dept of Labour, vol. 311, file 19(78) and vol. 115, file 600.02–106, 'The Winnipeg Construction Conference,' Jan. 1921; Building Industries Conference, *Proceedings*, xxxi; Hamilton *Herald*, 19, 26, 27 and 28 Apr., 10, 12 and 20 May 1920; Hamilton *Spectator*, 27 Apr., 3, 5, 10, 11, 12, 15, and 25 May 1920; *LL*, 14 May, 18 and 25 June, 9 and 23 July 1920

36 *LL*, 3 and 24 Oct. 1919, 19 Mar., 7 May, 6 and 13 Aug., 17 Sept., 1 and 29 Oct. 1920, 22 July 1921; Hamilton *Spectator*, 5 and 25 May, 5 and 16 July 1920; Hamilton *Herald*, 9 and 21 July 1920; NA, RG27, Dept of Labour, vol. 322, file 20(263), vol. 323, file 20(316)

37 *LOC* (1916), 52, 57; *Amalgamated Sheet Metal Workers' Journal* (Kansas

City, Mo.) 21 (Mar. 1916), 94; *LL*, 13 Feb., 17 Dec. 1920, 28 Oct.
1921, 21 Apr. 1922; Hamilton *Spectator*, 13 July 1921; McMaster University Archives, Bricklayers' and Mason's Union, Local No. 1, Ontario, Hamilton, *Letterbook*, F., Woods to E.B. Osborne, 8 July 1921, F.
Woods to Wm Dobson, 20 Aug. 1923.

38 NA, RG27, Dept of Labour, vol. 323, file 20(356); *LL*, 5 Nov. 1920
39 *London Advertiser*, 23 July 1920; *LL*, 27 May 1921; *LOC* (1922), 296;
   Globe, 15 Feb., 28 Mar. 1921; *Mail and Empire*, 16 and 19 Feb. 1921;
   Star, 18 Feb. 1921; *Toronto World*, 19 Feb., 14 Mar. 1921; NA, RG27,
   Dept of Labour, vol. 324, file 21(44); Building Industries Conference,
   Proceedings, 78; *LL* 6 Jan. 1922, 16 Mar. 1923
40 *Amalgamated Sheet Metal Workers' Journal* 27 (Jan. 1922), 5–6; NA,
   RG27, Dept of Labour, vol. 327, files 22(1), 22(1A), vol. 329, files
   22(42), 22(53); *IB*, 27 Jan. 1922; *Amalgamated Sheet Metal Workers' Journal* 27 (Feb. 1922), 5; *LL*, 15 and 29 July 1921, 3 and 31 Mar., 21
   Apr. 1922
41 NA, RG27, Dept of Labour, vol. 115, file 600.02-106, 'The Association of Canadian Building and Construction Industries, Report of Conference Labor Committee, adopted by Conference at Hamilton, Jan.
   20th, 1922'
42 Canada, Dept of Labour, 'Report of a Conference on Industrial Relations, Held at Ottawa, Feb. 21st and 22nd, 1921' (Ottawa 1921, 11,
   13–14, 20, 34
43 Richard Edwards, *Contested Terrain: The Transformation of the Workplace in the Twentieth Century* (New York 1979), 130–62; Sanford M. Jacoby,
   Employing Bureaucracy: Managers, Unions and the Transformation of Work in American Industry, 1900–1945 (New York 1985). See also David M.
   Gordon, Richard Edwards, and Michael Reich, *Segmented Work, Divided Workers: The Historical Transformation of Labor in the United States* (Cambridge 1982), 100–227; Daniel Nelson, 'The Company Union Movement, 1900–1937: A Reexamination,' *Business History Review* 56
   (Autumn 1982), 336.
44 Margaret E. McCallum's 'Corporate Welfarism in Canada,' *Canadian Historical Review* 71 (Mar. 1990), is based largely on *Industrial Canada* and *Labour Gazette* reports. See also Neil Tudiver, 'Forestalling the Welfare State: The Establishment in Programmes of Corporate Welfare,' in Allan Moscovitch and Jim Albert, eds, *The Benevolent State: The Growth of Welfare in Canada* (Toronto 1987).
45 Associate Committee on Industrial Fatigue of the Honorary Advisory Council for Scientific and Industrial Research, 'Survey of General Conditions of Industrial Hygiene in Toronto' (Ottawa 1921)

46 Ibid., 7; Ontario, Dept of Labour, 'Survey of Industrial Welfare in Ontario' (Toronto 1929), 3, 14, 36; AO, RG7, Dept of Labour, VII, 1, Research Branch, Senior Investigator, General Files, vol. 8, 'Miss Marion Findlay's Papers – re 'Survey of Industrial Welfare in Ontario'' '

47 *LG* 20 (Jan. 1920), 3, (Feb. 1920), 107; Canada, Dept of Labour, 'Report of a Conference on Industrial Relations,' 9–11; AO, RG7, Dept of Labour, VII, 1, Research Branch, Senior Investigator, General Files, vol. 8, 'Miss Marion Findlay's Papers – re "Survey of Industrial Welfare in Ontario" '; *MMJ* 32 (Feb. 1920), 132–3; Social Service Council of Canada, *Co-Management Experiments in Canadian Industry*, 'Advance Copy' (Jan. 1921), 10; Cecil Howard Aikman, *The Automobile Industry of Canada* (Toronto 1926), 14, 23–4

48 NA, RG27, Dept of Labour, vol. 320, file 20(143); *MMJ* 32 (July 1920), 629–30

49 David Montgomery, *Fall of the House of Labor: The Workplace, the State, and American Labor Activism, 1865–1925* (Cambridge 1987), 389

50 *Border Cities Star*, 19, 23 and 24 Apr., 3, 7, 12, 13, and 30 May, 4 June 1919; *Star*, 3 and 13 May 1919; *Globe*, 13 May 1919; AO, RG23, OPP, E-30, 'Strikes and Agitation, 1913–1921,' file 1.4, 'Strikes 1919,' Superintendent, OPP, to James Anderson, 6 May 1919; *IB*, 18 July 1919; *Sarnia Canadian Observer*, 4 Sept. 1919

51 NA, RG27, Dept of Labour, vol. 319, file 20(10)

52 *FP*, 5 June 1920; *SN*, 3 July 1920; *Globe*, 10 May 1920; NA, RG27, Dept of Labour, vol. 320, file 20(121), vol. 321, file 20(214), vol. 322, file 20(244); *Globe*, 14 June 1920; *IB*, 25 June 1920; *London Free Press*, 16 June 1920; London *Advertiser*, 17 June 1920; *LL*, 20 June 1920

53 AO, Irving Abella Tape Collection, Arthur Overs, interviewed by S. Bourden, Toronto, 11 Sept. 1971; NA, RG27, Dept of Labour, vol. 325, file 21(62); *International Union News*, 7 May 1921

54 NA, RG27, Dept of Labour, vol. 324, file 21(32), vol. 327, file 21(178); *LL*, 25 Feb., 11 Mar. 1921; Amalgamated Clothing Workers of America, *Proceedings* (1922), xxii, (1924), 138–40, 263; *LL*, 16 June 1922; *Advance* (New York), 9 Nov. 1923, 1 Feb., 21 Nov. 1924

55 Barbara Roberts, *Whence They Came: Deportation from Canada, 1900–1935* (Ottawa 1988), 71

56 OPP, file 1.5, 'Strikes 1921,' Wm. Greer to Jos. E. Rogers, 13 Feb. 1921; *Star*, 15 Feb. 1921

57 John Flett cited in *St. Catharines Standard*, 17 Feb. 1921. As the OPP noted, such use of 'special constables' from outside the municipality was against the law, OPP, E-30, file 1.5, 'Strikes 1921,' 'Memo for Su-

perintendent Rogers: Re Thorold Strike,' 17 Feb. 1921

58 NA, RG27, Dept of Labour, vol. 324, file 21(19), S.A. Wallace to H.L. Howard, 16 Feb. 1921

59 *Mail and Empire*, 19 Mar. 1921; OPP, E-30, file 1.5, 'Strikes 1921,' Wm. Greer to Joseph E. Rogers, 22 Mar. 1921 and 'Memorandum For the Honorable the Attorney-General,' Superintendent, 17 Mar. 1921; *Thorold Post*, 15 Feb. 1921; *LL*, 4 Mar. 1921; *St. Catharines Standard*, 15 and 23 Feb. 1921

60 *Toronto World*, 2 Feb. 1921; Toronto *Telegram*, 6 Feb. 1921; *Globe*, 21 Feb. 1921; NA, RG27, Dept of Labour, vol. 326, file 21(160A)

61 Sally F. Zerker, *The Rise and Fall of the Toronto Typographical Union, 1832–1972: A Case Study of Foreign Domination* (Toronto 1982), 178–204; *Star*, 16 Aug. 1924; Allen, *Social Passion*, 175–96; for strike statistics see Appendix.

62 Montgomery, *Fall of the House of Labor*, 408

63 NA, RG27, Dept of Labour, vol. 559, file 1, 'Canadian Railways, General, 1921'; *London Free Press*, 27 July 1922; *MMJ* 23 (Nov. 1921), 887–8; Canada, Dept of Labour, 'Government Intervention in Labour Disputes in Canada' (Ottawa nd), 20; Harold A. Logan, *Trade Unions in Canada: Their Development and Functioning* (Toronto 1948), 128–9; *CAR* (1922), 124–6; TDLC, *Minutes*, 17 Aug. 1922; *CCJ*, 1 (Nov. 1922), 577–8

64 *LN*, 21 Mar. 1919

8 Labourism Tested

1 Queen's University Archives, Andrew Glen Papers, box 5, file 23, 'Manifesto Issued by the Labor Representation Political Association,' Toronto 1923

2 *Globe*, 21 Oct. 1919

3 E.g., L.A. Wood, *A History of Farmers' Movements in Canada* (Toronto 1924), W.L. Morton, *The Progressive Party in Canada* (Toronto 1950)

4 Peter Oliver, 'Sir William Hearst and the Collapse of the Ontario Conservative Party,' *Canadian Historical Review* 53 (Mar. 1972), 23, 41; Peter Oliver, *G. Howard Ferguson: Ontario Tory* (Toronto 1977), 144

5 Craig Heron, 'Working-Class Hamilton, 1895–1930' (PhD diss., Dalhousie University 1981); Charles Johnston, *E.C. Drury: Agrarian Idealist* (Toronto 1986); Michael Piva, 'Workers and Tories: The Collapse of the Conservative Party in Urban Ontario, 1908–1919,' *Urban History Review* 3 (Feb. 1977), Martin Robin, *Radical Politics and Canadian Labour, 1880–1930* (Kingston 1968), and Brian Tennyson, 'The Ontario

General Election of 1919: The Beginnings of Agrarian Revolt,' *Journal of Canadian Studies* 4 (Feb. 1969), and his 'The Political Career of Sir William H. Hearst' (MA thesis, University of Toronto 1963)

6 This is particularly true of the Liberal Party, although Margaret Prang does not tend to analyse the divisions in these terms in *N.W. Rowell: Ontario Nationalist* (Toronto 1975).

7 NA, MG30, A31, Tom Moore Papers, 'Speeches, Memoranda and Clippings, 1918–46,' Broadside 1919

8 *MMJ* 31 (Dec. 1919), 1126; Thomas Fisher Rare Book Library, University of Toronto, J.S. Woodsworth Collection, Thomas Tooms Papers, Peterborough ILP Executive, *Minutes*, 20 Oct. 1919; John McPhee, 'The Labour Movement,' in Ronald Borg, ed., *Peterborough, Land of Shining Waters* (Toronto 1967), 293; *IB*, 14 Mar. 1919; *Parliamentary Guide*, 1920, 313

9 Oliver, 'Sir William Hearst,' 24

10 Francis Graham Stevens, 'A History of Radical Political Movements in Essex County and Windsor, 1919–1945' (MA thesis, University of Western Ontario 1948), 51–5; *MMJ* 31 (Apr. 1919), 263–4; *IB*, 12 Sept. 1919; *LOC* (1919), 59; PAM, MG10, A14/1, R.B. Russell Papers, Skidmore to Russell, 15 Apr. 1919; *IB*, 22 Mar. 1918, 2 May 1919, 11 June 1920; *MMJ* 31 (Mar. 1919), 273–4; *OLN*, 1 May 1919.

11 *LN*, 31 Oct. 1919; *LL*, 31 Oct. 1919, 9 Apr. 1920; Fern A. Sayles, *Welland Workers Make History* (Welland 1963), 82; *IB*, 31 Oct., 7, 14, and 28 Nov., 26 Dec. 1919, 27 Feb., 26 Mar. 1920

12 *IB*, 9 Apr., 11 June, 9 and 30 July, 13 and 27 Aug. 1920; Thomas Tooms Papers, Peterborough ILP Executive, *Minutes*, 2 Dec. 1919

13 J.L. Rutledge, 'The Birth of a Labor Party,' *Maclean's* 33 (Jan. 1920), 84; *IB*, 27 Apr. 1917; Queen's University Library, 'Declaration of Principles, Constitution and By-Laws, the Independent Labor Party of Ontario, as Adopted in Hamilton, July 2nd, 1917, and Amended in London, Apr. 3rd, 1920,' 3; *Industrial Union News* (Detroit), 29 Nov. 1919

14 Cited in *IB*, 16 Apr. 1920

15 Cited in *IB*, 23 July 1920

16 *Brantford Expositor*, 10 Nov. 1917, 29 May 1919; NA, RG27, Dept of Labour, vol. 311, file 19(50)

17 *IB*, 25 Apr. 1919; *LN*, 2 May 1919; *Brantford Expositor*, 5 May, 5 June 1919; *OLN*, 15 May 1919

17 *Brantford Expositor*, 30 Oct., 1 and 12 Nov. 1919; *IB*, 31 Oct., 7 and 28 Nov. 1919; Rutledge, 'Birth of a Labor Party, 23; *LL*, 7 Nov. 1919

18 *Brantford Expositor*, 22 and 23 Jan. 1920; *LL*, 23 and 30 Jan., 18 June

1920; *ND*, 28 Jan. 1920; *IB*, 30 Jan. 1920; *CAR* (1920), 532–3

20 E.C. Drury, *Farmer Premier* (Toronto 1966), 174–5

21 Johnston, *E.C. Drury*, 99–124

22 Ibid., 99; Morton, *Progressive Party*, 71; David Laycock, *Populism and Democratic Thought in the Canadian Prairies, 1910 to 1945* (Toronto 1990)

23 Morton, *Progressive Party*, 194; Johnston, *E.C. Drury*, 48–9, 141–8; Drury, *Farmer Premier*, 140–2

24 Laycock, *Populism and Democratic Thought*, 26

25 Johnston, *E.C. Drury*, 127

26 See Morton, *Progressive Party*; C.B. Macpherson, *Democracy in Alberta: Social Credit and the Party System* (Toronto 1953); William Irvine, *The Farmers in Politics* (1920; Toronto 1976)

27 Johnston, *E.C. Drury*, 47–8; AO, RG18, D-I-24, Special Committee on Proportional Representation, 1921

28 Loren M. Simerl, 'A Survey of Canadian Provincial Election Results, 1905–1981,' in Paul Fox, ed., *Politics Canada* (Toronto 1982); Johnston, *E.C. Drury*, 190–2

29 Drury, *Farmer Premier*, 108

30 Canada, *National Industrial Conference* (Ottawa 1919), 72; Alice Kessler-Harris, *Out to Work: A History of Wage-Earning Women in the United States* (Oxford 1982), 184. For a discussion of such 'moral' concerns see Susan Trofimenkoff, 'One Hundred and Two Muffled Voices: Canada's Industrial Women in the 1880's,' *Atlantis* 3 (1978).

31 *LG* 19 (Jan. 1919), 3; Marion Findlay, 'Protection of Workers in Industry,' in W.P.M. Kennedy, ed., *Social and Economic Conditions in the Dominion of Canada* (Philadelphia 1923); J.L. Rutledge, 'The Birth of a Labor Party,' *Maclean's* 33 (Jan. 1920), 81; Elizabeth Jane Campbell, '"The Balance Wheel of the Industrial System": Maximum Hours, Minimum Wage and Workmen's Compensation Legislation in Ontario, 1900–1939' (PhD diss., McMaster University 1981), 299

32 *IB*, 5 Aug. 1921; *LL*, 29 July, 30 Sept. 1921; Hamilton Public Library, Hamilton Central *ILP* branch, *Minutes*, 'Report of the Selection Committee,' 7 Nov. 1921. The Hamilton ILP, in fact, carried on this campaign for some time, *LL*, 17 Mar. 1922. Campbell is incorrect in claiming that labour demanded only a minimum wage for women; Campbell, '"Balance Wheel," ' 286.

33 *LL*, 21 Apr. 1922

34 *CCJ*, 2 (Feb. 1923) 55–6

35 *IB*, 31 May 1918; *Worker*, 17 May 1924

36 NA, RG27, Dept. of Labour vol. 3130, file 89, Third National Con-

vention, Workers' Party of Canada, 18 Apr. 1924, 'Report of Secretary at Annual Meeting of Toronto Women's Labor League. 18 Apr. 1924'; *People's Cause*, 20 Apr. 1925; *Worker*, 10 Jan. 1925; Margaret E. McCallum, 'Keeping Women in Their Place: The Minimum Wage in Canada, 1910–25,' *Labour/Le Travail* 17 (Spring 1986)

37 *LL*, 29 July, 7 and Oct. 1921, 21 Apr. 1922

38 *IB*, 7 Mar. 1919, 23 Jan. 1920; Ontario, Report of the Mother's Allowance Commission, 1921, 5

39 *IB*, 7 Nov. 1919

40 *LG*, 21 (Aug. 1921), 982

41 *Star*, 29 May 1919; NA, RG27, Dept of Labour, vol. 558, file 20(149)

42 *Globe*, 14 and 17 May 1920

43 AO, RG18, B-60, Inquiry into wages and living conditions of the men employed by the Hydro-Electric Power Commission at the Queenston-Chippawa Development (1920), *Proceedings*, 36; AO, RG3, Prime Minister's Office (Drury), box 23, file, 'Hydro-Electric-Chippawa Dev't,' MacBride to Drury, 27 May 1920, Drury to MacBride, 28 May 1920, and box 39, 'Minority Report'

44 *Star*, 21 June, 3 July 1920; *IB*, 25 June 1920; *Niagara Falls Review* 28 June 1920; *LL*, 24 Sept. 1920

45 *CAR* (1921), 530; Johnston, *E.C. Drury*, 113–14; *LL*, 23 July 1920

46 *LL*, 13 Aug. 1920, 14 Jan., 11 Feb. 1921; *LN*, 25 Apr. 1921; *IB*, 29 Apr. 1921; *ND*, 4 May 1921

47 *LL*, 29 Oct., 5 and 26 Nov., 17 Dec. 1920; Glen Papers, box 1, file 4, MacBride to Glen, 3 Nov. 1920; *LN*, 28 Oct., 25 Nov. 1920; *Herald*, 4 Nov. 1920; *ND*, 16 Dec. 1920

48 Peter Oliver, 'The New Order: W.E. Raney and the Politics of "Uplift,"' in his *Public and Private Persons: the Ontario Political Culture, 1914–1934* (Toronto 1975); Gerald A. Hallowell, *Prohibition in Ontario, 1919–1923* (Ottawa 1972)

49 *LN*, 9 Apr. 1920; *IB*, 9 Apr. 1920

50 *LN*, 9 Apr. 1920

51 *IB*, 9 Sept., 25 Nov. 1921; *LL*, 28 Oct., 29 Nov. 1921; *Herald*, 5 Dec. 1921

52 John English and Kenneth McLaughlin, *Kitchener: An Illustrated History* (Waterloo, Ont. 1983), 119–20, 122–3; *LL*, 17 Oct. 1919, 28 Oct., 11 Nov., 2 Dec. 1921; *IB*, 14 Oct., 25 Nov. 1921

53 *LL*, 11 Nov. 1921; *IB*, 14 Oct. 1921; UWO, London TLC, *Minutes*, 16 Nov. 1921; McMaster University Archives, Amalgamated Transit Workers, Div. 107, *Minutes*, 22 Oct. 1921; TLCC, Executive Council, *Minutes*, 11 Jan. 1922

54 *LL*, 7 Oct. 1921

55 *LL*, 29 July, 19 Aug. 1921

56 UWO, London TLC, *Minutes*, 20 Nov. 1918; *LL*, 5 Sept. 1919, 6 and 30 Jan. 1920; UWO, Arthur Mould Papers, 'Reminiscences of Arthur Mould' (typewritten) 71; *LL*, 30 Jan. 1920; *Herald*, 12 May 1921; *OBU Bulletin*, 17 Jan. 1920

57 UWO, London TLC, *Minutes*, 21 Apr., 1 Sept., 6 Oct., 15 Dec. 1920, 1 June 1921; *Herald*, 16 and 23 Sept., 7 and 21 Oct., 4, 11 and 25 Nov. 1920, 21 Apr., 12 May, 1 Dec. 1921; *IB*, 6 Feb. 1920, 29 Apr. 1921; UWO, Arthur Mould Papers, 'Reminiscences,' 71

58 *Herald*, 16 and 30 Sept., 7 and 14 Oct., 11 Nov., 16 Dec. 1920, 12 May 1921

59 *LL*, 21 Jan. 1921, 21 Sept. 1923; UWO, London TLC, *Minutes*, 5 and 19 Sept., 20 June, 4 July, 15 Aug. 1923; UWO, Arthur Mould Papers, Burke to F. Morrison, 6 and 23 July 1923, Morrison to Burke, 20 July 1923, and 'Ruling of Tom Moore'; *London Advertiser*, 5 July 1923

60 *LL*, 7 Apr., 24 Nov., 1 Dec. 1922; NA, MG28, I44, TDLC, *Minutes*, 6 July 1922, 'Minutes of the Meeting of the Executive Committee of the Ontario Section of the Canadian Labor Party, Toronto, Sept. 10, 1921'; *Herald*, 5 Dec. 1921

61 *LL*, 21 Oct., 16 Dec. 1921; TDLC, *Minutes*, 15 Dec. 1921; *IB*, 30 Dec. 1921

62 Glen Papers, box 2, file 9, 'Affiliated with LRPA,' and 'Executive Report, Annual Convention of the Independent Labor Party of Toronto' (20 Oct. 1923); *LL*, 4 May 1923

63 Ian Angus, *Canadian Bolsheviks: The Early Years of the Comunist Party of Canada* (Montreal 1981), 69; Glen Papers, box 1, file 4, 'I.L.P. Forum, 1920–21,' box 2, file 7, 'Central Executive Report, Annual Convention of Ind. Labor Party of Toronto, Sat. 21st, Oct. 1922,' 'I.L.P. Forum. Session 1921–22,' and 'Forum Meetings Session 1922–1923,' box 2, file 9, Glen to J.S. Woodsworth, 3 June 1923, 'Executive Report, Annual Convention of the Independent Labor Party of Toronto' 20 Oct. 1923, and 'Statement re: Dale v. Telegram Case,' box 5, file 24, 'Labor Songs,' box 6, file 'Pamphlets, Broadsides, Newsletters,' 'Songs of Labor'; *LL*, 28 Jan., 11 Feb. 1921; *IB*, 6 May, 9 Sept. 1921

64 *IB*, 22 Feb. 1922; *LL*, 3 Mar. 1922

65 *LL*, 10 and 17 Mar., 12 May 1922; Hamilton Public Library, ILP branch, *Minutes*, 27 Oct. 1922; *LN*, 27 Oct. 1922; London *Advertiser*, 8 and 13 May 1922; *Workers' Guard* (Toronto), 10 Dec. 1921

66 *LOC* (1922), 221–2; *LL*, 21 Apr. 1922; Glen Papers, box 2, file 8, Independent Labor Party of Ontario, *Proceedings* (1923); *LN*, 27 Apr.

1923; *CCJ*, 2 (June 1923), 251–2; St Catharines Historical Museum, Labor Educational Association of Ontario, 'Official Annual Labor Review, 1924,' 41

67 AO, RG3, Prime Minister's Office (Drury), box 34, file, 'Labour Conference 1923,' James Simpson to Drury, 27 Feb. 1923; *LL*, 2 Mar. 1923; *Worker*, 15 Mar. 1923. On the early history of the Workers' Party, later renamed the Communist Party, see Angus, *Canadian Bolsheviks*, and Walter Rodney, *Soldiers of the International: A History of the Communist Party of Canada, 1919–1929* (Toronto 1968).

68 *Worker*, 15 May 1922

69 TDLC, *Minutes*, 21 Sept. 1922, broadside, 'James Simpson Makes Uncalled for atack on Joe Marks'; *LL*, 17 Mar., 31 Mar. 1922, 4 and 18 May 1923; *Worker*, 15 Apr. 1922; *CCJ* 2 (June 1923), 252; *CAR* (1923), 533; Margaret J. Watson, 'The United Farmers of Ontario and Political Co-operation with the Independent Labour Party, 1919–1923' (Unpublished paper, York University 1984), 51

70 MTL, John Warburton Buckley Papers, Rollo et al. (members of the ILP caucus) to John Buckley, 1 Feb. 1922; *CAR* (1923), 576; Hamilton Public Library, Hamilton Central ILP branch, *Minutes*, 11 May 1923; *LL*, 18 May, 8 June 1923; *LN*, 25 May 1923; *CCJ* 2 (June 1923), 230; *Brantford Expositor*, 12 May, 20 June 1923; Glen Papers, box 5, file 23, 'Manifesto Issued by the Labor Representation Political Association'

71 *LL*, 10 Oct. 1919, 20 Aug. 1920, 18 Feb. 1921, 15 June 1923; *IB*, 29 Apr. 1921; *Workers' Guard*, 17 Dec. 1921; *OBU Bulletin*, 16 Nov. 1922; *LOC* (1922), 72, (1923), 69; *FP* 27 Jan. 1922

72 *LOC* (1924), 195

73 *LL*, 29 June 1923

Conclusion

1 *Canadian Labor World*, 2 Aug. 1923

2 *Worker*, 15 Mar. 1922

3 *LL*, 28 Aug. 1921

4 *Workers' Guard*, 17 Dec. 1921

5 NA, MG28, IV, 4, Communist Party of Canada, vol. 8, file 5, Tim Buck to E. Hewlit, 17 May 1924

6 London *Advertiser*, 5 July 1923; *LL*, 18 May 1923, 4 July 1924

7 NA, MG28, III, 56, Toronto Board of Trade, *Minutes*, Jan. 1922; NA, MG30, A31, Tom Moore Papers, file: 'Speeches, Memoranda and Clippings, 1918–1946,' clipping, Norman Reilly Raine, 'Tom Moore, Safety Valve of Labor,' *Maclean's*, 1 Apr. 1925, 72; *IB*, 16 Aug. 1918;

William Rodney, *Soldiers of the International: A History of the Communist Party of Canada, 1919–1929* (Toronto 1968), 152–3

8 *IB*, 27 May 1921; NA, MG28, I44, TDLC, *Minutes*, 16 Sept., 6 Oct. 1921; *LL*, 16 Sept., 14 Oct. 1921; *LN*, 28 Apr. 1922

9 On the Immigration Act see David J. Bercuson, *Confrontation at Winnipeg: Labour, Industrial Relations, and the General Strike* (Montreal 1974), 163, and Donald Avery, *'Dangerous Foreigners': European Immigrant Workers and Labour Radicalism in Canada, 1896–1932* (Toronto 1979), 90–4. The Criminal Code amendments served mainly as a threat until the late 1920s, Lita-Rose Betcherman, *The Little Band* (Ottawa nd), passim.

10 *OBU Bulletin*, 14 May 1921; *IB*, 29 Apr. 1921; *LL*, 29 Apr. 1921

11 *LOC* (1920), 103–4, (1923), 203–4; *Herald*, 28 Oct. 1920; *LL*, 29 Oct. 1920; *MMJ*, 33 (Mar. 1921), 237–8, (May 1921), 403; NA, MG26, I, Arthur Meighen Papers, vol. 32, Meighen to Tom Moore, 5 Nov. 1921

12 *Canadian Labor World*, 2 Aug. 1923

Note on Sources

Despite the relative paucity of secondary work on Ontario history in this period, the issues raised in this study touch upon a range of historical debates in labour, political, business, and women's history, most of which have been cited in the text or notes. The purpose of this brief note is to discuss the more important primary sources used, as well as those secondary sources essential to the study. A fuller bibliography is available in my doctoral dissertation (York University 1988).

The single most important source for this study was the lively labour press of the period, both for its often polemical editorial comment and for its reporting upon working-class activities. This includes the *Industrial Banner*, *Canadian Forward*, the *Labor Leader*, *Ontario Labor News*, and the *Worker* (along with its predecessors, *Workers' Guard* and *Workers' World*), all published in Toronto; *Labor News* and the *New Democracy* (renamed *Canadian Labor News*) of Hamilton; the *Workingman's Newsletter* and the *Herald*, both of London, the *One Big Union Bulletin* from Winnipeg, and the *International Union News* published in Detroit and New York. Trade-union journals, usually published in the United States, also often carried extensive reports from Canadian organizers and union locals. Of particular note are the *Machinists' Monthly Journal*, the *Journal of Electrical Workers and Operators*, the *Plumbers, Gas and Steam Fitters' Journal*, and the garment-trades papers, *Advance*, *Justice*, and the *Garment Worker*, although many others would have occasional reports of strikes in Ontario or letters from Canadian workers. Published proceedings of unions were also useful, particularly those of the Provincial Council of the United Brotherhood of Carpenters and Joiners and the Annual Trades and Labor Congress of Canada. The TLCC's *Canadian Congress Journal* is available from 1922. Business periodicals consulted included *Industrial Canada* and the *Financial Post*. Among the most useful local newspapers for this study were the *Toronto Daily Star* and the *Brantford Expositor*.

A number of manuscript collections at the National Archives of Canada were consulted. These include prime ministers' papers (R.L. Borden and W.L.M. King), N.W. Rowell, George Keen, J.W. Flavelle, Tom Moore, J.S. Willison, and John Bruce. Records of the Canadian Reconstruction Association, the Trades and Labor Congress, the Canadian Manufacturers' Association, the International Moulders and Allied Workers Union, the Toronto Board of Trade, and the Communist Party of Canada are also deposited at the National Archives. Federal government records used include those of the Department of Labour and the Department of the Secretary of State, Chief Press Censor.

At the Ontario Archives are the papers of Frank Beer and A.W. Roebuck, as well as premiers Hearst and Drury. As well, records of various commissions, including the 1920 inquiry into wages and working conditions at the Hydro Commission's Chippawa development, are available, as are the papers of the Ontario Provincial Police for this period. Queen's University Archives has a further collection from J.W. Flavelle as well as the papers of Andrew Glen. Printed materials, including a number of ILP or CLP pamphlets, are at the Douglas Library at Queen's. The Metropolitan Toronto Library has James Simpson's and John W. Buckley's papers, while the Robert S. Kenny and James S. Woodsworth Memorial Collections in Rare Books and Special Collections at the University of Toronto Library contain several useful items including, in the latter case, papers of Thomas Tooms and James McArthur Conner. The Regional Collection at the University of Western Ontario has the papers of Arthur Mould. The One Big Union and R.B. Russell papers at the Provincial Archives of Manitoba, as well as the file on the One Big Union in the University of British Columbia's Special Collections give an insight into the strength of the OBU in Ontario. Local trades councils were the scenes of many of the most lively debates, and the minutes of the Toronto council (at the National Archives) and the London council (at the University of Western Ontario) were invaluable. In other cases, local newspapers often carried extensive reports. Except for annual conventions reported in the labour press, no minutes of the Independent Labor Party appear to exist, except for those of the Central Hamilton Branch at the Hamilton Public Library.

Among government publications, those of the federal Department of Labour were the most helpful. The department's Industrial Relations Series includes reports on employee magazines, industrial councils, and various conferences. The annual *Report on Labour Organization in Canada* and the *Labour Gazette* are invaluable, although the Strike and Lockout files in the Department of Labour records at the National Archives give a far fuller picture of industrial activity. The transcripts of the National Industrial

Conference were published and are available, while only a typescript edition of the evidence presented to the Royal Commission on Industrial Relations is available through the Labour Canada Library. The annual reports of various Ontario government departments and boards were also consulted, as was the Ontario Department of Labour's *Survey of Industrial Welfare*, which appeared, belatedly, in 1929.

Employers pursued the propaganda war largely in pamphlet and magazine form. Publications of the Canadian Reconstruction Association are in the association's records in the National Archives, while a good collection of employee magazines (as well as constitutions and documents of various welfare bodies) are in the Department of Labour papers in the Ontario Archives. Other important contemporary publications include the *Survey of General Conditions of Industrial Hygiene in Toronto* by the Associate Committee on Industrial Fatigue of the Honorary Advisory Council for Scientific and Industrial Research (Toronto 1921); Tim Buck, *Steps to Power: A Program of Action for the Trade Union Minority in Canada* (Toronto 1925); the Imperial Munitions Board, *Women in the Production of Munitions in Canada* (1919); the Social Service Council of Canada, *Co-Management Experiments in Canadian History* (1921), and Mackenzie King's *Industry and Humanity*. Also see H. Mitchell, 'Profit-Sharing and Producers' Co-operation in Canada,' in the *Bulletin of the Departments of History and Political and Economic Science in Queen's University* (1918); Margaret Mackintosh, 'Government Intervention in Labour Disputes in Canada,' *Queen's Quarterly* 31 (1924); W.L. Grant, 'The Education of the Workingman,' *Queen's Quarterly*, 27 (1919), and J.L. Rutledge, 'The Birth of the Labor Party,' *Maclean's*, 33 (1920).

The best national overview of this period remains R.C. Brown and R. Cook, *Canada 1896–1921: A Nation Transformed* (Toronto 1974). Background is also provided by Richard Allen's *The Social Passion: Religion and Social Reform in Canada, 1914–1928* (Toronto, 1973); Michael Bliss, *A Canadian Millionaire: The Life and Times of Sir Joseph Flavelle, Bart., 1858–1939* (Toronto 1978); Paul Craven, *'An Impartial Umpire': Industrial Relations and the Canadian State, 1900–1911* (Toronto 1980); John English, *The Decline of Politics: The Conservatives and the Party System, 1901–1920* (Toronto 1977); Desmond Morton and Glenn Wright, *Winning the Second Battle: Canadian Veterans and the Return to Civilian Life, 1915–1930* (Toronto 1987); Doug Owram, *The Government Generation: Canadian Intellectuals and the State, 1900–1945* (Toronto 1986); Margaret Prang, *N.W. Rowell: Ontario Nationalist* (Toronto 1975); Daphne Read, ed., *The Great War and Canadian Society: An Oral History* (Toronto 1978), and Tom Traves, *The State and Enterprise: Canadian Manufacturers and the Federal Government, 1917–1931* (Toronto 1979). Key articles include Michael Bliss, 'The Methodist Church and

World War I,' *Canadian Historical Review* 49 (1968); R. Matthew Bray, '"Fighting as an Ally": The English-Canadian Patriotic Response to the Great War,' *Canadian Historical Review* 61 (1980), as well as various contributions to Frances Swyripa and John Herd Thompson, eds, *Loyalties in Conflict: Ukrainians in Canada during the Great War* (Edmonton 1983).

With some important exceptions, Ontario's history is less well served. See Ian M. Drummond, *Progress without Planning: The Economic History of Ontario from Confederation to the Second World War* (Toronto 1987); Gerald A. Hallowell, *Prohibition in Ontario, 1919–1923* (Ottawa 1972); Charles M. Johnston, *E.C. Drury: Agrarian Idealist* (Toronto 1986); Peter Oliver, *G. Howard Ferguson: Ontario Tory* (Toronto 1977), as well as Barbara M. Wilson's collection of documents, *Ontario and the First World War, 1914–1918* (Toronto 1977). Several articles by Brian D. Tennyson examine the election of 1919; the most relevant of these is 'The Ontario General Election of 1919: The Beginnings of Agrarian Revolt,' *Journal of Canadian Studies* 4 (1969). Oliver's 'Sir William Hearst and the Collapse of the Ontario Conservative Party,' *Canadian Historical Review* 53 (1972), and Michael Piva's 'Workers and Tories: The Collapse of the Conservative Party in Urban Ontario,' *Urban History Review* 3 (1977), similarly analyse this election.

The flowering of working-class history has, of course, profoundly influenced this study, but surprisingly little work by the 'new working-class historians' has been undertaken on this important period until very recently. David J. Bercuson has set the tone of debate on post-First World War labour activism in his two works, *Confrontation at Winnipeg: Labour, Industrial Relations, and the General Strike* (Montreal 1974; rev. 1990) and *Fools and Wise Men: The Rise and Fall of the One Big Union* (Toronto 1978), and an important article, 'Labour Radicalism and the Western Industrial Frontier,' *Canadian Historical Review* 58 (1977). Gregory S. Kealey has challenged Bercuson's 'western exceptionalism' in '1919: The Canadian Labour Revolt,' *Labour / Le Travail* 13 (1984). Also see Bryan D. Palmer, *A Culture in Conflict: Skilled Workers and Industrial Capitalism in Hamilton, Ontario, 1860–1914* (Montreal 1979); Michael Piva, *The Condition of the Working Class in Toronto* (Ottawa 1979) Craig Heron, *Working in Steel: The Early Years in Canada, 1883–1935* (Toronto 1988), and Craig Heron and Bryan D. Palmer, 'Through the Prism of the Strike: Industrial Conflict in Southern Ontario, 1901–1914,' *Canadian Historical Review* 58 (1977). Working-class politics and radicalism are dealt with in Ian Angus, *Canadian Bolsheviks: The Early Years of the Communist Party of Canada, 1896–1932* (Montreal 1981); Donald Avery, *'Dangerous Foreigners': European Immigrant Workers and Labour Radicalism in Canada, 1896–1932* (Toronto 1979); Norman Penner, *The Canadian Left: A Critical Analysis* (Scarborough Ont. 1977); Martin Robin, *Radical Poli-*

tics and Canadian Labour, 1880–1930 (Kingston 1968), and William Rodney, *Soldiers of the International: A History of the Communist Party of Canada, 1919–1929* (Toronto 1968). There is, however, little serious work on labourism except for Craig Heron's 'Labourism and the Canadian Working Class,' *Labour / Le Travail* 13 (1984).

Most of the secondary sources on employer strategies are American. These include Clarence E. Bonnett, *Employers' Associations in the United States: A Study of Typical Associations* (New York 1922); James Weinstein, *The Corporate Ideal in the Liberal State, 1900–1918* (Boston 1968); Stuart D. Brandes, *American Welfare Capitalism, 1880–1940* (Chicago 1970); Sanford M. Jacoby, *Employing Bureaucracy: Managers, Unions, and the Transformation of Work in American Industry, 1900–1945* (New York 1985); Daniel Nelson, *Managers and Workers: Origins of the New Factory System in the United States, 1880–1920* (Madison, Wis. 1974); Richard Edwards, *Contested Terrain: The Transformation of the Workplace in the Twentieth Century* (New York 1979), and David M. Gordon, Richard Edwards, and Michael Reich, *Segmented Work, Divided Workers: The Historical Transformation of Labor in the United States* (Cambridge, Mass. 1982). Other relevant studies of the United States include David Brody, *Labor in Crisis: The Steel Strike of 1919* (Philadelphia 1965); Valerie Jean Conner, *The National War Labor Board: Stability, Social Justice, and the Voluntary State in World War I* (Chapel Hill, NC 1983); Gwendolyn Mink, *Old Labor and New Immigrants in American Political Development* (Ithaca, NY 1986); David Montgomery, *Workers' Control in America: Studies in the History of Work, Technology, and Labor Struggles* (Cambridge 1979), and his *Fall of the House of Labor: The Workplace, the State, and American Labor Activism, 1865–1925* (Cambridge 1987), and Christopher L. Tomlins, *The State and the Unions: Labor Relations, Law, and the Organized Labor Movement in America, 1880–1960* (Cambridge 1985). On Britain, Alan Fox's *History and Heritage: The Social Origins of the British Industrial Relations System* (London 1985) is particularly helpful. There are few works on corporate welfare in Canada, with the exception of Bruce Scott, '"A Place in the Sun"; the Industrial Council at Massey-Harris, 1919–1929,' *Labour / Le Travailleur* 1 1976). Two overviews are Margaret E. McCallum, 'Corporate Welfarism in Canada, 1919–39,' *Canadian Historical Review* 71 (1990), and Neil Tudiver, 'Forestalling the Welfare State: The Establishment of Programmes of Corporate Welfare,' in Allan Moscovitch and Jim Albert, eds, *The Benevolent State: The Growth of Welfare in Canada* (Toronto 1987).

This study has also benefited from the development of women's history. In this regard, the various contributions to Linda Kealey, ed., *A Not Unreasonable Claim: Women and Reform in Canada, 1880s–1920s* (Toronto 1979), Carol Lee Bacchi's *Liberation Deferred? The Ideas of the English-Canadian Suf-*

fragists, 1877–1918 (Toronto 1983), as well as Cela Ramkhalawansingh, 'Women during the Great War,' in Janice Acton, Penny Goldsmith, and Bonnie Shepard, *Women at Work: Ontario, 1850–1930* (Toronto 1974), are directly relevant. Joan Sangster addresses many parallel issues in her *Dreams of Equality: Women on the Canadian Left, 1920–1950* (Toronto 1989), as does Linda Kealey in 'No Special Protection – No Sympathy, Women's Activism in the Canadian Labour Revolt of 1919,' in Deian R. Hopkin and Gregory S. Kealey, *Class, Community, and the Labour Movement: Wales and Canada, 1850–1930* (Aberystwyth 1989). Studies on protective legislation include Margaret E. McCallum, 'Keeping Women in Their Place: The Minimum Wage in Canada, 1910–1925,' *Labour / Le Travail* 17 (1986), and Veronica Strong-Boag '"Wages for Housework": Mothers' Allowance and the Beginnings of Social Security in Canada,' *Journal of Canadian Studies* 14 (1979). The best recent contribution to the family wage debate is Alice Kessler-Harris, *A Woman's Wage: Historical Meanings and Social Consequences* (Lexington, Ky 1990).

Finally, there are a number of unpublished theses that were important to this study. These include two Bachelor of Commerce theses prepared at Queen's University in the 1920s: W.J. Brown, 'Industrial Council Massey-Harris Co. Limited and Additional Personnel Features of the Same Firm' (1927), and Andrew Purdon, 'The Functions of the Industrial Relations Department of the International Harvester Company of Canada, Limited' (1929). Also used were Craig Heron, 'Working-Class Hamilton, 1896–1930' (PhD diss., Dalhousie University 1981); Elizabeth Jane Campbell, '"The Balance Wheel of the Industrial System": Maximum Hours, Minimum Wage and Workmen's Compensation Legislation in Ontario, 1900–1939' (PhD diss., McMaster University 1981); Jean MacLeod, 'The United Farmer Movement in Ontario, 1914–1943' (MA thesis, Queen's University 1958); Peter E. Rider, 'The Imperial Munitions Board and Its Relationship to Government, Business and Labour, 1914–20' (PhD diss., University of Toronto 1974); D. Wayne Roberts, 'Studies in the Toronto Labour Movement, 1896–1914' (PhD diss., University of Toronto 1978); Myer Siemiatycki, 'Labour Contained: The Defeat of a Rank and File Workers' Movement in Canada, 1914–1921' (PhD diss., York University 1986); T. Gerald J. Stortz, 'Ontario Labor and the First World War' (MA thesis, University of Waterloo 1976), and Brian D. Tennyson, 'The Political Career of Sir William H. Hearst' (MA thesis, University of Toronto 1965).

Index